THE WORLD GUIDE TO
Antiquities

THE WORLD GUIDE TO
Antiquities

by Seymour Kurtz

ACKNOWLEDGMENTS

The author gratefully acknowledges the research contributions of Thomas J. Cuddihy, Eugene J. Cotter, W. Scott Morton, Kathleen Zaborowski, Paula Gerson, Alfred Grossman, Thomas M. Shaw, Elizabeth A. Lehmann, and Ruth M. Kurtz.

Front of jacket: Etruscan art: Acroterion. Terra cotta with whitish slip and painted decoration. 5th century B.C. From Caere. (Gregorian-Etruscan Museum, Rome)

Back of jacket: Egyptian art: "Shrine of the Statues of the Royal Couple," detail. Gold-sheathed wood. 18th Dynasty. From Tutankhamon's Tomb, the Valley of the Kings, Thebes. (National Museum, Cairo)

Front jacket flap: Greek art: Tetradrachm of Alexander. From mint of Amphipolis. Ca. 333 B.C. (British Museum, London)

Half title page: Aztec art: Mask of Xipe-Totec, god of spring and fertility. Carved basalt. 14th century A.D. (British Museum, London)

Frontispiece: Chinese art: Bear. Gilt bronze. 1st century B.C. (British Museum, London)

Title page: Indian art: Siva. Bronze. 10th century A.D. (British Museum, London)

First published 1975 by
Octopus Books Limited
59 Grosvenor Street, London W1

An original work produced by
Vineyard Books, Inc.
159 East 64th Street
New York, N.Y. 10021

ISBN 0 7064 0462 9

Printed in Italy by Arnoldo Mondadori Editore SpA

PICTURE CREDITS: Kodansha Ltd., Tokyo (jacket cover and back, pp. 1, 2, 3, 5, 9, 10, 12, 15, 16 b, 18, 19, 22, 23, 25 l, 28, 30, 33 b, 34, 36, 37, 38 r, 38 l, 39, 43, 44, 47, 48, 50, 51, 55, 58, 62, 64, 66, 67, 68, 70, 71, 72 t, 72 b, 73 t, 77 b, 79, 80, 82, 83, 93, 94, 95, 97, 98, 99, 100, 101, 106 t, 110, 112, 123 t, 124, 126, 127, 132, 133 b, 138, 139 t, 142, 145, 146, 150, 151, 152, 154, 157, 158, 160, 162, 163 t and b, 164, 165, 169, 170, 171, 174, 175 t, 175 b, 177, 179, 180, 181, 183, 185, 186, 188–89, 190, 195, 197, 198, 200, 203, 205, 206, 209, 211, 212 t, 214 l, 214 r, 215, 217, 222, 226, 227, 228, 229, 232, 234–35, 236, 238, 242, 245, 246 b, 246 l, 247 b, 249, 250, 252, 254, 258, 265, 266 l, 270, 271, 275, 277, 283, 286, 290, 291 t, 294, 298, 303, 307, 309, 312, 313, 319, 321, 322); I. Graham (jacket flap); Held (pp. 4, 14, 26, 45, 60, 84 t, 84 b, 134, 191, 194, 204, 216, 278); Cleveland Museum of Art (p. 6 t); Paul Hamlyn (pp. 6 b, 148); Mondadori (pp. 7, 13, 25 r, 78, 85, 86, 106 b, 107, 114, 137, 187, 202 b, 207, 208, 219, 221, 222, 223, 225 b, 239, 255, 268, 295, 296, 304, 306, 314); Holle Verlag (pp. 8, 11); Metropolitan Museum of Art, New York (pp. 16 t, 31, 87, 247 t); Vineyard Books (p. 17); Mella (pp. 20, 272); British Museum (pp. 21, 74, 115, 133 t, 141, 192, 212 b, 230, 262, 273, 292, 300, 301); Mansell, London (p. 24); Bevilacqua (pp. 27, 69, 128, 131, 136, 156, 218, 231, 280); Museum of Fine Arts, Boston (p. 29); Werner Forman, London (p. 32, 267); Scala (pp. 33 t, 61, 108 r, 266 r, 269); Librairie Hachette (p. 35); Françoise Foliot (p. 41); Lavaud, Paris (pp. 42, 104); Holford (pp. 46, 52–53, 89, 111, 159, 176); IPAS (p. 54); Costantino Reyes Valerio (pp. 57, 77 t, 261); John Veltri (pp. 59, 103, 121, 241, 305); National Museum, Copenhagen (pp. 63 t, 130); Aufsberg Sonthofen in Allgarii (p. 63 b); Nelson Gallery, Kansas City (p. 73 b); Editorial Herrero (pp. 76, 199); Giraudon (pp. 81, 96, 317); Hans Hinz (pp. 88, 182, 184); Alinari (p. 91); Dr. P. H. Beighton (p. 92); Percival David Foundation (p. 102); Ist. Etruscologia Università, Rome (pp. 105, 109 b); Pedone (p. 108 l); Pucciarelli (pp. 109 r, 113, 123 b, 125, 129, 257); Horniman Museum (p. 111); Dan Grigorescu (p. 117); John Ross (p. 119); Salchow (p. 139 b); American Museum of Natural History, New York (p. 143); American Indian Museum, New York (p. 155); National Museum, Tokyo (p. 161); Tomsich (p. 172); Zoltan Wegner, Paris (p. 178); Museo Pignorini, Rome (pp. 193, 202 t); Jean Willemin (pp. 213, 223, 253, 260, 324); Museo delle Terme, Rome (p. 220); State Museum, West Berlin (p. 224); Larousse (p. 225 t); Museo de la Venta, Tabasco (p. 233); Soprintendenza Belle Arti, Salerno (p. 237); Linden Museum Stoccarda (p. 240); Novosti (pp. 243, 284); Osterreisches Museum for Kunst, Vienna (p. 248); Sekai Bunka (p. 281); Aerofilms, London (p. 288); Hirmer Verlag (pp. 291 b, 311); Camera Press, London (p. 293); Jean Dominique Lajoux (p. 297); Naturhistorisches Museum, Vienna (p. 315); Universitates Oldsaksamling, Oslo (p. 316).

If any oversight in the credits has occurred, the author and publisher extend their sincere apologies.

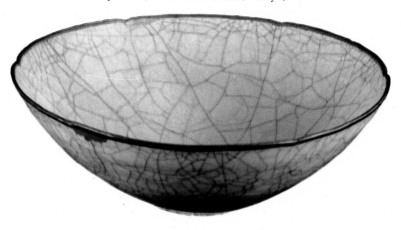

Chinese art: "Kuan" chiaotan-blue cup. Sung Dynasty, 12th century A.D. (National Museum, Tokyo)

Introduction

Many of the values that have been accepted as the basis of Western Civilization for a thousand years or more are today being called in question, and one of the results has been a new interest in other cultures. These form a disparate group whose main common denominator is that they are not based on Christianity. They can be conveniently considered under three main headings—the civilizations of the ancient world, of the Orient, and of those primitive peoples isolated from other civilizations by the accident of geography. Our knowledge of these ancient or primitive cultures is, to a large extent, based on the objects they produced, and this book is an attempt to provide in ready-reference form a conspectus of ancient, Oriental, and primitive art and artifacts.

The term *antiquities* is commonly used to denote objects made by the ancient peoples of Europe and the Near East from the earliest times up to the collapse of the Roman Empire at the end of the 5th century A.D., but the usage may also be extended to cover pre-Columbian material from Central and South America. Those sections of this book that deal with Oriental material concentrate on the period from pre-history to the 16th century A.D. but also include later material in such major fields as Chinese porcelain, Indian miniatures, and Japanese woodcuts. The artifacts of such primitive peoples as the Eskimos, the various African tribes, and the islanders of the Pacific come under the general heading of Ethnographica and are usually of much later date—from the 17th century A.D. almost up to the present day.

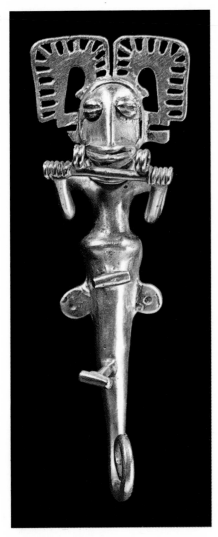

Incan art: Pendant representing a crocodile with the head of a frog. 14th–15th centuries A.D. From Colombia. (Courtesy the Cleveland Museum of Art)

Roman art: Cameo by Dioscorides, of Augustus. (British Museum, London)

Because this book combines what are usually taken as three separate subjects, the treatment has had to be selective. But the coverage is still extremely wide, including as it does architecture; sculpture in all materials, ranging from colossi to amulets an inch high; pottery and porcelain; tools and weapons; and articles for personal adornment as different as barbaric masks and fine Etruscan earrings. From all this mass of material the inquiring reader will be able to trace his own patterns, seeing a Modigliani in a Cycladic idol, or a Picasso ceramic in a pre-Columbian vase, tracing the two-way traffic between the cultures of East and West from the orientalizing patterns on Greek vases to the hellenizing influence on Indian sculpture of the conquests of Alexander.

The understanding of cultures through their artifacts is, of course, limited by what has survived and also, to some extent, by the purpose for which surviving objects were originally made, and here there are considerable variations between the three different areas covered by this book.

Antiquities come from graves, tombs and sanctuaries or from inhabited sites, destroyed by invaders, by natural disasters such as the eruptions that suffocated Pompeii, or simply by the passage of time. Funerary objects can be everyday possessions but were frequently specially made for their purpose so that they can reflect daily life only indirectly. Votive offerings were also usually produced for this particular purpose, though, as many of them took the form of sculpture, they should be representative of the plastic arts of their time. Invading armies are likely to have removed portable objects of any value, but the larger or more ordinary pieces, which they left, are often of great historical value. For our knowledge of everyday life it is often the rubbish dump that can provide most information, particularly when the inhabitants constantly rebuilt on the same site so that a datable sequence can be established by excavation of successive layers.

In the early periods grave goods can also be a major source for orientalia, but during the Middle Ages the temple became increasingly important, particularly for sculpture. Then arose a new class of rich collectors—rulers and their court—for whom works of art were consciously created and, valued as such, were passed down from generation to generation. Ethnographica can be divided into two main sections—cult objects and such possessions as weapons and articles for personal adornment.

Many of the former tend to be made from wood, which accounts
for the fact that comparatively little has survived from the more
distant past.

A great deal of the material covered by this book is still
available for the collector of modest means. Although today it is
illegal to export most antiquities and much orientalia from the
countries of origin, vast quantities of both were looted during
the hundred years preceding World War I, and this material
recirculates constantly as old collections are broken up.
Regrettably also, tomb-robbing and smuggling remain
flourishing industries in many parts of the world, often
encouraged by the overrigid application of laws designed to
conserve a country's cultural heritage.

The increased interest in ancient and primitive works of art
has, not unnaturally, resulted in a parallel increase in forgeries,
and the only advice that can be given to the would-be collector
is to buy from reputable dealers prepared to give unequivocal
guarantees of authenticity.

No single volume can hope to be more than an introduction to
the subjects dealt with in the pages that follow, but this book
will have served an admirable purpose if, by showing the reader
a bird's-eye view, it leads him or her to more detailed study of a
chosen sector. For this is a landscape in which every byway
provides fascination enough for a lifetime.

Greek art: Adonis and Aphrodite. Red-figure hydria attributed to the Meidias Painter. Ca. 400 B.C. (National
Archaeological Museum, Florence)

A

ABBEVILLIAN, a long-lasting, early paleolithic period. Some of the oldest known stone tools made by man were first discovered in 1832 by Jacques Boucher de Perthes in the gravel beds of the Somme Valley at Abbeville in northern France. These were hand axes, roughly chipped from a core of rock to form a point at one end, while the other end was rounded to fit the palm of the hand. Abbevillian man was a hunter who probably migrated to Europe from Africa during a warm interglacial. His tools are found associated with the bones of semitropical animals, such as the elephant, rhinoceros, and hippopotamus. Chronology is uncertain, but the Abbevillian era is thought to date from about 500,000 B.C.

ABORIGINE CULTURE, a culture that once covered the continent of Australia. The aborigines lived in the vast and now arid continent for perhaps 20,000 years prior to the arrival of European colonists in 1788. They remained largely nomadic hunters and food-gatherers, managing to sustain themselves with simple but efficient tools and weapons. The aborigines believed in a mythical Dreamtime, a paradisaical prehistoric period when ancestral beings lived on earth. In northern Australia these ancestral beings were called *wondjina*. The rich aboriginal songs, myths, and chants wistfully recall Dreamtime. Tribes of aborigines established special relationships with animals and natural objects called totems. They decorated their everyday objects, such as boomerangs, atlatls, and clubs, and adorned sacred rock shelters with paintings and drawings. Bark paintings were also made.

ABRI PATAUD. The word *abri* means a shelter, and hence this site is a rock shelter rather than a full cave. Abri Pataud is in the Vezere Valley in the Dordogne, France, a region that has some of the richest paleolithic remains in the world. The Aurignacian level at Abri Pataud (about 30,000 B.C.) showed dish-shaped hollows—with hearths in the center—which were living areas. The Magdalenian level, about 16,000 to 15,000 B.C., contained skeletal remains.

ABU SHAHRAIN. See ERIDU.

ABU SIMBEL, an Egyptian temple site in Nubia, constructed around 1250 B.C. during the reign of the 19th Dynasty pharaoh Ramses II. It consists of two pillared

Aborigine culture: Rock painting. Australia.

Abu Simbel: Colossal statue of Ramses II.

Abydos: Votive palette. Carved schist. Predynastic Egypt. (National Museum, Cairo)

halls and a chapel, hewn from cliffside rock on the Nile shore and dominated by four colossal statues of Ramses, each about 60 feet high. The main temple was situated so that morning sunlight could penetrate its deepest recesses. During the 1960s the site was dismantled and reconstructed on a higher ground level to prevent the temples from being inundated by rising Nile waters caused by construction of the giant Aswan Dam.

ABYDOS, ancient Upper Egyptian city, prominent over a wide span of Egypt's history, especially from the 1st through the 19th dynasties. Memorials to 1st Dynasty rulers were erected here, mainly steles covered with relief carving. An unusual ivory figure about 14 inches high, from Abydos, depicts a 1st Dynasty king and is now in the British Museum. Osiris, god of death, had his chief sanctuary at Abydos; and especially during the Middle Kingdom era; important personages commonly sought burial here. The great temple of Sethi I dates from the 19th Dynasty (about 1300 B.C.), although it was consciously built in an archaic style made to resemble structures of the Old Kingdom.

ACANTHUS, a decorative leaf carving of ancient Egyptian origin used widely in the Classical world, especially by the Romans for their Corinthian capitals. Apart from ancient Greek gravestones, the first use of the acanthus as a minor ornamental element for Greek temples appeared on the Parthenon and the Erechtheum on the Athenian Acropolis.

ACHAEANS. See MYCENAEAN CIVILIZATION.

ACHAEMENID DYNASTY, empire-building dynasty of ancient Persia stemming from King Achaemenes (7th century B.C.). The senior line included Cyrus I, who overthrew the Babylonian empire in the early 6th century B.C.,

and Cyrus II, the Great (559–530 B.C.), who conquered the Medes. Darius I established the junior line, and under his son Xerxes the empire stretched from the Danube to the Indus rivers. Darius, however, failed to conquer the Greeks at Marathon (490 B.C.), as did Xerxes at Salamis ten years later, and thereafter the empire eroded. The dynasty was ended and the empire overthrown with the defeat of Darius III by Alexander the Great in 331 B.C. Achaemenid art and architecture are among the glories of Persian civilization. Outstanding monumental remains include the tomb of Cyrus the Great at Pasargadae and the city of Persepolis, the ancient and splendid Persian capital built by Darius I.

ACHEULIAN, an early paleolithic period in Europe, probably the last phase of the Abbevillian. It is thought that Abbevillian man was gradually driven south by advancing glaciers over thousands of years. About 300,000 B.C., during a warm interglacial, man returned to northern Europe, bringing with him a technically superior hand axe. Acheulian man is named for his type site at St. Acheul on the Somme River in northern France, where his prehistoric tools were first found. The immense time lapses involved give an idea of the extremely slow rate of change in the old stone age.

ACROPOLIS, literally the "upper town." It identifies the citadel or stronghold of a Greek city. The Acropolis of Athens, crowned by Pericles' 5th-century B.C. temple to Athena (the Parthenon) and other temples, statues, and altars, is by far the best known.

ACROTERIA. See ATHENA NIKE.

ADAD, a major Babylonian and Assyrian sky god. He was the giver of life as rain-bringer, the destroyer as god of storms. Adad was depicted on Mesopotamian cylinder seals in his destructive aspect, brandishing a thunderbolt.

ADDAURA, near Monte Pellegrino in Italy, is the site of mid-paleolithic (before 35,000 B.C.) rock art. Its discovery followed upon the accidental explosion of an old ammunition dump. There are animal and human figures portrayed, the latter performing what may be a human sacrifice. The technique is similar to that seen in the prehistoric art of the Sahara.

ADZE, a flat and heavy cutting tool, used by woodcarvers in prehistoric and primitive societies. It consists of essentially two parts—a wooden handle and a blade of stone, shell, or metal—attached to form an acute angle. Ceremonial and decorative adzes are sought as collectors' items.

AEGEANS. See MINOAN CIVILIZATION, MYCENAEAN CIVILIZATIONS and CYCLADIC CULTURE.

AFRICAN MASKS, the carved spirit, human, and animal faces worn widely throughout western and central

Africa on ritual occasions. Masks served a variety of magical functions and uses. They instructed at initiation rites, officiated at funerals, judged in civil matters, and some drove witches away from the village. In nearly all ritual events the wearer of a mask was thoroughly concealed, his identity plainly subordinate to the power of the mask itself. Wood was the preferred material, though some masks were cast in metal. In form, African masks ranged from naturalism to cool abstraction; in expression, from refined serenity to stark hostility. Generally, masks were abundant in African tribes that lacked a strong central authority. Their supernatural properties, therefore, did not conflict with the personal rule of a chief or king. When masks and royal authority did coexist, masks remained under the control of the king or chief.

AGORA, the marketplace and civic center of a Greek city, the focus of commercial, political, and religious life. It was usually located at the foot of an acropolis and was the site of temples, public buildings, and stoas—long, narrow shelters with shops opening onto and outlining the more-or-less square area of the agora. Excavations at the Athenian agora have yielded many antiquities.

AGUADA CULTURE, the most advanced Pre-Columbian culture of northwest Argentina, which lasted from the 7th to the 11th centuries A.D. The Aguada people produced fine pottery, with both painted and incised decoration. However, they are most noted for their skill in working bronze and copper. Distinctive metalwork includes ceremonial copper axes and cast copper plaques. The latter depict, in low relief, an anthropomorphic figure flanked by two felines. The great abundance of jaguarlike representations that appear here has led scholars to conclude that the inspiration for Aguada art was derived from the late Nasca style of Peru and ultimately from Chavin civilization.

AHRENSBURG CULTURE. In late paleolithic times between 10,000 and 8000 B.C. the ice cap was receding northwards and the tundra was giving place to forests of birch in northern Europe. Men were migrating northwards and at the same time inventing new tools to deal with new situations. At Ahrensburg, near Hamburg, Germany, discoveries were made of 25 axes of stone mounted on handles made of reindeer antlers. These were apparently used to cut down small trees in the new birch forests. Along with the axes there were innumerable other tools of flint with tangs or pointed shanks designed to fit into hollowed-out handles. This culture spread to Britain, which in early post-glacial times was joined to the continent by a land bridge.

AHRIMAN, in Zoroastrian religion, the Evil Spirit, representing chaos, darkness, and death. In the struggle for the world he will eventually be defeated by Ahuramazda, the god of light.

African masks: Secret Society mask. Wood and cowries. Kuba, from central Zaire. (Rietberg Museum, Zurich; Von der Heydt Collection)

Ajanta caves: West-central India.

AHURAMAZDA, supreme god of Zoroastrianism, a religion founded in Persia 600–500 B.C. He represented truth, light, and life. Fire was one of his symbols, and he was sometimes depicted in conjunction with a winged disk. His defeat of Ahriman is foretold in the Persian *Avesta*.

AIHOLE, a small village in the central Deccan of India, once the capital of the early Chalukyas, the dynasty that ruled southern India until the 8th century A.D. The 70 or so Hindu temples scattered throughout the village and surrounding forests date from the 5th to 7th centuries A.D. and show the growth of Chalukya period architecture from carpentry and cave architecture towards Gupta style masonry. The epic sculpture here is considered among the finest in Indian art. Notable structures include the Ladh Khan, Durga, and Haccappya temples.

AINU, the aboriginal people of Hokkaido, southern Sakhalin, and Kurile Island, near the Arctic Circle in northern Japan. The time of their arrival in this area is uncertain, but their race is certainly of extreme antiquity, and they share many traits in common with what is known of prehistoric man in Japan. The best known of their sacred rites is the bear ceremony. A young bear is caught, tended with great care and reverence, and then ritually killed when it grows to suitable size. As special offerings to the gods, and as a way of communicating with them, the Ainu carve sticks of living wood, known as Inau. These resemble batons or wands with a cloak of wood shavings around them. Some of the Inau, however, are stylized effigies of human beings and may be related to clay figurines found at prehistoric Japanese sites. The Ainu decorate utilitarian objects with profuse carving and weave distinctive fabrics.

AJANTA, site of 29 rock-carved caves, mostly Buddhist, near Aurangabad in west-central India. Carved into the horseshoe curve of a high escarpment, the caves date from the 2nd to the 6th centuries A.D. and contain elaborate Gupta sculpture and perhaps the finest of all Indian wall paintings. The polychrome murals depict scenes from the life of Buddha in a manner combining both secular and sacred material, thus resurrecting, in part, the past of ancient India. The style of painting is flat, with some modelling of figures against a stylized background. The caves were rediscovered in 1819.

AKKADIANS, ancient inhabitants of the northern portion of Mesopotamia, of which the southern section was Sumer. The Akkadians, a Semitic people, settled between the Tigris and the Euphrates where the two rivers approach most closely; the name Akkadian derives from the city of Agade, not specifically located but some 30 miles north of Babylon. Under their great ruler, Sargon I, in the 3rd millennium B.C., the Akkadians absorbed the city-states of Sumeria, expanded to the north, and, indeed, created the first great historical empire. Their language, Akkadian, written in cuneiform, became the *lingua franca* of the Near East. Akkadian sculpture under Sargon and, especially, his grandson Naramsin demonstrates enormous force and vigor. Assimilating but transcending Sumerian traditions, the Akkadian seals, stele, and one notable surviving bronze head vividly display a stern world of animals, men, and gods.

ALABASTER, a whitish or grayish translucent stone of either calcite or gypsum used for sculpture, architectural embellishment, and utilitarian objects. It was most commonly used in ancient Egypt, Greece, and Rome.

ALABASTRON, a long, slim vessel with narrow neck used in an ancient Greek home to hold fragrant ointments. Frequently made of alabaster, it was round at the foot and was supported by a stand.

ALACA HUYUK, a major Anatolian site in north-central Turkey, east of Ankara. It was probably settled as early as 4000 B.C. and later had relations with the city of Troy. Among the many finds here were 13 "royal tombs," perhaps the prototypes for the Shaft Graves of Mycenae. Richly furnished with rare art objects of gold, copper, and bronze, these tombs date from about 2500 B.C. Copper and bronze figurines of women, stags, and lions were found; the animal figurines were designed to fit atop poles, probably in religious ceremonies, and are called "standards." Gold vases and decorative weapons were also discovered. The figurines are among the earliest representational works of Anatolia. Alaca Huyuk was later occupied by the Hittites, probably early in the 2nd millennium, who left various reliefs and, most strikingly, a rugged fortified gate, embellished with sphinxes carved in stone.

ALASKA. See **IPIUTAK**.

ALBA LONGA, a legendary Italian city said to have been founded by Ascanius, son of the Trojan hero Aeneas, in the 12th century B.C. It was located southeast of Rome in the Alban hills near modern Castelgondolfo, summer residence of the popes. It was supposedly destroyed by Rome in the 7th century B.C. and never rebuilt, although modern Albano preserves its name. Alban wine and building stones were well known in ancient times, and, in his *Aeneid*, the Roman poet Vergil suggests that the descendants of Aeneas moved their capital from Alba Longa to the present site of Rome. In ancient annals Alba Longa is given as the birthplace of Romulus and Remus.

ALEMANNI, a Germanic tribe once located at the headwaters of the Rhine and the Danube in modern Swabia. They threatened the Roman frontier in 213 A.D. and were defeated by Caracalla. Several inroads on the Rhine region were made later in the 3rd century, and in 258 they laid waste parts of Gaul and northern Italy, one group almost reaching Rome. They probably occupied Alsace in 350 but were defeated by the Emperor Julian a few years later. Alemanni graves consisting of tomb chambers, or small mounds enclosing a coffin, have been found.

Alabaster: Perfume container. Egyptian. (National Museum, Cairo)

ALEPPO, in northwest Syria, an ancient commercial center of the Near East. Commanding a fortified height, the city owed its prosperity to its position at the crossroads of the caravan route from the Mediterranean to Mesopotamia. Aleppo is mentioned in accounts of the early 2nd millennium B.C. (usually as Khalap or Haleb), when it was the capital of an Amorite kingdom. It was subsequently taken by the Hittites, the Hurrians, and briefly, in the 15th century B.C., by the Egyptians. Later, it passed to the Assyrians, Persians, Seleucids, and Romans. Of the Hellenistic-Roman city there remain only the foundations of a perimeter wall. Aleppo was conquered by Islamic Arabs in 637 A.D. and reached its zenith under their domination. After Damascus, Aleppo is the Syrian city richest in Moslem monuments, including some of the most beautiful covered bazaars in the Near East. The ancient section of Aleppo, dating from the early 2nd millennium B.C., still awaits excavation.

ALEXANDRIA, an Egyptian city founded in 332 B.C. by Alexander the Great. It was the most famous and important of the many cities of that name. A Mediterranean port, it prospered and became Egypt's capital under the Ptolemies, developing into a center of commerce, industry, and learning. Alexandria's museum and library were

14

Altamira: Cave painting, detail. Magdalenian period. Northern Spain.

unique in ancient times, and it was the site of one of the seven wonders of the ancient world, the Pharos (lighthouse), nearly a mile offshore. A great center of Hellenistic and Jewish culture, it soon outgrew Carthage and became the largest city in North Africa. Alexandria was the only city in Egypt that had any importance for the Romans, who annexed it in 30 B.C. Antiquities from Alexandria are often called Alexandrine.

ALLAH, the Arabic word for God. The prophet Mohammed (7th century A.D.) preached the sole divinity of Allah, the unique creator and judge of the world. The major religion founded by Mohammed is known as Islam, "surrender to God." Its holy book is the Koran. Allah is never depicted in Islamic art.

ALMERIA, a province in southeast Spain, containing remains which indicate that in neolithic times, about 2700 B.C., it may have been colonized by newcomers of a Mediterranean race. The finely polished stone axes, sickles made of flint, and large jars of plain pottery found in Almeria show that these invaders had connections with Egypt and were probably the first wave of neolithic settlers and farmers to reach Europe. Other finds in Almeria include microlithic tools of indigenous peoples already living in Spain in the previous mesolithic era, about 4000 B.C.

ALPERA, a rock shelter in the province of Albacete in southeast Spain, containing drawings of the so-called Spanish Levantine type. This art is possibly of the same date as the Magdalenian art of France and northern Spain (15,000–10,000 B.C.) but shows a clear cultural connection with the Capsian drawings found in Africa, in the central Sahara, and as far south as Rhodesia. Scenes depict highly active hunters, often with bows and arrows, pursuing game which thrive in a warm climate, as opposed to the arctic fauna of more northern prehistoric art.

ALTAMIRA, near Santander in the Cantabrian Mountains of northern Spain, is the site of cave paintings acknowledged to be among the finest executed by prehistoric man. In the polychrome paintings of Altamira, Cro-Magnon artists took advantage of natural bumps and hollows in the cave roof to achieve remarkable three-dimensional effects. Bison, a predominating subject, show impressive bulk and are drawn with consummate skill, exact anatomical observation, and deep artistic feeling. This cave displays examples, also known elsewhere, of a man's left hand laid on a rock and outlined in color by a painter evidently right-handed. Remains of palette shells have been found with colors of ochre and charcoal-black mixed with animal fat still in them. The cave art at Altamira was the subject of bitter controversy

Amarna: Fish effigy. Glass. Egyptian, 18th Dynasty. (British Museum, London)

when first reported in 1897, and its authenticity was not acknowledged until similar mid-Magdalenian art (12,000 B.C.) had been discovered in the Perigord region of France. Altamira and Lascaux rank as the greatest examples of prehistoric cave art known to mankind.

AMARAVATI, site of the ancient captial of the Satavahana Empire from the 1st century B.C. to the 3rd century A.D. Andhra monuments here are considered the high point of south Indian Buddhist art. Located in the central Deccan, near Nagpur, the site was rediscovered in 1796. Most famous of the monuments is the huge Great Stupa. Its carved decorations depict scenes from Buddha's life in the Amaravati style—elongated, yet voluptuous and precise figures—which greatly influenced south Indian, Ceylonese, and southeast Asian sculpture.

AMARNA, an Upper Egyptian tell, site of a brilliant city established by the 18th Dynasty pharaoh, Akhenaten (or Amenhotep IV), a social, religious, and intellectual reformer of the 14th century B.C. Although abandoned a few years after Akhenaten's death, Amarna was the center of a radically new Egyptian artistic style, somewhat colored by Minoan-Mycenaean and western Asian influences. Sculpture is highly naturalistic, and several figures of the youthful but ascetic Akhenaten survive. Remains of palaces and of temples to Aton—the one god, as interpreted by Akhenaten—contained delicately colored murals of far more graceful execution than any preceding Egyptian art. Amarna's boundaries were set off by a number of finely carved steles. The city extended about five miles along the Nile and was roughly a half mile wide. The so-called Amarna letters, an extensive cuneiform correspondence between the Egyptian pharaoh and Near Eastern kings, are of great historical importance.

AMBER, fossilized pine resin, found mainly on the southeastern shores of the Baltic and along the North Sea. It was used for ancient jewelry and later as a varnish. Finds of amber have suggested patterns of prehistoric European trade routes.

AMMONITES, a Semitic, monotheistic people living east of the Jordan River whose civilization flourished from the 13th to the 6th centuries B.C. In constant conflict with the Hebrew tribes of Palestine, they were the "sons of Ammon" of the Old Testament and were frequently denounced by Prophets therein. They were defeated in battle but not demolished as a power by Saul and David. Primarily a pastoral people, they also possessed some agriculture. Archaeological investigation has revealed the remains of several fortified towns.

AMON, also Amen or Amun; chief deity of Egypt's Middle and New Kingdoms, patron of the city of Thebes; often associated with the more ancient sun god, Ra, and called Amon-Ra. From the Middle Kingdom era, Amon was closely associated with the monarchy, and pharaohs commonly incorporated his name into their own. Amon is generally depicted in human form, together with a ram.

AMORITES, a Semitic people of the ancient Near East. Originally desert-dwelling barbarians from Arabia, they moved, around 2000 B.C., to control Mesopotamia and were one of the causes of the downfall of the Sumerian civilization of Ur. They dominated the area under a myriad of petty rulers and many tribal groupings. The Amorites also conquered portions of Syria and Palestine, where they mixed and amalgamated with the Canaanites. Their ancient name was Amurru.

AMPHORA, a large eight- or nine-gallon oval, two-handled vessel, used by the ancient Greeks for the stor-

Amulet: Carved stone. Melanesian, 19th century A.D.
(British Museum, London)

age of oil, honey, and especially for fermenting wine
drawn from the vats. The Panathenaic amphora, with a
broad body tapering sharply downwards and a relatively
thin neck, was given as a prize at the annual Panathenaic
games at Athens. It was regularly decorated with the
figure of Athena and a scene depicting the event for
which the prize was given.

AMULET, object believed to have magical powers for
healing and protection against evil. Originally natural
substances like shells or semiprecious stones, they later
were carved objects or inscribed papers worn as a locket
necklace.

ANASAZI CULTURE. Along with the Hohokam and
Mogollon, the Anasazi provided one of the main cultural
traditions of the prehistoric American Southwest. Although the early stages of Anasazi culture date back to
100 B.C., its more characteristic traits do not begin to
appear until 400 A.D. Anasazi culture reached its peak
between 1100 and 1300 A.D. with the construction of large
villages with houses of several stories and populations of
more than 1,000. The most famous of these is Pueblo
Bonito, in Chaco Canyon, New Mexico. Anasazi people
also produced beautiful pottery, weaving, and objects of

Amphora: Panathenaic black-figure ware. Greek, 4th
century B.C. (Metropolitan Museum of Art, New York;
Fletcher Fund)

Anasazi culture: Painted pottery. From Arizona. (Museum of Primitive Art, New York; gift of Mrs. Gertrud A. Mellon)

shell and turquoise which show some Mexican influence. Modern-day Pueblo culture is a direct offspring of the Anasazi.

ANATOLIA, the large mountainous plateau of Asia Minor, now in Turkey, and one of the world's richest archaeological regions. For untold centuries Anatolia served as the bridge between Asia and Europe and saw the passage, invasion, or occupation of many different peoples: Trojans, Hittites, Sea Peoples, Phrygians, Assyrians, Lydians, Armenians, Greeks, Persians, Romans, and others. Among its numerous archaeological sites are Troy, Hacilar, Catal Huyuk, Beldibi, Gordion, Karatepe, Urartu, Kultepe, Alaca Huyuk, and Boghazkoy. Farming began here in the 7th millennium B.C., thus placing Anatolia in the vanguard of the neolithic agricultural revolution. Recent excavations at Hacilar and Catal Huyuk reveal the transition from food-gathering to food-growing cultures. The genesis of Anatolian visual arts also seems to begin with the people of Hacilar and Catal Huyuk. These enigmatic settlers painted wall murals, created a highly decorative pottery, and modelled remarkable clay figurines of the Mother Goddess, the central divinity of these very early Anatolians. However, the ancient art of Anatolia reached its zenith only after 2500 B.C. with the metalwork of Troy and Alaca Huyuk, where royal tombs have yielded extremely fine objects of gold, silver, and bronze. The most impressive stone monuments of this historic plateau date from the Hittite period of the 2nd millennium B.C. Although noted as metalworkers—the Hittites are said to have been the first to use iron weapons and implements—the Anatolians also crafted terra cotta and glass, as can be seen in the objects excavated at the Phrygian city of Gordion, of about 1200 B.C. In the 8th century B.C., after the Assyrians won control of Anatolia, the indigenous arts of the region, with but few exceptions, suffered a general decline.

ANCESTOR WORSHIP, rite commemorating dead forebears and promoting the solidarity and continuity of the family and clan. It is a particularly important aspect of religion in China and India and in African and Polynesian regions. Chinese ancestor worship, which dates, at least, from the Shang culture before 1000 B.C., emphasizes filial piety as the most admired of virtues. Early rites included animal sacrifice, libations, and consulting oracle bones about particular ancestors; rites now contain prayers, offerings, and grave visits. Sraddha, the rite of Indian ancestor worship, dates back to Vedic times. Carved ancestor figures were made in many different parts of the world.

ANDHRA, a culture of the Satavahana Empire, dating from the mid-1st century B.C. to the 4th century A.D. in the northwestern Deccan of India. Probably of Dravidian origin, Andhra culture, at the height of its influence,

stretched from coast to coast and its people were engaged in shipping and foreign trade. The early Andhra period (72–25 B.C.) produced the ornate sculptured gateways of the Great Stupa at Sanchi. The later period (25 B.C.–A.D. 320) saw the development of many of the monuments at Amaravati, including the Great Stupa there. Characteristic Andhra pottery was a painted, rouletted, wheel-made ware.

ANDRONOVO CULTURE, actually a group of related early Eurasian cultures, identifiable during most of the 2nd millennium B.C. and covering an area approximately encompassing Soviet Kazakhstan and parts of southwestern Siberia. The people of Andronovo were seminomadic, predominantly breeders of cattle, sheep, and horses, who engaged in some farming and had established villages. Their most noteworthy artistic output coincides with the development of tin and copper mining in the 14th century B.C., at which time they began producing ornamental metal objects. Tomb sites have revealed utensils, weapons, and objects for personal adornment in gold, bronze, and tin that show marked sophistication in metalworking. Earliest objects have abstract geometric designs, which rather abruptly gave way to a distinctive animal-style steppe art, probably introduced by neighboring Karasuks.

ANGHELU RUJU is a large copper-age cemetery of rock-cut tombs on the island of Sardinia in the Mediterranean. Its earliest artifacts are similar in type and date to those of Sicily of the 3rd millennium B.C. The tombs in Sardinia, in general, are hemispherical chambers cut out of rock with a narrowing portal entered by stepping down into a small pit. At Anghelu Ruju, however, an

Angkor Wat: Khmer. Northwest Cambodia.

antechamber and small cells off the main chamber are often found as additions. The main cultural influences here are from Crete, of which Sardinia may have been a colony. These influences are seen in marble statuettes in the Cycladic style and in carved symbols on some of the Anghelu Ruju tombs showing the head of a Minoan bull and high-prowed Minoan ships. The rock tombs of Sardinia may have played a role in the development of Megalithic culture in Spain and in other coastal areas of Europe.

ANGKOR, site in northwest Cambodia, the seat of several ancient Khmer capitals and the center of Khmer civilization from the 9th century until the 16th century A.D. It is now one of the world's great archaeological treasures. Its most famous ruins include Angkor Wat and Angkor Thom, which contain lavish Khmer palaces, temples, and governmental buildings. Angkor, extending over a 40-square-mile area, was, in a sense, the basis of Khmer life; its vast system of irrigation canals provided the water for growing rice. The king, as the image of God on earth, assured continual water, and the temples in the form of elaborately carved stone ''sacred mountains'' existed as a symbol of the king's power and divinity. However, Angkor also contributed to the Khmer downfall, for with grander building projects, neglected irrigation trenches, and people enslaved to building, the

weakened Khmers finally succumbed to Cham and Thai invasions. The Bayon Temple, a Buddhist and Hindu sanctuary in the center of Angkor Thom (built in the 13th century A.D.), is probably the most imposing monument in Angkor.

ANGLO-SAXON PEOPLES, a union of Germanic tribes—the Angles and Saxons—who invaded England from the North Sea region of what is now Germany soon after 400 A.D. This invasion was at least partly connected with the massive upheaval in northern Europe following the collapse of Imperial Rome. The Anglo-Saxons gradually displaced the island's native Britons and Roman and Celtic populations and by about 600 A.D. were the rulers of Britain. They set up a number of small regional kingdoms, most of which retained independence and individuality for several centuries. The Anglo-Saxons came to England as a roving, warring, seafaring society that left few architectural remains or examples of monumental art. Nevertheless, they put care and imagination into their sagas and legends—Beowulf and the Anglo-Saxon Chronicle—and into portable objects, such as weapons and armor. With precision and an instinct for design, they carved their oar-driven ships, their chief means of transport, and the carts in which they traveled on land or used for ceremonial occasions. After arrival in England they began to mingle with the Celts and the Romano-British peoples already there, and they adopted these peoples' settled life. The major Anglo-Saxon kingdoms included those of Northumbria, Mercia, and Wessex. One of the few remaining Anglo-Saxon archaeological

Anglo-Saxon peoples: Purse lock. Gold, garnets, glass, and enamel. Found at Sutton Hoo. (British Museum, London)

20

Animal style: Bronze elk. Eurasia.

hoard, found almost intact. The Sutton Hoo hoard, now in the British Museum, is sufficiently varied to give a reliable picture of Anglo-Saxon art. It shows it to be both native and derivative, with a Germanic and barbaric love of display and intricate design, apparent in the find of gold and jeweled mountings of swords and helmets and in objects of personal adornment. Celtic art strongly influenced the Anglo-Saxon, as can be seen in the recurring tendril motifs on the page margins of the Anglo-Saxon Book of Durrow (Trinity College, Dublin) and on some silver pieces from Sutton Hoo. The supreme example of Anglo-Saxon mingling of cultural themes, their combining of native and borrowed style elements in a single work of art, is in the so-called Franks Casket, donated to the British Museum by Sir A. W. Franks in 1867. Carved about 700 A.D. from the bones of a whale cast up on England's Northumbrian coast, this small casket, only about nine inches long, displays a mixture of several cultural elements. There is an iconography of Roman inspiration (Romulus and Remus), of Nordic pagan (Weyland the smith at his forge), and of Christian (the Adoration of the Magi). However, the over-all style is Anglo-Saxon, with bands of runic inscriptions sharply carved in relief above and below the various scenes. Depictions of hooded and bearded figures dressed in kiltlike garments, as seen on the Franks Casket, are totally unlike any figures in Roman art.

ANIMAL STYLE, a term describing the art of various Eurasian nomadic cultures that flourished in the south Russian steppes through central Asia to the Ordos region of western China. The style began at least as early as with the Karasuk culture of the 2nd millennium B.C. and reached its zenith with the art of the Scythians in the late 1st millennium B.C. It remained viable for perhaps another thousand years in the art of succeeding waves of mounted nomads who swept across Eurasia. As the name implies, the subjects of animal style were animals—horses, birds, stags, cattle, etc.—most of which had economic or religious significance for the nomads. Animal figures were made of bronze, iron, gold, silver, wood, etc., and in eastern regions they were often cut from leather and appliquéd on textiles. Almost without exception the animal figures are highly stylized and often contorted into semigeometric shapes. Animal style was the art of people who did not build permanent communities; thus the objects were portable, primarily for personal adornment, or for wagon, chariot, or weapon decoration and horse trappings.

ANIMISM, in primitive religion, the belief in the existence of spirit beings. These may be gods, the ghosts of ancestors, and even the souls of inanimate objects or natural phenomena. Their essential quality is that they are supernatural and mysterious. Since these spirits have benevolent and malevolent powers, special rites are necessary to control them. Often this has resulted in the

sites is at Yeavering—from the kingdom of Northumbria—which dates after 600 A.D. The site, excavated in the 1950s, consisted of a great timbered palace or assembly hall, with smaller adjoining buildings. Of even more interest is the East Anglian royal ship burial, dating from the 7th century and found at Sutton Hoo on England's Suffolk coast. Before the end of the 7th century, Mercia established dominance over most other Anglo-Saxon kingdoms. However, it was the kingdom of Wessex that most nearly unified the Anglo-Saxon world under its famous King Alfred in the 9th century. Anglo-Saxon influence and prestige declined after the Viking invasion of England in 1016, then disappeared entirely with the epochal Norman conquest of 1066.

Anglo-Saxon Art and Antiquities. The Anglo-Saxons left little in the way of permanent art for examination by posterity; and before 1939 and the dramatic discovery at Sutton Hoo, Anglo-Saxon art of significance was practically unknown. Central to Sutton Hoo was a memorial burial boat, long since disintegrated, and a rich treasure

creation of a wealth of ritual art objects, among them sculptured figures, masks, and elaborate costumes.

ANKH, among the most common Egyptian hieroglyphs, shaped like a "T" surmounted by an oval. Its meaning is "life," and in ancient Egyptian art, gods and kings are often depicted carrying an ankh to prolong or renew life. In later times it was often confused with a crucifix.

ANLO, a site on Drenthe Heath in Holland associated with some of the earliest neolithic cultures of northern Europe. Anlo was occupied by a long succession of peoples beginning in the 4th millennium B.C. A cattle pen of late neolithic times (after 3000 B.C.) has been found, also a settlement of the Beaker People. It was finally occupied by the Urn People in about 1200 B.C.

ANSE AU MEADOW. It was often stated that Vikings sailing from Greenland discovered America. However, no indubitable remains from the Viking period in North America were known. Then excavations at Anse au Meadow on the northern tip of Newfoundland turned up a spindle whorl (a wool-spinning weight), iron nails, and a ring-headed pin. These objects, dated by the radiocarbon method, along with remains of houses of Viking type at the same site, establish Anse au Meadow as a permanent settlement of Vikings in the 10th century A.D. This date corresponds with that in the Norse sagas for the discovery of America, which the Vikings called Vinland.

ANTIOCH, a major Hellenistic city in Asia Minor. It was founded around 300 B.C. in the northeast corner of the Mediterranean coast, about 15 miles from the sea. The city was a prosperous trade hub (wine, olive oil, silk) and an important center of art from the Hellenistic period down to the 5th century A.D. The city was personified in the famous bronze statue of Tyche by Eutychides, now lost but known in some 20 Roman copies (one is in the Vatican Museum). During the 1st century A.D., artists here developed a refined technique of polychrome mosaic that rivaled painting. The Drinking Contest of Dionysius and Heracles, a superb floor mosaic (32" by 59") from the Atrium House at Antioch, is one of the most advanced renderings of light and shadow in mosaic that has come down to us. Now in the Worcester Art Museum, in Massachusetts, it dates from about 75 A.D.

ANTIQUITY. As used in this book, the term refers to a work of art—not merely an artifact—that is pre-Christian or non-Christian in origin. Antiquities range in age from more than 25,000 years ago to art objects made in Africa and Oceania prior to the Second World War.

ANTONINE WALL, a Roman frontier wall in Scotland, farther north than the better-known wall of Hadrian. Built at the order of the Emperor Antonius Pius in 142 A.D., it had small, close-spaced forts and smaller signalling platforms occurring in pairs at its high points. The

Romans pulled back to Hadrian's Wall after heavy losses were inflicted on the Scots in 185 A.D.

ANU, the father and king of Sumerian gods. Originally god of the heavens, he became the leading figure in a triad, with Enlil (earth) and Ea (waters). The great temple at Warka is believed his.

ANUBIS, an ancient Egyptian god, represented as having a jackal's head and a man's body. He is considered the guardian of the dead, as well as of tombs, embalming, and burial.

ANURADHAPURA, site of the royal capital of Ceylon from 200 B.C. to A.D. 780. Its ruins include the huge Buddhist stupa, Abhayagiri Dagoba, and the Ruvaneli Dagoba. A visiting Indian prince introduced Buddhism here around 200 B.C. by planting a shoot from the original bodhi tree, under which Buddha found enlightenment. The site was abandoned in the 8th century due to Tamil raids from southern India.

ANYANG, one of the earliest centers of Chinese civilization and the capital of the Shang Dynasty after 1400 B.C. Located in northern Honan, the site was first excavated in 1927–36, providing evidence that the Shang were real,

Anubis: "The Weighing of the Souls," detail. From the *Book of the Dead of Ani*. Egyptian, 19th Dynasty. (British Museum, London)

not legendary. Findings included oracle bones inscribed with the names of Shang rulers, superb bronze vessels, jade carvings, circular dugout houses, cemeteries, and horses and chariots. Civilization developed more rapidly at Anyang than in other areas of East Asia because it was a cultural crossroads of the eastern agricultural Chinese, the southern forest dwellers, and the northern and western nomads.

AOSTA, a Roman town founded in 25 B.C. by the Emperor Augustus to house the 3,000 discharged veterans of his Praetorian Guard. Located 50 miles north of Turin, near the foot of Mt. Blanc, it was originally called Augusta Praetoria; its well-preserved fortification wall testifies to Aosta's military origin. Temples, storehouses, and baths have been excavated, as well as a roofed theater dating from the last decade of the 1st century B.C. The town gate (Porta Praetoria) is one of the largest and most beautiful known; an arch, with Corinthian columns and Doric frieze and cornice, it straddles the approach road to the city.

APELLES, a 4th-century B.C. Greek painter—the favorite artist of Alexander the Great. In Apelles' "Alexander with a Thunderbolt," painted for the magnificent Temple of Artemis at Ephesus in Asia Minor, the bolt is said to have projected realistically from the picture. The special tone of his paintings was thought to have been brought about by a secret varnish he invented. His painting of Aphrodite Anadyomene, the goddess rising from the sea, was said to have been a masterpiece. Apelles' works are no longer extant.

APENNINE CULTURE, a bronze-age Italian culture of about 1500 B.C., which extended, in differing local forms, the length of Italy down the spine of the Apennine Mountains. A distinctive form of this culture was found in the *terramara* ("rich earth") sites near the northern part of the mountain chain just south of the Po River. These village settlements were built on wooden platforms, probably to avoid flooding. The inhabitants were expert in metallurgy and agriculture and had domesticated a number of animals, including dogs, horses, sheep, oxen, and fowl. They cremated their dead. The Indo-European language of the *terramara* people affected the languages of a number of the later tribes of Italy, such as the Latins, the Sicels, and the Venetians. (The terms "Apennine culture" and "terramara culture" are sometimes used interchangeably.)

APHRODITE, the irresistible Greek goddess of love, wife of Hephaestus and unfaithful to him with Ares. In art she appears nude, rising from the sea or leaving her bath. The most famous statues of her are the Aphrodite of Melos (Venus de Milo), now in the Louvre, and that of Praxiteles (Aphrodite of Cnidos), known only through Roman copies. The lost Aphrodite Anadyomene ("rising from the sea"), a painting by the Greek Apelles, was said to have been a masterpiece. In Roman times she was known as Venus.

APHRODITE OF CNIDOS. See PRAXITELES.

APIS, sacred bull of ancient Egypt. The animal was the primary symbol of power and fertility. Many were buried at the necropolis, Saqqarah, near Memphis. Bull-worship ultimately spread throughout the Mediterranean world.

APOLLO, Greek sun god. Originally the protector of flocks, he was subsequently worshipped as the god of archery, medicine, music, and prophecy. He had no close Roman counterpart and was thus adopted by the Romans with his Greek name. He was the founder of cities, promoter of colonization, giver of laws, and punisher of wrongs. His oracle at Delphi was specially influential in the 6th and 5th centuries B.C. Apollo was a popular subject in Greek art from the 7th century B.C. and is usually depicted as a handsome youth, naked or robed, with bow or lyre, alone or with Artemis, his sister.

Aphrodite: Marble. Greek, workshop of Praxiteles, 4th century B.C. (Museum of Fine Arts, Boston; Bartlett Collection)

Apsara: Dancing figure. Bronze. (Museum of Fine Arts, Boston)

APOLLODOROS, a 5th-century B.C. Greek painter who is called the "shadow painter" for his graduated shading of light and dark. He is said to have been the first to give figures the appearance of reality, to have used shadows and perspective, and to have worked with mixed colors instead of pure ones. None of his works survives, and only two of his pictures are mentioned in ancient sources. However, his importance was fully recognized in antiquity.

APOLLO OF BELVEDERE, a Roman copy of a 4th-century B.C. Greek statue of Apollo. The god is nude except for a cloak around his shoulders which drapes over his extended left arm. A magnificent Greco-Roman statue, it is so named because it now stands in the Belvedere courtyard of the Vatican Museum in Rome.

APOXYOMENOS. See LYSIPPUS.

APPIAN WAY. Considered by Roman historians to be their oldest formal road, the Via Appia was built by the Censor Appius Claudius in 312 B.C. It ran south from Rome down the west coast to Capua and later was extended inland over to the eastern shore—i.e., through Beneventum to Brundisium (modern Brindisi). Near Rome it was lined with ancient monuments.

APPLIQUE, technique in which an ornament or object is attached to a base material. The materials may be the same, as cloth on cloth, or different, as cloth on leather. Applique is commonly used in embroidery and in sculpture as, for example, metal on stone.

APSARAS, voluptuous Hindu nymphs who are the mistresses of gods and men. As heavenly dancers, they are the counterparts of the gandharvas, male heavenly musicians. Apsaras are popular subjects of Hindu painting, sculpture, and literature.

AQUAMANILE, an effigy vessel, used for the pouring of liquid in prehistoric and ancient times. It was generally associated with religious rites. Minoan and Greek rhytons are some examples of aquamaniles.

ARABIAN CIVILIZATION. The pre-Islamic culture of the Arabian people in the vast, hot, and hostile Arabian peninsula was primarily nomadic, a way of life made possible by the domestication of the camel around the middle of the 2nd millennium B.C. Nomad social organization was based on clans, combined in loose tribal confederations. Such law as prevailed was largely that of communal vengeance, in which wrongs would be repaid in kind, "life for life, eye for eye, tooth for tooth," thus strongly reinforcing the essentiality of clan and tribal solidarity. The religion of the nomadic Arabs was primarily animistic; gods and spirits were worshipped in natural objects: trees, wells, and rocks (the Black Stone at Mecca, later the center of Islamic devotion, was long one of these animistic shrines). Although the more formal pantheons of surrounding cultures no doubt impinged on the religious consciousness of the bedouin Arabs, such organized religion was essentially linked to the settled rhythms of agriculture and was thus irrelevant to nomadic existence. In marked contrast to the unrooted life of the central and northern Arabs were the cultures that grew up in the southwestern rim of the peninsula, where climate and geography favored settlement. Here, in what the Romans came to call Arabia Felix—Fortunate Arabia—such civilizations as the Sabaean, the Minaean, and the Kataban flourished. These were roughly contemporaneous, rising about 400 B.C. By the end of the 1st century B.C. the Sabaeans had absorbed the other kingdoms of what is now Yemen. The area, in addition to a prosperous agriculture, engaged in extensive trade westward to Africa across the Red Sea and thence to Mesopotamia and the Mediterranean. The prosperity of the region was diminished by the invasion of Christian Ethiopians in 525 A.D., and its agriculture was devastated by the collapse of the Marib irrigation dike system in 575 A.D. Under these blows, a large portion of the population fled northward to take up the life of the Arab nomads, whose greatest age coincided with the rise of Islam in the 7th century A.D.

Arabian Art and Antiquities. Nomadic life in the desert precluded by its nature the creation of graphic art on any significant scale; the major creative emphasis of the nomad was on poetry, preserved in oral tradition. It was in the settled southwestern portion of the Arabian peninsula and at Petra and Dedan in the north, settlements on the borders of Palestine, that works of art were created and have survived. Of these antiquities one of the most notable is the great temple at Marib in the south. The south has also left a number of statues and statuettes, probably of religious use or significance, as well as rather primitive reliefs. Most notable of southern Arab artifacts were probably their small works of art in gold, silver, and bronze—goblets, lamps, and vases, as well as gold jewelry and coins in considerable quantity.

ARAMAEANS. A Semitic people who, from the 11th to the 8th centuries B.C., spread out from the Syrian desert to occupy large areas of Syria and Mesopotamia. For centuries they were bitterly embattled with the Assyrians, but the Aramaean threat was largely ended by the victory of Sargon II of Assyria in 720 B.C. Although the Aramaeans generally adopted the culture of the resident peoples they overran, their language, Aramaic, which was allied to Hebrew and Phoenician and written in the Phoenician alphabet, came to succeed Akkadian as the *lingua franca* of the Near East. In Palestine it became the language of the common people; it was spoken by Jesus and his disciples.

ARA PACIS, one of the great monuments of Roman art, completed at Rome in 9 B.C. Also called "The Altar of Augustan Peace," it was erected by the Senate to commemorate the Emperor Augustus' victorious return from Gaul and Spain. The walls surrounding the altar carry marble reliefs which are among the most important in all of Augustan art. Among other scenes, the consecration-day procession includes superb portraits of the Imperial family and of Augustus himself. The whole monument was reconstructed near its original location in 1938.

ARAWAKS, an indigenous Caribbean peoples who had settled most of the Greater Antilles by 1000 A.D. and formed the dominant group there when Columbus arrived. Arawak pottery style suggests that they originally came from South America, and certain cultural traits, among them the ritual ball game, indicate contact with Mexican peoples. The Arawaks lived in towns of up to 5,000 people and were ruled by chiefs called caciques. They excelled in sculpture, and the guiding principle of the Arawak artist was to handle his material in such a way that its inner "spirit" was released. Wood was carved into standing idols and ceremonial stools of anthropomorphic form known as Duhos. In addition, the Arawaks produced a large body of stone sculpture, including mysterious three-pointed stones; these are thought to be Zemis, the idols used by Arawak shamans to communicate with the spirits.

ARCHAIC PERIOD, in Greek art, the epoch from the mid-7th century to the end of the Persian wars in 479 B.C.

Ara Pacis: "The Altar of Augustan Peace," detail. Roman, ca. 9 B.C., Rome.

Archaic period: "Calf Bearer" (Moschophorus). Marble. Greek, ca. 570 B.C. From the Athenian Acropolis. (Acropolis Museum, Athens)

It was an era of rapid development of Greek culture, with progress in every area—political, social, economic, and especially artistic. Archaic art has been compared with the Romanesque period in early Christian art—i.e., little artificiality or convention, direct and expressive, yet with still unpolished techniques. Greek vase painting became more ornate and naturalistic, showing Egyptian and Assyrian influence; the painted human figure acquired more realism; and growing importance was attached to over-all composition. Although still characterized by a rigid frontality, sculpture displayed a greater anatomical reality. Concurrently, temple architecture also began its evolution from wood to stone, seeking the proportions that would lead to 5th-century B.C. perfection.

Archaic smile: Marble head. Greek, 6th century B.C. From the Athenian Acropolis. (Louvre, Paris)

ARCHAIC SMILE, a distinctive feature of Greek sculpture of the Archaic period. To some the "smile" seems to be a happy accident—the result of the sculptor's habit of finishing the mouth with a deep point at its corners. When sculptors later employed gradual modelling techniques between the corner of the mouth and the cheek, the so-called smile disappeared. However, many scholars believe that the archaic smile was intended and thus expressed a spiritual meaning for early Greek culture.

ARES, Greek god of war. Ares represents the passionate response to battle, its irrational frenzy, and its horrors. Though the son of the Greek gods Zeus and Hera, he is commonly the helper of foreigners (the Trojans) or unusually fierce people (the Amazons). In art he is often depicted with Aphrodite, goddess of love, and symbol of another human passion. In Roman times he was known as Mars.

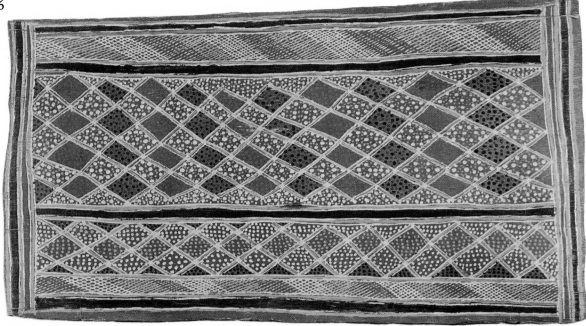

Arnhem Land: Painting on bark. Australia. (Musée Ethnographique, Geneva)

ARGOS, a small Greek city, founded by Dorians on the Peloponnesus and which flourished during the early 1st millennium B.C. Its citizens worshipped Apollo, Athena, and Hera; and Argos had one of the earliest temples to Hera in the Greek world. Its artists played a major role in the creation of the Doric-style temple and the development of Greek sculpture. Traditionally, the earliest Greek coins are supposed to have been minted by Pheidon, the 7th-century B.C. king of Argos. Traces of temples to Apollo and Athena are extant, as is an adjacent terraced sanctuary and altar.

ARIKAMEDU, site of an iron-age settlement in southern India, near Pondicherry. Excavations of this site revealed evidence of Roman trade in the form of Arretine pottery and allowed cross-dating with similar objects at other sites to establish accurate dating of south Indian cultures, especially the previously puzzling megalithic tombs. Conclusions were that the south Indian stone age ended about 200 B.C., followed by the iron-age megalithic culture to the mid-1st century A.D., then the Andhra culture.

ARMENIANS, an ancient Indo-European people of Asia Minor who may have descended from the Phrygians or the people of Urartu. Armenians are first noted in Assyrian annals of the 7th century B.C. as being settled in Urartu, a kingdom of eastern Anatolia, centering around Lake Van. The Biblical Ararat, Urartu has a mountain on which, it is said, Noah's Ark came to rest. In 612 B.C. the first Armenian state, under King Parvir, was established near Lake Van, and from then onwards Armenia grew in power and importance. By the 1st century B.C. Armenian might, as described in Roman annals, had reached its peak, especially during the reign of Tigranes the Great. Little remains of pre-Christian Armenian art and architecture, other than a magnificent coinage and some ruins of palaces. Among these is the spectacular summer palace of the Armenian kings at Garni, in Soviet Ar-

menia. Its ruins include massive fortifications, a Hellenistic temple with a richly carved frieze, and a Roman bath with a beautiful mosaic floor. In the early 4th century A.D. Armenia was converted to Christianity; thus it became one of the world's first Christian nations.

ARNHEM LAND, a broad peninsula of northern Australia, including the offshore Wessel Islands and Groote Eylandt. The aborigines who inhabit this region are prolific craftsmen. Their art is expressed in several media encompassing paintings on bark or in caves and rock shelters and figures carved in wood and in bark or molded in wet sea sand. Some paintings bear a vague resemblance to the stick figures of the African Bushmen. Characteristic of Arnhem Land is the so-called X-ray style of painting which shows the skeletal structure of animals.

ARPACHIYAH. See **HALAFIAN CULTURE.**

ARRETINE WARE, a class of Roman pottery, designed in plain, wheel-thrown form or relief-molded. It was produced in Arretium (modern Arezzo), a city of Etruria in northern Italy. It is characterized by its red-gloss, often glazelike finish. Handleless cups, bowls, and plates were the most popular forms. Arretine ware was often modelled after Roman metalwork, and from 30 B.C. to 50 A.D. it dominated the Roman domestic and international markets.

ARTEMIS, Greek moon goddess, the twin sister of Apollo. Artemis was the chaste goddess of wildlife and especially of the young of all living things. She was revered as the virgin goddess of birth and invoked by women in labor. Tall and slender, she is often depicted with her brother, Apollo, and her attributes are the crescent moon and the bow and quiver. When taken overseas by colonizing Greeks, her cult often changed, and at Ephesus in Asia Minor she was revered and represented as Artemis Polymastos (many-breasted), a mother goddess of the

Near Eastern type. She was known as Diana among the Romans.

ARTEMIS OF EPHESUS, a large and unusual marble cult statue of the Greek goddess Artemis, once the object of veneration in the famous Temple of Artemis in Ephesus. Possibly carved in the 6th century B.C., the statue depicted Artemis as having many breasts, an eccentric iconography more related to Mesopotamian and Anatolian influence than to that of Greece. The many-breasted Artemis that stands in the museum at Ephesus may be a copy of the original or the original itself.

ARYANS, a seminomadic, Indo-European people of Central Asia who began migrating in several directions in the 2nd millennium B.C. A tall, fair, long-headed people who drove horse-pulled chariots and worshipped sky gods, they invaded Europe, Anatolia, and also India, where they overthrew the Indus Valley civilization in the northwest and established Vedic culture, 1500–800 B.C. When Aryan priests composed the *Rigveda* (the sacred Hindu texts) about 1500–1000 B.C., India's written history began. Aryans stressed the purity of their blood and their superiority over the local Dravidian population; this attitude led to the development of the Hindu caste system. By 500 B.C. the Aryans were absorbed into the Indian population.

ARYBALLOS, a small, spherical bottle with a narrow neck. A Greek vessel, it was used for unguents and scented lotions. Large numbers were produced at Corinth from 575 to 525 B.C. Their decoration is usually mechanical and not of high quality.

ASHANTI, one of several Akan-speaking African peoples of southern Ghana. About A.D. 1697 the Ashanti formed a strong confederation under the leadership of Osei Tutu and successfully waged wars against their neighbors until their defeat by the British in 1896. Gold was the traditional medium of exchange, and many art objects from these highly aristocratic people were made of gold. Small brass figures used as gold weights are prized art works. Perhaps their most sacred object is the so-called Golden Stool, which is said to have descended from heaven. Ashanti wood carvings include fertility figures and decorative stools. Colorful kente cloth, woven from silk threads, is of high quality.

Ashanti: Decorative ornament. Gold. From southern Ghana. (British Museum, London)

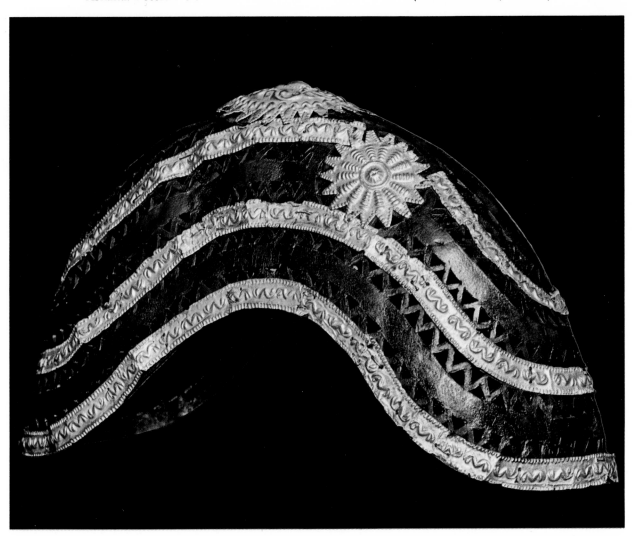

Ashikaga period: "History of Seikoji," detail. Scroll-painting on paper. Japanese, 15th century A.D. (National Museum, Tokyo)

ASHIKAGA PERIOD, in Japanese history, a brilliant epoch (1338 to 1573 A.D.) of cultural development, rapid economic growth, and reunification between the northern and southern imperial courts. It is also called the Muromachi period. Ashikaga art was dominated by Zen Buddhism and "the cultivation of the little." The tea ceremony, Noh drama, landscaping, Sung-style landscape painting (particularly by Shubun and Sesshu), the Kano school of painting, the development of handicrafts, and the establishment of commercial towns are all products of this era. The Ashikaga feudal system came under attack in 1467, and the period ended with a century of war.

ASHUR, the chief god of the Assyrians. He was a sun god, and his symbol was the winged solar disk, a device also widely used by the Egyptians and the Hittites. He was a warrior, leading his people in battle and punishing their enemies. He later became identified with Bel-Marduk, the chief deity of Babylonia.

ASKELON, a city of the Philistines on the Palestine coast near present-day Gaza. It is the only Philistine city excavated as yet. Investigations indicate that the site was once occupied by the Canaanites, whose settlement was destroyed by the Sea Peoples around 1200 B.C. The Philistines followed and were in turn replaced by a Greco-Roman culture.

ASKOS, in the Classical period, a small Greek oil pitcher with a low, flat-bottomed body curving toward a vertical spout at one side. An arched handle above this convex curve is joined to the neck of the spout. The name is also used for various earlier vessels in the shape of a sack, skin, or animal.

ASMAR, a tell on the site of the ancient city of Eshnunna, northeast of Baghdad. The city was first occupied around 3000 B.C. and grew into a place of some importance, with shrines and palaces. It struggled with varying success to remain an independent city-state but was apparently abandoned about a century after being conquered by

Hammurabi of Babylon around 1761 B.C. The "Laws of Eshnunna," an inscribed code found at the site, probably precedes by a few generations the Code of Hammurabi.

ASMAT, an aggressive people living principally along the southwestern coast of New Guinea. The Asmat first became known to outsiders in the 1930s because of their violent assaults on their more peaceful neighbors. Central to every Asmat village was a large ceremonial men's house called a *yeu*. All important festivals and dances centered around the *yeu*. The Asmat had an extremely varied wood sculpture. Relying on red, white, and black as dominant colors, they created intricately carved ceremonial shields bearing abstract mythic symbols. Ancestral bisj poles, drums, canoe prows, and masks stand out among the vast array of their carved household and ritual works.

ASSUR, the religious capital of the Assyrians, named for the god Ashur, who was its patron and whose temple was the city's most prominent building. It was sited on the west bank of the Tigris, 60 miles south of modern Mosul in Iraq. Founded late in the 3rd millennium B.C., it became the first capital of the Assyrian Empire, losing its political but not its religious primacy in the 9th century B.C. It was destroyed by the Medes around 614 B.C. Parts of the city, its temples, and its palaces remain.

ASSYRIAN CIVILIZATION, the long-lasting and influential Mesopotamian power originating in the ancient city of Assur on the Tigris River in the late 3rd millennium B.C. and persisting with some temporary losses of influence until its final collapse around 612 B.C. Its people venerated many deities, generally depicting them in animallike forms. However, religion was apparently less central to Assyrian culture than the more practical pursuits of military conquest and the development of an iron-working technology, which gave Assyria superior weapons for warfare. In addition to Assur the Assyrians built grandiose capital cities at Nineveh, also on the Tigris, and at Nimrud, near modern Mosul, Iraq. Both Nimrud and Nineveh were excavated in the 19th century, revealing remains of great Assyrian monuments, palaces, and temples, many of which contained large-scale stone sculpture, as well as small and delicate ivories and similar art objects. Nineveh also displayed large palace libraries containing inscribed cuneiform clay tablets yielding much information about various aspects of the Assyrian world. Throughout its entire history Assyria's culture was militaristic; thus its periods of greatness were those of territorial expansion and victories in battle. Its first important rulers were of Amorite ethnic origin and included Ishme-Dagan, who briefly made Assyria the strongest power of its time before its conquest in 1790 B.C. by Hammurabi of Babylon. A major resurgence

Assyrian Civilization: Ashurbanipal II. Carving. 883–859 B.C. (Museum of Fine Arts, Boston)

Assyrian art: "Lamassu." Winged, human-headed bull.

of Assyrian power, occurring in the 13th century B.C. under King Shalmaneser, marks what is often called the First Empire. It lasted until around 858 B.C. and is marked by expansion to Urartu (within modern Turkey) and northeast to Armenia. The brief but glorious Second Empire lasted roughly a century and a half, starting in 746 B.C., when Tiglath-pileser III came to power. He consolidated Assyria politically, creating the complex administration needed to govern the now vast territorial empire, extending from the Persian Gulf nearly to the Black Sea and including outright annexation of Assyria's traditional enemy, Babylon. Further territorial expansion and subjugation of neighboring kingdoms continued until the reign of Ashurbanipal (668–627 B.C.), who, despite many victorious campaigns, lost certain important satellite kingdoms, notably Egypt. Ashurbanipal was the last of Assyria's many great kings. Following his death the empire, beset by many of the peoples it had previously conquered, crumbled rapidly. The city of Nimrud was destroyed by the Medes in 612 B.C., and less than a decade later the last traces of Assyrian power had disappeared from the face of the earth.

Assyrian Art and Antiquities. A distinctly Assyrian art style began emerging in Mesopotamia by the 14th century B.C. The Assyrian world view had two opposed aspects, reflected in religious art as contrasted with secular art. Religious expression was mainly architectural. Temples, called ziggurats, were built on artificial elevations, demonstrating a basic Assyrian attitude towards the great distance between the gods and man. Secular art—mainly sculpture—appeared by the 9th century B.C.; this move away from exclusively religious sculpture constituted an innovation in western Asian art. All Assyrian sculpture was relief, the secular works nearly always being palace adornment intended to glorigy the kings who commissioned them. Subjects express the preoccupations of Assyrian nobility—warfare and hunting. Battle scenes, although primitive by classical standards and showing no grasp of perspective, nevertheless have a vivid sense of action and narrative power. Also striking are large, winged, human-headed bulls in high relief, guarding palace entrances. The only extant examples of Assyrian painting are a few nearly ruined frescoes on palace walls, dating from about the 8th century B.C. The British Museum has a world-famous collection of Assyrian antiquities.

ASTARTE, in the Canaanite pantheon, the goddess representing the female principle. She united a diversity of attributes not always strictly compatible, such as virginity and maternity, as well as fertility, love, sex, and war.

Assyrian art: "Naval Expedition," detail. Alabaster bas-relief. Reign of Sargon II. From Khorsabad. (Louvre, Paris)

Many reliefs and figurines bear her representation. The Ashtoreth of the Bible, she is equated with other like goddesses, including the Babylonian Ishtar.

ASUKA PERIOD, in Japanest history, a century (538 to 645 A.D.) in which Buddhism was introduced and influenced Japanese art. The Yamato state opened relations with the three kingdoms of Korea, linking Japan with the northern Wei Dynasty of China. Most Asuka art bears the Wei imprint—a stern approach with fine proportion and stylization. Perhaps the most outstanding expression of Asuka art is the Sakyamuni Triad, a statue of Buddha also known as the Tori Triad. It can be seen at the Horyui-ji temple in Nara.

ASWAN, an Egyptian town on the Nile's northernmost cataract; of some importance since the 3rd millennium B.C., when it was an outpost of the 1st Dynasty's domain. Aswan's granite quarries served ancient Egypt as a source of building material. Dams at Aswan since 1898, supplanted in the 1960s by the world's largest dam, have resulted in the submersion of some ancient monuments, such as those at Philae, beneath man-made lakes. Other edifices (e.g., the Abu Simbel temples) have been relocated beyond the new high-water levels.

ATCHANA, a settlement site, anciently called Alalakh, in south Turkey near the Syrian border. Excavations here have revealed buildings and artifacts dating from the mid-3rd millennium B.C. to around 1200 B.C. Atchana

Athena: Vase ornament. Gilded bronze.

was once an independent state and later became a lesser capital of the Hittites. A number of carved ivories found here show a variety of influences, Egyptian, Hittite, and Aegean. Most notable of the finds is a very fine stone head, thought to be of Yarimlin, a local ruler in whose palace the statue was found; it is executed in a style far in advance of its time and place.

ATESTE. See ESTE.

ATHENA, virgin goddess of Athens, protector and champion of that city but worshipped throughout Greece. Fearing a son stronger than himself, Zeus swallowed his consort, Metis, and Athena sprang fully grown from his head. Leader and defender in war, patroness of arts and crafts, and later the personification of wisdom, Athena first appears in the 7th century B.C. in sculpture and on vases and coins. Her most famous temple, the Parthenon, held both the masterful chryselephantine Athena Parthenos of Phidias and the frieze depicting her important festival—the Panathenaea. Phidias' formidable 40-foot bronze Athena Promachos, as well as the classically serene Athena Lemnia, also adorned the Acropolis. The Romans identified Athena with Minerva.

ATHENA LEMNIA, a Greek bronze statue of Athena by the 5th-century sculptor Phidias. A masterpiece of Greek art, it was dedicated and placed on the Acropolis in Athens by the Athenian colonists who left to settle on the Aegean isle of Lemnos between 451 and 448 B.C. Ancient critics, who knew Phidias' Zeus at Olympia and the famous statue of Athena in the Parthenon, called Athena Lemnia the sculptor's finest work. We know it only through two marble statues in Dresden and a beautiful head in Bologna, which are thought to be Roman copies.

ATHENA NIKE, a small Ionic temple on a bastion of the Athenian Acropolis, built about 410 B.C. It was dedicated to Athena as goddess of victory (*nike*). Despite its small size, the temple had pedimental figures and golden roof decorations (*acroteria*), as well as a finely executed frieze (part of which survives) picturing the struggle of the Greeks against the Persians. So careful had been the ancient construction of Athena Nike that modern restorers were able to reconstruct the temple by fitting together the fragments of its ruins.

ATHENS. A small Ionian town in the 2nd millennium B.C., Athens by the 5th century B.C., and especially under the rule of Pericles, had grown into the artistic and intellectual center of the Greek world. In the early 6th century B.C. Solon liberalized Athenian laws, which ultimately led to the founding of Athenian democracy in 507 B.C. A magnificent city-state, destined to become one of the world's most historic places, Athens twice defeated the Persians in the early 5th century B.C. At its height of greatness, Athens patronized the tragedies of Aeschylus, Sophocles, and Euripides, the paintings of Polygnotos, the sculpture of Phidias, and the architecture of Ictinus.

Athena Nike: Greek Ionic temple, ca 410 B.C. Athenian Acropolis.

Under Pericles the Athenian Acropolis was rebuilt, and such superb buildings as the Parthenon, the Erechtheum, the Athena Nike, the Propylaea, and the Chalkotheke, a repository for bronze votive offerings, were erected. Other remains from the 5th century B.C. include the theater of Dionysus, on the south slope of the Acropolis, and the temple to Hephaestus, the so-called Theseum, in the Athenian Agora. The Agora, or marketplace, has been under excavation since 1931, and finds there date from the 6th century B.C. to the 3rd century A.D.; they include a completely reconstructed stoa of the 2nd century B.C. Outside the Dipylon Gate is the Kerameikos, the ancient cemetery of Athens, where many antiquities have been found. The Pynx, a hill west of the Acropolis, was the meeting place of the Athenian assembly. The building of an empire, the constant warfare, especially with Sparta, the Macedonian invasions of Philip and his son, Alexander the Great, and several plagues finally exhausted Athens. The city was sacked by the Roman Sulla in 86 B.C.

ATLANTES, the term used to describe the large sculptured male figures used as building supports or columns in the ancient world. They are the opposite of caryatids, or maiden columns. Atlantean figures appear in the temple architecture of ancient Greece. Enormous atlantes, some in the form of four-sided columns depicting male warriors, were introduced into the art of ancient Mexico by the Toltecs of Tula.

ATLATL, the New World term for a spear-thrower, an artifact also used in prehistoric Europe. It is a long stick, which serves as an extension of the arm, thus affording the thrower more leverage. Atlatls are often elaborately decorated and thus are highly prized as collectors' items.

ATON, Egyptian god introduced by the 18th Dynasty pharaoh, Akhenaten (or Amenhotep IV), who worshipped him as the one and only god, a radical departure from traditional Egyptian polytheism. The god took the form of the sun disk and was a derivation from the ancient god Amon. Aton appears in art as a disk with oddly shaped rays or wings.

ATRIUM, main feature of a Roman house. It was an unroofed or partly roofed court, entered from the vestibule, which opened onto the street. A usual feature in the developed atrium is the *impluvium*, a large basin set in the floor to catch rainwater from the opening in the roof (*compluvium*).

ATTICA, the easternmost region of central Greece. Its chief city was Athens, which dominated the area by the 7th century B.C. Attica's wealth was due to its natural resources—excellent clay, abundant marble, and silver

Aton: "The God Adored by Akhenaten and Family," detail. Limestone relief. Egyptian, 18th Dynasty. From Amarna. (National Museum, Cairo)

and lead from Laurium. Many archaeological finds of the 6th century B.C., such as sculpture and pottery, show Athenian artistic and political pre-eminence in the Attic countryside, although Eleusis, to the west, retained a prominent religious position because of the goddess Demeter, who is said to have first brought grain to man here.

AUGUSTAN PERIOD, in Roman history, the beginning of Imperial Rome, dating from the reign of the Emperor Augustus (27 B.C.–14 A.D.) and regarded as Rome's golden age of art and culture. The period was marked by the general acceptance of Greek standards of artistic excellence by the Romans. Restraint, elegance, and technical assurance were the hallmarks of Augustan sculpture and painting. Portraiture, as exemplified by the figures sculpted on the Ara Pacis, reached an artistic peak with vivid realism complementing the exaltation of the emperor, a combination of attitudes which, in later times, was expressed in the emperor-cult. Augustan style was Greek in inspiration, but realistically portrayed faces were distinctively and inevitably Roman. Highly romanticized landscape paintings reached new heights during the Augustan age and were much favored by the aristocracy as wall murals. The city of Rome was transformed architecturally as marble replaced sun-dried brick in the construc-

tion of many new and important buildings. The triumphal arch was established as a conventional form of Roman monumental art and subsequently became recognized as a characteristic of Imperial Rome. An extremely fine example of portable Augustan art is the so-called Portland vase.

AURIGNACIAN. The name of this prehistoric upper-paleolithic culture is derived from the village of Aurignac in the Haute-Garonne region among the foothills of the Pyrenees. The culture was widespread in Europe and flourished between 30,000 and 20,000 B.C. in the late old stone age. Cro-Magnon Man appeared in Europe during this period. Finely worked stone tools were made, as well as bone and ivory carvings and cave art. Magdalenian culture followed that of the Aurignacian.

AURORA. See EOS.

AVARS, a people probably originating in central Asia—or perhaps as far east as Mongolia—who established control in the Danube Valley from the 6th through the 9th centuries A.D. before being supplanted by the Magyars. Avar art is primarily metalwork used for personal adornment, saddle decoration, etc. The two dominant motifs in Avar art are fighting animals or griffins and

Attica: Hydria, detail. Black-figure ware. Greek, ca. 510 B.C. (Museum of Fine Arts, Boston; William Francis Warden Foundation)

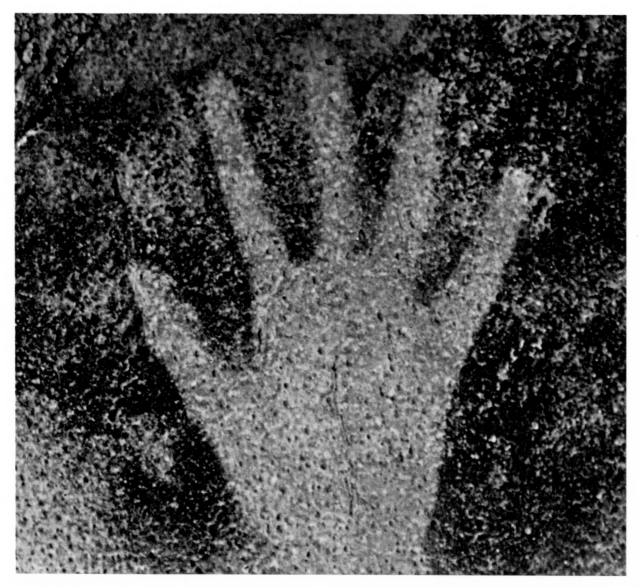

Aurignacian culture: Handprint. Ca. 25,000 B.C. Gargas Caves.

stylized vine shoots or palmettes. Both motifs are often contorted into circular shapes. Their inspiration appears to derive from Scythian and Sarmatian origins.

AVEBURY, in Wiltshire, England, is the site of one of the largest megalithic ceremonial centers in Europe, although its stones, some 14 feet high, are not so massive as those of Stonehenge. A 20-foot bank of chalk soil encloses an area of about 29 acres. Within the bank is a ditch 30 feet deep. In the center a ring of 100 slabs of sarsen, a local sandstone, encloses two smaller stone circles. A remarkable avenue (50 feet wide and a mile long) leads towards the circle and was probably the scene of ritual processions. Avebury was erected by Megalithic Builders and dates from about 2000 to 1600 B.C.

AXUM, a city in northern Ethiopia and center of the ancient kingdom of Axum, which began before 500 B.C.

and lasted through the 1st millennium A.D. During the reign of King Ezana (around 330–350 A.D.) Axum became Christianized, and most subsequent art and architecture shows Christian influences. However, the earliest art and monuments of Axum are from pagan times and involve the worship of the stars. Noteworthy are thin basalt funerary steles, which vary greatly in height. The largest stele still standing is about 70 feet high, dating from the 5th century B.C. Another—still larger but lying in fragments in Axum's ruins—stood 109 feet, which makes it the largest known ancient stele. The temples—and, later, the churches—are stone and usually massive. Many temples contain sculpted thrones and stone figures in an early South Arabian style.

AYUTHIA, the southern cultural center of the early Thai kingdom. The city flourished from the 13th through the

Aztec Civilization: Mask of Xipe. Carved basalt. 14th century A.D. (British Museum, London)

16th centuries A.D. and was located roughly 50 miles north of Bangkok. Its art and architecture is an amalgam of three influences: the Thai, who invaded the region from the north in the early centuries A.D.; the Khmer, or Cambodians; and the Sukhodaya, who preceded the Thai as the region's dominant political power. The chief religious influence in Ayuthia was Hinayana Buddhism; the city's oldest surviving structures are 13th-century Buddhist temples.

AZILIAN CULTURE, a mesolithic culture spread widely in southern and central Europe and named for its type site, the cavern of Mas d'Azil near the French Pyrenees. It began about 8000 B.C. and was roughly contemporaneous with that of the Maglemosian in northern Europe. Azilian man hunted and fished with spears of bone or wood carrying tiny flint points, or microliths; flat bone points were also used. The most distinct element of the Azilians, however, was their geometric paintings, in red ochre, on smooth pebbles.

AZTEC CIVILIZATION, the last, great civilization of Pre-Columbian Mexico. At its height, prior to the Spanish Conquest of 1521, the Aztec Empire held sway over most of present-day Mexico, ruling and demanding rich tribute from many diverse nations and peoples, to say nothing of the endless flow of sacrificial victims exacted from vassal states for Aztec altars. From the most humble, even miserable, origins the Aztecs, a band of nomadic barbarians, built a powerful empire within the space of a few centuries. The Aztecs, or Tenochcas, as they called themselves, entered central Mexico in the 12th century A.D., following the decline and fall of the Toltec Empire. By about 1350 they occupied a swampy island in the middle of Lake Texcoco; the Aztecs attributed their choice of site to divine instructions from their god, Huitzilopochtli, but in fact this was the only land their more powerful neighbors would allow them. Here they founded their capital, Tenochtitlan, which soon grew to be a great and populous imperial city; in later times it was renamed Mexico City. From the beginning of their meteoric rise to power the Aztecs manifested bizarre contradictions of character. They aspired to high culture and refinement while enjoying the most savage of religious practices. Their overwhelming desire to rule led them into alliances, betrayals, and, finally, bloody conquests, conquests which brought them the trappings of more civilized peoples, whom the Aztecs despised. From the fallen Toltec Empire to the north they borrowed a foreign pantheon of gods, while they remained devoted to their own gods, Huitzilopochtli and his monstrous mother, Coatlicue, who demanded a constant stream of blood sacrifice to keep the sun aloft in the heavens. Military expansion was the hallmark of Aztec civilization, and after a great victory in 1430 the Aztec king Itzcoatal ordered all historical records rewritten to establish descent from the prestigious Toltecs. Aztec society was rigidly classified. Most important were the *pilli*, or nobility, all members of the royal family, from whose ranks kings, priests, and warrior chiefs were chosen; the *pochteca*, or merchants, conducted trade, as well as espionage in time of war; the *macehuales*, or commoners, were the most populous class; and finally there were the serfs and the slaves. All Aztec men were required to serve as warriors, and success or failure in battle could drastically alter their social position. However divided Aztec society

Aztec art: Two-headed serpent. Mosaic. 15th century A.D. (British Museum, London)

became—and through the decades the gulf between nobles and commoners widened—the Aztecs were held together by the fear of punishment by sacrifice but, above all, by their faith in themselves as a chosen people with a divine mission to maintain the sun in its heaven. In the years just before the Spanish Conquest this once proud warrior state suffered famine, economic collapse, widespread rebellion, omens of destruction, and, with it, enormously increased human sacrifice. These disastrous events, coupled with the mistaken belief held by Montezuma II, the last great Aztec emperor, that the Spaniard Cortez was a returning god, so weakened the Aztec Empire that it fell easy prey to the Spanish, who were backed by subject peoples no longer willing to abide Aztec oppression.

Aztec Art and Antiquities. Although there are many examples of Aztec antiquities, especially in stone, the Aztecs were an eclectic people who absorbed art styles from

Aztec art: Coatlicue. Basalt. 1324–1521 A.D. From Coxcatlan. (National Museum of Anthropology, Mexico City)

several different nations, particularly those of the Toltecs and the Mixtecs, and consequently it is sometimes difficult to discern that which is essentially Aztec. It is generally accepted, however, that the Aztecs combined foreign traditions with an imperial style of their own invention to form an art of great vigor and technical perfection calculated to convey the power and grandeur of the Aztec state. Aztec stone sculpture ranges in style from the extremely realistic, such as representations of men, animals, and plants, to abstract but terrifying stone statues of divinities. Probably the most famous of these is the huge statue of Coatlicue, the Aztec mother goddess, now in the National Museum of Anthropology, Mexico City. The Aztecs were skilled in the carving of jade and obsidian, the casting of gold, the making of featherwork, and in the creation of startling mosaic masks. Unfortunately, most Aztec architecture, much of their goldwork, and almost all of their painted codices were destroyed by the Spanish.

Aztec art: Shield. Gold with feather mosaic. 1324–1521 A.D. From Mexico City. (National Museum of Anthropology, Mexico City)

Aztec art: Skull mask of Tezcatlipoca. Human skull with turquoise and obsidian mosaic. 15th–16th centuries A.D. (British Museum, London)

B

BA, a Bantu prefix applied to tribal names in west and central Africa. It means simply "the people." Elimination of the prefix in this reference work reflects current preferred usage. See, for example, Kuba rather than Bakuba.

BAAL, the leading god of the Canaanite pantheon. Although the name, meaning "master," was applied to various god figures, Baal proper was the deity of storm, lightning, and rain. He was often depicted as a young warrior with horned helmet. A famous stele showing him was found at Ugarit.

BAALBEK, an ancient Roman colonial city in Lebanon, containing some of the Near East's most impressive Roman architectural ruins. Notable examples include a Temple of Jupiter (built around 60 A.D.), whose standing remains are six magnificent columns, 65 feet high, supporting a lintel; a colonnaded Temple of Bacchus (211–217 A.D.), decorated with intricate relief carving; and a delicate, domed, circular Temple of Venus (2nd or 3rd centuries A.D.), fronted by a Corinthian arch and columns.

BABYLONIAN CIVILIZATION, the seminal and durable civilization of southern Mesopotamia, recognizable as a distinct entity by 1792 B.C. It grew from its capital, Babylon, and endured until its extinction by the Persians in 539 B.C. Babylon's major impact was as the leading cultural force of the ancient Near East. The city of Babylon was on the Euphrates River, about 50 miles south of modern Baghdad; and during its final centuries of existence, when it was at its largest, it had a population of about 100,000 and an area of perhaps 500 acres. Babylonian civilization, which from its earliest extended far beyond the city's confines, originated on approximately the same territory as its ancestral but distinctly separate Sumerian civilization. Babylon's so-called Old Empire was created by the Amorite king Hammurabi, who reigned for over 40 years, beginning in 1792 B.C., consolidating territories from the Persian Gulf to the northernmost regions of the Tigris and Euphrates rivers. Law of the land was the Code of Hammurabi, which, despite its emphasis on extremely harsh punishment to fit criminal acts, was probably the world's most sophisticated body of law to that time. Astronomy, mathematics, and scholarship flourished in the Old Empire, as did many kinds of magic and astrological divinations. Hammurabi was followed by a succession of mediocre kings who presided over Babylon's decline and, in 1595 B.C., its destruction by neighboring Hittites. Babylonian civiliza-

tion was insignificant for about a millennium, as Assyrian military might and culture reigned supreme throughout Mesopotamia. A dramatic Babylonian rebirth occurred, beginning around 604 B.C., under Nebuchednezzar II, who founded what is called the New Babylonian Empire. He extended Babylonian territory to the Mediterranean coast, twice capturing Jerusalem and in 586 B.C. deporting its people to Babylon. The city of Babylon and its civilization experienced its golden age during this period. Babylon was a city of splendor, containing fine temples and palaces, as well as the fabled Hanging Gardens. Its major street was a wide avenue bordered with blueglazed tile walls periodically embellished with animal reliefs. Babylon's gods, mainly inherited from Sumerian civilization and shared with other Mesopotamian peoples, included Marduk, patron of Babylon; Ishtar, goddess of love; and a virtual galaxy of others. But by the mid-6th century B.C., Persia was rapidly becoming western Asia's dominant power. In 539 B.C. Cyrus the Great of Persia took Babylon without a struggle. The city was totally abandoned before the time of Christ.

Babylonian Art and Antiquities. Although several distinct cultures waxed and waned in the forcing ground of world civilization—Mesopotamia—it was Babylonian art and culture, founded largely on the earlier Sumerian tradition, that dominated. Examples of Old Empire animal and human sculpture in terra cotta and bronze have been found at numerous sites, notably the palace ruins at Mari (modern Tell Hariri) and Larsa (modern Senkera). Probably the era's best surviving object is a technically excellent rendition of a head in granite, possibly representing Hammurabi. Ruins of the New Empire at Babylon have revealed a surprising scarcity of art objects, partly because of looting and destruction preceding Babylon's fall and also because a favored sculpture medium was brick, which survives poorly. The most informative ruins include Nebuchadnezzar II's great palace; a small part of the Marduk Ziggurat, thought to be the Biblical Tower of Babel; and the Ishtar Gate, decorated in colored tiles with images of bulls, lions, and dragons.

BACCHUS. See DIONYSUS.

BACTRIA, an ancient region that encompassed parts of modern Turkestan, the Soviet Union, and Afghanistan. It was a major meeting point for early Eastern and Western civilizations. Following conquest by Alexander the Great in 328 B.C., it stood as an eastern outpost of Hellenistic culture. Although soon separated from the West when the Parthians expanded their territories into Iran, Bactria remained culturally Greek until about 135 B.C., when it was overrun by an Asian tribe, the Saraks. There is academic dispute about Bactria's importance as a feeder of Greek art influences into India via nearby Gandhara.

BADEN CULTURE, in central Europe, a period when seminomadic warriors moved in from the north upon the

Babylonian Civilization: "Code of Hammurabi," detail. Black basalt stele. 18th century B.C. (Louvre, Paris)

Bambara: Chiwara mask. Carved wood. (Pierre Vérité Collection, Paris)

settled neolithic peasants of the rich Danubian culture some time prior to 2000 B.C. The resultant mixed culture spread westwards and in its Austrian phase is known as the Baden culture. Pottery associated with it has high, ornamental handles and fluted decoration on the body of the vessel. This distinctive form of handle and ornament was carried forward and reproduced in vessels of the succeeding European bronze age.

BAGA, a West African people living in coastal Guinea. Although they have lived along the coast for several hundred years, the Baga have legends that recall their migration from a homeland near the source of the Niger River. Baga art, politics, and religion are concentrated in the secret Simo Society. A visually striking mask of the Simo Society is the *nimba*, a huge beaked mask with large breasts; it is known as the maternity figure. The *banda* mask, used in initiation ceremonies, is also fearsome in appearance. Long and worn horizontally on top of the head, it is a composite of human, crocodile, and antelope features.

BALDR, a Nordic god, son of Odin and Frigg, and a favorite with all the Nordic gods. He was the god of light and so handsome that he shed radiance all around him. Frigg tried to protect him by having all plants, animals, and stones swear never to do him harm. The demon god, Loki, however, discovered that mistletoe had been excepted from this oath and with a wand of that plant succeeded in bring about the death of Baldr.

BALI, a small island off the east coast of Java in Indonesia and an outpost of Hindu culture since about 1500 A.D. Earlier, in 1293, the Hindu dynasty of Majapahit came to power in neighboring Java and continued to rule there for about 200 years, until driven away by Islamic powers from India. The Majapahit survivors took refuge on Bali, which they previously had ruled only nominally. A difficult target for military invasion, Bali was ignored by potential Islamic attackers, and its transplanted Hindu culture remained relatively undisturbed. It has fine examples of Hindu art and architecture.

BALKAN CULTURE. The most important fact about the prehistoric Balkan area is that it was one of the two routes by which farming and pottery-making were introduced into Europe as part of the slow spread of the neolithic agricultural revolution. The other route was from North Africa through Italy and France. The Balkan cultural region shows constant early contact with neolithic Aegean, Anatolian, and Mesopotamian cultures and with Minoan civilization in Crete. Pottery of various kinds, burnished, incised, and painted, is found in Macedonia, Thessaly, up to the significant settlements of Vinca near Belgrade and Starcevo in Rumania, which form the starting points for the spread of Danubian culture to the north. Danubian culture, beginning about 4500 B.C., may be considered an outgrowth of the earlier culture of the

Balkan farmers. There was also a flowback of painted pottery from the Danube down south to Thessaly and the Aegean area.

BALL GAME, in Pre-Columbian religion, a ritual game played over a wide area of America from as early as 1000 B.C. until the time of the Spanish Conquest. It reached its greatest elaboration in the regions of modern-day Mexico and Guatemala. The game was played by two teams, each composed of three to seven players. The ball symbolized the sun, which had to be kept aloft through the efforts of men. It could be struck only with the elbows, knees, and hands of the players. Failure to keep the ball in play, an omission punished by death, meant that the sun had gone to the underworld, where its light would be extinguished. Various aspects of the game are depicted in carved relief panels, painted codices, and portable sculpture. The ball game was the inspiration for some of the finest stone sculpture to come from ancient Mexico: yokes, hachas, and palmas, all thought to be ceremonial paraphernalia associated with it.

BALUCHISTAN, an ancient trade-route region, situated between principal cities of the Indus Valley and Mesopotamia. The area included territory along the modern Iran-Afghanistan border. Remains of trading posts in this area date back to 4000 or 3500 B.C. and contain copper and stone objects similar to those found in such widely separated regions as Persia and Mohenjo-Daro. Baluchistan's earliest known natives include the Kulli, a copper-age people whose main extant art is painted earthenware pottery.

BAMBARA, an African people living in Mali. The Bambara, whose name means "infidels," formed two strong kingdoms in the 17th and 18th centuries A.D. The older and stronger of the two was at Segou; the other was farther north at Kaarta. They served as bulwarks against the rising tide of Islam in West Africa. The Bambara produced many works of art, including ancestor figures, fertility figures, and intricately carved pulleys. In addition, they had a wide variety of masks associated with their various secret societies. The jewel among Bambara masks was the Chiwara, an elegant antelope mask, said to represent the mythical being who taught agriculture to the Bambara.

BAMILEKE, an African people of south-central Cameroons. The Bamileke fled to their present mountainous homeland after the 17th-century A.D. invasions by the warlike Fulani. In the relative security afforded by their new home terrain they established several small chiefdoms. Many art objects, such as wood and bead-encrusted stools, served the need of local royalty. Beads also adorned some Bamileke masks. The Bamileke achieved an especially successful union of art and architecture. The door frame and roof-supporting pillars of the chief's house were profusely carved with human images.

BAMIYAN, the site of unusual Buddhist cave monasteries in northern Afghanistan. The world's two most colossal statues of Buddha, 175 feet and 120 feet tall respectively, are also there. Bamiyan's statues, monasteries, and temples were carved out of a sandstone cliffside. The Buddhas seem to date from about the 3rd century A.D., but the monasteries and temples are probably older, having architectural styles deriving from ancient Iranian and Greco-Roman sources. However, the paintings within the temples are Indian in style.

BANDKERAMIK WARE is the name given to a neolithic pottery of the Danubian farming culture which spread over the loess lands of central Europe in the 4th millennium B.C. In the Bandkeramik style ribbons, or bands, of linear ornament decorate gourd-shaped pots and vessels. The ware occurs in several German sites and derives its name from the German. The ornamentation has been dated from about 3000 B.C. and thoroughly classified at the site of Koln-Lindenthal on the Rhine.

BANGWA, an African people of the southwestern Cameroons. The Bangwa were not a unified tribe but consisted of nine chiefdoms, the most important of which

Bamiyan: Bodhisattva. Detail of cave painting. Northern Afghanistan.

44

Battersea Shield: Gilded bronze with enamel. Celtic, 1st century B.C. (British Museum, London)

was Fontem. Situated in rugged mountains, the chiefdoms deterred Europeans until 1897. The Bangwa carved many masks used by various societies. One such group was the so-called Night Society, which oversaw proper succession to the chieftaincies. Elaborately carved stools for the chiefs and ancestor figures were prominent among their art objects. Bangwa style is heterogeneous. Some works are related to western neighbors such as the Ekoi; others look more like Bamileke art.

BANTUS, the largest division of African peoples, they inhabit a vast area covering central, eastern, and southern Africa. The term "Bantu" is most precisely a linguistic, not a racial, description. It embraces a wide variety of cultures, ranging from the simple village Kota to the empire-building Lunda. The majority of Bantu-speaking peoples are settled farmers.

BARKAER, site on the northeast coast of Jutland, in Denmark, where the earliest traces of European neolithic farming north of Switzerland were found. Pollen analysis shows that forests were cleared and grain grown. Two remarkable longhouses of 26 rooms, lining a stone-cobbled "street," were discovered at the site. Collared pottery flasks and jars, amber beads, and copper pendants of about 2500 B.C. were also found, the last presaging the imminent arrival of the bronze age.

BARK CLOTH. See TAPA CLOTH.

BARK PAINTING, in primitive art, a painting applied to the inside of a bark surface. The technique is found over parts of Melanesia, most notably in the Lake Sentani, Humboldt Bay, and Gulf of Papua regions of New Guinea. Bark painting is especially common in north and northeastern Australia, where its style varies widely according to location. The most distinctive bark paintings are probably those in the X-ray style of Arnhem Land, Australia, which depict the internal organs of living creatures. In general, bark paintings are divided into two classes: those that are cult symbols and can be viewed only by initiates and others that may be enjoyed by the entire community as decorative, as well as magical, objects.

BARROW, a term, originating in England, used to describe ancient burial mounds, some round, others long and rectangular in shape. In some barrows, mounds of earth are heaped up over inner tombs built of stone, or over cairns of loosely piled stones.

BARUMINI, an archaeological site in Sardinia, dating from the mid-2nd millennium B.C. There are nuraghes, or towers of massive masonry, surrounded by a stone wall. In the late 6th century B.C. the settlement was captured by the Carthaginians but reoccupied thereafter by Sardinians until Roman times.

BASALT, a volcanic rock, ranging in color from green through brown and black. Where available it was often

used by primitive societies and ancient cultures to make art objects.

BASARABI CULTURE, a major iron-age culture in Rumania. The Hallstatt cemetery in Austria is definitive for typing the Basarabi culture further east, and this eastern version of Hallstatt is named for Basarabi on the Danube. The cemeteries and settlements of this epoch in Rumania are dated from 800 to 650 B.C. Bronze was still used in this period for ornaments, but swords and other weapons were of iron.

BASILICA, a large public hall found in almost every city of the western Roman Empire. Often of rectangular form with a roofed hall, the basilica usually formed one of the boundaries of a Roman forum. It had commercial, religious, and military purposes but is generally associated with the administration of justice. The derivation of large Christian churches called by the same name is not so direct or certain as was once thought.

BAS-RELIEF, low-relief sculpture. The term ranges in application from extremely low relief to a sculptural projection of about half of a subject's actual proportions. In all cases, the forms stand out from a plane or a curved background surface. In many civilizations there is a development from bas-relief to high relief to free-standing sculpture.

BASTET, the Egyptian cat goddess worshipped mainly in the region of the Nile Delta. Numerous cat figurines survive; typical are bronzes from Egypt's late period (712 B.C. to about the Christian era).

BATIK, a technique of fabric decoration widely practiced in Indonesia, particularly on Java. Certain portions of the cloth are covered with wax so that they do not absorb color when dyed. The waxing and dyeing process is repeated several times and ends in an elaborate pattern, including cursive animal and plant designs. The origins of batik art are uncertain; however, temple ruins in Java, up to 1,200 years old, have yielded fragments of stone figures wearing garments with batik designs. Modern machine-made batiks fail to duplicate the intricate and rich designs found on earlier, hand-made versions of the art.

BATTERSEA SHIELD, a Celtic shield of bronze, with embossed decoration and red enamel studs, dredged up from the Thames River at Battersea and dating from about the 1st century B.C. The "tendril" ornamentation is characteristic of Celtic decoration and is found also on swords in Switzerland and on captive shields depicted on a Roman arch at Orange in southern France. Nearly three feet high, the shield is now in the British Museum.

BATTLE-AXE PEOPLE. At about the same time as the Beaker People were spreading over Europe, at or before 2000 B.C., nomadic peoples from the east were also moving in. Large numbers of their characteristic battle-axes of stone have been found in barrow graves in Denmark, in other parts of Scandinavia, in Germany, indeed all over north, central, and eastern Europe and as far south as northern Turkey. The axe heads are six to eight inches long, with a blade at one end and a hammer or knob at the other and with a hole to take the shaft. They are made of porphyry, greenstone, and granite, beautifully cut and polished. The Battle-Axe People tended cattle and horses, cultural traits developed on the Russian steppes. They may have been among the earliest of Indo-European people to enter Europe.

BATTLE OF THE ISSUS, a famous Roman floor mosaic found in 1831 in the House of the Faun at Pompeii. The clear but crowded composition represents with a vivid sense of drama the battle of Alexander the Great against the Persian king Darius III at the river Issus in 333 B.C. The mosaic is derived from a celebrated 4th-century Greek painting either by Philoxenos or Aristeides of Thebes and mirrors that period's skillful use of foreshortening and the effects of light and relief obtained with a few fundamental colors on a dun background. The accuracy of costumes and weapons and the careful portraits of Alexander and Darius clearly reflect the Roman love for realistic detail. Though it served as a floor decoration, this large mosaic (it measures almost nine feet by seventeen feet) now hangs like a painting on a wall of the Naples Museum.

BAULE, an Akan-speaking West African people living in southern Ivory Coast. Their identity as a people began in the mid-18th century A.D. when they separated from the Ashanti and migrated westward under the leadership of Queen Aura Poku. The elegant and graceful Baule art style, long admired by Europeans, best exhibits itself in so-called ancestor figures. Gold and brass pendants were made of fine filigree or cast by the cire-perdue process. Distinctive, too, was a large round and flat mask with stylized animal features and a monkey deity carved in the round.

BAYON TEMPLE. See ANGKOR.

BEAKER PEOPLE. Drinking vessels, or beakers of bell shape, finely made of brown or red clay, with a capacity of two to three pints and decorated with incised geomet-

Baule: "Monkey deity" mask. Painted wood. (Museum of African and Oceanic Art, Paris)

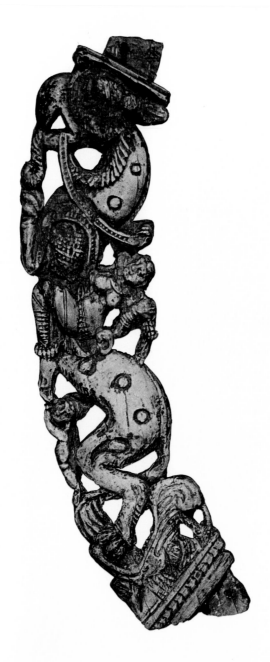

Begram: Ivory-inlay plaque, ca. 2nd century A.D. (Musée Guimet, Paris)

BEEHIVE TOMB. See THOLOS.

BEGRAM, ancient Kushan capital in Afghanistan. It was originally a Persian town but was annexed to Bactria after Alexander's conquest. The Kushans, who were related to the Sarak destroyers of Bactria, flourished in and around Begram from the 2nd century B.C. until about 241 A.D. The city was culturally international, its art showing Greco-Roman, Indian, and Syrian influences. Major extant art objects include delicate Indian-style ivory plaques. Some Buddhas from Begram of the 2nd and 3rd centuries A.D. resemble late Roman and early Christian sculpture.

BEHISTUN, a village in Iran, 30 miles east of Kermanshah. Near here, on a precipitous rock face 300 feet above ground, Darius the Great had carved, in 516 B.C., a commemoration of his victories in winning control of the Persian Achaemenid Empire. A colossal bas-relief shows Darius confronting his shackled, defeated enemies as the god Ahuramazda blesses him. More important, there are carved cuneiform inscriptions in Old Persian, Babylonian, and Elamite describing Darius' triumphs. In the mid-19th century, Sir Henry Rawlinson managed with great difficulty the dangerous task of copying these inscriptions and began deciphering them. Rawlinson's work on the Behistun inscriptions was the crucial key that opened the long-dark mysteries of cuneiform.

BELDIBI, an archaeological site on the southern coast of Anatolia, dating to the mid-7th millennium B.C. The Beldibi peoples lived in rock shelters, practiced primitive agriculture, and made simple pottery, a craft they undoubtedly learned from the more advanced culture at Catal Huyuk on the Anatolian plateau. Beldibi is remarkable in that it is the only area of the Near East where cave art, similar to that of the Magdalenian in western Europe, has been found. These simple wall paintings, chiefly rock engravings of bulls and stags, as well as small portable objects such as figurines, incised stones, and decorated weapons found at Beldibi, have led scholars to conjecture that the Beldibi and the Magdalenians were actually of the same race.

BELGAE, peoples of north Gaul between the Seine and the Rhine, first known through Julius Caesar's account. Most were of Celtic origin, but Caesar characterizes some eastern branches as Germans who had migrated across the Rhine. Some sections of the tribe inhabited Britain. The names of many branches of the Belgae survive in present-day place names, as Bellovaci in Beauvais, Suessiones in Soissons, Remi in Rheims, and Ambiani in Amiens. Attacked by Caesar in 57 B.C., they formed a defensive alliance but were finally subdued in 46 B.C. Augustus set up Belgicas as a separate province in northern Gaul in 16 B.C. Well-furnished Belgae tombs, containing high-quality metalwork, have been found.

ric designs, have been unearthed all over Europe. The people who made these beakers seem to have originated in central Spain in about 2000 B.C. and to have spread widely, travelling as traders to France, Austria, Holland, and Britain. They brought with them not only their distinctive beakers but also short daggers made of bronze, which proved to be the first metal objects seen in many parts of Europe. They may also have spread the art of brewing beer. Single buttons associated with their graves may indicate the use of a loose woolen garment fastened by a button at the neck. Their beakers are often found at the sites of the Megalithic Builders.

Benin Civilization: Two leopards. Ivory and copper. 19th century A.D. (British Museum, London)

BELLA COOLA, a North American Indian tribe settled in northern British Columbia. The Bella Coola shared the distinctive traits of the Northwest Coast culture, including an economy based on the sea and forest, a well-developed social system, and the production of elaborate art objects. They are especially famous for bold, dramatic wooden sculptures and the use of vibrant colors to emphasize their features. The Bella Coola also produced a distinctive type of mask with movable or interchangeable parts, used in their winter dances.

BENA LULUA. See LULUA.

BENI HASSAN, site of a rock-cut temple and several tombs in Middle Egypt. The temple was constructed by the queen, Hatshepsut (reigned about 1505–1484 B.C.), and dedicated to a cat goddess, Pakhet. The tombs are earlier, built for noblemen of around 1900 B.C., most

notable among them being that for the prince, Khnumhotep. The burial chambers are beneath chapels bearing columned porticoes. Chamber walls are covered with paintings depicting Egyptian life, including battle scenes, peasants in the fields, and skilled craftsmen at work. A few burial chambers were converted into Coptic chapels in early Christian times.

BENIN CIVILIZATION. Centered on the city of Benin in southwest Nigeria, the Benin kingdom was a powerful and remarkable African state. It first appears in history about 1400 A.D., when the Bini people sent for a new king from Ife, the sacred Yoruba city. Oranmiyan (or Oranyan) arrived, but finding life difficult among an alien people, he returned to Ife. His son, nevertheless, grew up to be installed as the first Benin Oba, or king. He and his successors ruled a large area from their palace in the

Benin art: Head of a Queen Mother. Cast bronze. 15th–16th centuries A.D. (British Museum, London)

art were made for the Oba and his court. Among the more celebrated bronzes are free-standing statues and narrative wall plaques, which decorated royal buildings. They depict the Oba often attended by palace chiefs, royal musicians, court retainers, and soldiers; even Portuguese soldiers figure prominently in Benin bronzes. Of the more sacred objects were elaborate bells and intriguing bronze heads, assembled for royal altars at which the Oba honored his ancestors in annual ceremonies. These heads supported ivory tusks intricately carved with images of former Obas. Ivory was also used for masterful carved masks and for royal sistra. Lively debate centers on the origin of Benin bronze-casting. Legend holds that it derived from Ife during the reign of Oba Oguola. Close examination of Benin and Ife objects, however, demonstrates great differences between the two art styles.

BERBERS, an indigenous Caucasoid people of North Africa. Although they are quite widely spread, they tend to live largely in mountainous areas. It is estimated that there are some five million people speaking the Berber language, which is a member of the Hamitic linguistic group. Berbers are fiercely independent; they are organized into self-sufficient families, clans, communities, and tribes. Berbers tend to be primitive Moslems, although their women are far less subservient than in traditional Moslem societies. Berbers produce rugs, blankets, and pottery decorated with distinctive geometric patterns.

BERLIN PAINTER. See GREEK CIVILIZATION.

BERNARDINI TOMB, an Etruscan burial vault at Praeneste (Palestrina), in central Italy, dating from the 7th century B.C. and holding an unusual number of fine gold, ivory, silver, and bronze objects. It is named after the Bernardini brothers, who financed its hasty and highly unscientific excavation in 1876. The wealth and type of grave goods from the tomb suggests that it held several burials, probably of Etruscan warriors. The style and motifs of the treasure, which includes silver relief bowls, glass, faience, and gold jewelry and weapons, show the effect of eastern Mediterranean influences (Cypriot, Phoenician, and Syrian) on Etruscan art. Most of the Bernardini pieces are now in the collection of the Villa Guilia in Rome.

BERNOUS, a cave near Bourdeilles in the Dordogne, France, which contains some of the earliest cave art known. It is dated in the Aurignacian period, approximately 30,000 B.C., and includes depictions of mammoth, bear, and rhinoceros.

BETHEL, an ancient Palestinian city about ten miles north of Jerusalem. Although cited in Genesis as the approximate site of Abraham's altar to God, the town was rejected as the site for a holy city by the Israelite King David around 1000 B.C. However, Bethel soon gained importance as a Hebrew religious sanctuary, becoming the temporary seat of the Ark of the Covenant. After the

fortified capital city. Benin's fluid borders encompassed at times such non-Bini peoples as Yorubas and Ibos, over whom the autocratic Oba had the power of life and death. He maintained a monopoly over trade and specifically excluded all foreigners. Twice a year every village was required to send tribute to the Oba, and any village refusing to do so was considered in revolt and faced the wrath of the Oba and his menacing armies. Rigid hierarchical ordering of offices, both hereditary and nonhereditary, marked the political structure. Benin became wealthy through trade in ivory, pepper, palm oil, and slaves. It was notorious for its slave trade and the practice of human sacrifice. Benin first came to be known to Europeans in 1485 through the written accounts of the Portuguese explorer Affonso de Aveiro. Its history of independence came to an abrupt end in 1897 when a British punitive expedition invaded the capital; a brief struggle was concluded with the destruction of Benin and exile for its defeated Oba.

Benin Art and Antiquities. Benin art ranks with the finest in Africa. Their bronzes, skillfully crafted in cire perdue, testify to the past greatness of the culture. As bronze-casting was a royal monopoly and prerogative, works of

death of Solomon and the subsequent collapse of his unified kingdom, Bethel became a religious center rivalling Jerusalem in importance.

BIBLICAL ARCHAEOLOGY, a term applied to that branch of archaeology concerned with the reconstruction and illumination of events described in the Old Testament. Excavations in and around Palestine have revealed the substantial accuracy of the Old Testament as a historical record of the ancient Hebrews. Among the major Biblical sites of the region are Jericho, Samaria, Megiddo, Lachish, Mersin, and Hazor. Of a much earlier time are the finds from Mesopotamia, which predate the great Palestinian period by many centuries. There, thousands upon thousands of written clay tablets have been unearthed at sites such as Nuzi, Mari, Ugarit, and Ur, which carry stories of the Biblical Flood, the narrative of Jacob, prophecies (later adopted by the Hebrews), and poems and psalms which also found their way into the Old Testament. It is possible that the ancient Hebrews, a group of desert tribes, migrated to Mesopotamia in the 3rd millennium B.C. and there were taught the arts of civilization by the Sumerians, the most advanced people of their time. Biblical archaeology enjoyed its greatest triumph with the astounding discovery of the Dead Sea Scrolls. Found near Qumran, these manuscript scrolls not only support and enhance the history of the Old Testament but also shed a penetrating light on the genesis of the New Testament.

BICHE DE BALZOTE. See IBERIAN PEOPLES.

BIERI. See FANG.

BIRKA, a site on an island in the Malar Lake in Uppland, Sweden, the most northerly major trade center in Europe during the Viking age. It flourished between 800 and 975 A.D. In the 1,200 graves outside its walls that have so far been excavated, evidence of coins, pottery, jewelry, metalwork, glass, skins, and many other objects testify not only to the work of local artisans but to trade connections with all of western Europe, Byzantium, and the Arab world.

BISJ POLE, a tall, totemlike pole carved by the Asmat people of southwestern New Guinea to commemorate their ancestors. The usual iconography of the bisj pole is of slender and tall ancestor-figures with long, attenuated limbs. A flaglike openwork structure juts out from the top. The bottom of the pole is carved in a stylized figure 8, which is said to represent the roots of the sacred banyan tree. The pole is carved from a banyan after it is ritually "hunted and killed."

BISKUPIN, a complete village of the iron age in Poland, discovered near the modern town of Biskupin northeast of Poznan. The village was built in 700 B.C. on an island in a lake with a causeway of 150 yards leading to the shore. Solidly constructed ramparts of earth-filled timber frames surrounded the settlement to protect it from enemies and from the waters of the lake. The houses, on long log-paved streets, were constructed of tongued and grooved timbers and thatched with reeds. They had stamped clay floors and contained a stone hearth, a raised common bed, and a place for a loom opposite the door where there was maximum light. One of the first plows known in Europe was found at Biskupin, as well as stone querns for grinding grain, iron and bronze implements, amber and glass beads, and finely worked articles of bone. The main food was grain and pork, and there was little hunting. The waters of the lake gradually gained on the town and it had finally to be abandoned.

BITIK HUYUK, an archaeological site, located near modern Ankara, Turkey, where the famous Bitik Vase was found. It is now in the Archaeological Museum in Ankara. Dating from the last half of the 2nd millennium B.C., it is one of the few vases with relief decoration to survive intact from the pre-Hittite period. The neck, shoulders, and body of the vase are decorated with three continuous bands of relief, each about six inches wide, with depictions of religious ceremonies. The reliefs show vestiges of polychrome painting, which may suggest the presence of colored stucco reliefs or wall paintings in Bitik's temples and palaces.

BLACK-FIGURE VASES. See GREEK CIVILIZATION.

BLACK OBELISK, a monument erected by Shalmaneser III (859–824 B.C.) of Assyria to commemorate his discovery of the sources of the Tigris. Found at Nimrud, the obelisk celebrates the event in 24 oblong relief panels and an inscription. In relief is the only known depiction of an ancient Hebrew king, Jehu. The obelisk is in the British Museum.

BLACK PAGODA. See KONARAK.

BOBO, an African people living principally in Upper Volta. The Bobo, unknown to Europeans until 1887, comprise several tribes that differ from one another noticeably in their art. The Bobo Fing or Black Bobo, for instance, carve a relatively realistic wood helmet mask sometimes surmounted by a crest. This mask is worn at funerals or at initiation rites for young men. The Bwa (or Bwaba) display many masks during ceremonies of their Do Society, a secret governing organization. These colorful and highly abstract masks are decorated with lines and chevrons; their huge penetrating eyes are heavily accented with concentric circles. All of the Bobo people carved free-standing human figurines.

BODHGAYA, among the most sacred of all Buddhist sites, located on the outskirts of the Indian town of Gaya. Buddhist scriptures relate that Siddhartha Gautama found enlightenment here while seated under the legendary Tree of Wisdom (and after 49 days of meditation on the meaning of existence). He thus became Buddha—one who is fully enlightened—and spent the remaining 40 years of his life teaching the precepts he had attained at Bodhgaya.

Bodhisattva: Detail of painting in colors on silk. Japanese, Heian period. (National Museum, Tokyo)

BODHISATTVA, a Buddhist term designating spiritual beings usually incarnated as men. They live among suffering humanity as powers of goodness, dedicating themselves to mankind. In this way they postpone their entry into the state of pure spirituality and enlightenment of a Buddha and thus are considered saintly but not divine. They are common subjects in Buddhist painting and sculpture.

BODHI TREE. See **BUDDHIST ART AND ANTIQUITIES.**

BODROGKERESZTUR, a site in east Hungary that gives its name to a culture which succeeded that of Tisza, or Theiss, and forms part of the Hungarian copper age from about 2800 B.C. This culture was formed by a combination of the Schneckenburg culture of Rumania and the Tisza culture of Hungary. Largely a cemetery site, Bodrogkeresztur is noted for its metal tools and battle-axes, its pottery with pedestals, and its jars with characteristic small lugs on cylindrical necks. The men in the graves were laid on their right sides, the women on their left.

BOEOTIA, an ancient region of central Greece bordering Attica (the district of Athens). Archaeological evidence indicates that it was important in the Greek bronze age (2500 to 1100 B.C.). Homer names 29 of its towns in the *Iliad,* but, in Classical times, there were only about a dozen towns, of which Thebes was the most significant. Boeotia was artistically backward but produced several poets, Hesiod and Pindar among them. Its coins display an ox hide as a symbol, a punning allusion to the resemblance between the name of the region and the Greek word for ox (*bous*). Boeotian terra-cotta figurines, usually in the form of abstract gods or animals, are plentiful.

BOGHAZKOY, a Turkish village east of Ankara near the site of Hattusas, the ancient capital of the Hittites. The place was first inhabited in pre-Hittite times, about 3000 B.C. From the 16th to the 13th centuries B.C. it was the residence of the Hittite kings and the center of their empire. Excavations have revealed massive defensive walls, gates, temples, and more than 10,000 clay tablets bearing cuneiform inscriptions, from which comes most of our information on Hittite history and culture. The rock sanctuary of Yazilikaya, with many relief figures and hieroglyphics, lies nearby. Hattusas fell with the Hittite Empire around 1230 B.C.

BOHUSLAN. Carvings on smooth slabs of rock in the Bohuslan province of south Sweden were identified in 1906 as being connected with sun worship in the bronze age. A typical depiction represents the solar disc carried on a ship at night, from sunset to sunrise, guarded all the while by men with battle-axes. The sun was believed to traverse the heavens in a chariot drawn by horses and to return by sea at night. Similar rock carvings are widespread in Norway and Sweden.

BONAMPAK, an ancient Mayan ceremonial site, with several ruined temples, in the Mexican state of Chiapas, near the Guatemalan border. It is renowned for its miraculously preserved polychrome wall paintings, executed about 800 A.D. Scenes of the robing of priests, a great battle, the sacrifice of prisoners, and a festival, including a dance and bloodletting ceremony, cover temple walls. In addition to their great artistry in composition and their richness of color, the Bonampak murals are famed for the wealth of information they yield about Mayan customs.

BONPO. See **LAMAIST ART AND ANTIQUITIES.**

BOOK OF THE DEAD, in Egyptian archaeology, the term given to those papyrus scrolls, some measuring 75 feet in length, found in ancient Egyptian tombs. Fre-

Bonampak: Fresco, detail. Mayan. Temple of the Frescoes.

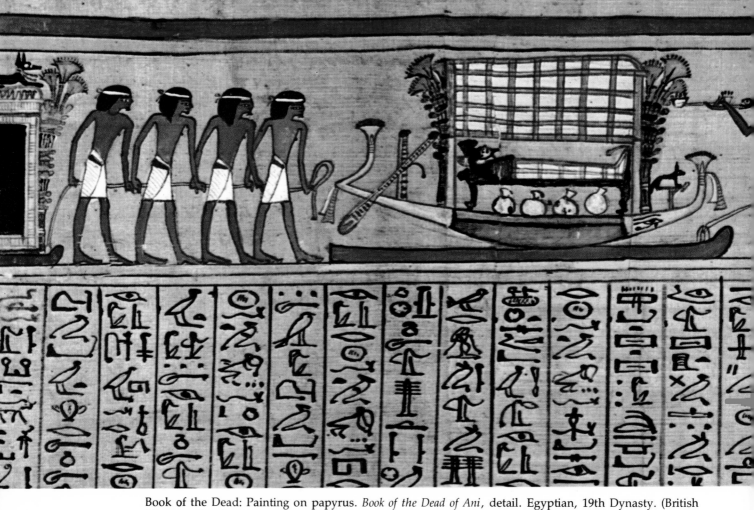

Book of the Dead: Painting on papyrus. *Book of the Dead of Ani*, detail. Egyptian, 19th Dynasty. (British Museum, London)

quently illustrated, they offer magic spells and incantations for the deceased. The term sometimes includes coffin and tomb inscriptions as well as scrolls. A Book of the Dead was inserted in a tomb to aid the deceased in his efforts to cope with the afterlife. The practice originated during the 18th Dynasty, in the New Kingdom, although its early versions—the Pyramid Texts—date from the 5th and 6th Dynasties. There is no uniformity of content or arrangement regarding various parts of the Book of the Dead.

BOOMERANG, a weapon used chiefly by the aborigines of Australia. A flat, slightly curved object made of hard, close-grained wood, the boomerang was used as a missile and for hitting or striking. It was very often decorated with incised geometric designs that were stylized emblems of totems.

BOROBUDUR, a great Buddhist temple in central Java and that island's most important Buddhist monument. The grandeur of Borobudur's architecture and iconography places it among the supreme masterpieces of Asian art. Its origin is shrouded in mystery, although it was probably built in the 8th century A.D., at the time when the area was ruled by a dynasty founded by Shailendra, an expatriate from India. The temple apparently was abandoned around 1000 A.D. and forgotten by history

until its discovery in the 19th century. It was fully excavated by the Dutch East Indian administration in 1907–11. Borobudur is in the shape of a huge, many-terraced pyramid, the walls of which are covered with intricate bas-reliefs, and domed and niched to hold a total of 72 Buddha statues. At the structure's summit is the main stupa, a peaked dome containing an unfinished Buddha.

BOSCOREALE HOARD, a treasure of 94 pieces of silver plate of Alexandrine and Roman workmanship, unearthed in 1893–94 in the ancient villa of Boscoreale. Situated near Pompeii, the villa was buried by the eruption of Vesuvius in 79 A.D. The treasure could have been deposited in Boscoreale by those fleeing the volcanic disaster. The Boscoreale hoard is in the Louvre.

BOYNE, a river in Ireland, about 25 miles north of Dublin, on the bank of which is a bronze-age cemetery of chambered tombs, called Brugh na Boinne, and dating from some time after 2000 B.C. They form the finest group of prehistoric ritual monuments in Ireland and include New Grange. The tombs were robbed of their treasures by Norse invaders in 861 A.D.

BRAHMA, the highest personification of god in Hindu religion and the term used to denote the Universal Soul in Hindu philosophy. Early Hindu writings, or *Vedas*, contain legends in which Brahma is given a somewhat man-

like personality. More sophisticated Hindu philosophy, spelled out in the *Upanishads,* sees Brahma as the ultimate reality, totally immaterial and without individuality.

BRAHMAGIRI, a major archaeological site in southern India, excavated in 1947. Three distinct cultures were found here. The earliest dates from before 2000 B.C. and used stone tools. The second, dating from the 1st millennium B.C., employed copper instruments and buried its dead in chambers similar to those found as far away as Palestine and Europe. The third, dating from about 200 B.C. and later, shows evidence of trade with ancient Rome.

BRAK, an archaeological site in eastern Syria north of the Khabur River. It was occupied from very early prehistoric times until the mid-2nd millennium B.C. The most striking finds here are a very large number of small—about two inches high—alabaster figurines of vaguely human shape whose major feature is the eyes (hence the "Eye Temples" associated with them) and a curious painted cup representing a man's visage.

BRIGANTES. See STANWICK BRONZES.

BRITONS. The name refers to the early inhabitants of Britain, but because of successive waves of migration the term is not easy to define. There are remains of the work of man in Britain in all the major divisions of prehistoric time, such as the paleolithic, particularly in the south of England and Creswell Crags in Derbyshire, and neolithic and bronze-age remains of the Megalithic Builders and the Beaker People. But the name "Britons" takes on more meaning, and is usually used, when opposed to invaders such as the Romans and the Anglo-Saxons. The tribes in Britain who faced the Romans in the 1st century A.D. were related to the peoples of Gaul, sometimes called Celts. Those who faced the Anglo-Saxons in the 5th and 6th centuries A.D. were Celtic Britons who were gradually forced by the invaders to take refuge in the western parts of Britain, such as Cornwall, Wales, Ireland, and the west of Scotland. In other instances they remained where they were and mingled with their new masters.

BRITTANY. This northwest corner of France is celebrated for its great megalithic monuments—namely, alignments of thousands of stones, menhirs, dolmens, and passage graves of the bronze age about 2000 B.C. The center of what must have been a great religious cult was at Carnac in the Morbihan. The south coast of Brittany has many more megalithic remains than the north, though tombs in the Channel Islands form an exception. There is a close linguistic and cultural connection in later Celtic civilization between Brittany and Britain, as for instance

Bronze age: The Solar Chariot. Bronze and gold leaf, ca. 10th century B.C. From Trundholm. (Danish National Museum, Copenhagen)

between the name Cornwall in Britain and the festival of Cornouailles at Quimper in Brittany. The region was an important site of the Megalithic Builders.

BRONZE, an alloy of copper and tin; probably the first metal alloy employed by man upon emergence from stone-age cultures. Bronze frequently develops a beautiful patina. The earliest and finest bronze urns, statuettes, etc., were produced by the Mesopotamians, Anatolians, and Chinese starting in the 3rd millennium B.C.

BRONZE AGE, in archaeology, the technological period between the stone and iron ages. Copper was probably the first metal man learned to smelt and use, while he was also still using stone and flint tools. But copper is soft and does not hold a sharp edge. It is also difficult to cast, since gas bubbles form easily in the process. Copper ores that happened to contain a small portion of tin proved better. Metal founding or casting was practiced in the Near East by 3500 B.C. By about 2500 or earlier metalworkers in Anatolia and the Near East were consciously using copper alloyed with 10 or 12 percent of tin to make the harder metal, bronze. Its use for both weapons and tools spread gradually through Crete, Greece, the Balkans, and Spain to Europe, although bronze did not penetrate to such places as Brittany in northern Europe until about 1750 B.C. The bronze age in the Near East lasted until after 1000 B.C., when iron began to supplant bronze, particularly for weapons. Since the so-called bronze age varies in time from region to region and in some world areas never appeared, absolute dating is not to be implied.

BRUNIQUET, a cave in the Tarn-et-Garonne department of France, distinguished by examples of late-paleolithic art objects of about 12,000 B.C. These include engravings on limestone plaques, spear throwers, and perforated bones decorated with subtle animal figures.

The holes in the bones were possibly used for straightening arrows.

BUBALUS. See SAHARAN ROCK DRAWINGS.

BUCCHERO WARE, a distinctive type of pottery produced in abundance by the Etruscans in the 7th and 6th centuries B.C. Its finish is a lustrous black, and decorations are in relief or engraved. Early Bucchero seems to be modelled after bronze or ivory Etruscan vessels. In later times the ware became less fine, the shapes clumsier, and decorations (in relief) repetitious. Found from Africa to ancient Britain, the pottery provides evidence of extensive Etruscan trade routes.

BUDDHA, founder of the Buddhist religion. He was born a north Indian prince, Siddhartha Gautama, in the mid-6th century B.C. and died in 483 B.C. While a young man he abandoned his wealth, became an ascetic and devoted his life to the suffering poor. His life changed direction once again after his enlightenment at Bodhgaya, and he began teaching the precepts of Buddhism. This religion, a reaction against the traditional Hindu faith of India, stressed love of mankind and repudiated the caste system.

BUDDHIST ART AND ANTIQUITIES span a wide range in time, in geography, and in style. Buddhist art accompanies the religion of Buddha from India west to Afghanistan, north through central Asia and China, south to Ceylon and Indochina, and as far east as Japan. On a time scale, major Buddhist monuments, such as the stupa, were produced in India from the years following Buddha's death (5th century B.C.) until about the 8th century A.D. In China, Buddhist art stands among the few

Buddhist art: Head of Buddha. Stone. 5th–6th centuries A.D. From Sarnath. (National Museum, New Delhi)

C

CADBURY, in Somerset, England, is the site traditionally identified with Camelot, the capital of King Arthur. It is a large hill-top fort, surrounded by steep, multiple ramparts. Recent excavations have revealed a neolithic phase of the site, possibly as early as 3000 B.C., a bronze age, and a Roman iron-age period of occupation. New defenses and pottery remains correspond with the Arthurian period of 500 A.D., when Britons were defending the site against Anglo-Saxon invaders. Not surprisingly, little has been unearthed that can be indubitably connected with King Arthur.

CADDO CULTURE. At its peak, around 500 A.D., the Caddoan cultural area included southern Arkansas and parts of Louisiana, Texas, and Oklahoma. It is speculated that this region was the center of the Southern Death Cult of later times, a religious movement which spread over the southeastern United States. The cult was obsessed with death and characterized by Caddoan art objects with morbid, haunting motifs. The Caddoans were especially noted for their pottery, which, although made without a wheel, was distinguished by its balanced proportions and fine modelling.

CAERE, one of the wealthiest of the 12 Etruscan cities, situated 30 miles north of Rome. Caere (now the modern Cerveteri) reached the zenith of its power between the 7th and 5th centuries B.C. Excavations here have revealed elaborate chambered tombs laid out in streets like houses in a town. Their frescoes are outstanding and provide ample evidence of the artistic achievement in Etruria. The port of Caere was Pyrgi (modern Santa Severa), where were found in 1964 three now famous sheets of gold leaf, one inscribed in the Phoenician language, the other two in the mysterious and yet unsolved Etruscan language.

CAIRN, in European archaeology, a pile of stones that sometimes acts as a landmark but more often as a memorial to the dead. In prehistoric times cairns of various shape were heaped over tombs and graves.

CALENDAR STONES, large circular stones representing the solar disk which were carved in ancient Mexico during Aztec times. Eighteen of these, in varying degrees of elaboration, have been found to date in all parts of Mexico. The most famous, known simply as the Aztec Calendar Stone, weighs 20 tons, measures 13 feet across, and is richly carved with symbols representing the Aztec conception of the universe. Another monolith found in Mexico City and measuring more than three feet high shows a similar stone set on top of a pyramidal structure. Both stones are now in the National Museum of Anthropology, Mexico City.

CALLICRATES. See ICTINUS.

CALLIGRAPHY, the art of beautiful handwriting. A minor art in the West since the invention of the printing press, calligraphy in China is on an artistic level with fine painting. Chinese characters are made with a brush rather than a pen, and various schools and theories of calligraphy have existed since antiquity. In Islamic art calligraphy reached a high point.

CALUMET, the ceremonial pipe of the North American Indians. Typically it consisted of a hollow tube made of wood to which a stone bowl was attached. Its long stem was carefully crafted and decorated with elaborate carvings and symbolic materials. The Indians considered the pipe a religious object, part of the personal "medicine" of the owner, and forbade women to look at it. Its most famous use was to ratify alliances and treaties, from which it acquired the name "peace pipe."

CAMELOT. See CADBURY.

CANAANITES, an ancient Semitic people who occupied much of the eastern Mediterranean—the areas of Palestine and Syria—from roughly 2000 to 1200 B.C. They were recipients and transmitters of influences from adjacent cultures, notably Egyptian, Mesopotamian, and Hittite. They were succeeded by the Israelites and Philistines in

Calendar stones: Aztec calendar. Basalt, 15th century A.D. From Mexico City. (National Museum of Anthropology, Mexico City)

the south and merged with the Phoenicians in the north. Experienced maritime traders, the Canaanites made an effort to forestall oblivion by establishing colonies in Cyprus, Sicily, Sardinia, and elsewhere in the Mediterranean, but these collapsed within a few hundred years. El, Baal, and Astarte were among their chief deities.

CANOE PROWS, the curved frontal ends of boats. Especially in cultures that bordered on the Pacific Ocean these prows were richly carved with protective human or animal figures which would aid in fishing or in war. Carved prows are also found in other sea cultures—for example, in that of the Vikings. Canoe prows are highly prized art objects.

CANOPIC JARS, Egyptian containers used to hold the internal organs of the dead who were mummified. The jars were typically of finely carved alabaster, although wood, limestone, pottery, and faience were used. They were entombed with the mummy, each organ (liver, kidneys, stomach, etc.) having its own jar. The earliest canopic jars are from the Old Kingdom, of about 2500 B.C.

CAPITAL, the uppermost element of a Greek column upon which the entablature rests. Its shape is the main, but not the only, way of distinguishing the Doric, Ionic, and Corinthian orders. The Romans developed a fourth type, the Composite Order, a more elaborate combination of Greek elements. Capitals are often richly carved and thus are sought by collectors.

CAPITOLINE, the smallest of the seven hills of Rome. It was earlier known as the Saturnian Hill and originally had two peaks—the Capitolina and the Arx. More a citadel and religious center than an inhabited area, it was the site of the Capitol, a late 6th-century B.C. temple to Jupiter, Juno, and Minerva. Only a corner of the ancient temple platform remains. The hill and its temple were imitated in many Roman provincial cities.

CAPPADOCIA, a wild and mountainous region in what is now eastern Turkey. Its soil was poor, its terrain ill-suited for agriculture; it was largely ruled by tribal chiefs. It became part of the Persian Empire in the 6th century B.C., was conquered by the Macedonians in 322 B.C., came under the nominal rule of the Seleucids in the next century, and eventually became a Roman client kingdom and then province. A notable example of Hittite rock relief, showing winged disks, was found at Imamkulu in Cappadocia.

CAPSIAN CULTURE, a stone-age culture of North Africa, named from its type site at Gafsa, Tunisia. Its earliest period dates from around 10,000 B.C. The Capsians were hunters, food-gatherers, and stone workers; their middens, containing numbers of blades, burins, and scrapers shaped of stone or obsidian, are found throughout much of Mediterranean Africa. Their early dwellings were shallow caves, on the walls of which they drew simple hunting scenes. Around 5000 B.C. animals were domesticated and pottery introduced. There are examples of Capsian art in Alpera, Spain, and as far south as Rhodesia.

CARACALLA'S BATHS, Roman public baths, or *thermae*, built by the Emperor Caracalla in the 3rd century A.D. Far more elaborate than baths found in provincial Roman towns, Caracalla's baths had impressive interiors, with rich mosaics, rare marbles, and gilded metals. It could accept 1,600 bathers at one time. The ruins are still in use today for opera productions. Baths were found everywhere in the Roman Empire and were enjoyed by all classes of society. They were more than mere bathing places but were instead the centers of social life in a city. Like modern Turkish baths, there were rooms of varying temperatures, as well as reading rooms and places for exercises and games.

CARBON 14. See RADIOCARBON DATING.

CARCHEMISH, an ancient city-state on the west bank of the Euphrates where the river crosses from Turkey to Syria. Its notable tell has provided rich evidence of the history of the area. Although long occupied, the site became important under the Hittites; its citadel and walls commanded an important crossing of the Euphrates and

dominated trade routes. After the fall of the Hittites it was much fought over and finally conquered by Assyria in 717 B.C. The buildings of the city bore large numbers of reliefs and inscriptions, with both Hittite and Assyrian characteristics.

CARNAC, in Brittany, a main European center of the Megalithic Builders. It is the site of long avenues of standing stones (or menhirs) of granite, arranged in three groups which seem to have formed one vast system when erected towards the end of the neolithic period, between 4000 and 3000 B. C. The Menec group consists of 11 lines of stones extending 1,100 yards, the Kermario group of ten lines of approximately the same length, and the Kerlescan group of 13 lines, 880 yards long. Each alignment ends in a stone circle. In the Carnac region there are also passage graves and barrows of neolithic date.

CARRARA MARBLE, a famous marble quarried in the mountains near Carrara in northwestern Italy. It was first exploited by the Romans in the middle of the 1st century B.C. Augustus used this marble in rebuilding Rome. Carrara marble has an untransparent denseness that some find unattractive compared with the luminous quality of Greek marble, especially that from the isle of Paros.

CARTHAGE, ancient North African city, archrival of Rome, and Rome's opponent in the three Punic wars of the 3rd and 2nd centuries B.C., until finally defeated in 146 B.C. Carthage was founded by Phoenicians from Tyre in the 8th century B.C. in a strategic spot midway along the North African coast, near modern Tunis. The city grew fast and monopolized trade in the western Mediterranean. She fought intermittently with the Greeks and Etruscans over Sicily and the sea routes from the west. Commercial treaties guided peaceful relations with Rome until Hannibal led Carthage in an inevitable but unsuccessful war in the 3rd century B.C. The final struggle ended with the destruction of the city in 146 B.C. Its attractive site was recolonized by Julius Caesar and Augustus and became the capital of proconsular Africa, second only to Rome in the western Mediterranean. This preeminently commercial state traded in Tyrian purple, gold, ivory, pottery, bronze, perfumes, and textiles but never developed an art of its own.

CARTOUCHE, an Egyptian symbol consisting of an oval resting on a horizontal line. The oval was drawn large enough to contain hieroglyphics, designating a royal name, which was supposed to be preserved eternally by the cartouche's sacred power. The cartouche shape is said to have represented the sun on the horizon.

CARYATID, the Greek term for an architectural column carved in the form of a clothed woman. The most famous examples are those of the south porch of the Erechtheum, an unusual 5th-century B.C. Ionic temple on the Acropolis at Athens. One of the six caryatids from this porch is a

Caryatids: Greek, 5th century B.C. South porch of the Erechtheum, Athenian Acropolis.

copy, the original being in the British Museum. The opposite of a caryatid is an atlantean male figure.

CASTELLAZO DI FONTANELLATO. See **URN PEOPLE.**

CASTEL SANT'ANGELO. See **ROME.**

CASTILLO, the site of a decorated, prehistoric cave, near Santander in northern Spain. It is chiefly famous for animal paintings of the great age of cave art in the mid-Magdalenian period about 12,000 B.C. However, at the mouth of the cave excavations have shown habitation by Neanderthaloid man about 40,000 B.C. and have even uncovered Acheulian tools, which would take human use of the site back to about 200,000 B.C.

CATACOMB, an underground burial area with galleries whose sides are lined with stacks of coffinlike niches. The catacombs are usually associated with Rome and the early Christians, but similar subterranean burial places, excavated before the birth of Christ, have been found elsewhere—e.g., Sicily, Malta, North Africa. The term itself comes from the Greek *kata kumbas* ("at the hollows").

CATAL HUYUK, a major site in south-central Turkey, excavated in 1961–65, revealing one of the world's oldest settlements. The structures there spanned a millennium from around 6700 B.C. to around 5650 B.C. and revolutionized concepts of the origins of civilization in the Near East. Twelve building levels were dug, the rectangular mud-brick houses being contiguous and doorless, entered through the roofs. The settlement had a fully developed agriculture, growing various grains. In addition to hunting, sheep and cattle were bred. There were rich wall decorations, many shrines, and figurines of the Mother Goddess.

CAVE ART is a term applied to the art of paleolithic man as seen in drawings, paintings, and engravings on the walls of caves, found mainly in central and southern France and in Spain but also in regions of North Africa and East Europe. This art shows great variation in date and style, though the earlier art is not always the more primitive. The beginning of cave art is found in the Aurignacian period about 30,000 B.C., and it reaches its height artistically with the great animal paintings in the caves of Altamira in Spain and of Font-de-Gaume, Lascaux, and others in the Dordogne region of France in the Magdalenian period, 15,000–10,000 B.C. Representations of men and animals were still being executed on rock faces as late as the copper age in Spain in 2400 B.C. The paintings of the great Magdalenian artists exhibit a remarkable sophistication, a knowledge of anatomy, and a feeling for the personality of animals. Their nature and position, often in the darkest recesses of the caves, indicate that the paintings were not done for show nor as self-expression on the artist's part but for magical and religious reasons; cave paintings promoted the fertility of game and the success of the hunter, upon which the existence of the tribe depended.

CAVES OF THE THOUSAND BUDDHAS, site of countless wall paintings decorating a vast honeycomb of caves at modern Kizil, Turkestan. The paintings probably were executed when the caves were part of the Buddhist principality of Kucha. In the 7th century A.D. that independent state was overrun by the Chinese, who called the cave site Ming Oi, or thousand caves. The paintings show evidence of highly diverse artistic styles. Some very fine works, including sensuous human figures painted in an Indian style, were removed in 1926 and housed in a Berlin museum, only to be destroyed in the Second World War.

CAVE TEMPLES, a mainly Buddhist form of religious architecture, less often used for Hindu and Jain edifices. Such temples are not natural geological formations occupied for religious purposes but are man-made and carved into rock hillsides and cliffsides. The first were cell-like sanctuaries for Buddhist monks and date from the early Buddhist era. Later examples became more elaborate and by the 1st century B.C. began assuming a size and shape similar to a typical Christian basilica—a resemblance that is purely coincidental. India's important cave temples are in the west, roughly from Hyderabad to the vicinity of Bombay. The most famous include those at Ajanta and Ellora. In Wei Dynasty China (5th century A.D.) imposing Buddist cave temples were cut into limestone at Tatung, Yunkang, and Tunhuang in the northern provinces. Cave temples were often decorated with impressive statuary and wall paintings.

Cave art: Deer and Ibexes. Detail of cave painting. Magdalenian. Cognac, France.

Celtic peoples: Pillar. Coarse-grained limestone. 5th or 4th century B.C. From Pfalzfeld. (Rheinisches Landesmuseum, Bonn)

CAYLA DE MAILHAC, a hilltop site in southwest France near Narbonne with a sufficiently clear and long series of occupations from 700 to 100 B.C. to give a key dating sequence for the late bronze age and the early iron age in this region. Connections begin with the Urnfield culture and continue with Hallstatt and then La Tene affinities in the iron age. Certain levels contain Greek black-figure ware and Etruscan pottery that can be independently dated to the 6th century B.C.

CELLA, a rectangular room which formed the inner sanctuary of a Greek temple. It housed the cult statue of the god or goddess to whom the temple was dedicated. In later Greek temples the cella was regularly surrounded by columns and had a vestibule-porch at the front and at the back.

CELTIC PEOPLES, an historic and imaginative group of Indo-European tribes who, along with their distant relatives, the Slavic and Germanic peoples, probably descended from the Battle-Axe culture, which arose in southern Russia in the 3rd millennium B.C. By the early 2nd millennium B.C. the Celts, who had spread widely over western Europe, were recognizable as a cultural entity, with closely related languages, religious customs, and forms of artistic expression. Celtic physical characteristics included tall statures, fair complexions, wavy hair, and heavy beards. Among the many tribes and cultures that predate and anticipate the formation of the Celtic nation are the Beaker people, named for those tribes of early Europeans who buried drinking vessels with their dead, and the Urn people, whose burial grounds have yielded cremation urns. However, it is only with La Tene culture—named for a major Celtic site in Switzerland—that Celtic dominance of much of Europe and the British Isles becomes apparent. In the 3rd century B.C. Celts, known then as Galatians, were raiding the Greek city-states, and in France, where they were called Gauls, and in northern Italy they often engaged the legions of Rome. Fierce warriors, the Celts were finally subjugated by Julius Caesar in the mid-1st century B.C. While Imperial Rome spelled the end of Celtic militancy in Europe, Celtic culture continued to flourish throughout much of western Europe, including the British Isles. The most advanced areas of the Celtic world existed in what is now France and England during the late 1st millennium B.C. and the first few centuries of the Christian era. During this time Celtic society had a strong economic basis in agriculture; physical outlines of some of their once prosperous farms can still be seen on the chalk downs of southern England from Sussex to Dorset. The Celtic religion was Druidism, which was based on the worship of forest spirits and included such elements as divination by means of human sacrifice, a rich mythology, and reverence for such monster deities as the man-eating image found at Noves in southern France. When Rome began to collapse and its Imperial legions departed

from Britain in the 4th and 5th centuries A.D., the Celtic peoples of Roman-British culture carried on life much as before until gradual pressure from the more barbaric Anglo-Saxons, the Jutes, and, later, the Danes forced them to retreat west—to Cornwall, Wales, Ireland, and the west coast of Scotland. These places, along with Brittany on France's west coast, became the final refuge of Celtic culture. There, Celtic traditions have retained some

62

Celtic art: Mirror-back. Incised and patinated bronze. 1st century B.C. From Desborough, England. (British Museum, London)

of their life to the present day, especially in the languages of Gaelic, Erse, Welsh, and Breton.

Celtic Art and Antiquities achieved their distinctiveness, hence their artistic importance, with La Tene culture, spanning the period from about 500 B.C. until the 2nd or 3rd century A.D. Although La Tene artists excelled as metalworkers (e.g., shields, weapons, mirrors, jewelry, horse and carriage adornments, helmets, wine vessels, etc.), they also left noteworthy stone sculpture. In strong contrast to the neighboring Greco-Roman world's emphasis upon realism in human representation, Celtic art offered abstract and asymmetrical design, and even images of men and animals were executed by Celtic artists in relatively abstract terms. Celtic sculpture and metalwork were created primarily for tribal chieftains, who were noted for their ostentation. However, some major Celtic art objects are of a monumental nature and probably had religious significance. Well known in this category are the stone pillars found at Entremont, France, dating from the 3rd century B.C. and decorated with numerous carvings of men's heads in the highly simplified style that is unmistakably Celtic. Many decorative metal objects (e.g., bronze cauldron mountings, jewelry, etc.) take the form of fantastic birds and animals and closely resemble the animal style of the Scythians, from which they probably derive. The famous La Tene site in western Switzerland yielded a large number of bronze and iron votive offerings when excavated in the early 20th century. Many other Celtic sites—including Gloucester, England; Vaucluse, Vix, Somme-Bionne, and Eure in France; Malomerice in Czechoslovakia; Saarbrucken in Germany; Gundestrup in Denmark, etc.—testify to the widespread diffusion of Celtic art and culture across the European continent. In its late, or post-La Tene, period Celtic art was touched by Roman influences. For example, a fine metal Celtic vessel found at Aylesford, England (where it still can be seen), has small bronze heads that are Celtic adaptations of Roman style, while the frieze around the bucket's top shows animals facing each other along with abstract curvilinear embellishments that are purely Celtic.

CEMPOALA. See **TOTONACS.**

CENOTAPH, an empty Egyptian tomb built to commemorate the death of a pharaoh who was actually buried elsewhere. Abydos, in Upper Egypt, is one of the most important sites of Egyptian cenotaphs. The cenotaph form was also used in later civilizations.

CENOTE, a circular well, formed by the collapse of underground caves. Cenotes were the principal source of water for the Maya of the Yucatan peninsula in Mexico. As such, they were a major factor in determining the

Celtic art: Base of the Gundestrup cauldron. (National Museum, Copenhagen)

Celtic art: Ritual object. Beaten gold with repousse decoration. Ca. 900 B.C. From Schifferstadt. (Historisches Museum der Pfalz, Speyer)

location of population centers, and in many cases they took on a religious significance. The most famous of them is the Sacred Cenote at Chichen Itza. Excavators here have found great quantities of gold and jadite art objects, which had been thrown into the Sacred Cenote as offerings to the rain god.

CENTURIPE VASES. See **LIPARI.**

CERES. See **DEMETER.**

CERVETERI. See **CAERE.**

CHACMOOL, a monumental Pre-Columbian stone sculpture in the form of a reclining anthropomorphic figure. The figure's head is upraised, and its hands hold a receptacle or rest on a depression in its stomach. It is thought that these receptacles or hollows were used for burning incense or for receiving the hearts of sacrificial victims. Chacmools were first introduced into Mexico by the Toltecs.

CHALCEDONY, a smooth, fine-grained stone resembling agate and occurring in many colors. It takes a high polish and has been used since ancient times in all regions where available to make small sculptured art objects.

CHALCOLITHIC. See **COPPER AGE.**

CHALDEES. See **UR.**

CHALKOTHEKE. See **ATHENS.**

CHALUKYA PERIOD, in Indian history, a Deccan dynasty that lasted for about 200 years, beginning in the mid-6th century A.D. The Chalukya Dynasty was among the more powerful of several feuding Hindu kingdoms that arose to fill the vacuum left by the collapse of India's great Gupta Dynasty. The Chalukya capital was at Vatapi, now called Badami, and its greatest king was the feudal leader Pulakesin II.

CHAMBER TOMB, in European archaeology, a large vaultlike structure with many burials, covering a long period of time. The Megalithic Builders made elaborate chamber tombs of various shapes with great slabs of stone, nearly all covered with cairns of loose stones or mounds of earth. Some have doorways of stone with round portholes in the center. The practice of building chamber tombs was first introduced into Spain about 2400 B.C., probably from the eastern Mediterranean, and spread mainly by sea routes up the west coasts of Europe as far as Ireland and the north of Scotland.

CHAMPA, a kingdom that extended over much of modern Vietnam from the 2nd through the 14th centuries A.D. Its people, the Chams, were of Indonesian origin. By about 400, under King Bhadravarman, their culture was recognizably Indian, their major religions being worship of the Hindu god Siva and, later, of Buddha. Their enduring art consists of a number of temples containing sculpture, built mainly in the 9th and 10th centuries at such locations as Mi Son, Binh Dinh, and Huong Qua.

Chacmool: Carved stone, detail. Maya-Toltec. From Chichen Itza. (National Museum of Anthropology, Mexico City)

The temples are typically tall brick structures with intricately pavilioned towers.

CHANCHAN, capital of the Chimu Empire and the largest city ever built in ancient Peru. Located near the present city of Trujillo, the vast ruins of streets, houses, pyramids, and reservoirs hint at its highly developed urban existence. The city was divided into ten or more walled districts, covered about ten square miles, and had a population of about 50,000. Mysteriously, there seems not to have been any entrance through the mammoth 50-foot-high walls that enclosed the districts. Geometric and animal designs in low relief, and occasional wall paintings, decorated many buildings.

CHANDELA PERIOD, in Indian history, a northern dynasty governing in and near the city of Khajuraho from the 10th through the 13th centuries A.D. The Chandela kings' chief cultural contribution was their building of 85 beautiful temples dedicated to Hindu and Jain deities during the 10th and 11th centuries. About 28 of these shrines survive to the present, and although they are towerlike in shape, they are relatively small, usually no more than 100 feet high.

CHANDI, a Javanese term designating an ancient, sacred shrine that houses an icon, usually of Indian religious origin. The earliest chandis were small, one-chambered structures, having a portico and a peaked or towered roof. In later examples, antechambers were added, often vastly increasing the chandi's total size.

CHANGSHA, a town in Hunan Province, China. It was the capital of the small southern feudal kingdom of Chu until the latter was absorbed by the Han Dynasty, which became dominant throughout China in the late 3rd century B.C. Excavated tombs at Changsha dating roughly from the early Han period have been found to contain some of the earliest known examples of lacquered manlike figurines that were buried with the dead for religious reasons.

CHASSEY CULTURE, in French prehistory, is of neolithic date and takes its name from the fortified camp at Chassey in the Saone-et-Loire department of central France. The innovations of French neolithic culture spread northwards from the Mediterranean and reached Chassey from the Rhone Valley. The site has yielded plain, round-bottomed pottery, clay spoons, handles of antler "sleeves" into which small stone axes were inserted, and decorated pottery of about 2300 B.C.

CHAVIN CIVILIZATION, the oldest civilization of South America and, with the Olmec of Mexico, one of the earliest of the New World; its beginnings may date from 1200 B.C. Chavin, the first pan-Peruvian civilization, flourished from about 900 B.C. to 200 B.C. and takes its name from the modern town of Chavin de Huantar, nestled in a fertile valley high in the Andes. Nearby are the remains of the largest Chavin ceremonial center. Chavin civilization was dominated by religious fervor, especially that surrounding the cult of the jaguar-god. His religion was spread by zealous missionaries through

the highland and coastal regions of north and central Peru; its influence was felt even as far south as the Paracas peninsula. Although conversion seems to have been the probable means of Chavin expansion, military conquest cannot be ruled out. Central to the religion were temples constructed of dressed stones, field stones, or adobe. The principal temple at Chavin, a vast, decorated building known as the Castillo, shares features with other temples found at Cerro Blanco, La Copa, Pacopampa, and Mojeque. The Lanzon, a sacred granite block with the jaguar-god carved in relief, is in the temple complex at Chavin. The areas around Chavin temples were normally ceremonial centers and did not support a large, permanent population. The enigmatic origin of the Chavin is a subject of considerable debate. Some scholars look to the Olmec culture of Mexico as a source. Others have suggested the eastern side of the Andes and even the Chou Dynasty in China as possible origins.

Chavin Art and Antiquities. Stone reliefs and carvings, as well as textiles and ceramics, provide ample evidence of the awesome quality of Chavin art. The jaguar-god is often portrayed, as are humans, birds of prey, caymans, and serpents. Various combinations of these beings were carved in monumental stone reliefs or were used as the dominant decoration for ceramics. The Great Image, or Lanzon, and the monstrous Tello Obelisk stand out as masterpieces of relief carvings. The characteristic ceramic form was the stirrup-spout bottle. A special ceramic style that developed in the coastal regions of northern Peru— under Chavin influence—is known as Cupisnique.

CHENG CHOU, the early capital of China's ancient Shang culture, located on the south shore of the Yellow River. It predates Anyang, the most important Shang capital. Cheng Chou is the earliest known site of China's bronze-age culture, ritual bronze vessels being the most important art objects found there. The city was rectangular, approximately 5,700 feet by 6,600 feet, and enclosed within an earthen wall. Cheng Chou served as the Shang capital until about 1384 B.C., the year believed to mark the founding of Anyang.

CHENLA, a southeast Asian feudal leader of the 6th century A.D.; also the name of the kingdom he founded. Chenla overthrew the Funan kingdom, situated along the Mekong River in what is now Cambodia. Chenla culture was initially Indian, but gradually its architecture and sculpture began to take on an individual character showing Indonesian traits. The Chenla kingdom apparently disintegrated in the 8th century. It was gradually reorganized, emerging in the late 8th century under the leadership of Jayavarman II. This marked the beginning of the Khmer (Cambodian) kingdom.

CHEOPS PYRAMID. See GREAT PYRAMID.

Chavin Civilization: Decoration on the exterior wall of the Castillo, Chavin de Huantar.

CHERT, a type of quartz having properties similar to flint. Like flint, it was used for weapons and tools by stone-age cultures. Some very fine-grain chert was polished to make art objects.

CHERTOMLYK BURIAL, an outstanding Scythian gravesite located north of the Black Sea in the Soviet Ukraine. The 60-foot-high burial mound, dating from the 4th century B.C., contained several chambers, holding skeletons of a chieftain, attendants, and horses, as well as a hoard of precious objects. Unusually fine gold and silver antiquities show a blending of Greek, Persian, and Scythian styles. Possibly the single most important piece is a 27½-inch-high silver amphora with reliefs of Scythian horse trainers, executed in undeniably Greek style; later embellishments include Scythian-style lion heads, which detract from the amphora's aesthetic beauty but tell much about the meeting of cultural influences in the Dnieper River Valley. Items of pure Greek craftsmanship include a gold plaque showing Herakles fighting a lion and a golden sword scabbard showing Greeks and Persians in battle. All pieces cited here are housed in the Hermitage, Leningrad.

CHIA, type of Chinese bronze vessel made during the Shang and Chou eras. They were supported on three or four legs and were used for ritual purposes.

CHIAHSIANG HSIEN, the location of important Han Dynasty tomb sites in China's Shantung Province. Tombs of Chinese noblemen, dating from the 2nd century A.D., have yielded information about the society and culture that permeated China during the Han period. Interior walls of tomb chambers are covered with paintings or relief sculptures depicting both the everyday life of the period and the religion and mythology of the people.

CHIBCHA CULTURE, a culture of the Colombian and Peruvian highlands that existed for only a few centuries prior to the Spanish Conquest. The Chibchas were organized into small political chiefdoms. Their religion focused on the worship of the sun and on a culture hero called Bochica, who shares many of the characteristics of the Mexican Quetzalcoatl. The Spanish chroniclers wrote glowing reports of Chibcha political organization, architecture, and wealth. However, archaeologists have so

Chichen Itza: Detail of the Temple of the Warriors' pyramid. Maya-Toltec, 11th century A.D.

Chichen Itza: The Caracol (foreground). Maya-Toltec, 9th–10th centuries A.D.

far uncovered little evidence to support Spanish claims. Chibcha ceramics are not distinctive. Their metallurgy is less advanced than that of other areas of Colombia. Chibcha goldwork is easily recognizable for its application of soldered wire embellishments to the flat unpolished surface of figures.

CHICHEN ITZA, the most splendid of Mayan ceremonial centers, located in the northern Yucatan peninsula near the modern Mexican city of Merida. Its arts reflect the fusion of two civilizations—the ancient Maya and the Toltec. The oldest buildings at the site, the so-called Nunnery complex, the Iglesia, and the Caracol, date to the 9th and 10th centuries A.D. and reflect the curvilinear, ornate, Puuc style in architecture. During the late 10th century A.D. Chichen Itza came under strong Toltec influence from central Mexico, and legend states that the city was actually conquered by Toltec lords. The Toltecs altered the Caracol and erected the structures known as the Castillo, the Courtyard of a Thousand Columns, the Skull Rack, the Great Ball Court, and the Temple of the Warriors, which is almost identical to a building at the

Toltec capital of Tula. The character of the wall painting and sculpture at Chichen Itza also changed under Toltec domination. They introduced the sculptural forms of the Chacmool and monolithic square columns in the form of feathered serpents. Motifs are concerned with death, violence, and militancy and are essentially non-Mayan in character. Rare examples of Mayan wall painting can also be seen at Chichen Itza. They depict scenes of daily life and are of great ethnographic interest. Chichen Itza is perhaps most famous for its Sacred Cenote, a deep well into which offerings were cast. Excavations here have yielded beautiful jades and some of the few known pieces of Mayan goldwork. These are mostly large, finely embossed gold disks with Toltec warrior motifs. Other pieces suggest trade with Central America and Colombia. Chichen Itza collapsed, for still unknown reasons, during the 13th century. Political dominance shifted to the city of Mayapan, but the Maya were never again to achieve the level of artistic excellence found at Chichen Itza.

CHIMU, a powerful and despotic empire that covered the northern coast of Peru for more than 200 years until its

69

dismemberment and absorption by the Incas in about 1470 A.D. Its exact boundaries are unknown, but it may have extended from Tumbes to the Chillon Valley. Its greatest city and capital was Chanchan, but each irrigated coastal valley had its own urban center—cities being a characteristic development of the Chimu. Chimu culture, essentially industrial in nature, seems largely to have been a revival of the Mochica. Effigy vessels, such as the common stirrup-spout bottle, were often standardized and reflected imitations of earlier designs. Few painted vessels exist; most are black ware. Gold and silver Chimu art objects have been found.

CH'IN DYNASTY, rulers of China between 221 and 206 B.C. and the initiators of the First Chinese Empire. One of several warring states, it became dominant between 230 and 221 when its armies defeated all rivals. The Ch'in king named himself First Emperor, forging an administration that effectively unified all China. A despotic government, it stressed military prowess and restricted citizens' rights. The First Emperor's personal control was so total that his dynasty could not survive his death. Except for completion of the Great Wall, little of cultural importance derives from the Ch'in era.

CHIN DYNASTY, leaders of northern China between 1126 and 1234 A.D. It was originated by the Jurched tribe of Manchuria. Rising against Manchuria's Liao Dynasty and destroying it in 1125, the Jurched moved into ter-

ritories south of China's Great Wall, ending Sung domination in northern China. Although semibarbaric, the Jurched adopted the Chinese dynastic name Chin and ultimately made peace with the southern remnant of the Sung Dynasty. Art surviving from the period is primarily of Sung origin. Both powers were extinguished by the Mongol invasion in 1234.

CHINESE CIVILIZATION, the oldest living civilization in the world and among the most brilliant ever created by man. It spans perhaps as many as four millennia, with 2205 B.C. traditionally given as the beginning year of China's first dynasty, a prehistoric and legendary regime called the Hsia Dynasty. Archaeology offers evidence that Chinese civilization originated in the Yellow River Valley of northern China, where prehistoric farmers grew grain and raised pigs, cattle, dogs, and fowl for food. Two cultures appeared here before 2000 B.C.: the Yangshao, or Painted Pottery culture, in what is now northern Honan Province, and the Lungshan, or Black Pottery culture, along the coast from the Wei River basin to modern Hangchow. It is possible that the Hsia Dynasty may be identified with one of these cultures, although supporting archaeological data is inconclusive. However, the last Hsia rulers were probably historical personages. According to legend the Hsia were overthrown by revolution and were succeeded by the Shang Dynasty, China's earliest historical culture, which took China into the bronze

Chimu: Funeral mask. Gold with emerald pendants. (Miguel Mujica Gallo Collection, Lima)

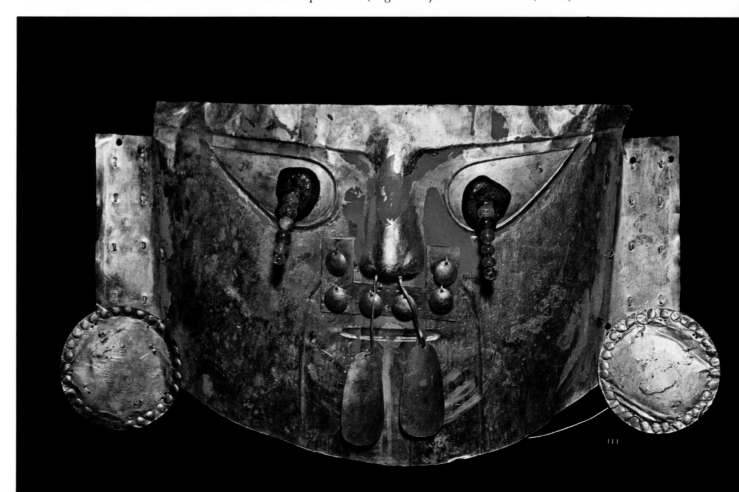

Chinese bronze: Yu vessel. Ca. 1100–1000 B.C. (National Museum, Tokyo)

Tang Dynasty, a force that restored order throughout China by 628. At about this time the great Tang leader Tai Tsung also subjugated the Mongols and took their title, "Heavenly Khan," for himself. From the late Tang through the Sung Dynasty (960 to 1279) China enjoyed its golden age, roughly equivalent to Europe's Renaissance. Literature, architecture, and painting manifested a supreme artistry, and after preceding centuries of development the art of ceramic-making approached perfection in Sung porcelain. The Mongols of Genghis Khan swept down from the north in the 13th century, ultimately destroying the Sung Dynasty and conquering China but failing to assimilate with the Chinese people or their culture. Mongol rule in China was consolidated in the Yuan Dynasty but waned after 1271 and disappeared in 1367. Its last remnants were defeated by the founders of the Ming Dynasty, who gained preeminence in the late 14th century and, after 1421, governed China from Peking. Ming rule gave China a long period of relative peace, during which time the arts and technology flourished in full maturity. However, Ming rule gradually grew reactionary and decadent, collapsing in the mid-17th century, when the Manchu, or Ching, Dynasty replaced it and endured to the early 20th century.

Chinese Bronze and Metalwork. Bronze-working was more highly developed in early China than in any other ancient civilization; the most important pieces date from the Shang and Chou eras. Typical bronzes of these periods are elaborately decorated ceremonial vessels. Shang bronzes invariably have a heavy green patina, due to their great age and to the earth from whence they were excavated. It is often difficult to distinguish between Shang and Chou bronzes, although many Chou vessels are unusually large and sometimes less artfully designed than their Shang predecessors. With the dawn of China's Han Empire in 206 B.C. the making of bronze vessels declined, although the metal continued to be used to make mirrors and statuary. Finest examples of Han metalwork are in gold rather than bronze.

Chinese Ivory and Jade. Ivory carving dates back to antiquity in China but reached its height during the Ming Dynasty. The finest Ming ivories are portrait-type statuettes of men, highly naturalistic in style. The distinctively Chinese craft of jade carving had become a sophisticated art as early as the Chou era and continued to be practiced over the centuries. It reached perfection during the Ching Dynasty in the 18th century. From earliest times, pendants and statuettes of jade have been especially valued by the Chinese, who regard jade in much the same way that Western peoples value diamonds. Most of

age. The Shang Dynasty lasted about 300 years, beginning around 1400 B.C. China's earliest known written records date from the third dynasty, the Chou, which was founded in either 1122 or 1027 B.C. By the late 6th century B.C. Chou rule had declined and numerous rival states battled for supremacy, most of them claiming descent from Chou ancestry. Despite political chaos, the 6th through 2nd centuries B.C. mark China's classical age, seeing the birth of Confucian and Taoist thought. Imperial China began with the Ch'in Dynasty, whose invincible armies unified China in 221 B.C. and who established a strong central government with its capital at Hsien-yang. A Ch'in emperor completed construction of China's Great Wall to defend his realm from northern nomadic tribes. Sudden administrative collapse ended Ch'in rule in 206 B.C., but the Chinese Empire was continued by two succeeding Han dynasties. The Han era extended to 222 A.D. and saw vast Chinese territorial expansion into central Asia to the west and Korea to the east. The Later Han Dynasty declined in the 3rd century A.D. and was followed by three centuries of political disunity but also by the introduction and flowering of Buddhism in China. The country's Second Empire came with the rise of the

Chinese painting: "Birds and Flowers of the Four Seasons," detail. Ming Dynasty. (National Museum, Tokyo)

Chinese ceramics: Amphora. Glazed earthenware. Tang Dynasty, 8th century A.D. (National Museum, Tokyo)

the raw jade carved in China had to be imported, probably from central Asia or Siberia.

Chinese Painting. The history and styles of Chinese painting are as diverse as European art styles, and its evolution is analogous to Western painting. Just as European medieval painting was devoted to Christian purposes, most Chinese painting before the Tang era was religious, often executed on walls and largely associated with temples and gravesites. Buddhist influence extended well into the Tang period. Chinese painting reached full flower during the Sung Dynasty (10th through 13th centuries), when the art became secularized, ceasing to be religion's servant. Innumerable fine Tang and Sung painters prospered under royal patronage. Landscape and calligraphic art reached sublime heights during the Sung and the following Yuan period. In Ming China numerous new trends developed, including the elegant and ultra-simple bamboo-scroll painting. Quality, variety, and quantity of Chinese painting remained high into the Ching Dynasty, which ended in 1912.

Chinese Porcelain, the ultimate expression of China's long history of superb ceramic-making, first appeared during the late Tang Dynasty—in the mid-9th or early 10th century A.D. Porcelain's invention was at least partly due to the fact that the Yueh, a semibarbaric people to China's south, with a highly advanced ceramic technology, were absorbed by Tang China in the 8th century. Porcelain's development arose from two major events: the construction of kilns in China that could produce unprecedented temperatures (above 1450° F.) and the discovery of kaolin, a very fine white clay which, when fired at extremely high temperatures, becomes porcelain, a ceramic of unsurpassed hardness and delicacy. Porcelain may be given a translucent quality, and porcelain objects often have paper-thin walls. The first Chinese porcelain factories were at Kingtehchen (modern Fowliang), in Kiangsi Province, where glazed white vessels, in the manner of Yueh ware, were produced. Porcelain-making was greatly refined after 960 A.D. when the Sung Dynasty rose to power. Delicately colored glazes, with surfaces of satinlike softness, crackle-grain, or high mirrorlike finishes, adorned Sung vases. Most often decorated with subtle and shaded patterns, on a white, green, or brown background, Sung porcelain achieved artistic heights only occasionally equalled, but never surpassed, anywhere in the world. In the Yuan era, coming after the Sung, Chinese porcelain typically had stylized floral or dragon motifs—sometimes left unglazed—in colors contrasting with backgrounds. In Ming China, from about 1392 to 1644, porcelain-making reached its full maturity,

Chinese porcelain: "Kuan" chiaotan-blue bowl. Sung Dynasty, 12th century A.D. (National Museum, Tokyo)

Chinese jade: Ornamental disk. Chou Dynasty. (Nelson Gallery, Kansas City)

Chinese sculpture: Bodhisattva. Painted wood. Sung Dynasty, 12th century A.D. (Museum of Fine Arts, Boston; Harvey Edward Wetzel Foundation)

and objects were made in shapes, sizes, colors, and glazes of virtually limitless variety. Ching Dynasty porcelain was also of generally excellent quality, and in the 18th and 19th centuries it was designed to order for foreign markets. Such Ching porcelain often bears Western decorative devices despite its Chinese manufacture.

Chinese Sculpture is largely mythological and religious in subject matter, the most notable work having been executed from the Han through the Tang periods. The earliest sculpture in the round appears in the Han Empire and includes massive horses and mythological animals found at tomb sites. By the 5th century A.D. Chinese sculpture was Buddhist, and many colossal Buddha statues were sponsored by the Buddhist-oriented Wei Dynasty which then flourished. Rigidity and extreme stylization began to disappear from Chinese Buddhist sculpture in the Tang era, giving way to more intimate and human forms. Secular sculpture had become fairly common during the preceeding Six Dynasties era (4th through 6th centuries) and prevailed into the Tang period. Animal figures erected around tombs of important Tang leaders are quite naturalistic.

Chinese Terra Cotta dates from prehistoric times and shows a high state of craftsmanship from the late 3rd millennium B.C. The Chinese claim, probably inaccurately, to be the first culture to use the potter's wheel; at any rate, they were certainly among the first. Fired pottery from the prehistoric Yangshao culture was delicately shaped and painted with intricate abstract designs in red and black pigments. Many outstanding examples, found in graves, survive to the present. Lungshan pottery, contemporary with Yangshao, is black and unpainted, but its delicacy of design often excels even that of Yangshao vessels. Terra-cotta urns of Shang vintage are often shaped and decorated like bronzes and typically are of light-colored clay baked nearly to stoneware hardness.

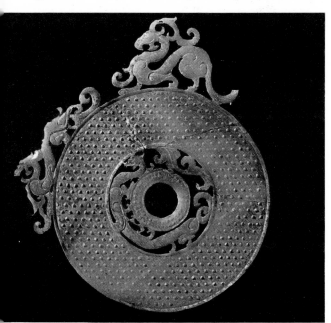

Ceramic vessels and statuettes, notably horses, dragons, etc., have been found at Chinese gravesites dating from many historical periods, but by the Tang era (10th century) the best work was being done in the newly invented material, porcelain.

CHING DYNASTY, lords of China from 1644 to 1912. They originated as a Manchu power, developing complex relations with Ming Dynasty China by the early 17th century. Under their military leader, Dorgon (1612–50), the Manchus invaded northern China, establishing their government in Peking in 1644. Administrators, previously loyal to the Ming government, began defecting to the new Ching Dynasty. Transition between Ming and Ching cultures was gradual, and the arts of both eras are similar. Many fine porcelains and important paintings survive from Ching China.

CHIRIQUI, a regional art style of Panama that flourished in the centuries prior to the Spanish Conquest. Chiriqui cemeteries are noted for gold and gilded copper pendants, which are similar in style to Veraguas pieces. In addition to metalwork, Chiriqui graves have yielded ceremonial stone metates in the form of stools and in effigies of the jaguar-god.

CHIUSI, town in central Italy and formerly one of the 12 Etruscan cities. The Romans called it Clusium. Many Etruscan antiquities have been found here. Tradition claims that one of its rulers, Porsenna (probably a title, not a person), ruled Rome for a while, and this might reflect an actual period of friendly relations between Rome and Etruria. Chiusi was a center of decorative bronze-working and a major center of stone-carving.

CHIWARA. See BAMBARA.

CHOKWE, an African people living principally in northern Angola and southern Zaire. A chain of small chiefdoms, the Chokwe were invaded and absorbed by the powerful Lunda Empire during the 17th century. Their independence was restored with the demise of the Lunda Empire at the end of the 19th century. The artistic Chokwe craftsmen fashion elaborate thrones and articles of regalia for their chiefs. Also they carve wood human figurines, some of which are said to represent the legen-dary hero Tshibinda Ilunga. The *mukanda,* or initiation rites through which all Chokwe males pass, requires the presence of masks. These are made mostly of wood and raffia. The name Chokwe, a striking example of the problems of transliteration, has more than 40 variant spellings, including Vatshiok, Bajok, and Quihocos.

CHOLA PERIOD, extending from 864 to 1279 A.D. in southern India but was at its height under its monarchs Rajaraja the Great (985–1014) and Rajendra I (1014–82). The Cholas then controlled territory from Ceylon to the Ganges and held outposts in Burma. This period saw the resurgence of Hinduism, following the decline of Buddhism in India. Hindu architecture and sculpture flourished, assuming a highly baroque quality. The greatest Chola edifice is the Rajrajesvara Temple to Siva, erected at Tanjore around the year 1000. The best examples of Chola sculpture are bronzes, notably of dancing, many-armed Sivas.

CHOLULA, one of the most important religious centers of Pre-Hispanic Mexico, located near the modern city of Puebla. The first traces of settlement here date to 600 B.C. Near the beginning of the Christian era construction began on a great pyramid, which over the years grew to become the largest in the New World. In its final state the pyramid covers 25 acres, stands 180 feet high, and is presently crowned by a Spanish colonial church. By 900 A.D. Cholula was the center of the Mixteca-Puebla art style, and local craftsmen produced fine gold, elaborate mosaic work, and beautiful ceramics. The Aztec emperor Montezuma would eat only from Cholula polychrome plateware. Recent excavations near the great pyramid have uncovered painted murals dating from 200–300 A.D. Dubbed "The Drinkers," they depict what is probably a planting or harvest ceremony. The figures are shown seated and reclining while drinking pulque, an intoxicating Mexican beverage. These murals are considered to be among the most original and naturalistic of Pre-Columbian painting.

CHOU DYNASTY, controller of China from 1122 or 1027 B.C. until about 400 B.C. The Chou attained power after destroying the Shang Dynasty. Like the Shang, their most notable surviving art objects are bronze urns and ritual vessels. In 771 B.C. the Chou capital, Hao, was destroyed by obscure barbarians. Although the royal line was re-established at Loyang, Chou power drastically declined, its authority challenged by numerous rival dynasties. Cultural historians distinguish between Western Chou (pre-771 B.C.) and Eastern Chou (post-771 B.C.) dynasties.

CHRYSELEPHANTINE, a Greek term for statues made of gold (*chrysos*), to depict garments, and ivory (*elephantos*), to evoke flesh. They were supported by internal wooden forms. The two most famous chryselephantine statues were of Zeus in the temple at Olympia and of Athena Parthenos in the Parthenon at Athens. Both, by the great 5th-century Greek master Phidias, are lost.

75

CIEMPOZUELOS, a site in central Spain, not far from Madrid, where finely polished pottery finds, incised and decorated, mark the beginnings of Beaker culture about 2000 B.C. Pottery of this type spread all over Europe, accompanied by finds of bronze daggers and other metalwork.

CILICIA, an ancient region of Asia Minor, roughly the eastern half of the southern coast, between the Mediterranean and the Taurus mountains. The area was under the domination of the Assyrian Empire before it was annexed by the Persians. Apparently settled by Greeks after the Trojan War, it is perhaps best remembered as a pirates' haven from the 2nd century B.C. until they were suppressed by the Roman general Pompey in 67 B.C. The province was made part of the Roman Empire by the Emperor Vespasian in 72 A.D. Besides being fertile, it was important strategically as the only land route from Asia Minor to Syria. Tarsus was its major city.

CIMMERIANS, the earliest important tribe of mounted nomads of the Eurasian steppes, identifiable from perhaps 1000 B.C. As rulers of the area north and northeast of the Black Sea, they commonly exacted tribute from the indigenous sedentary peoples there—possibly forerunners of the Slavs. Cimmerian origins are uncertain, but after the 8th century B.C. they were displaced by a new nomadic wave, the Scythians. In the process of retreating, the Cimmerians moved westward, raiding cities and towns in Asia Minor. Although there are no known art objects that can be identified with certainty as Cimmerian, these people probably had an animal-style art prefiguring and resembling that of the Scythians. Some art scholars equate the early Cimmerians with the Lurs, a people who inhabited Luristan, a territory between the Caspian Sea and Mesopotamia, around 1000 B.C. and who made outstanding bronzes, often having animal and demonic motifs.

CIRCUS MAXIMUS, the earliest example in Rome of a circus—an oval enclosure for chariot racing, games, and public shows, shaped much like a modern race course. The scene, too, of brutal gladiatorial contests, it was enclosed on three sides with tiers of seats and divided lengthwise by a barrier (spina). The Circus lay in the valley between the Aventine and Palatine hills and possibly dates back to the 6th century B.C., though it was rebuilt by Julius Caesar. It was over 2,000 feet long and 600 feet wide and held about 300,000 spectators.

CIRE PERDUE (lost wax) is an ancient method of metal casting. A model of the figurine, statue, vessel, etc., is made in wax, for solid casting, or in wax on clay, for hollow metalwork. The model is covered with moist clay, vents are inserted, and the whole is baked in a kiln. The melting wax drains through the vents and is replaced by molten metal, usually bronze. When the metal solidifies, the outer clay form is chipped away to reveal the finished casting.

CIST BURIAL, in European archaeology, a single grave often lined and roofed with stone slabs to form a "chest" or "kist," as opposed to larger chamber tombs where many members of a family or clan could be interred together. Cist burials were often covered by an earthen barrow. The practice of prehistoric cist burial was very widespread.

CIVILIZATION, a term often discussed but rarely defined. As used in this book the word implies a complex society—with a structured social order—usually governed by rulers, be they democratically elected or otherwise, such as kings, princes, priests, or paramount chiefs. It employs professional artisans who produce a range of sophisticated works. There is a permanent, central organization, often a literate one, based on the rulers' palace, the priests' temple or ceremonial center, or, most importantly, on an urban community, living in a city. Cultures generally appear as stages prior to the formation of a civilization; they lack large towns, monumental buildings—such as temples, palaces, and public halls—and writing. However, works of art are frequently created. Sumerian civilization was probably the first in the world, while the Chinese enjoy the world's oldest living civilization.

CLASSICAL ANTIQUITIES, a generic term for the many and varied art relics and monuments of ancient Greece and Rome. Included would be temples, statues, mosaics, paintings, vases, etc., which have some artistic or historical importance. Etruscan antiquities are often included with those of Greece and Rome.

CLASSICAL PERIOD, in Greek history, the golden age of Greek culture. Centered at, but not limited to, Athens, the era lasted from the second quarter of the 5th century to the last quarter of the 4th century B.C. and included the period of Pericles. Drama (Aeschylus, Sophocles, Euripides), the writing of history (Herodotus, Thucydides), oratory (Isocrates, Demosthenes), and philosophy (Plato, Aristotle) reflected a preoccupation with man, his rights and responsibilities, and with the ultimate issues of life. The art of the period shows the same concerns. Classical art is simple, restrained, clear, and perfectly executed. Balance and harmony shine forth in temples (the Parthenon), sculpture (Phidias' statues of Athena Lemnia and Athena Parthenos), painting (the work of Apollodoros and Apelles), and in the other arts. Never again did Greek art and architecture reach these sublime heights.

CLEOPATRA'S NEEDLES, name given to two red-granite Egyptian obelisks, which once stood at Heliopolis, where they had been erected by Pharaoh Thutmose III in the 15th century B.C. In 14 B.C. they were removed to Alexandria by Roman troops. As gifts from a 19th-century Egyptian sultan they were carried from Alexandria to their present sites—one in London, the other in New York City's Central Park. They each measure about 70 feet in height and are covered with hieroglyphic inscriptions; the inscriptions have been greatly eroded by urban air pollution.

CLIFF PALACE. See **MESA VERDE.**

CLOISONNE, an ancient style of decoration, using thickly applied enamel and outlining each colored shape

Codex: Page from the *Codex Nuttall*. Mixtec culture. (Bodleian Library, Oxford)

with thin strips of metal, often silver, gold, bronze, or copper; it was common in eastern Mediterranean cultures.

COATLICUE, Aztec goddess whose name meant "serpent-skirted." Although considered the mother of the god Huitzilopochtli, she was more monstrous than maternal. Sculpted images of her displayed prominently severed hands and excised hearts of sacrificed victims. A colossal and terrifying statue of Coatlicue is in the National Museum of Anthropology, Mexico City.

COCLE, one of the best-known indigenous art styles of Panama, which flourished from 500 A.D. until Hispanic

times. The type site of the style is Sitio Conte, where numerous graves, richly stocked with polychrome pottery and gold ornaments, were found. Among the gold pieces are spectacular pendants depicting humans, alligators, frogs, and bats. The technique and style of the goldwork is closely related to the Quimbaya style of Colombia.

CODEX, a distinctive book created by the peoples of Pre-Columbian Mexico. Codices consisted of a continuous length of animal hide or plant-fiber paper, which folded horizontally like a screen. Genealogies, legendary and historical events, economic accounts, and calendrical

Colima culture: Dog-effigy vessel. Painted clay. Western Mexico. (National Museum of Anthropology, Mexico City)

matters are represented in brightly painted cartoonlike scenes with symbolic writing. Examples of codices created by the Aztec, Maya, and Mixtec peoples still exist and have given scholars a wealth of historical information. Sadly, the vast majority of codices were burned by the Spanish, who, unable to understand their content, considered them to be the works of the devil. The word *codex* is also used to describe papyrus scrolls from ancient Egypt and Mesopotamia.

COLIMA CULTURE, a culture developed in the state of Colima, along the west Mexican coast. It is noted for the production of large, hollow pottery figures which date between 350 B.C. and the 3rd century A.D. These are beautifully polished, vigorously modelled, and carefully incised. The range of subject matter is wide; priests, flute players, sea creatures, animals, vegetables, and men and women in a variety of naturalistic attitudes are all depicted. The most famous of Colima subjects are the hairless Mexican dogs, which were fattened for consumption by the Colima nobility. They are portrayed sleeping, playing, growling, wearing masks, and in a variety of other

stances. The Colima people also produced large bowls with vegetable motifs and life-size face masks of stone and clay.

COLOSSAL HEADS, monumental stone heads carved between 1000 and 400 B.C. by the Olmec people of ancient Mexico. To date, some 20 heads have been recovered, the majority from the sites of La Venta, Tres Zapotes, and San Lorenzo. They range in height from five to ten feet and weigh up to 40 tons. The heads are superficially alike; all have heavy, thick-lipped, somewhat negroid features and wear a head piece that resembles a modern football helmet. However, they differ subtly in facial proportions, expressions, and motifs carved on their helmets. Like much of Olmec art their meaning is still uncertain, and scholars have speculated that these most impressive sculptures might be representations of warriors, humanized gods, especially the jaguar-god, or idealized portraits of rulers.

COLOSSEUM, the medieval name for the Flavian amphitheater in Rome and so called because of a colossal statue of Nero that stood nearby. One of the greatest works of architectural engineering left to us by the Romans, it was begun by the Flavian Emperor Vespasian and dedicated by the Emperor Titus in 80 A.D. The exterior, originally sheathed in marble (later looted for other buildings), used all three architectural orders (Doric, Ionic, Corinthian) for the half-columns of the first three

Coatlicue: Basalt. Aztec, 15th century A.D. From Mexico City. (National Museum of Anthropology, Mexico City)

Colosseum, Rome.

arcaded stories of the façade. The fourth story was a masonry wall, topped by masts for the awning that provided shade from the sun. Three tiers of seats held about 50,000 spectators. The arena was floored in timber, covering cages for beasts, elevators, and drains. When the populace tired of its gladiatorial shows, the arena would be flooded for mock seabattles.

COLUMN KRATER. The Greek term *krater* was used for vessels in which wine was mixed with water; the ancients almost never drank wine undiluted. Kraters were fairly large, with wide necks and bodies and two strong handles. The column krater takes its name from handles shaped like architectural columns, which seem to support the rim of the vessel.

CONSTANTINE'S ARCH, a commemorative Roman monument built near the Colosseum in 312 to 315 A.D. to mark the victories of the Emperor Constantine. The triumphal arch was common in ancient Rome, but Constantine's Arch is unique, for it reuses relief sculpture and architectural ornaments from a number of earlier Roman structures, along with contemporary Constantian work. Two strips of the "Great Trajanic Frieze," from Trajan's forum (110 A.D.), depict the Dacian wars, with Trajan's features altered to resemble those of Constantine. Historical reliefs from the time of Hadrian and Marcus Aurelius, in the Classical style, are also included. Scenes of Constantine leaving Milan, entering Rome, and distributing gifts in the Forum are done in a surprisingly unclassical and popular style—large compact heads, drapery chiseled in deep furrows—by artists of native Roman tradition. Classical modelling and ideal proportions are missing, but the insignificance of human beings and the solemn majesty of the emperor are both vividly expressed. The monument is an anthology of the major stages of Roman historical relief. Its contemporary Constantian carvings mark the beginning of a new orientation in art—laws of perspective and spatial illusion giving way to conventional laws of visibility and hierarchic order.

CONSTANTINOPLE. See **BYZANTIUM.**

COPAN, the southernmost and once one of the largest of Mayan cities, located in present-day Honduras. The earliest inscriptions found here date from the 5th century A.D. Copan is famous for a unique style of Mayan stone sculpture that first appeared in the mid-7th century A.D. It is characterized by an abundance of carving on stelae, altars, and as architectural embellishment in relief so high that it approaches three-dimensional sculpture. This contrasts with the low relief typical of most other Mayan sculpture. Human faces are portrayed frontally, in a naturalistic and expressive manner, but surrounded by a complexity of ornament and symbol so lavish that it almost obscures the portraits. The most outstanding example of integrated Mayan sculpture and architecture is at Copan. Called the Hieroglyphic Stairway, it rises 90 feet from the base of a pyramid to its crowning temple; the risers of the stairs are completely covered with hieroglyphic relief, relating the history of the city. Five life-size stone sculptures of Mayan rulers decorate the stairs at set intervals. Sculpture from Copan so impressed early American and European explorers that a good deal of it was removed to private collections. Among these pieces is the "Head of the Young Maize God," acknowledged to be one of the most sensitive portrayals in Mayan art; it is now in the Peabody Museum of Harvard University.

COPPER AGE, in archaeology, a short technological period between the stone and bronze ages. The copper age is sometimes called the Chalcolithic (Greek for copper and stone) because men were using both copper and stone implements. The copper age may be dated as beginning in Europe about 2200 B.C., although the use of the metal was known long before in western Asia. Copper objects in Europe first appeared in Hungary, Switzerland, north Italy, and north-central Spain. In Spain the Beaker People were using the metal while surrounded by other peoples still living in caves and using only stone tools.

COPTS, an Egyptian people identifiable by the 3rd century A.D., or slightly earlier, and still an Egyptian minority group. The word *Copt* is an Arabic corruption of the Greek word *Aegyptos* for the native population of Egypt. The Coptic language—important to Egyptian scholarship—is a remnant of ancient Egyptian and is written with the Greek alphabet plus six demotic characters. Coptic provides clues regarding how the early Egyptians pronounced their language. Egyptian art of early Coptic times included mummy portraits, painted in encaustic on wood in an interesting Greco-Roman style. But Coptic style *per se* is a distinctive kind of abstract ornamental carving (in wood, ivory, etc.) found in Coptic churches and sometimes in Islamic mosques.

CORBELLED, a type of roof or archway in which stone blocks are situated so that they project outward from the face of the wall to support the building's higher structural parts.

Copan: Stele. Carved andesite, dated 782 A.D. Mayan.

Copts: "Daphne." Marble relief, 5th–6th centuries A.D. Fragment from Sheh Abahd, Egypt. (Louvre, Paris)

CORINTH, a cosmopolitan Greek city, strategically sited on the isthmus between central Greece and the Peloponnesus, with harbors on both eastern and western seas. Corinth was preeminent as a shipbuilding center in the 7th century B.C., and Corinthian exports were a vital factor in Mediterranean markets. Her pottery was especially popular, and the attractive vases used to ship her olive oil and perfumes have been found widely in the Classical world; its pale buff clay is decorated with lively animals in red, black, brown, yellow, and white. Lions, sphinxes, and birds are surrounded by clusters of starlike dots and flowers. The best Corinthian vases show a refined and delicate decorative sense and careful attention to detail. Mass pottery production in Corinth led to less careful work, and, after 550 B.C., Athens captured the market. The city became synonymous with sensuous luxury and gave its name to the most luxuriant of the three architectural orders, the Corinthian. "Corinthian bronze" was a costly alloy of gold, silver, and copper used for expensive ornaments. Corinth was razed by Romans in 146 B.C., refounded as a Roman colony in 44 B.C., and was finally destroyed by an earthquake in 521 A.D.

CORINTHIAN CAPITAL, a special feature of one of the three Greek architectural orders. All four faces of the capital were identical, with curved volutes rising vertically from luxuriant bands of acanthus leaves. A baroque capital, it was first discovered on a free-standing column in the 5th-century B.C. temple of Apollo at Bassae in the northwestern Peloponnesus. It did not really suit Greek taste, but the Romans used the column widely in their buildings, and it became the foremost order of the empire.

COWRIES, small white seashells found in the Indian Ocean or the Red Sea. In pre-European times these shells, symbolizing the female vulva, were used widely in Africa and in Oceania as currency. They also served as ornaments for costumes and art objects.

CREMATION, disposal of the dead by burning. This was a common custom in several ancient cultures, including Indian, Japanese, Greek, Etruscan, and among the Roman aristocracy.

CRESWELLIAN CULTURE, a name derived from Creswell Crags, a type site in Derbyshire, England. In a ravine here are several caves that have yielded remains from both the paleolithic and the mesolithic ages, including flint knives and microliths. In these caves two of the earliest known examples of cave art, engraved bone fragments, in Britain were found; one depicts a reindeer, the other a male human figure, probably a sorcerer associated with hunting magic. They date from about the 10th millennium B.C.

CRETE. See **MINOAN CIVILIZATION.**

CRO-MAGNON MAN, a true *Homo sapiens* of the Aurignacian and Magdalenian periods whose remains were first discovered in 1868 at the rock shelter of Cro-Magnon in the Dordogne, France. The original findings consisted of five skeletons—those of a woman, a child, and three men. They lay surrounded by tools, weapons, and necklaces of shells and teeth. Since then numerous Cro-Magnon remains have been widely discovered in Europe. Cro-Magnon Man was more than six feet tall, with a broad forehead, firm chin, and a cranium greater in size than that of present-day man. The plane of his face was more vertical, with a less projecting jaw, than that of earlier Neanderthal Man. Cro-Magnon Man, an old-stone-age hunter who first appeared about 25,000 B.C., had mastered the arts of drawing and painting, in contrast to Neanderthal Man. He is generally credited with having created the cave art of Lascaux and Altamira. Recent discoveries, especially those in the Istallosko Cave in Hungary, indicate that the heartland of Cro-Magnon Man was probably southeastern Europe.

CROMLECH, a Welsh or Breton term describing, at first, a crooked stone, then applied to single standing stones, and finally to a circle of standing stones. In the religious center of the Megalithic Builders at Carnac in Brittany, for instance, the circles that terminate the alignments, or rows of standing stones, are named cromlechs.

CROTONA, ancient Croton, an 8th-century B.C. Greek colony on the "toe" of Italy, famous for its doctors and athletes and its cult of Heracles. In the 6th century B.C. it rose to prominence under the government of the religious brotherhood founded there by the Greek philosopher Pythagoras.

CTESIPHON, an ancient ruined city on the east bank of the Tigris across from Seleucia, about 15 miles southeast of modern Baghdad. Once a legendary city of splendor, Ctesiphon in the 2nd century B.C. became the summer residence of Parthian kings and in the 3rd century A.D. the capital of the Sassanians. The Arch of Ctesiphon, its most notable remain, is an enormous single-span vaulted hall that once served as the throne room of the Sassanid palace. Ctesiphon was taken and plundered by the Arabs in the 7th century A.D.

CUCUTENI CULTURE. The neolithic farmers of the Danube Valley in the 4th millennium B.C. were attracted northwards and eastwards by the fertile loess plains of Rumania and south Russia. At the settlement of Cucuteni near Iasi in northeast Rumania some of their remarkable pottery was discovered. It developed from the more primitive pottery found at Starcevo and consists of jars and bowls raised high on pedestal bases with beautifully linked spiral designs in red, warm yellow-browns, and black, sometimes over a white slip or underlayer on the red clay. Cucuteni was fortified by a rampart and ditch.

CULT STATUE, the image of the deity placed in the cella of Greek or Roman temples. Popular worship centered around the statue, which offered the ancients a concrete idea of their gods. Since few cult statues survive, knowledge of them has depended on descriptions and small reproductions, particularly Roman copies of cult masterpieces by Phidias and Polyclitus.

CULTURE. See CIVILIZATION.

CUMAE, the earliest of the Greek colonies in southern Italy. Founded around 750 B.C., it prospered and colonized much of the district, including Naples. The famous Sibyl made her home here, and the cave of the oracle was excavated in 1932. Taken by the Romans in 338 B.C., Cumae supported them in their wars with Hannibal and with the Italian cities in southern Italy. As nearby Puteoli became more important, Cumae declined.

CUNEIFORM, the earliest known system of writing, probably developed by the Sumerians in Mesopotamia by the 4th millennium B.C. Basically ideographic, its wedge-shaped characters were generally incised on wet clay with a split reed, or stylus, the clay tablets then being hardened by baking or exposure to the sun; later cuneiform was also inscribed on stone and metal. Cuneiform was used for a number of languages in addition to Sumerian, including Akkadian (very widespread), Elamite, Hittite, and Babylonian. Rawlinson's work at Behistun was crucial to the modern decipherment of the script.

CUPID. See EROS.

CUPISNIQUE CULTURE, a regional variation of Chavin civilization, with sites in several coastal valleys of northern Peru. It flourished between 900 and 200 B.C. Cupisnique ceramics are highly prized and closely resemble those of highland Chavin. Typically they are thick-walled and massive and of a somber black or gray color. Decoration consists of the manipulation of the surface of the vessel, either by low-relief modelling, incision, or roughening. Shapes include the stirrup spout and a jar with a long, narrow neck. The earlier Cupisnique vessels usually have Chavin jaguar-god motifs. Later examples are in high relief and bear the forms of animals, humans,

Cuneiform: Script from Mesopotamia.

Cyprus: Fertility goddess. Clay. 3rd millennium B.C.
(Louvre, Paris)

plants, and buildings and thus represent the beginning of a 2,000-year-old tradition of effigy-modelling on the Peruvian north coast.

CUZCO, the ancient capital and administrative center of the Incan Empire, in south-central Peru. Although the legendary founding of Cuzco took place around 1200 A.D. (by the first Inca emperor, Manco Capac), its basic grid-like plan, which continued until the Spanish Conquest, was laid out by the Incan emperor Pachacuti. Besides its imperial palaces, which were built around the central Huacapata Plaza, there were houses for nobility, for workers, and for rulers of conquered peoples. The principal buildings, the Temple of the Sun and the House of the Virgins of the Sun, were lavishly decorated with gold ornamentation. The unwalled city was guarded by the fortress Sacsahuaman, which overlooked Cuzco from a nearby hill. Cuzco was plundered by Pizarro in 1533.

CYBELE, the ''Great Mother,'' a Near Eastern goddess of nature, worshipped in the form of a block of stone. The Greeks identified her with Rhea and the Romans with Ops.

CYCLADIC CULTURE, the neolithic way of life that dominated the more than 200 islands dotting the Aegean Sea between mainland Greece and Crete. Arising about 4000 B.C., Cycladic culture reached its height between 2600 and 1100 B.C., long before Greek culture became important. Cycladic wealth was derived from an active maritime trade and from valuable deposits of marble and metals. The people here shared many cultural traits with other Aegean peoples, including the cult of the mother-goddess and that of the sacred bull. Excavations at the town-site of Phylakopi, on Melos, have yielded tools, weapons, and pottery very similar to Minoan artifacts from Crete, although far from the same level of artistic excellence. The great thrust of Cycladic artistic activity was dedicated to a cult of the dead, who were buried in collective tombs with offerings of highly distinctive, elegant figurines. By 1700 B.C. Cycladic culture was almost completely under the domination of Crete. Some 500 years later Cretan influence was replaced by Mycenaean, and Cycladic culture fell into a decline.

CYCLADIC IDOLS, a unique type of marble figurine, originating on the Cycladic Islands in the 3rd millennium B.C. They scale from one to five feet in height and most often depict a standing nude female with arms folded across her chest. Slender, abstract, and elegant, these statuettes differ considerably from the heavy, voluptuous mother-goddess figures produced in the eastern Mediterranean of the same period. Seated men, playing musical instruments, are also the subject of Cycladic

marble carvings. Associated with the Cycladic cult of the dead, these so-called idols are found in Aegean graves and in Crete and Greece. Cycladic idols are often copied and then sold as originals.

CYCLOPEAN, a method of stone masonry employed by many ancient peoples. Uncut stones of massive size were used in building a structure, with pebbles and rubble packed between them in place of mortar.

CYPRUS, an eastern Mediterranean island (about 3,500 square miles) that fell, in ancient times, within the sphere of Minoan, Egyptian, Persian, and Greek civilizations. Settlement dates from the 6th millennium B.C. and sites of that period, such as Khirokitia, have yielded vessels and idols made of stone. The Cypriote bronze age (roughly 2400–1050 B.C.) saw the island as the Mediterranean world's major source of copper, a metal that derives its very name from the island. Originating in this period was Cyprus's characteristic pottery, a fine, red-polished ware, often globular and high-necked, with incised or low-relief decoration. The early 1st millennium B.C. witnessed large-scale Greek colonization and predominantly Greek artistic styles. Pottery was mainly of Greek geometric style. Notable sculpture included life-size votive figures, usually in terra cotta or limestone.

Cycladic idol: Head of an idol. Marble. Cycladic culture, ca. 2000 B.C. From Amorgos. (Louvre, Paris)

84

D

DACIA, ancient kingdom north of Macedonia, in the lower loop of the Danube. The Emperor Trajan immortalized his two successful campaigns against the Dacians (101–102, 105–106 A.D.) in the elaborate spiral frieze of the 130-foot column he set up in the forum at Rome in 113 A.D. The Emperor Aurelian abandoned Dacia to the Goths in 270 A.D.

DAEDALUS, a legendary Athenian artist, craftsman, and inventor of pre-Classical times. He fled Athens for Crete, where he built the famous Labyrinth for King Minos and designed the thread, or clue, with which Ariadne saved Theseus. King Minos imprisoned Daedalus and his son Icarus, but they escaped with two pairs of wings Daedalus made from wax and feathers. Icarus flew too near the sun, the wax melted, and he was drowned in the Aegean. Many archaic Greek temples and statues were thought to be by Daedalus, and the term *Daedalic* is applied to a type of early statue or figurine with an unusually low forehead. Daedalus is depicted on vases, gems, and sculpture in Greece, in Etruria, and in Roman wall paintings.

DAGOBA. See **STUPA.**

DAGON, a god of various ancient Near Eastern peoples, particularly the Philistines. He had temples at Ashdod, Gaza, and Ras Shamra. Dagon was frequently conceptualized as half man, half fish. He is several times referred to in the Old Testament.

DAHOMEY, a former West African kingdom that ruled over much of the southern part of modern Dahomey. Established in the early 17th century A.D., this kingdom of the Fon people maintained its power with a large army, the hard core of which was an elite corps of women, often referred to as Amazons. The omnipotent rulers of Dahomey were deeply involved in the 19th-century slave trade and in the annual sacrifice of humans. The kingdom collapsed in 1893 when the French invaded and exiled the last Dahomey king, Behanzin.

DAIBUTSU, in Japanese, a colossal statue of Buddha. The Great Buddha of Kamakura, one of the largest bronze statues in the world, is a 52-foot-high seated Buddha and was built about 1252 A.D. during the revival of Buddhism in Japan. An earlier Daibutsu is at Nara.

DAMA DE ELCHE. In the summer of 1897 workmen levelling ground at Elche, Alicante, on the east coast of

Dahomey: Fon tapestries. From Dahomey. (Museum of African and Oceanic Art, Paris)

Spain, unearthed a small bust of sandstone in the ruins of a Roman house. It was sold to the Louvre but returned to the Prado in Madrid in 1941. This now famous statue, the Dama de Elche, shows a woman of wealth with a high comb and mantilla, elaborate jewelry, and large ornamental discs over her ears. The face by contrast is severe, calm, and aristocratic with finely chiselled features. The attribution may be Roman, but the emphasis in the ornament of the bust is strongly Iberian. It is possible that the work dates from as early as the 4th century B.C.

DAMASCUS, the present capital of Syria and one of the most ancient cities in the world. Excavation has disclosed pottery dating from the 3rd millennium B.C. The first historical mention of Damascus comes from Amarna, where hieroglyphs list it as one of the cities conquered by Egypt in the 15th century B.C. Damascus has been ruled by many peoples and molded by many cultures: Aramaeans, Assyrians, Persians, Greeks, Romans, Arabs, and Ottoman Turks.

DAN, a West African people, formerly called the Yakuba, who live in the central Ivory Coast and in Liberia. They are most famous for a realistic type of mask much sought after by collectors of African art. Dan masks, with their delicate oval face, their sensitive rounded features, and smiling, although elegant, expression, are typically painted in highly polished black. The Dan also make a horrible terror mask, similar in style to that of their the Ngere. The Dan show great skill as metalworkers, and their works include copper statuettes of various subjects, among them female figures.

DANEGELD. According to the Anglo-Saxon Chronicle the Vikings from Scandinavia made attacks on England almost every year from 835 A.D. onwards. In 865 the first payment of a political bribe, or protection money, was made to the Danes in the form of Danegeld. King Alfred of Wessex paid Danegeld in 868 and afterwards but gradually built up sufficient power to defeat the Danes and divide England with them at the Peace of Wedmore. Danegeld was also extracted from the Byzantines by the Vikings in Russia. Foreign antiquities found in Viking graves may have come to Scandinavia as loot, as trade items, or, quite possibly, as a form of Danegeld.

DANILO, a neolithic village site on the Dalmatian seacoast in Yugoslavia. Two types of prehistoric pottery have been found here, both of which have counterparts on the Italian side of the Adriatic. One has geometric designs in black and wide bands of red on a buff ground; the other is a burnished ware with incised designs.

DANUBIAN CULTURE. The inhabitants of central and eastern Europe, for untold centuries hunters, fishers, and food-gatherers, began about 4500 B.C. to learn agriculture from peoples and ideas that flowed from the Aegean and the Near East. These influences mixed with early Danubian cultures and produced in the Balkans such neolithic settlements as Vinca and Starcevo near the Danube. From the Danube region, particularly from centers in Moravia and Slovakia, farming spread gradually northwards over

Dama de Elche: Sandstone. 4th–3rd centuries B.C. Found at Elche, Alicante. (Prado, Madrid)

the great loess-soil plains of central Europe until it reached the Baltic region by about 2500 B.C. The peasant farmers of this neolithic Danubian culture did not know the use of metal. They used stone tools, particularly hoes of shoe-last shape, and bone and flint implements. They lived in well-built timber houses and had already domesticated cattle, sheep, goats, and pigs. Their pottery is at first comparatively simple, often copying the shape of gourds, a mark of the southern origin of the culture. Pottery forms and decoration gradually became more complex and beautiful. Bandkeramik ware is typical of Danubian culture, as is Tisza pottery.

DEAD SEA SCROLLS, a collection of texts, mainly in Biblical Hebrew, Aramaic, and Greek, discovered since 1947 in 11 caves at Qumran, on the northwestern shore of the Dead Sea. They are possibly the most important archaeological finds of our time. The scrolls, which contain books of the Old Testament, apocryphal books, Old Testament commentaries, hymns, and theological works, seem to have been written from about the mid-2nd century B.C. to about the mid-1st century A.D. and are about 1,000 years older than any previous manuscripts of the Old Testament. Some of the scrolls are complete—the great scroll of Isaiah is seven and one half yards long—but most are in small fragments that must be painstakingly reassembled and deciphered. Apparently, they were written and cared for by a sect of Essenes, a mystical monastic community, living at or near Qumran. The scrolls have been dated by two methods. The first, radiocarbon dating, performed on some of the scroll linens, indicate a date of 33 A.D. ± 200 years. Subsequent excavations in the Khirbet Qumran, about one-half mile south of the scroll caves, yielded a jar identical to storage jars found in one scroll cave, along with one coin that could be dated precisely at 10 A.D. More extensive excavations yielded 500 coins in a 200-year sequence, enabling archaeologists to give the scrolls fairly accurate dates and simultaneously providing a history of the site. The scroll community occupied Qumran from the last quarter of the 2nd century B.C. until 68 A.D., with the exception of one brief period of abandonment (31–5 B.C.) following an earthquake. Qumran's inhabitants apparently hid the scrolls when Roman troops occupied the site—and the scrolls were then forgotten until their modern discovery. The Dead Sea Scrolls are the most important source in the study of the genesis of Christianity. It is thought that John the Baptist was an Essene. Dead Sea Scrolls are on display in the Shrine of the Book in Jerusalem.

DEER PARK. See SARNATH.

DELHI SULTANATE, a period of Moslem rule in India from A.D. 1206 to 1526. By the 14th century these Turkish sultans controlled all of north India and the Deccan to Cape Comorin. Their control disintegrated, and north India finally fell to the invading Moghuls. The Delhi Sultanate was a period of autocratic rule, marked by the oppression of Hindus. But Islam could not obliterate Hindu culture, and the Hindus could not assimilate Islam. The sultans built many mosques and palaces in the Indo-Saracenic style—a combination of Indian, Turkish, and Persian influences; they include the Qutb-Minar and the Quwwat-ul-Islam Mosque, both in Delhi.

DELPHI, site of the oldest and most important Greek oracle of Apollo. It lies at the foot of Mt. Parnassus near the north coast of the Gulf of Corinth. Its sacred navel stone (*omphalos*) was supposed to mark the center of the earth. The ruins of the temple of Apollo seen here are from the 4th century B.C.; it was the third or fourth structure on the same foundation. The Delphian precinct also has numerous miniature temples ("treasuries") presented to the gods by the cities of Greece. Decorative reliefs from these buildings offer fine examples of Archaic and Classical art, as do the pedimental sculptures from a no-longer-extant 6th-century Apollo temple and a 5th-century bronze charioteer, now in the Delphi Museum. A club room of the Cnidians, scene of one of Plutarch's dialogues, was once decorated with famous paintings by Polygnotus.

DEMETER, the Greek goddess of agriculture (Ceres for the Romans) and the mother of Persephone (Roman: Prosperpina). She is variously the wife of Poseidon, Zeus, or Hades. In Greek Archaic and Classical art, she is shown with Triptolemus, whom she sent through the world to teach the art of farming, and Persephone, carrying ears of grain or a torch scepter. Eleusis, in Attica, was sacred to Demeter.

DEMOTIC, Egyptian script used from about 800 B.C. to the 5th century A.D. It replaced the older hieratic script, which was based on hieroglyphics. Demotic appears on public documents, stelae, and obelisks and is found on the Rosetta Stone. It most frequently occurs on papyrus.

DENDERA, site of an ancient Upper Egyptian city, notable for its temple to the goddess of women, Hathor, and also for its 6th Dynasty tombs, built mainly of brick. Although the original Hathor Temple dates from the Middle Kingdom, the structure now standing is from the Ptolemaic period (late 2nd century B.C.), with later additions from Roman times. The names of the Roman em-

Diadoumenos: Marble. Roman copy of a bronze original by Polyclitus. (Metropolitan Museum of Art, New York)

Delphi: Remains of a temple sanctuary.

perors Domitian and Trajan appear on the gateway, and a 2nd-century A.D. limestone relief depicts Trajan dressed in the garments of a pharaoh.

DENDROCHRONOLOGY, in archaeology, the use of tree-ring patterns to date wood at a particular site. Because the width of tree-trunk rings varies according to climate, a plotting of tree-ring patterns can be made in a particular area. Then timbers and wood recovered from a site in the same area can be compared with the master plotting for dating. The method can be used only in areas where the climate has varying temperature and rainfall and where timber has been used and preserved. The technique is often used to cross-check radiocarbon dating.

DENDUR. See NUBIA.

DEVI, the Hindu mother-goddess who is the daughter of Himavat and the consort of Siva. In her benevolent aspect she is called Mahadevi or Parvati and is depicted as a beautiful woman. She is Durga and Kali in her terrible aspect and is shown as a horrible hag.

DIADOUMENOS, a well-known bronze statue of the 5th-century B.C. Greek sculptor Polyclitus, showing a young athlete "binding a ribbon around his head" (*diadoumenos*). Though the original has not survived, several Roman copies hint at the harmony of proportion and the attention to detail for which Polyclitus was famous.

DIANA. See ARTEMIS.

DINOS, a large Greek vessel, oval in shape and without handles, used for mixing wine.

DIOCLETIAN'S BATHS, a monumental building constructed in Rome by the Emperor Diocletian around 302 A.D. A fairly typical example of a grandiose Roman bath, it consisted of some 3,000 rooms, with very high ceilings of intersecting barrel-vault design, supported largely by Corinthian columns. Aside from the baths' functional features, consisting of bathing pools—some of them heated—the structure's walls were originally decorated with mosaics, its interior adorned with colossal sculpture, etc. In the mid-16th century the building's remains were converted into a magnificent Christian church, S. Maria degli Angeli, by Michelangelo. While Christian decoration largely erased that of Imperial Rome, the building's original main lines were preserved. **DIOCLETIAN'S PALACE,** the fortified retreat on the coast of Yugoslavia (at modern Split, or Spalato) built for the Emperor Diocletian about 300 A.D. and to which he retired in 305 A.D. The massive walls remain and show a large rectangular enclosure, quartered by two broad colonnaded streets running north-south and east-west. It contained housing for the Imperial guard, the emperor's apartments, his octagonal mausoleum, a tiny Corinthian temple to Jupiter, a great hall with domed vestibule, all forming an impressive and compact complex within. An ambitious and scenic gallery ran between the corner towers on the seaward side of the enclosure. Arches springing directly from columns—a device known but not exploited before—are here used for the first time on a monumemtal scale.

Dionysus: Amphora. Black-figure ware. Greek, ca. 535 B.C., signed by the Amasis Painter. From Vulci (The National Library, Paris)

DIONYSUS, in Greek religion, god of fertility and wine, also called Bacchus and identified by the Romans with Liber. The worship of Dionysus was celebrated with music, dancing, and drunken orgies. He is a very popular figure in vase-painting. In the Archaic period he is depicted as a bearded and majestic old man, but in later times he is often shown young and nude, with long clustering hair crowned by the grapevine or ivy, and with a fawn or panther skin over his shoulder and a wine cup or some grapes in his hand. Nymphs and satyrs often accompany Dionysus. He was associated with various religious cults and festivals.

DIPYLON STATUE. See KERAMEIKOS CEMETERY.

DISCOBOLUS, a bronze statue of a discus-thrower by the 5th-century B.C. Greek sculptor Myron, an older contemporary of Phidias and Polyclitus. It is known only through Roman copies, the best preserved of which is in the Terme Museum in Rome. The Discobolus dates from about 460 B.C., and his dynamic pose contrasts with the serenity of sculpture from the early Classical period.

DOGON, a West African people who live on the Bandiagar cliffs in Mali. The Dogon are a refugee people who settled their cliff villages about 500 years ago and gradually supplanted the prior inhabitants, the Tellem. The complex and rich cosmology of the Dogon remained hidden from outsiders until the 1940s when Marcel Griaule, a French anthropologist, began to study them. Dogon cosmology provides a framework and explanation for many aspects of their culture, such as art, architecture, and traditional customs. A granary, for instance, is a container for food, a symbol of woman, a replica of the structure of the universe, and its form relates to a basket used by the Dogon. Many wood sculptures of freestanding figures, doors, and pulleys show the *Nommo,* or ancestral spirits, from whom the Dogon are descended.

DOLMEN, in prehistory, a type of monument in which two or more large stone slabs are set on end (or edge) and support a flat slab to form an arch or roof. Dolmens date from the neolithic period and are found mainly in Europe and North Africa. The word is of Celtic origin.

DOLNI VESTONICE, an ice-age site in Moravia where remains of prehistoric mammoth-hunters of the Gravettian period, about 25,000 years ago, have been found. A rather impressive range of implements in bone, antler, and mammoth ivory turned up here, as well as a small portrait head carved in ivory and several animal and Venus figures. Bones notched in five-count groups have also been unearthed.

DONGSON CULTURE, a southeast Asian bronze-age culture dating from about 500 B.C. to the 2nd century A.D. Located mainly in Than-Hoa province of Vietnam, on the Tonkin Plain, it produced the first true Indochinese art. Excavations of Dongson sites in 1926 yielded a characteristic bronze containing about 20 percent lead alloy and

Dogon: Mask. Painted wood. (British Museum, London)

fashioned into drums decorated with scenes and geometrical designs. Dongson culture fell under the influence of Ch'in Dynasty China, and Chinese artifacts of the Han period have been found at Dongson sites.

DORAK, an archaeological site in northwestern Asia Minor, Turkey, where reputedly was found a fabulous treasury of antiquities. The Dorak treasure was apparently discovered in two royal tombs, similar to those at Alaca Huyuk. From the remains of a gilded wooden throne found in association with the hoard, the collection is dated to 2480 B.C. Included in the treasure were five female figures fashioned from electrum, silver, and bronze, elaborately decorated cups, richly ornamented swords and daggers, and a quantity of gold jewelry in the style of Troy, as were scepters, ceremonial axes, and other art objects. After its excavation the Dorak treasure vanished, causing one of the greatest scandals of modern archaeology. It is presumed that the hoard is in the hands of a wealthy private collector.

DORDOGNE, a region in southwest France particularly rich in prehistoric remains. The Dordogne River, which gives its name to the region, flows from the foothills of the Massif Central westwards to the Atlantic at Bordeaux. In its valleys, particularly that of the Vezere River, are a number of prehistoric sites in caves and overhanging rock shelters where bones, artifacts, and cave paintings have been found, pointing to human occupation from perhaps 125,000 years ago. The lifelike figures of horses and bison, some in color, in the cave at Lascaux are among the most celebrated examples of prehistoric art.

DORIANS, the last of the northern peoples to enter Greece, in about 1100 B.C. They displaced or merged with the Mycenaeans, who were culturally superior but probably akin to the Dorians. The so-called Dorian Invasion is now seen more as a gradual infiltration and transformation of very early Greek culture that finally led to the Greek city-state of the 8th century B.C. The Dorian element in Greek art is identified with an austere restraint and sober solidity that blended well with the delicate grace of the more elaborate Ionic strain in architecture, pottery, and sculpture. The Geometric period in Greek archaeology is often associated with the Dorians, as is the Doric Order of architecture.

DORIC CAPITAL, the distinguishing feature of the earliest Greek architectural order. It consisted of the *echinus*, a simple convex molding swelling out from the top drum of the column, and topped by the *abacus*, a flat, rectangular slab upon which rested the horizontal architrave supporting the eaves of the roof. The Doric capital, and a few inches of the drum below, were carved from a single block of stone. It may be related to surviving Mycenaean capitals. Doric is the usual order for Greek temples on the mainland of Greece, in Sicily, and southern Italy. It takes its name from the Dorians of mainland Greece.

DORYPHOROS, the most famous statue of Polyclitus, the 5th-century B.C. Greek sculptor, second only to Phidias in reputation. This bronze masterpiece depicts a powerful-looking youth "carrying a spear" (*doryphoros*).

It was accepted as the canon, or standard, of Greek excellence and served as a model for later artists. Known only through Roman copies, the most complete Doryphoros was found at Pompeii and is in the Naples Museum.

DOWRIS, a bronze-age site in Ireland near Athlone, where gold and bronze articles were found in a hoard. Some of these may have been made at Dowris between 800 and 600 B.C. and show great skill in casting and in working with sheet metal. Two discs connected by a curved bar formed an ornamental cloak-fastening worn at the neck and found at many Irish sites. Cauldrons, pins of sunflower pattern, horns, and shields with both U- and V-shaped notches were among the objects discovered here.

DRAVIDIANS, one of the earliest peoples inhabiting India. They are a mixture of mongoloid and black aborigine stock. The Aryan invasion of the 2nd millennium B.C. pushed the Dravidians south, where they remained predominant for a long period. By 500 B.C. Indian culture was a mixture of Dravidian and Aryan elements. Dravidians today are represented by Tamil, Telegu, Malayam, and Kanarese languages. Dravidian contributions to Hinduism include naturalism, the cult of the mother-goddess, and the worship of images of specific deities. Their architectural dolmen-form is a forerunner of the later chaitya-hall of Indian temples.

DREAMTIME. See ABORIGINE CULTURE.

DROMOS, in archaeology, a term first used in connection with the ancient tombs at Mycenae. It describes a cut or walled passageway, without a roof, leading into the entrance of a roofed tomb, usually built of stone, as in the tombs of the Megalithic Builders in many parts of Europe.

DRUIDS, priests and judges of the Celtic tribes of Gaul and Britain. They are first mentioned as "the philosophers among the Celts" by Sotion of Alexandria in 200 B.C. Julius Caesar, in his account of the conquest of Gaul in 50 B.C., said that the Druids met annually near Chartres under an archdruid and acted as a unifying force among the independent tribes. As priests they conducted the worship of the Celtic gods, often in sacred groves. The oak, and the mistletoe growing on it, were regarded as holy. Human sacrifices were carried out by the Druids and divination practiced by observing the death struggles of the victims. In the only early account of Druids in Britain, Tacitus describes the capture by the Romans of the island of Mona off the north coast of Wales, which was a Druid stronghold. In this account there is a suggestion that the Druids supported the national resistance of the Celts against foreign invaders. The association of the Druids with Stonehenge and Avebury and various elaborate descriptions of their priestly functions there have no basis in fact.

DUHOS. See ARAWAKS.

DURA-EUROPOS, a major caravan center in the Syrian desert, near the Euphrates. Founded in about 300 B.C. by the Seleucids, it was successfully occupied by the Parthians, the Romans, who established a garrison here, and

Dying Gaul: Marble. Roman copy, ca. 220 B.C., of bronze original once at Pergamon. (Capitoline Museum, Rome)

the Persians, who destroyed the city in 258 A.D. In 1922 Yale University began a continuing series of excavations at Dura-Europos that has revealed a startling collection of wall paintings on temples, homes, a synagogue, a mithraeum, and on a small Christian house-church, the oldest such church known to date. The paintings of Biblical scenes in the synagogue are not only completely unexpected but bear the mark of high artistic quality, as do the Christian paintings in the house-church. Obviously influenced by Hellenistic and Roman styles, the paintings shed a much needed light on Jewish and early Christian painters of the Roman catacombs. The wall paintings were removed from Dura-Europos and are now in the Damascus Museum. However, a complete set of copies may be seen at Yale University.

DUR SHARRUKIN. See KHORSABAD.

DVARAVATI, a Buddhist kingdom in Thailand. At first part of the Funan Empire, it became independent in the 7th century A.D. The people of Dvaravati probably were Mons, and by the 10th century they were assimilated into the Khmer kingdom. The principal archaeological sites of the kingdom are S'i Tep, Pra Pathom, and P'ong Tuk, where many small works of art have been found; these sculptures generally show Indian stylistic influences.

DYING GAUL, a marble copy of a bronze statue of the 3rd century B.C., set up at Pergamon in Asia Minor to commemorate the victory of King Attalus I of Pergamon over invading Gauls. The mortally wounded warrior is portrayed sympathetically, and the statue is typical of Pergamene production in the 3rd century B.C.—intense, vigorous, somewhat unrefined, and preoccupied with violence and death. The marble copy is in the Capitoline Museum, Rome, and dates from about 220 B.C.

E

EA. See ENKI.

EAST ANGLIA, a flat region of the east coast of England between the Wash and the Thames estuary. It has geographical characteristics similar to those of the Netherlands. The early archaeological deposits of this region include some of man's earliest stone tools, discovered near Ipswich and Norwich. Gold torques and armlets of twisted gold, made in about 1600 B.C., have been found at Grunty Fen, Cambridgeshire. But the greatest single treasure dates from the time of the Anglo-Saxon invasions in 650 A.D.—namely, the Sutton Hoo hoard. Decorated weapons, a helmet, purse, and other priceless objects in gold, silver, enamel, and garnets accompanied the ship burial of a Saxon chief. The body was absent and it is thought he may have been drowned at sea. Alfred the Great (871–899) was forced to include a large part of East Anglia in his grant of the Danelaw land to the Viking invaders.

EASTER ISLAND, a small Polynesian island located in the eastern Pacific Ocean, some 2,000 miles off the coast of Chile. Inhabited probably in the 5th century A.D., the island, one of the loneliest in the world, received its name when Dutch explorers reached it on Easter Day, 1722. Gigantic stone statues of humans, some weighing more than 50 tons, have given the island an aura of mystery. Hewn from single blocks of stone, these megalithic colossi, some measuring 30 feet in height, rest on stepped ceremonial platforms (of finely fitted masonry) and display incredible engineering skill. Because these statues, as well as numerous petroglyphs and other archaeological remains, differ so widely from the culture of the rest of Polynesia, some scholars advance the theory that settlement originated from the coast of Peru. Voyages of Thor Heyerdahl have demonstrated the possibility of such a migration. Among small works of Easter Island art are the *kavakava,* carved images of slightly bent and emaciated humans.

ECBATANA, an ancient Persian city on the site of the modern Hamadan in western Iran. It was the splendorous capital of the Medes until conquered and plundered by Cyrus the Great in 550 B.C. It became the summer residence of the Achaemenid kings following Cyrus and was lost by them to Alexander the Great in 330 B.C. Among the few remains found here were Median rock-cut tombs and inscribed plaques and column bases, dating from the period of the Achaemenid Dynasty. Ecbatana was the site of the Median royal treasury, as yet unexcavated.

EDOMITES, a Semitic people whose kingdom in the extreme southeast of Palestine flourished from the 13th to the 8th centuries B.C. An agricultural and commercial civilization, it left pottery remains of a high order of excellence, as well as figurines of fertility deities. Frequently mentioned in the Old Testament, the Edomites were at almost constant war with Judah, primarily for control of trade routes and copper and iron deposits. Weakened by these conflicts, the Edomites were, by the 4th century B.C., conquered by the Nabataeans.

EDO PERIOD, in Japanese history, also called the period of the Tokugawa Shogunate, which lasted from 1603 to 1868. It represented an epoch of great prosperity, peace, and cultural isolation in Japan. Originating with the rise of Tokugawa Ieyasu, who was officially given the title of shogun by the emperor in 1603, the period reflected the power of the new middle class, which demanded art works to its own tastes. Confucian thought, stressing a tranquil and ordered society, dominated. Buddhism declined, and Japanese sculpture virtually disappeared. However, painting flourished. The Kano school (founded by pre-Tokugawa artist Kano Masanobu) achieved formal perfection in its Chinese-style screen landscapes. Most significant was a new movement, the

Easter Island: Stone colossi.

Edo period: Dish, detail. Nabeshima porcelain. Japanese, early 18th century A.D. (National Museum, Tokyo)

Egyptian Civilization: Portrait of Hesira. Wood relief. 3rd Dynasty. From Saqqarah. (National Museum, Cairo)

ukiyo-e ("pictures of the fleeting world"), which produced both paintings and wood-block prints. Subjects reflected tastes of the new bourgeoisie and included domestic and street scenes and portraits of popular Kabuki actresses. Artists such as Hiroshige, Kiyonaga, Utamaro, Hokusai, and Korin were popular. Noteworthy porcelains were produced, and new textile techniques were introduced. In all, Edo art attained high levels of craftsmanship and richness. Ancient Edo is now called Tokyo.

EGYPTIAN CIVILIZATION, one of the most durable and wealthy civilizations of the ancient world, second only to the Sumerian of Mesopotamia as the world's earliest civilization. It arose sometime before 4000 B.C. along the fertile banks of the Nile in northeast Africa, a river valley protected by impressive natural frontiers—mountains and deserts to the east and west. Geographically isolated, the Egyptians created a unique society, conservative and theocratic, that was destined, in later times, to become a major cultural influence in the development of the eastern Mediterranean and Near Eastern worlds. Egyptian civilization first becomes recognizable as such during the so-called Predynastic era (roughly 4000 to 3200 B.C.), when two distinct Nile kingdoms evolved. One, in Lower Egypt (the northern Delta region and environs), centered around the ancient holy city of Heliopolis; the second was in Upper Egypt (extending for a few hundred miles south of the Delta), where there flourished two successive related cultures, sometimes called Nagada I and II, after a major archaeological site of that name. Around 3200 B.C. the semilegendary King Menes established the 1st Dynasty, uniting the Upper and Lower kingdoms and creating an administration in

which control and exploitation of the Nile for irrigation of farmland became organized and widespread. Egypt's civilization was largely the result of the successful effort to channel the yearly rise and ebb of Nile waters by construction of irrigation dikes. Material abundance, based on the cultivation of grains and flax, led to the growth of Nile city-states and to the fostering of such crafts as stone masonry and textile production. Flax was the basis of Egypt's linen craft, a trade which was to become famous throughout the world. Egyptian civilization is generally divided into three great periods. The first of Egypt's major historic periods—called the Old Kingdom—began with the 3rd Dynasty pharaoh, Zoser, and lasted from about 2780 to 2280 B.C., with its political base in the Lower Egyptian capital, Memphis, and its religious center at nearby Heliopolis. By this time, and throughout Egypt's subsequent history, the pharaoh had established unquestioned secular authority and religious leadership that became increasingly identified with divinity. Egypt's religion was polytheistic and state-oriented; its major gods were personifications of the natural forces. The Egyptian's observation of the annual recurrence of agricultural life cycles, embodied in the ebb and flow of the Nile, led him, by analogy, to form the religious concept of life after death. The Old Kingdom became the great era of pyramid construction, and pyramids to such pharaohs as Zoser, Cheops, etc., were intended to serve pharaonic needs in the afterlife. Egypt's second major period, the Middle Kingdom, lasted roughly from 2052 through 1778 B.C. and originated when Memphis-based rule in Lower Egypt was eclipsed by that of Thebes in Upper Egypt. The founder of Theban government, Mentuhotep I, established the 11th Dynasty. His successors were several pharaohs named either Amenemhat or Sesostris. The invasion of Middle Kingdom Egypt in the 18th century B.C. by Near Eastern semibarbarians, called the Hyksos, opened a period of foreign rule. The Hyksos were finally driven out of Egypt by Ahmosis in 1580 B.C., who then re-established the 18th Dynasty at Thebes, thus inaugurating Egypt's third and final period of historical importance, the New Kingdom. This era, lasting to about 1085 B.C., was Egypt's greatest period of conquest and imperial expansion, which reached beyond the Nile Valley into western Asia. It was a significant period artistically—a time of monumental sculpture and elaborate temple architecture built to glorify state leaders, notably at such Egyptian sites as Karnak and Luxor. Unique among New Kingdom pharaohs was Akhenaten, who built a brilliant new city at Amarna and defied traditional polytheistic precepts by stating belief in only one god. This possible precursor to the more important Judaic monotheism only just survived Akhenaten's reign. After

Egyptian Civilization: The sanctuary of Amon, Karnak. New Kingdom.

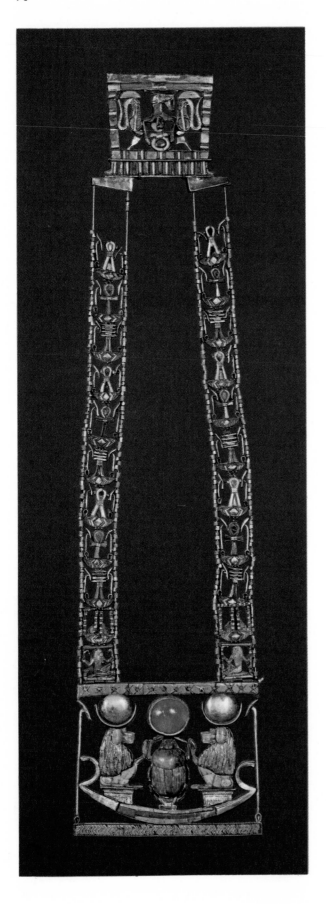

his death the heresy of his views was underlined when his successors had his city destroyed. The New Kingdom was also a period of extensive Hebrew immigration into Egypt and their subsequent persecution which culminated probably during the reign of Ramses II, when Moses led the Hebrews out of Egypt. After 1100 B.C. Egypt's imperial power waned. In 664 B.C. the country was invaded by the Assyrians. From 525 B.C. until the arrival of Alexander the Great in the 4th century B.C., Egypt was little more than a Persian colony. Ptolemaic rule, inaugurated by one of Alexander's generals in 304 B.C., gave Egypt a Greek dynasty until the country was annexed to the Roman Empire.

Egyptian Metalwork. While stone was abundant in Egypt, metal was scarce, and although a metal-crafting tradition arose in the early centuries, chiefly based on Nubian gold or Sinai copper, statuary of stone was the predominant medium of sculptural expression. However, many fine Egyptian objects of metal exist, especially those revealed in the New Kingdom tomb of Tutankhamon, where extremely rare silver vases, sarcophagi, and trumpets were found. Gold played a role in Egyptian art from Old Kingdom times, particularly in jewelry and in art objects specifically made for royalty. Egypt's goldsmiths were as sophisticated in their craft as their counterparts of our time, and in addition to jewelry their most notable work included inlays on furniture and statuary. Bronze statue-casting existed as an art from prehistoric times but did not become important until the Middle Kingdom (about 2000 B.C.); the best bronzes are representations of royalty or animal figurines, the latter generally associated with deities.

Egyptian Painting. Known to us mainly as frescoes in temples and in tomb chambers—and less often in private dwellings—Egyptian paintings were in tempera or sometimes in encaustic. Vivid colors are often beautifully preserved, partly because of the high quality of Egyptian pigments but also because a dry climate and the darkness of the paintings' repositories inhibited deterioration and fading. Since Egyptian painting was a vital art over several millennia, styles are widely varied and subject matter was virtually limitless, encompassing religious and secular themes, landscape art, and portraiture. Perhaps the most distinctive feature of Egyptian painting is its narrative element. Much can be learned about Egyptian households—both aristocratic and humble—and about Egypt's craftsmen and farmers at labor, its royalty enjoying the hunt and at leisure, by viewing Egyptian frescoes. The light of outdoors dominates Egyptian painting. Naturalistic landscapes, including animals in their habitats, were a recurring subject, probably having their fullest expression in the Middle Kingdom masterpieces of the 19th century B.C.

Egyptian metalwork: Collar with pectoral. Gold, faience and carnelian. New Kingdom, 18th Dynasty. From Tutankhamon's tomb, the Valley of the Kings. (National Museum, Cairo)

Egyptian painting: Garden with fish pond. New Kingdom. 1580–1314 B.C. From tomb at Thebes. (British Museum, London)

Egyptian Sculpture. Ranging from colossal stone pharaoh figures (for example, the portrait of Ramses II at Abu Simbel, the Giza Sphinx, etc.) to exquisite alabaster and ivory figurines, and the equally small ushabti funerary figures of wood, terra cotta, ivory, or faience, Egyptian sculpture is among the finest in the world. Early relief sculpture includes scenes carved on slate palettes (slabs used, probably by royalty, for grinding cosmetics); the most famous of these are the so-called Nagada (about 3200 B.C.) and Narmer (about 3000 B.C.) palettes. Subsequent relief sculpture was produced in abundance for tombs, temples, and palaces. Typical Old and Middle Kingdom sculpture in the round are stiff and static pharaoh figures, often about life-size. Development into a more expressive style came with the New Kingdom's

brief but important Amarna period (mid-14th century B.C.), begun by the heretic king Akhenaten. The human face here assumed individual, naturalistic features, and the Amarna sculptures are among the finest in Egypt's history. The subsequent era of the Ramses saw sculpture assume huge, virtually architectural scale, a fitting reflection of the New Kingdom's imperial success.

OVERLEAF—Egyptian sculpture: *Page 98:* Princess Nofti, detail. Painted limestone. Old Kingdom, 4th Dynasty. From the tomb of Rehotep at Meidum. (National Museum, Cairo) *Page 99:* Carved schist. Old Kingdom, 4th Dynasty. From a temple at Giza. (National Museum, Cairo)

EKOI, an African people living in eastern Nigeria and southern Cameroon. Little is known of the origin of these people, as their loosely organized society did not emphasize the continuity of history through oral traditions. The Ekpe Society, a secret male governing body, stimulated the production of masks. Some of these masks were strikingly aggressive, with clenched metallic or bone teeth, hair, and long twisting and curling horns. The mask is normally covered in animal skin, but in former times the appropriate material was human skin.

EL, the supreme god of the Canaanite pantheon. The name was a Semitic common noun meaning simply "god" and appears elsewhere in such formations as the Hebrew Elohim and the Arabic Allah. The Canaanite El was a somewhat remote and distant figure, infrequently symbolized.

ELAMITES, an ancient Near Eastern people who lived in what is now southwest Iran. Much of what is known of the Elamites comes from excavations at Susa. Culturally, the Elamites were largely dominated by Mesopotamia. Their art and architecture were at best variants of Mesopotamian themes. However, warfare and political conflict between the Elamites and other Mesopotamian peoples were very frequent. The Elamites helped overthrow the 3rd Dynasty of Ur around 2000 B.C. and invaded as deeply as Babylon in the 13th century B.C., but these successful incursions were temporary. The Elamites were absorbed into the Achaemenid Empire in the 6th century B.C.

EL ARGAR CULTURE. For many centuries the province of Almeria in southeast Spain was a center of chalcolithic culture, when stone and copper were both used for weapons and tools. However, by 1700 B.C., as evidenced by the remains of the hill-fort site of El Argar, the true bronze age arrived in Spain, probably from the Aegean. Two other sites in Almeria, El Oficio and Fuente Alamo, show the same El Argar bronze objects. In about 200 years this bronze-using culture spread all over Spain. Triangular bronze daggers, awls, arrowheads, axes, and, especially, halberds were found at El Argar and other sites, as well as smooth, dark pottery, silver rings and diadems, beads of stone, shell, and wire, and even of Egyptian faience.

ELATEIA, the earliest known neolithic site in central Greece, dating from around 5500 B.C. It was first excavated in 1959. Three major stratified levels were revealed in which the long, slow development of red-on-white pottery can be seen yielding to black polished and polychrome ware. Elateia may be linked with the Danilo culture of Yugoslavia.

ELECTRUM, an alloy of gold and silver which, according to Pliny, was one-fifth silver and four-fifths gold. The result was a metal whiter than gold and with a luminous quality. Art objects of electrum are rare, but the precious alloy was sometimes used for decorative vessels and coins.

ELEKTRA GATE. See THEBES.

ELEPHANTA, island site of Indian cave temples in Bombay harbor. Dating from the 8th to 9th centuries A.D., they are the last of the major cave temples excavated, as the cave form was being replaced by free-standing temples. Similar in style to Ellora, the main temple of Elephanta is 90 feet long; inside are ten large sculptures theatrically presented in deep boxlike niches. They commemorate the legend of Siva. The temple sanctuary was desecrated by the Portuguese in the 16th century.

ELEPHANTINE, a small rock island in the Nile River near Aswan, the southern outpost of ancient Egypt's Old Kingdom. A harbor with fortifications dates from the 12th Dynasty. Most temples, including one built by Amenhotep III, were destroyed in 1822, when a local bureaucrat used their stone for new construction. Re-

Elamites: Man-bull and goddess. Brick relief. 12th century B.C. From Susa. (Louvre, Paris)

Elgin Marbles: "Centaur and Lapith Fighting." Marble metope. Greek, 447–442 B.C. From the south side of the Parthenon, Athens. (British Museum, London)

mains still standing include a temple to Hekayeb—an Old Kingdom governor of Elephantine—and a granite gateway constructed by a son of Alexander the Great.

ELEUSIS. See ATTICA.

ELGIN MARBLES, sculpture of Classical Greek origin (mid-5th century B.C.), originally adorning the Parthenon and Erechtheum in Athens, now possessed by the British Museum. Between 1801–03 they were purchased by the Englishman Lord Elgin from the Turks, who then controlled Athens; hence their name. In 1816 Lord Elgin sold the sculptures to the British government. Their exhibition in the 19th century gave modern Western Europe its first close study of original Greek sculpture of the highest quality. The marbles, thought to be largely the work of the Athenian sculptor Phidias, include seated and reclining figures in the round of Aphrodite, Demeter, Persephone, and other deities, and friezes of horsemen and standing figures. Although largely mutilated over the centuries, the marbles are sufficiently intact to retain the magnificent qualities that distinguish Classical Greek art. On several occasions the Greek government has demanded return of the Elgin Marbles.

ELLORA, site of 34 rock-cut cave temples near Aurangabad in India. Carved in the 5th to 9th centuries A.D., the caves are Hindu, Buddhist, and Jainist. The earliest are Buddhist, dating from the 6th century; Visvakarma, a major temple site here, is a good example. The Hindu caves, which are from the mid–7th to 8th centuries, include the great Kailasanatha Temple, which is actually a free-standing building cut from the hillside; it is about the size of the Greek Parthenon and is completely covered with carvings. In its inner sanctuary is a giant lingam, the spiritual embodiment of the god Siva. The Jain temples here date from the 9th century and include the notewor-

Enamel: Double-gourd vase. Chinese, Ming Dynasty. (Percival David Foundation, London)

thy Indra Sabha. The Ellora site contains some of the finest of Indian sculptures. Traces of Ajanta-style paintings have been found in some of the caves.

EL TAJIN, ancient Totonac ceremonial center on the Gulf of Mexico near Veracruz. Its many buildings—a stepped pyramid, with niches; ceremonial platforms; and several sacred ball courts—were mainly built between the 7th and 10th centuries A.D. El Tajin was mysteriously abandoned around the 13th century, and its vast ruins await extensive excavation. The so-called Pyramid of the Niches is a high point of Totonac genius and one of the most interesting examples of religious architecture in Pre-Columbian Mexico. The square building rises in six stepped stories on top of which is a small temple. Deep niches, numbering 365, give the building its characteristic appearance. The niches probably corresponded to the days of the Totonac calendar. Among the many stone sculptures found at El Tajin are objects associated with the ritual ball game.

ELYON, in the Aramaean pantheon, a god derived from the Canaanite supreme god El. (A considerable number of Canaanite gods were absorbed by the Aramaeans.) Elyon, or some variation thereof, was an element in the names of many Aramaean kings.

EMBLEMA, the central illustration of a large mosaic, usually laid into the floors of fine Roman villas. Also the central design or decorative motif on such objects as vases, plates, etc., of ancient Greek or Roman origin.

ENAMEL, glassy substance heated to melt and join to metals such as gold, silver, and copper. Enamel can be inlaid, transparent, or painted and is used in many techniques, such as cloisonne and champleve.

ENCAUSTIC, technique of painting in hot materials, such as wax, usually on ceramic, wood, or stone. The word is derived from the Greek *enkaustikos*, meaning "burning in." Greco-Egyptian mummy portraits from the Fayum are executed in encaustic.

ENKI, one of the three chief deities, with Anu and Enlil, in the pantheon of Sumer. His chief seat was at Eridu, and he presided over wisdom and sweet water. He was also known as Ea.

ENKOMI, an important bronze-age site on the east coast of Cyprus. The settlement here lasted from 1900 to 1200 B.C., when it suffered a Mycenaean invasion. Fortifications from the 13th century B.C. are impressive, and excavations have revealed a rectangular network of streets testifying to city planning of a high order. The "Apollo Alasiotas," a bronze figurine of a horned god found in a sacred building here, dates from the 13th century B.C. and is now in the Nicosia Museum.

ENLIL, the most important god of the Sumerians until replaced by the Babylonian deity Marduk in the 13th or 12th century B.C. He was the patron of the city-state Nippur and was particularly concerned with the skies and storms.

ENTREMONT. See CELTIC PEOPLES.

EOS, Greek goddess of the dawn, mother of Memnon, who was slain by Achilles. She laments him by shedding tears each morning, bedewing the earth. In art, she appears winged, hovering in the sky, riding in her chariot, moving with a torch before Ares, or sprinkling the earth from a vase. The Romans called her Aurora.

EPHESUS, ancient Greek port city in western Asia Minor, probably founded by Ionian settlers around the 11th century B.C. and briefly controlled by Lydians, Persians, and, after 129 B.C., was Rome's provincial capital in Asia. The site is best known for its famous Temple of Artemis, a magnificent marble structure (with 96 columns) lauded as one of the seven wonders of the ancient world. Remains of this mid-6th century B.C. Ionic temple cover an area of about 180 feet by 370 feet. The temple housed the unusual cult statue of a many-breasted Artemis. The temple was burned in 356 B.C., rebuilt on the original scale, then destroyed by Gothic invaders in 262 A.D. Excavations at Ephesus have also produced pottery shards from the Greek Geometric period and Hellenistic remains of a town wall and broad arcaded streets, which the Romans restored in the 4th century A.D. A carved column-drum from the Temple of Artemis is in the British Museum and may be the work of the Greek master Scopas.

EPIGRAPHY, the deciphering and interpretation of ancient inscriptions, as on papyrus and parchment, stones, coins, seals, or monuments to gain information about a site or culture. Perhaps the most famous examples of this study were the deciphering of the Rosetta Stone, which unlocked the mystery of ancient Egyptian hieroglyphics, and the readings of the Behistun rock, which provided the key to cuneiform.

ERECH. See **URUK.**

ERECHTHEUM, a magnificent and unusual Ionic temple built on the northern slope of the Athenian Acropolis, opposite the Parthenon. Unlike any Greek temple built before or after 405 B.C., its completion date, the Erechtheum has an irregular plan, with chambers on different levels. It was named for Erechtheus, a mythical hero of Athens, who, with Athena and Poseidon, was a patron deity of the city; all three were worshipped in the Erechtheum. Its main rectangular cella has a portico of six Ionic columns on the east side; four columns partly engaged to a wall on the west (an architectural device rarely used by Greeks but to become popular with Romans); and an elaborately carved doorway on the north. On the south is an unorthodox but famous portico, known as the Porch of the Maidens, or Caryatids, since six sculptured female figures support the flat entablature; one of the original caryatids is now in the British Museum. The architectural decoration of the Erechtheum is especially rich and executed with great delicacy. There are fine floral carvings, gilded stone, inlaid glass beads in different colors, and a carved external frieze with white marble figures attached to a background of black Eleusinian limestone. The irregularity of the Erechtheum's site and the inclusion of several pre-existing shrines in its ground plan may explain the temple's puzzling and unprecedented design.

ERIDU, the oldest city of Sumer, located 12 miles southwest of Ur in what is now Iraq. On this site is the very important tell of Abu Shahrain. Here excavations have revealed an urban and religious center dating back to the middle of the 6th millennium B.C. A succession of increasingly elaborate mud-brick temples were found, displaying from the beginning such Sumerian characteristics as

The Erechtheum: The south porch. On the Athenian Acropolis.

Eskimos: Mask. Painted wood and feathers. (Private collection, Paris)

niches and buttresses. Also discovered was a quantity of painted pottery decorated with geometric, animal, and floral designs. The city declined in importance with the rise of the 3rd Dynasty of Ur around 2100 B.C.

EROS, god of love in Greek myth, the youngest of the gods, son of Aphrodite by Ares or Hermes. A symbol of a dangerous passion, he often appears as a winged figure in vase paintings striking lovers with axe or whip. Rendered as a youth in the Archaic period, he grows progressively younger, and in the Hellenistic period he lets fly his arrows of love as a playful infant. The Romans identified him with Cupid.

ESHNUNNA. See ASMAR.

ESKIMOS, an Arctic people, with a long, continuous development beginning before 1000 B.C. Through the centuries these people, who are related to Siberian Arctic tribes, have lived in scattered bands and followed the seasonal migrations of seals, caribou, whales, and fish. The overwhelming influence on their life and art is the harsh, Arctic environment, which the Eskimos attempted to control with magic and ritual. The long nights, weird natural phenomena, and constant dangers of the Far North made these people especially susceptible to dreams, visions, and messages from the supernatural. Their art bears this spiritual imprint. Almost all Eskimo art, generally carved sculpture in ivory, walrus tusk, or tooth, is connected with ritual. While extremely small in scale, the objects are monumental and bold in feeling. The high point of Eskimo art was probably reached by about 1000 A.D. The pieces then were simple in design, sparing in ornamentation, and seemed to have been highly specialized magical objects. In later times, fantastic and elaborate wooden masks were created by the Eskimos of the Alaskan coast under the influence of Northwest Coast art styles.

ESQUILINE, one of the seven hills of ancient Rome and largest hill of the city's eastern district. Long used as a cemetery, Esquiline's 8th- and 7th-century B.C. tombs have yielded numerous bronze and ceramic vessels, statuary, friezes, etc., and tomb paintings dating from throughout the Republican period. The so-called Esquiline Venus, found on the Esquiline in 1847 and now in the Capitoline Museum, Rome, is a Roman copy of a 5th-century B.C. Greek work. This hill was the location of the homes of several notable Romans of the 1st century B.C., including Vergil and Horace. From the Imperial period are ruins of the once great bath of Titus; and the valley between Esquiline and Palatine is the site of the Flavian Amphitheater—popularly called the Colosseum —dating from the late 1st century A.D.

ESTE, known to the Romans as Ateste, was one of the principal towns of northern Italy in the 9th century B.C. and for 700 years the most important commercial and artistic center of the district of Venetia. About 20 miles from Padua, Este was noted for its production of sheet bronze, especially bronze situlae, decorated in relief with scenes of monsters, sacred processions of warriors, priests, and chariots, done in a distinctive style. The city was peacefully annexed by Rome in 184 B.C.

ETHIOPIANS, inhabitants of the land south of Egypt, an early Hamitic people, also called Nubians. Ancient Egypt's late period saw Ethiopian (Nubian) rulers in the 24th and 25th Dynasties (8th century B.C.). In Ethiopia, from around the 7th century B.C., a Semitic South Arabian influx occurred and resulted in a kingdom with its capital at Axum. This Hamito-Semitic culture flourished for a millennium, declining after the 6th century A.D. but having subsequent periods of cultural rebirth. Christianity took firm hold in Ethiopia after 333 A.D. Archaeologically, Ethiopia is largely unexplored; thus there are gaps in the knowledge of its history and its culture. Notable pre-Christian monuments are towering obelisks, mainly at Axum. Christian churches in central Ethiopia—e.g., at Lalibala—are unusual, being solid rock-cut structures sunk below ground level.

ETRUSCAN CIVILIZATION, one of the most enigmatic in all history, flourished from about the 9th to 2nd cen-

Etruscan Civilization: Long Etruscan inscription. Gold. From Pyrgi.

turies B.C. on the Italian peninsula. A non-Italic people, with a language yet to be fully deciphered, the Etruscans were a lively and exuberant folk, much given to banquets, dancing, and games. Their origins, a much debated subject, remain cloaked in mystery. Some scholars believe the Etruscans were the successors to the ancient Villanovans, who, by 1000 B.C., had established a remarkable culture in and around present Bologna. Other experts, supported by Greek and Roman historians, look to the eastern Mediterranean, and especially to Asia Minor, for the original Etruscan homeland. In any case, by the 9th century B.C. the Etruscans were well settled in Etruria, now modern Tuscany, north of Rome. In the subsequent years the Etruscans, or Rasna, as they called themselves, made their power and influence felt from the Po Valley in the north to Campania in the deep south, enjoyed a foreign trade with central Europe, Greece, and Carthage, and established a confederation of rich city-states whose luxurious lifestyle became proverbial. Although tradition says that there were 12 Etruscan cities, including Tarquinia, Chiusi, Vulci, Veii, Palestrina, and Caere, recent aerial surveys reveal that virtually every defensible elevation in Etruria became the site of an Etruscan settlement at one time or another. In the 8th century B.C. the Etruscans conquered the hilltop towns of Rome, then occupied by the Italic Latins, and there organized a city-state. Etruscan ways of life played an enormous role in the development of later Roman civilization. The cities of Etruria were supported by an extensive agricultural hinterland, with wheat, grapes, and olives the chief farm products. Later, during the 7th and 6th centuries B.C., Etruscan wealth grew due to the mining and smelting of regional copper and iron deposits, the source of their foreign trade. Ships were built and maritime commerce encouraged. At its height, in the late 7th century B.C., Etruria controlled much of the Italian peninsula. Its cities were ruled by oligarchs, who governed the rich aristocrats, the poor laboring class, and the slaves with a light hand. A high level of sophistication was achieved in the arts, most notably in music, literature, painting, sculpture, and metalwork. In the 6th century B.C. Etruscan expansion was halted by the growing power of the Greek colonies of southern Italy, while, in Rome, the Latins overthrew Etruscan hegemony. Civilized, and more concerned with the arts of peace than those of war, the Etruscans lacked the military prowess necessary to maintain a long-lived empire. Their attempt in 525 B.C. to conquer the Greek colony of Cumae, near Naples, met with failure; in 475 B.C. they were defeated at sea by Syracuse. Veii, a major Etruscan city, fell to the Romans in 396 B.C.; and in about 390 B.C. the barbaric Gauls invaded Etruria. Thereafter, as the power of Rome waxed, that of Etruria waned, until finally Etruscan civilization was completely absorbed into the mainstream of Roman life. The most distinctive feature of Etruscan culture was religion. Although polytheistic, with a pantheon vaguely similar to that of the

Greeks and Romans, the Etruscans, unlike the Greeks and Romans, were deeply preoccupied by a death cult. This dark side of the Etruscan character expressed itself in magnificent tomb art, an art that survives to the present day in ancient Etruscan necropolises that were built more like towns for the dead than cemeteries.

Etruscan Bronze and Metalwork. From small polished mirrors to large chariots the Etruscans showed great ability as metalworkers. Their metalwork, like most of known Etruscan art, was fashioned for religious and funerary purposes. Decorative designs show apparent Near Eastern influence, tending to be rich and complex in detail, while in later times Greek elegance and simplicity can be seen. Early metal sculptures, dating from probably the 7th and 6th centuries B.C., include canopic urns—globular and covered vessels shaped to resemble the features of the deceased, whose ashes it contained. Notable examples of these are currently housed in the Archaeological Museum, Florence. Etruscan bronze household objects included braziers, candle holders, and bowls. Bronze statuettes of high quality and great expressiveness appear from the mid-6th through the 2nd centuries B.C., and frequently small human figures are added to the lids and feet of vessels. The finest Etruscan metalwork is in gold. Many Etruscan tombs have yielded ornate golden jewelry—bracelets, fibulae, etc.—sometimes embellished with repousse figures. The Etruscans were particularly known for their proficiency

Etruscan metalwork: Fibula. Rolled gold with repousse and applique work. 7th century B.C. From the Regolini-Galassi tomb at Caere. (Vatican Museum, Rome)

in the granulation technique, in which figures are decorated with lines of tiny gold granules. Examples of this craft include a 7th-century gold fibula from the Bernardini Tomb, decorated with lions, sphinxes, and griffins, and a gold bowl, also from the Bernardini Tomb, with sphinx handles.

Etruscan Painting, known from the many interior wall paintings of tombs, is naturalistic, with human forms the dominant subject matter. They may represent a narrative of the deceased in his earthly life or his future in the afterlife. The earliest known Etruscan tomb paintings are to be found in Tarquinia and date from the late 7th century B.C. Vigorous and lively, these compositions are among the best preserved of all ancient paintings. Modern scholarship generally places Etruscan painting as a provincial offshoot of Greek styles. While this is perhaps a safe generalization, Etruscan painting does differ from its Greek sources in that it shuns idealized human faces and forms and, in fact, often gives them a touch of parody. Etruscan painting was distinctive and important from the 7th through the 3rd centuries B.C., and during

that period it underwent almost continuous development. Early technique consisted of outline drawings filled in with flat washes of basic colors. An outstanding example of this style is the 7th-century "Boy on Horseback," from the Campana Tomb, Veii. Etruscan painting advanced to the use of halftones and broader depictions in subject matter by about the 6th century B.C., as can be seen, for example, in the painting of "Achilles Ambushing Troilus" in the Tomb of the Bulls at Tarquinia (c. 540 B.C.). Also at Tarquinia is the fresco in the Tomb of the Augers, where funeral games are played while mourners stand before a door symbolizing the entry to the other world. The most extraordinary wall paintings in Tarquinia are those in the Tomb of Hunting and Fishing (c. 500 B.C.). They form a panorama, encompassing a banquet and a fishing scene decorated with leaping dolphins and soaring birds of many colors. Dancers and musicians were also popular tomb subjects and can be seen in the Tombs of the Lioness, Leopard, and Triclinium. The beginning of the 5th century B.C. ushered in a more somber painting style, followed by a period during which there appears to have been no tomb painting at all. With the resumption of such work in the 4th century B.C. a new approach is evident. Scenes of banqueting in Hades become common, but a new theme of monsters and demons often fills the background, apparently reflecting changes in Etruscan religious beliefs and political power.

Etruscan Sculpture, like Etruscan painting, was predominantly sepulchral and was largely influenced by Greek styles. The preferred materials were terra cotta and bronze, with a relatively small amount of work executed in various local stones. Unlike the Greeks, Etruscan

Etruscan sculpture: Ara della Regina Temple. 4th–3rd centuries B.C. Tarquinia. (National Museum, Tarquinia)

Etruscan painting: "Funeral Dance." Fresco from Ruvo di Puglia. (National Museum, Naples)

Etruscan terra cotta: Canopic jar. From Sarteano. (Archaeological Museum, Florence)

Etruscan Terra Cotta. Few civilizations have so thoroughly explored the potentials of terra cotta as the Etruscans, who used it in sculpture while other cultures were more at home with stone. The earliest terra cottas of importance, found in 7th-century B.C. tombs, include the cinerary urn from Cetona, which has a modelled face on its lid (Archaeological Museum, Florence), and possibly some pieces from Caere, now in the British Museum. Terra-cotta works also appear extensively in temple sculpture and include not only large statues but also relief decorations taking fantastic shapes (gorgons, etc.), applied as protective covering to wooden temple walls. Temple art also included small votive groups, such as the Woman with Child in Her Lap, and the figures of Aeneas Carrying his Father. From the 4th century on, statues of everyday scenes become dominant (e.g., the Child Playing with a Bird), and by the 3rd century a major Roman art genre was anticipated in the form of realistic portrait heads. A comprehensive collection of Etruscan terra cotta is housed in the Villa Giulia, Rome.

EUPHRONIOS. See **GREEK CIVILIZATION.**

sculptors made only rare use of marble. Sculpture first appeared in Etruria in the 7th century B.C., the best work done by foreign artists or their local imitators. Examples include the Stone Centaur and the Standing Woman, from Vulci, reflecting influences from Greece and Asia Minor. During the 6th century B.C. Etruscan sculpture came into its own, with a unique approach to the Greek Archaic style. Large terra-cotta statues appear, like the sarcophagus from Caere, with its famous reclining husband-and-wife lid-figures. Veii became a major art center with the establishment there of the workshop of Vulca, an Etruscan sculptor who was called to Rome to decorate the Capitoline Temple of Jupiter. Associated with this workshop is the sculpture representing Herakles Stealing the Holy Hind of Apollo, executed for the temple at Veii around 510 B.C. This work shows a curious mixture of local and Greek influences. Although the face of the striding Apollo exhibits the Greek "archaic smile," the strength and power of the figure is very un-Greek. Etruscan sculpture of the 4th century shows a growing interest in realism, which prevailed into the Hellenistic period and ultimately became a major element in the evolution of Roman sculpture.

Etruscan terra cotta: Bucchero decanter. From the Regolini-Galassi tomb, Cerveteri. End of the 7th century B.C. (Vatican Museum, Rome)

Etruscan terra cotta: "Man and Wife," detail. Sarcophagus lid. From Caere. (Villa Giulia Museum, Rome)

Etruscan sculpture: Portrait of Silenus. From Pyrgi.

F

FAIENCE, a substance composed of clay and sand or ground quartz, developed by Predynastic Egyptians, who baked it in terra-cotta molds to make scarabs, beads, vessels, figurines. Faience has a glassy finish in shades of blue and green.

FALASHAS, the black Jews of northern Ethiopia. The origin of these anomalous people remains obscure. Although the Falashas believe they are direct descendants of Jews who migrated from Palestine in Biblical times, it is more probable that they were an indigenous Ethiopian people who were converted to Judaism. They apparently adhered to their religion even when the rest of Ethiopia adopted Christianity in the 4th century A.D. and still follow the prescribed rituals of Judaism. Falashas are known throughout Ethiopia as fine craftsmen, and they work as potters, weavers, blacksmiths, and masons.

FANG, an African people living principally in Gabon and Spanish Guinea. Although the Fang were originally a people who inhabited the interior of central Africa, they migrated to the seacoast, where they became important in overseas trade. They accomplished this in a series of mass migrations that ended about 1870. Their most distinctive art form was a wood-carved human figure called a *bieri*, which guarded the remains of Fang ancestors. Also important were masks of the Ngi Secret Society. These masks, with their serene, white elongated faces, had a major influence on the European cubist art movement.

FATYANOVO CEMETERY, an extensive burial ground of about 1800 B.C., discovered near modern Yaroslavl in Russia. The antiquities and grave goods unearthed here, one of the very few archaeological sites as yet located in central Russia, reflect a well-developed farming community, possibly Slavic in origin. The Fatyanovo people, whose religious practices included a cult of the dead, left metal weapons, ornaments, art objects, stone axes with characteristic drooping blades, bone tools, and amber pendants. However, they are best known for a thin-walled pottery, richly painted with rhythmic, geometric designs.

FAUNUS. See **PAN**.

FAYUM, a lake bed in Lower Egypt west of the Nile, presently only partly covered by Lake Moeris. It was the site of several prehistoric cultures dating from around the 5th millennium B.C., among which was the Gerzean. Fayum settlements show traces of oval mud dwellings

Faience: Hippopotamus. Egyptian, 12th Dynasty. (National Museum, Cairo)

and have yielded remains of pottery, shell jewelry, and flint and bone tools and weapons. There is also evidence of early grain cultivation and livestock breeding. The Fayum region has further yielded papyrus fragments from the Greco-Roman period, mainly early-Christian texts written in Greek.

FEATHERED SERPENT. See QUETZALCOATL.

FERTILE CRESCENT, a term coined by the American archaeologist James H. Breasted to designate the fertile area where the world's first civilizations originated. It extends from Egypt's Nile Valley northward around the eastern Mediterranean coastline through Palestine and Syria, then curves southward to encompass Mesopotamia.

FERTILITY FIGURES, magical objects used widely in the prehistoric and primitive worlds. Though many of these figures are associated with women—to ensure the birth of children and that they be healthy and beautiful—some are directed towards the increase of flocks and herds and the continued renewal of the land. Fertility figurines, often carved, are generally of high artistic quality.

FETISH, in primitive religion, an object believed to embody a magical power which, when properly invoked, can give protection, cure illness, wreak destruction, or perform other acts. The efficacy of the fetish is further enhanced by the addition of foreign substances, which may be such seemingly ordinary materials as seeds, teeth, fingernails, and hair. A fetish figure, generally a woodcarving, is often modelled in such a way as to provide a receptacle for magical substances. The most striking fetish figures are those from central Africa. These naturalistic wood images of humans, or sometimes of animals, are often completely covered with nails, knives, and sharp-bladed objects and are said to cause pain to those depicted. Voodoo dolls are a later development of African fetish figures such as the konde.

FIBULA, a metal garment clasp, a combination of brooch and safety pin, often with incised decoration on the catch plate. Although fibulae were less fashionable in Greece after the 6th century B.C., 4th-century examples from southern Italy have a semicircular bow and elongated catch with delicate filigree ornamentation.

FILITOSA, a prehistoric fortress of cyclopean masonry in Corsica. A wall of huge stone blocks, built on an outcrop of rock, encloses three *torre*, or towers, of similar masonry of about 1200 B.C. Carved slabs or stone pillars of an earlier date are built into the walls. The *torre* in Corsica are similar to the *nuraghe* in Sardinia.

FIRE-SPITTER. See SENUFO.

FIVE DYNASTIES PERIOD, 53 years of almost constant war in 10th-century north China. Centered around the capitals of Loyang and Kaifeng, the war (beginning in 907 A.D.) involved several small kingdoms and finally ended in 960 with the foundation of the Sung Dynasty. Despite the disruptions of war, Chinese culture developed steadily. Fine porcelains were produced, and landscape paint-

Fertility figure: Wood. Afo, northern Nigeria. (Horniman Museum, London)

Five Dynasties period: Ink on paper. Chinese, mid-10th century A.D. (National Museum, Tokyo)

ers, who were forced to the south for patronage, developed their art to a level of excellence that influenced Chinese painting for the next eight centuries.

FLUORINE TEST, in archaeology, a technique to determine the ages of different bones found at the same site. The test is based on the process that takes place when fluorine in the groundwater comes into contact with the calcium phosphate of bones. The fluorine collects in the bones; thus the longer the bones have been buried, the more fluorine they will contain. It must be used carefully, for it is not a universal standard and may not even be constant at one site. The fluorine test was instrumental in proving the Piltdown Man skull a forgery.

FLY RIVER, one of the longest rivers in New Guinea; it rises in the center of the island and flows southeast into the Gulf of Papua. The Fly River forms a border between two major art regions: the Papuan Gulf and the Torres Straits. Both of these areas enjoy a dramatic ceremonial life, with the ample use of masks, typically decorated with two-dimensional geometric designs. The island people of the Fly delta are noted for their production of elaborate masks and headpieces carved from tortoise shell.

FON, a West African people who were dominant in the former kingdom of Dahomey. Fon arts were stimulated by their royal court, which ruled for about 300 years beginning in 1600 A.D. Huge, brightly colored appliqué cloths served as tapestries and as historical narratives. Mud relief plaques, which decorated the walls of royal buildings, also told of past events. Small brass figures of humans and animals and elaborately carved thrones for the Fon kings stand out as major artworks. Also, almost life-size wood statuary of the last two Dahomey kings, Glele and Behanzin, represented respectively as an anthropomorphic lion and as a shark, are masterpieces. They can be seen at the Musée de l'Homme, Paris.

FONT-DE-GAUME, a Magdalenian cave site in the Perigord of France. It is embellished with numerous pictures of animals, many in color, dating from the last ice age, about 15,000 B.C. Magdalenian realism and sophistication are clearly seen here, with some 200 animals elegantly depicted with sweeping curves of tusk and horn.

The importance of various kinds of game to the Magdalenian hunter may be detected in the frequency of their occurrence on the cave walls. In descending order, there are bison, horses, mammoths, reindeer, wild cattle, antelopes, woolly rhinoceros, bear, wolf, and lioness.

FORTUNA, often called the Roman goddess of good luck, is better described as the goddess who brings fertility and increase (from *ferre*, to bear). This native Roman deity was identified in the Classical period with the Greek Tyche and, like her, is pictured with a cornucopia or ship's rudder, signifying either a bestower of blessings or a pilot of destiny.

FORUM, the center of most Roman towns, used for political meetings and business dealings. Usually a large, open rectangular area, it was surrounded and enclosed by important civic buildings, including basilicas and temples. The Greek marketplace, or agora, was similar.

FRANCO-CANTABRIAN, a term applied to the prehistoric art on the walls of numerous important caves on either side of the Pyrenees and the extension of the same chain in the Cantabrian Mountains of northern Spain.

FRANCOIS TOMB, a large, multichambered, carefully planned and elegantly furnished Etruscan tomb found in 1857 at Vulci, about 70 miles north of Rome, and named for its discoverer. The Etruscan frescoes that embellished its walls were moved soon after their discovery to the Villa Torlonia in Rome. Grim battle scenes in the T-shaped central room include an episode from a long-lost Etruscan history of Rome and the more usual scenes from Greek legend. Most interesting of these is that of Achilles slaying Trojan captives at the tomb of Patroclus.

The ghost of his comrade (Patroclus) appears beside the great Greek hero who is about to slit the throat of a nude Trojan. Inserted between them is the beautiful and compassionate death spirit (Vanth); behind the Trojan prisoner stands the horrible Etruscan demon Charun. The tomb dates from the 5th century B.C.

FRANCOIS VASE, a magnificent Greek volute krater of the early 6th century B.C., found in an Etruscan tomb at Vulci and named after its discoverer. Signed by the painter Kleitias and the potter Ergotimos, it is over two feet high and has six superimposed bands of careful and lively decoration. The scenes are mostly mythological, and the more than 200 figures include Achilles, Hephaistos, Ajax, and Artemis, along with pygmies, animals, and monsters. Most of the heroes and gods are identified by name. The vase is now in Florence.

FRANKS, a group of Germanic tribes who, before the 3rd century A.D., were settled in the Low Countries and in the lower Rhine Valley. Those living nearest the sea were known as the Salian Franks. The Franks migrated south and west from about 450 to 550 A.D. and conquered much of the area of modern France. They moved cautiously, however, retaining their home base at Aachen (Aix-la-Chapelle), and made a more permanent mark upon European history than the other tribes then invading the Roman Empire. The greatest early figure in Frankish history was that of King Clovis of the Merovingian house, who reigned from 481 to 511. The most remarkable and valuable of Frankish antiquities appear during and after the reign of Charlemagne.

FRANKS CASKET. See **ANGLO-SAXON PEOPLES.**

Francois vase: Black-figure ware, detail. Greek, early 6th century B.C. From Vulci. (Archaeological Museum, Florence)

Fujiwara period: The Phoenix Hall, at Uji, near Kyoto.

FRESCO, a wall-painting technique in which water-based pigments are applied to moist plaster. The paints then combine with the plaster and will not peel if exposed to moisture.

FREYJA, the Nordic goddess of love, marriage, and fertility, sister to the god Freyr. She is often confused with the goddess Frigg, the wife of Odin. Freyja was often depicted as riding in a chariot drawn by cats.

FREYR, a Teutonic and, especially, a Nordic god, who with his father, Njord, was associated with fertility. In Nordic mythology there are two races of gods—the Aesir, gods of battle, and the Vanir, gods of field and pasture, sunlight, and fertility, and to which group Freyr belongs. Freyr's chief seat was at Uppsala.

FRIEZE, a sculptured band located between the architrave and cornice of a building. Friezes are common on many kinds of architecture and are found worldwide. A famous example is the frieze of the Greek Parthenon.

FRIGG, a Nordic goddess, wife of the chief Scandinavian god, Odin. She shared his wisdom and foresight. Though the protector of marriage and giver of fruitfulness, she, as well as her husband, engaged in amorous adventures. The Germanic form of her name, Frija, simply means ''well-beloved' or ''spouse'' and gives rise to the name of the day Freitag—Friday.

FRISIANS, a Germanic people who, before the time of Christ, inhabited the islands and coasts of Holland and northern Germany. Closely allied to the Anglo-Saxons, they were involved in the invasion of England. They and the Salian Franks were the only Germans not subject as vassals to Attila the Hun in 440 A.D. The Frisians were ultimately conquered by the Franks in the 8th century.

FRIT, technique in which glass is inlaid on metal and ceramic, a forerunner to enamelling. It is often found on Egyptian and Assyrian art objects.

FUJIWARA PERIOD, a time of cultural brilliance in Japan lasting from 897 to 1185 A.D. During this period Chinese influences on Japanese art disappeared; the result was *yamato-e*, a purely Japanese painting style with flat-colored surfaces and simple flowing lines. Scroll art flourished, with elegant examples such as the Gengi-Monogatari scroll. The development of the Amida cult of Buddhism with its visions of the Pure Land served as an inspiration for artists to create works as beautiful as paradise. The Fujiwara period is often included with that of the Heian.

FUNAN CULTURE, from a kingdom in Southeast Asia, regarded as an early artistic phase of Khmer civilization. A mixture of Dongson, Indonesian, and Mon-Khmer elements, it lasted from the 1st to the 6th centuries A.D. Objects recovered from the Oceo site in South Vietnam indicate strong Indian influences. Temple architecture was tiered to create the ''sacred mountain'' image, and sculpture showed Greco-Buddhist influence in its naturalism and Indian traits in its deep relief style and its sensuality. Funan culture finally merged with the Chenla before being assimilated into the Khmer.

G

GAEA, or Ge, for the Greeks the goddess of the earth, mother of terrifying beings such as the Titans, Cyclopes, and Giants. She was especially honored as the mother of all and in Athens as the nourisher of children. The Romans identified her with Tellus and invoked her in time of earthquakes.

GALLA, an African people living in central and southern Ethiopia. Mostly a pastoral people for whom cattle had great ritual importance, the Galla migrated into their present homeland during the 16th century A.D. They established many small kingdoms which retained their independence until the 19th century, when they were absorbed by the Ethiopian empire. Among the Galla, craftsmen, such as potters and smiths, were held in contempt as manual workers and belonged to low-status castes.

GANDHARA, an ancient border region between Afghanistan and Pakistan. A Greco-Buddhist school of art flourished here from the 1st to the 5th centuries A.D. The area was invaded by the Persian Darius I in the 6th century B.C. and then by Greeks, Indians, Kushans, and finally the Huns in the 5th century A.D. Because Gandhara was at times isolated from Indian culture, its art was dominated by Western influences. Architectural styles were a mixture of both Hellenistic Greek and Indian; the best-known examples are the 700-foot-high stupa at Shah-ji-ki-Dheri and the Palace of Sirkap at Taxila, the capital. Gandharan sculpture, a superb encounter between East and West, is credited with producing the first anthropomorphic representation of Buddha and with influencing the art of Mathura.

GANDHARVAS. See APSARAS.

GANESHA, Hindu elephant-headed god. He oversees literature and education and is called upon at the start of all undertakings to remove obstacles. He is usually represented as having one broken tusk, four arms, and riding a rat.

GANGES CULTURE, in India, was almost fully developed by the 6th century B.C. in small kingdoms, notably in that of Kosla and Magadha. The Ganges Valley was then a place of intellectual and spiritual ferment, becoming the birthplace of two major religions—Buddhism and Jainism. The period's greatest leader, Bimbisara, brought his kingdom of Magadha to regional preeminence before his murder in 490 B.C. By the 4th century B.C. Magadha's

Gandhara: Reliquary. Chased gold with rubies. Gandharan school, ca. 2nd century A.D. (British Museum, London)

capital was Pataliputra, the major Ganges cultural center which remained so through the great—and Ganges-based—Gupta period (3rd–6th centuries A.D.).

GANYMEDE. In Greek mythology, the handsome son of Tros, carried off because of his beauty to be cup bearer to Zeus. The abduction scene showing Zeus in the form of an eagle was represented in a famous bronze by the 4th-century B.C. Greek sculptor Leochares, a marble copy of which is in the Vatican Museum.

GATEWAY GOD. See TIAHUANACO.

GAULS, a generic term for the Celtic tribes who once inhabited the regions of France, Belgium, and most of the Netherlands during the period of history when Rome was the dominant power. The Gauls, generally tall, often blond, were described by the Romans as turbulent and warlike. They invaded Italy and sacked Rome itself in 390 B.C. but thereafter were confined to the north of Italy, which became the Roman province of Cisalpine Gaul, and to the regions beyond the Alps called Gallia Narbonensis and Transalpine Gaul. Conquered with difficulty by Julius Caesar during the years 58–51 B.C., the Gauls, along with the Spaniards, ultimately became the most Romanized of all the non-Italic inhabitants of the Roman Empire. Gaulish cemeteries have been found in northern Italy and in France, with grave goods and antiquities similar to those of other Celtic peoples.

116

GEDI, an East African site dating from roughly the 13th through the 15th centuries A.D. on the Indian Ocean coast of modern Kenya. Gedi's culture, although colonial Arabic, showed a variety of influences imported from Asia and Indonesia. Ruins at Gedi include an Arab-style palace from the 15th century and large houses of slightly earlier construction. Earthenware vessels dating from the 13th century and later are red ceramic and include cooking and storage pots, oil lamps, etc., in a style of possible Indonesian derivation.

GEESE FRESCO, a masterpiece of ancient Egyptian painting, discovered in a mastaba at Meidum. Simple but elegant in design, this tempera mural, painted on a plaster panel almost six feet long, is now in the National Museum, Cairo. It dates from the 4th Dynasty (early 3rd millennium B.C.) and shows two groups of standing geese in mirror-like symmetry. Its style was repeated in later Egyptian painting where the desired effect was one of archaism.

GEOCHRONOLOGY, in archaeology, a general term for dating techniques based on the physical changes of the earth as derived from geophysics. Among these techniques are archeomagnetism, dendrochronology, fluorine test, obsidian dating, radiocarbon dating, thermoluminescence, and varve dating. For example, in the case of archeomagnetism, it is known that heating obliterates the magnetism of oxide iron, such as that in clay; when it cools, its structure is redetermined by the earth's magnetic field. Examination of ancient hearths by this technique may provide accuracy to within 50 years of a distant date.

GEOMETRIC PERIOD, named for the ceramic style dominating early Greek art from roughly 900 to 750 B.C. The geometric style originated chiefly in Attica and the Peloponnesus, although it ultimately pervaded most of the Greek world. Vases were painted with highly complex geometric motifs and, in later examples, with an intermingling of highly stylized men and animal figures. Floral or leaf motifs never occur. Typical human figures are wasp-waisted silhouettes. Some larger vases show highly detailed scenes, including ships, chariots, warriors, dancers, etc. The period also included some representative sculpture, mainly small, simplified, and stylized human and animal figures in bronze. Remains from the Kerameikos cemetery, near Athens, are the main source of Geometric-period antiquities. The evolution of the geometric style is usually attributed to the Dorians.

GERMANIC PEOPLES, a branch of Indo-Europeans that included numerous localized tribes—among them, Goths, Alemanni, and Franks—apparently having common early antecedents with Celtic, Nordic, Slavic, and Italic peoples. As such, the ancient forefathers of the Germanic peoples were probably farmers in southern Russia during the mid-3rd millennium B.C., growing cereal grains, domesticating cattle, sheep, and pigs, living in small villages, and burying some of their dead in kurgan graves. By the 1st millennium B.C. Germanic tribes inhabited areas of north and central Europe, generally east of territories dominated by the Celts. It should be noted, however, that most modern scholars hesitate to make any sharp cultural distinctions between Germans and Celts at this period—the only indisputable distinction being in their respective languages and geographic locations, as observed and recorded by Greek and Roman chroniclers. They were described by the Romans as tall, blond, and blue-eyed. The men dressed in a belted garment along with trousers and a mantle of wool or, occasionally, of fur. In the 2nd century B.C. German hordes invaded Gaul, partly displacing the Celts. In particular, three Germanic tribes—the Cimbri, Ambrones, and Teutons—moved into southern Germany between 113 and 101 B.C., from whence they mounted new invasions of Gaul and Italy. Defeat by Julius Caesar's army in the Rhineland in 58 B.C. was a major turning point in the incorporation of some Germanic peoples into the Roman world. However, as the Roman Empire declined in the early centuries A.D., Germanic dominance increased, so that by the 5th century A.D. Germans had virtual control of the entire Rhine Valley. By about 600 A.D. the Anglo-Saxons, a Germanic peoples, had become the ruling class of Britain. Pre-Christian Germans worshipped gods similar to those of the Nordic peoples—Wodan (Odin) and Donar (Thor) being their major deities.

Germanic Art and Antiquities in the pre-Christian era cannot be viewed as an important individual entity, since culturally no firm and clear differences exist among Germans, Celts, or Slavs on the basis of art and artifacts. Thus, in speaking of art and antiquities, it is more proper to speak of the cultures common to all of these peoples. First was the culture of the Battle-Axe People, who were settled in southern Russia in the 3rd millennium B.C. This was followed by the Unetice culture, of about 1900 to 1500 B.C., and then by the Hallstatt culture, from about 1200 to 600 B.C. The subsequent La Tene period, which dominated much of pre-civilized Europe beginning in about 500 B.C., is usually classified as Celtic and thus falls outside the scope of this article. Important Germanic objects from the 2nd and early 1st millennium B.C. are typically found in hoards at innumerable archaeological sites in northern and central Europe. Finds include metal items designed as personal jewelry or implements—bronze and copper rings, torques, and fastening pins being common. Tools and weapons include flanged axe heads and riveted daggers. During the final centuries of pre-Christian Europe the artistic contribution of Germanic tribes was limited. However, German blacksmiths were highly esteemed within their tribes, both as artists and craftsmen. Fine examples of their work are such objects as belts, fibulae, buckles, etc., made of various metals, including bronze, iron, gold, and silver. Typically, they were tooled with complex abstract designs, and the most ornate examples are sometimes studded with semipreci-

Germanic peoples: Buckle. Merovingian period. From Tressan, St. Germain.

ous stones and/or embellished with niello or cloisonné designs. Eurasian influences show in some later Germanic works in the form of fantastic animal designs; they appear as far west as England—for example, on some of the antiquities found at Sutton Hoo.

GERZEAN CULTURE of Predynastic Egypt dates from the mid-4th millennium B.C. It is named after its most important archaeological site—El Gerza in the Fayum—but its influence spread deep into Upper Egypt. Gerzean culture was apparently the immediate ancestor of Egypt's dynastic civilization. Clay pottery was often painted, typically with representations of ships then sailing the Nile, and shapes of some pottery show Near Eastern influence. Egypt's earliest known relief sculpture is Gerzean and was executed on stone palettes that were used as grinding bases for cosmetics.

GETIANS, also Getae or Daci, a Thracian people who lived along the banks of the Danube River in what is now Rumania and Bulgaria. They flourished from the late 1st millennium B.C. until about the 2nd century A.D., when they were finally conquered by Roman armies. Although noted by Roman historians for their gold and iron work, relatively little is known of Getian antiquities other than that they were influenced by Celtic and Scythian art styles.

GEZER, an ancient Canaanite city located just south of Lydda in modern Israel, on the site of Tell el Jazar. First occupied by cave dwellers, Gezer became a boundary town of the Philistines. Subsequently it was captured by Egypt (18th Dynasty) and later fortified and rebuilt by the Israelite King Solomon. It remained under Jewish control until Roman times, when it was gradually abandoned. Important discoveries at the site include Egyptian and Philistine tombs, the foundation of the castle of Simon Maccabeus, and the so-called Gezer calendar. This calendar, dating from the 10th century B.C., is a limestone plaque—four and one-fourth by three and one-eighth inches—inscribed with early Hebrew writing. The text enumerates the agricultural seasons.

GHANA, an ancient empire of West Africa. A state whose beginnings may date to the 4th century A.D., Ghana did not finally collapse until 1240 A.D. The empire's legendary wealth was based on its favorable location between the Arab and Berber traders of the north and the gold and ivory producers of the south. An elaborate system of taxation, best described as an export-import tax, kept the royal coffers full and the armies paid. Invasions by Berbers in the 11th century eventually led to internal disintegration and the decline of Ghana. Its last capital was at Kumbi Saleh, located about 200 miles north of the modern city of Bamako. The empire of Ghana was followed by that of Mali.

GHASSUL, an archaeological site, dating to the period between 3800 B.C. and 3350 B.C., located northeast of the Dead Sea in Palestine. Its inhabitants were simple farmers who painted their mud-brick dwellings with remarkable polychrome wall paintings which portray cult scenes, mythical and real animals, and geometric patterns. Their pottery was elaborate in style and is distinguished by a great variety of shapes, including vessels modelled in imitation of the water-skins used to carry liquids. The Ghassulian people also crafted a large number of copper objects and buried their dead beneath stone dolmens.

GIGANTIJA, site on the small island of Gozo, near Malta. A double temple here, built of great stone slabs forming two oval forecourts, connected by passages, and culminating in a corbel-roofed apse, may be the oldest extant stone temple in the world. It dates from about 3000 B.C. Its general shape is the same as that of rock-cut tombs in the Near East and in the mid-Mediterranean region. A conical pillar rises in one of the lateral apses, and there are the remains of a large stone table.

GILGAMESH, the hero of the best-known epic in Sumerian and Akkadian literature. His exploits were widely disseminated and long retold in ancient Mesopotamia. An early Sumerian text (on tablets) dates from the first half of the 2nd millennium B.C. The fullest text extant, in Akkadian, comes from Nineveh. The story tells of the adventures of Gilgamesh, half god and half man, and his friend Enkidu, the beast-man, as they confront gods and monsters, life and death. The Biblical story of the Flood comes from the Gilgamesh epic.

GIZA, an ancient Egyptian burial site across the Nile from modern Cairo. Main structures include the great Sphinx, dating from around 2500 B.C., and three major pyramids: that of Cheops, the world's largest, and those of Chephron and Mykerinus. Also at Giza are remains of workers' barracks, designed to hold about 4,000 men, and numerous underground tomb shafts, some of which are 80 feet deep.

GLASINAC, a cemetery site near Sarajevo in Yugoslavia. The graves are buried under mounds and are more numerous here than in almost any other ancient cemetery, amounting to more than 10,000 in number. Pottery and weapons of bronze and iron excavated here show wide connections between this Balkan necropolis and Greece, Italy, and the Danube region.

GLAZE, a glassy coating on porous pottery to make it impermeable and to protect its decoration. The pottery is coated with powdered glass after firing and then is refired to fuse the glaze.

GLOUCESTER HEAD, a carved limestone head of a man, dating from about the 1st century A.D., found at Gloucester, England, and now housed in the archaeological museum there. Of Celtic workmanship, the head, which is about eight inches high, is unusual in that it constitutes a fairly successful blending of two art styles usually considered incompatible—the realism of Roman art and the semi-abstract stylization that characterizes the Celtic idiom.

GOKSTAD SHIP BURIAL. In 1880 the burial of a 9th-century A.D. Viking chief within his oceangoing ship was discovered at Gokstad in southern Norway. The ship, and its remaining treasure, is now preserved in the Oslo Viking Ship Museum. A magnificent example of Viking craftsmanship, it is 75 feet long, with a 17-foot beam amidships, and draws only three feet of water when fully loaded at about ten tons. A replica, which was sailed to the United States in 1893, proved to be remarkably fast, logging ten to eleven knots with primitive rigging and small sail spread. The clinker-built oak planks were secured to the frame with spruce roots, giving the ship elasticity in severe sea conditions. Decking, mast (about 33 feet high), yards, and oars were of pine. Covering the oar ports, and still in place, were 32 shields, each circular, painted in yellow and black, and about three feet in diameter. Richly carved wood, textiles, and silverwork were uncovered here, but most of the burial treasure had been looted prior to modern discovery.

GOLDEN HORNS OF GALLEHUS. Two great golden horns, two feet nine inches long and one foot nine inches long, respectively, were found in 1639 and in 1734 in the same field of Tonder, south Jutland, Denmark. Unfortu-nately they were stolen in 1802 from the Royal Collection in Copenhagen and melted down. Gold reproductions have been made from earlier drawings and descriptions of these, the greatest of early Danish gold treasure yet found; the originals dated from the first half of the 5th century A.D. The curved horns, or lurer, had bands of decoration consisting of small human and animal figures.

GOLDEN HOUSE, the vast and luxurious villa with gilded porticoes built by the Emperor Nero in the heart of Rome after the disastrous fire of 64 A.D. Its sprawling complex of buildings, gardens, and colonnades had at its center an artificial lake, site of the future Colosseum. Suetonius' description of this imperial fantasy tells of rows of marble-lined sitting rooms, opening onto long colonnades, and inner chambers with stucco paintings in low relief; they were the first example of Roman wall painting to be uncovered in the Renaissance. Called grotesques, after the vaulted rooms (grottoes) in which they were found, these exquisite, dainty paintings became models for Raphael and his students, decisively influencing Roman palace decoration throughout the 16th century. Nero's pleasure palace shone throughout with opulent decoration in gems, gold, pearls, and shells. One room had a mysterious ceiling said to rotate like the heavens.

GORDION, ancient capital of the Phrygians, located in central Anatolia in modern Turkey. The Phrygians, a warrior people of Indo-European origin, had by 1000 B.C. established themselves as the successors to the Hittites of Anatolia. The kings of Phrygia were often called Midas. Exhaustive excavation of Gordion, begun in 1949, is not yet complete. Important known ruins include a city gate showing evidence of having been rebuilt several times during the 1st millennium B.C. and still intact up to about 26 feet. There are also traces of an altar used for fire worship and a number of tombs that have yielded wooden furnishings and bronze weapons and implements. Gordion came under Cimmerian rule in the 7th century B.C.

GORGONS, legendary figures of Greek origin, they were malevolent women having fierce facial expressions and snakes coiled in their hair. Their very gaze turned men into stone. Medusa was the most famous of Gorgons. Gorgoneion are ornamental representations of Gorgons' heads.

GOTHS, a Germanic people of northern Europe who, in the distant past, were settled in the Baltic region. The Goths moved south and were settled on the shores of the Black Sea by 200 A.D. The Visigoths, or Western Goths, feeling the pressure of Hun invasions, crossed the Danube and, by the use of cavalry, defeated the Romans at the battle of Adrianople in 378. They ravaged the Balkan peninsula and turned towards Italy. Rome was captured in 410 by their chief, Alaric. The Ostrogoths, or Eastern Goths, were defeated by the Huns but broke away in the mid-5th century. Their chief, Theodoric the

Great, educated in Constantinople, acted as an agent of the eastern Roman Empire in defeating Odovacar the Goth, who had driven out the last western Roman emperor, Romulus Augustulus, in 476. After Theodoric's death Justinian drove the Ostrogoths out of Italy, and they disappeared from history as a separate people. The Goths in their wanderings left few antiquities of their own.

GRAVETTIAN, named for its type site of La Gravette in the Dordogne, France. An upper-paleolithic culture, placed about 30,000 B.C., the Gravettian period is thought to have run concurrently with two other subdivisions of the Aurignacian: the Chatelperronian and the Aurignacian proper. Among the most famous artifacts of the Gravettian period are small female statuettes carved in ivory, probably fertility cult figures, with sexual characteristics emphasized. These Venus figures occur in association with Cro-Magnon Man in the Perigord, France, and in Predmost in the Danube Valley, and in other European sites.

GREATER VEHICLE. See MAHAYANA.

GREAT PYRAMID at Giza, Egypt, built for the 4th Dynasty pharaoh Cheops (or Khufu) and the largest tomb-pyramid ever constructed. Completed around 2800 B.C., it was then 481 feet from base to top and faced with white limestone slabs, each weighing some 5,000 pounds. The facing has long since been removed, making the pyramid's present height 475 feet. It has an unusually large number of internal chambers, of which the mummy chamber·is accessible through a vertical floor shaft. The

Pyramids at Giza.

royal burial chamber was discovered in the 10th century A.D. and its lavish artworks looted.

GREAT TOMBS PERIOD, the last phase of the Yayoi period in Japan, from the mid-3rd to the 7th century A.D. Its main cultural characteristic was the burial of notables in huge mound tombs. The mounds, which are about 1,500 feet long and 120 feet high, are either round, square, or in a keyhole shape and are surrounded by moats. The tombs excavated contained swords and carved jewels, or *magatana*, which are the symbol of the Japanese Imperial family, whose lineage dates directly from this period. Haniwa terra-cotta figures surrounded the tombs.

GREAT WALL OF CHINA, northern frontier defense built to prevent nomadic and Mongol tribal raids into China. The wall stretches 1,400 miles from southwest Kansu to southern Manchuria. Constructed of stone and earth and faced with brick, it is 20 to 30 feet high and has a 10-to-13-foot-wide road along its top. Sections of the wall were built during the late Chou period and were incorporated into one wall (450 miles long) under the First Emperor of Ch'in, Shih Huang Ti. Additional construction and rebuildings of the Great Wall continued until the 16th century.

GREEK CIVILIZATION, the great cultural awakening on the Greek peninsula that followed the Dorian dark age and which, by the 5th century B.C., was to attain peaks of artistic and intellectual perfection rarely equalled, and never surpassed, in world history. If the Romans gave Western civilization its mundane traditions, its laws and statecraft, its martial arts, its technical accomplishments, the things of the world, it was the Greeks who provided the spiritual thrust. In the 5th millennium B.C. Greece was occupied by non-Greek neolithic farmers, farmers who bore a striking resemblance to those of pre-Minoan Crete and to other agriculturalists of the myriad Aegean islands. The language and culture of these earliest inhabitants of the Aegean were destined to flower in the brilliant Minoan civilization of later times. Although it is thought that Greek Ionians were settled on the mainland by the mid-3rd millennium B.C., there is little evidence to support the theory. In about 2000 B.C. the warlike Achaeans, probably the first Greek-speakers on the peninsula, occupied Greece. Said to have been barbaric invaders from the north, the Achaeans conquered and then merged with the indigenous population, thus forming, under strong influence from contemporary Minoan Crete, Mycenaean civilization. The Mycenaeans, as described in the Homeric epics, came to dominate the Aegean, but by 1200 B.C., and exhausted by the long Trojan War, they became vulnerable to new Greek-speaking invaders from the north, the Dorians. Within a century the iron-sworded Dorians had put the cities and citadels of Mycenaean Greece to the torch. The fall of Mycenaean civilization marked the beginning of the Greek dark age, a harrowing time of strife, turmoil, and chaos that lasted for about 250 years. Not until 850 B.C. did the Greek peninsula see the dawn of a new era, of a unique renaissance which was to become Greek civilization: the summing-up of past Aegean civilizations and cultures. The Hellenes, as the Greeks then called themselves, built small city-states in the isolated and divided terrain of ancient Greece, and although they were often at odds or even at war with each other, the Hellenic city-states were bound by a common language, a common culture, and a common pantheon of Olympian gods. Writing reappeared under the Hellenes, but unlike their ancestors the Mycenaeans, who used a Minoan script, the new Greeks adapted the more efficient Phoenician alphabet to their language. From the very beginning the Greek city-state, or *polis*, was ruled by a hereditary landed aristocracy; in later times the *polis* became, more and more, a self-governing community; the word *democracy* is Greek in origin. However, democracy was never offered to all. The austere rigidity of the earliest city-states, such as Corinth, is reflected in the art of this, the Geometric period. Painted vases, decorated with abstract and symmetrical forms, bear static compositions almost Egyptian in feeling. The Geometric style reached its height in the Peloponnesus, which had long been settled by the Dorians and which was soon to become the homeland of their natural heirs, the Spartans. In the 8th century B.C. the Greek city-states, now bustling with activity, expanded trade with the Near East and Egypt and launched colonies in southern Italy and Sicily. Fresh and new winds from the eastern Mediterranean affected Greek art and life, and the so-called Orientalizing period was ushered in. Stone temples, based on earlier timbered structures, were designed and monumental sculpture made its appearance. In this period too a well-to-do merchant class emerged, with far-reaching effect on the broadening of Greek democracy. The landowners, farmers, soldiers, and seafarers of the typical Greek city-state were joined by determined entrepreneurs, who demanded greater participation in government. The first Olympic Games, a major unifying event in Greek national life, were held in the 8th century B.C. However, despite increasing prosperity, the average Greek family lived modestly in a simple house of stucco or baked brick, warmed by the Aegean sun. The streets of the *polis* were narrow and crowded and sanitation poor. This standard of life for the many was to continue throughout the history of ancient Greece. The Archaic age, issuing from the Orientalizing period in about 600 B.C., is said to mark the beginnings of true Greek civilization, although much had gone before. Archaic Greece saw the rise of Athens and Sparta as the dominant city-states, a historic event that would finally lead to the tragic Peloponnesian War; the final departure by force of autocratic rulers; and the development, in art, of black-figure vases and free-standing statuary. With the Persian wars of the early 5th century B.C., and especially with the famous Greek victory at

Greek Civilization: Doric columns of the Temple of Athena, Athens.

Marathon in 490 B.C., the Archaic spirit—now seemingly traditional and old-fashioned—gave way to a new *élan*, a new vigor, borne on the wings of victory. The golden age of Greece, the Classical period, arrived. An almost miraculous happening for its time and place, Classical Greece enjoyed a burst of creative energy never before seen in world history. Led by Athens but by no means limited to that city, the Greek spirit, which since the Orientalizing period of some 200 years before had been hampered by Egyptian and Near Eastern modes, asserted itself in a uniquely Greek manner. The past was shunned, humanity displaced divinity as the main force in Greek life, and man, the measure of all things, became the master of his own destiny. Magnificent temples were built, but while dedicated to the gods, they served the aesthetic pleasure of man. Artists, architects, poets, dramatists, historians, and scientists were elevated to positions of great importance, while philosophers, those noblest of Greeks, discussed the ideals of life, of man, of art, of politics in the marketplace. Open debate, as well as public competition, were the essence of Greek character. The citizens of the Greek *polis*, a community of born critics, selected and commissioned their own artists, poets, dramatists, and Olympic athletes: thus, for the first time in history, a public art and architecture, a public theater, and a publicly supported sports program appeared. The Classical aesthetic, the enduring expression of the 5th-century Greek city-state, was devoted to the ideals of balance and proportion and, above all, to the concept of beauty, both human and divine, based on an exquisite blending of the physical and the spiritual. The Greeks, unlike the Romans, abominated one-dimensional realism, the realism of the death mask. In Athens, especially under the statesman Pericles, who came to power in about 454 B.C., the Acropolis was re-built, the Parthenon added, and Athenian democracy broadened. However, the same confidence and assurance that were born of Athenian victory over the Persians—thus giving rise to the optimism of the Classical period—brought Athens, the queen of Greek city-states, the dream of imperial conquest. Harsh reality was supplied by Spartan troops in the long and disastrous Peloponnesian War, which finally ended with Spartan victory in 404 B.C. Although Classical ideals of art and thought persisted for another 50 years, the intellectual excitement that characterized the golden era was waning. In the mid-4th century B.C. a new wave of invaders from the north, the Macedonians, moved south. Under Philip and his son, Alexander the Great, the now vulnerable city-states were quickly united, albeit by sword and fire. The Hellenistic period of Greek history had begun. After joining the chronically feuding cities of Greece into something resembling a national state, Alexander, with an invincible army, conquered much of the known world. From Egypt to the south, through the Near and Middle East, and even to India, Alexander built an empire, a Hellenistic empire, which, although short-lived, left permanent imprints on the art and thought of many foreign peoples. In Greece, meanwhile, the mainland cities, such as Athens, were becoming, more and more, mere commercial centers, while the Greek cities of the eastern Mediterranean—Pergamon, Antioch, Rhodes, and Alexandria—grew as great centers of Hellenistic art. The canons of Hellenistic art differed widely from those of Classical Greece. Although the human form was emphasized, Classical balance, proportion, and serenity were replaced by Hellenistic agitation, drama, and realism. Soon after Alexander's death in 323 B.C. his empire crumbled; his heirs, the leading Macedonian generals, divided the imperial spoils. During the Hellenistic period Rome emerged as an international power in the central Mediterranean and by the 2nd century B.C. was threatening Greece itself, once again weakened by internal strife and conflict. In the ensuing years many Greek artists and intellectuals, as well as the Olympian gods, were drawn to the safer, more comfortable, and more affluent confines of Rome, where the extraordinary and glorious heritage of Greece was to find new voice. At the time the Roman general Sulla sacked Athens in 86 B.C., this once splendid city, shimmering in memory, was little more than a provincial backwater.

Greek Bronze and Metalwork, of excellent quality, was produced throughout ancient Greek history. In the Geometric period of the 9th century B.C. solid-cast votive statuettes, depicting men and animals, made their first appearance. Strongly influenced by Minoan styles, these bronzes are rather abstract and elongated in form but show great creative energy. In the subsequent periods—the Orientalizing, Archaic, and Classical—large-scale bronze statues eclipsed the smaller works of the Geometric. Many famous Greek sculptors worked in bronze, although stone was the more important art medium. In the Hellenistic period small-scale bronzes of extremely fine design reappeared in Greece and in Asia Minor. While gold and silver were used by Greek metalsmiths, they were used sparingly. Surviving bronzes of ancient Greece include large statues of nude males, draped females, athletes, and representations of the gods. A myriad of decorative statuettes, as well as relief-embossed vases, mirrors, household and ceremonial vessels, and armor, also remain. Gold and silver plateware, somewhat more rare, can be seen in major world museums.

Greek Mosaics, a minor art in Greece, were to find their finest expression in Roman art. The earliest known Greek mosaics were found at Olynthus in Macedonia and date from the 5th or 4th century B.C. Composed of colored pebbles, the Olynthus mosaics offer scenes of the chase, mythological subjects, and motifs of birds, animals, and flowers. Pebble mosaics have also been discovered at Olympia, Sicyon, and Corinth. Of a later time, about 300 B.C., are those mosaics from Pella in Macedonia, the birthplace of Alexander the Great, which have proved to be the finest and best-preserved pebble compositions in

Greek bronze: Aphrodite and Pan. Reverse of incised bronze mirror cover. Greek, 3rd century B.C. From Corinth. (British Museum, London)

Greece. Differing from the earlier mosaics, the Pella mosaics are less flat, more three-dimensional, and thin strips of lead were inserted for greater design definition. Among the best known of the Pella mosaics is the Stag Hunt, signed by Gnosis, the master Greek mosaicist. In the 3rd century B.C., in the Hellenistic centers of the eastern Mediterranean, marble cubes replaced pebbles in the building of mosaics, and with the new technique much greater pictorial freedom was achieved. The Hellenistic city of Antioch, in Syria, became a world center for the production of marble mosaics.

Greek Painting, a crowning achievement of the ancient Hellenes, failed, for the most part, to survive the ravages of time and war. Examples of Greek mural and panel paintings, of which there were many, exist today as a rarity and in the most fragmentary of states. Modern scholars, however, have reconstructed the development of Greek painting through the literary descriptions of Greek and Roman historians, artists, and critics. In the Archaic period, when wall paintings first appeared, the

Greek mosaics: "Nilotic" mosaic, detail. Hellenistic period, 2nd–1st centuries B.C. From Palestrina. (Archaeological Museum, Palestrina)

124

end, the illusion of reality. Apelles, the master illusionist, who was to set the standards of Hellenistic art, became the most respected painter of his day. In the Hellenistic period, while mythological and historical subjects persisted, landscape, genre, and still-life paintings came to the fore. Glimpses into the lost world of Greek painting are best had in Italy, in Etruscan and Lucanian tomb paintings, which were probably derived from Hellenic models, and, above all, in the wall paintings and mosaics of Pompeii, Herculaneum, and Stabiae.

Greek Sculpture, by far the best known and most admired of Greek art forms, began unpretentiously in the Geometric period of the 9th and 8th centuries B.C., with stone reliefs the major sculptural expression. In the 7th century B.C., during the Orientalizing period, the first free-standing statuary, heavily influenced by Egyptian and Near Eastern models, made its appearance. The art of free-standing figures continued its development in the Archaic age of the 6th century B.C., when the considerable wealth of the Greek city-states was applied to large-scale public architectural projects, and statuary, more and more, became anatomically perfect, while movement, as expressed in the human form, was still limited. Rigid frontality, as well as the so-called archaic smile, characterize statues of the period. After the Persian wars and the beginning of the Classical age, Greek sculptors turned away from static stone composition, so Egyptian in feeling, and sought a new concept, a new ideal form for the representation of both men and gods. Their search, as can be seen in the works of Myron, Polyclitus, and Phidias, ended with the flowering of Classical sculpture, perhaps the greatest sculpture the world has ever known. Naturalistic, harmonious, serene, and grand, the Classical ideal of sculpture, for future generations of men, came to epitomize the formal perfection, the unique spirit of Greek civilization. After the cataclysmic Peloponnesian War, Greek sculptors, such as Praxiteles, Scopas, and Lysippus, heralded a new age, the Hellenistic, and the monumental rigor of Classical stone was replaced by softer perceptions and a greater interest in human emotions. With the shift of power from mainland Greece to the coastal lands of the eastern Mediterranean at the time of Alexander's Hellenistic Empire, the Greek sculptor and artist, no longer supported by city-state patronage, became itinerants. Travelling from one Hellenistic city to another, the Greek sculptor attempted to emulate the Classical ideal, but local and regional tastes prevailed. No longer was there one Greek style but a multiple Hellenistic style, marred by eclecticism. Pergamon, in Asia Minor, emerged as the most popular sculpture center of the Hellenistic world, and its style of twisting and emotion-

Greek artist echoed the drawings found on black-figure ware of the same era, but his large-scale murals had more color, laid on in flat unmodulated fields. Possibly the finest example of this style can be seen in a tomb near the ancient Greek colony of Paestum in southern Italy. With the arrival of red-figure ware in the early 5th century B.C., which marks the beginning of the Classical age, vase drawing of the Archaic gave way to vase painting of the Classical. So too did mural drawing, filled with flat fields of color, disappear in favor of true painted murals. At Delphi was the *Sack of Troy,* a wall painting by Polygnotos, the great muralist, which is the first known expression of the new style: naturalistic, emotional, and with tentative attempts at foreshortening and spatial depth. Painting techniques developed rapidly, and by the end of the 5th century B.C. Apollodoros and Zeuxis were exploring three-dimensional effect, the mixing of colors, and the use of light and shadow. In the 4th century B.C. panel painting, especially in encaustic, became enormously popular. Figures were modelled realistically, a wide range of mixed colors was employed, and light and shadow were skillfully deployed to achieve but one

Greek metalwork. Gold. 4th century B.C. (Museum of Fine Arts, Boston; Pierce Foundation)

charged statuary, almost baroque in conception, came to dominate what was now the Greco-Roman world.

Greek Terra Cottas, found throughout the history of Greek civilization, were an exquisite medium for the Greek sculptor. Their development from the Geometric period follows the stylistic growth of large-scale bronze and stone sculpture. In their earliest phase Greek terra cottas were hand-modelled, and form reflected Egyptian and Near Eastern art canons, resulting in heavy and unarticulated human figures. Molded terra cotta, rather than hand-made, came to the fore in the mid-6th century B.C., and the human figure grew more and more naturalistic, a flow that climaxed in the sizable terra cottas of Classical Greece. Large, seated and standing gods and goddesses, beautifully proportioned, characterize the Classical age. Nearly all Greek terra cottas were painted, giving them a lively and vivid appearance. Purple, red, blue, yellow, and green, as well as black and white, were the standard colors. However, since colors were applied as a wash and not fired into the clay, extremely few painted terra cottas remain. For many centuries Boeotia, a region north of Athens, was a center of terra-cotta production. Boeotian statuettes often depicted groups of people or single individuals engaged in everyday occupations. From the 6th century B.C. is the charming Boeotian baker leaning over his oven, now in the Louvre, and a carpenter sawing wood, in the Copenhagen National Museum. In the Hellenistic period, from the late 4th through the 2nd century B.C., many elegant terra-cotta figurines were produced at Tanagra, Myrina, and Pergamon; some of these extraordinary statuettes still retain their delicate coloration. Terra-cotta reliefs were also made in ancient Greece, with mythological and historical scenes dominant. The reliefs are generally associated with temple architecture, although some, bearing everyday subjects, genre scenes, may have decorated private homes. According to Pliny, many Greek masters of terra cotta migrated to Etruria, a fact which, in part, may explain the enormous success of the Etruscan terra-cotta tradition.

Greek sculpture: Phidias and assistants, "Ilissos." Pentelic marble. Ca. 435 B.C. From the west pediment of the Parthenon, Athens. (British Museum, London)

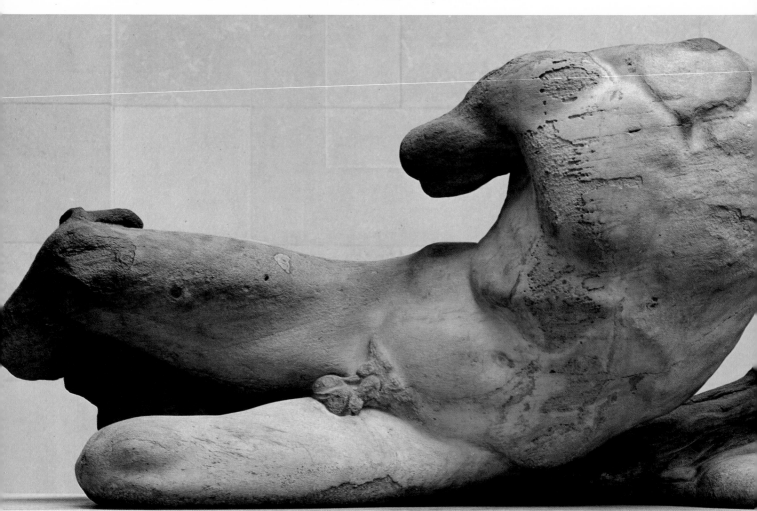

Greek sculpture: Aphrodite.
Bronze. Hellenistic period. Found
near Patras. (British Museum, London)

128

Greek Vases, in their myriad shapes and sizes, reached a formal perfection that surpassed even the best of Minoan ceramics. The shaping and painting of vases, from the very beginning, was a major art in Greece, and both potters and painters frequently signed their work. The study and appreciation of Greek vases in all their richness and abundance have provided scholars with a long and coherent view of Hellenic art development. From the Geometric period, of the 9th and 8th centuries B.C., are large vases unearthed in the Kerameikos cemetery, the so-called potters' field of Athens. With their bands of symmetrical ornamentation and complex linear patterns, Geometric ware was abstract and often somber; funeral processions, with wasp-waisted men and gods, in

Greek vases: Attic Dipylon vase. Geometric period, 8th century B.C. (National Museum, Athens)

silhouette, were a favorite subject. In the Orientalizing period, of the 7th century B.C., leaf and floral motifs, borrowed from Egypt and the Near East, made their first appearance. Freely drawn animals and men and brightly colored mythological subjects marked the new prosperity of the Greek world. Vivid Corinthian ware became dominant, and the sobriety of the Geometric was at an end. Another fine pottery of the period is termed Rhodian, after the island of Rhodes, said to have been the center of the new style. In the 6th century B.C., during the Archaic age, a new technique of vase-making emerged in Athens and Attica and elsewhere. Called black-figure ware, Attic pottery was adorned with black silhouetted figures in a brilliant glaze, placed directly onto the natural red clay of the vase. Simple and strong, black-figure compositions usually depicted a single dominant theme, with animals and monsters as common motifs. Human figures, as well as those of the gods, grew increasingly more realistic. However, the nature of the black-figure medium required the use of a pointed tool for the incision of details, thus limiting the possibilities of realistic portrayal. Even so, masterpieces of black-figure ware were produced by Kleitias, Lydos, and Exekias. In about 530 B.C., with the remarkable invention of red-figure ware, the pointed tool gave way to the brush, and true vase painting, rather than vase drawing, appeared. Reaching its height in the early Classical period, red-figure pottery was to provide the finest paintings on clay that Europe has ever known. Instead of black silhouettes on a red background, the Classical vase painter decorated his pottery with red figures on a black background, reversing the Archaic style of black-figure ware. Because of the new freedom, a freedom that reserved large areas of the vase for the painter's brush, pictorial composition became richer, figures more naturalistic, and details more accurately described. Shading, foreshortening, and scenes of vigorous action were now possible. Among the greatest of Classical vase painters were Psiax, Euphronios, Onesimos, Douris, and the so-called Berlin Painter. Advances in the figural and spatial aspects of vase painting led to revolutionary changes in Greek wall painting, which by 430 B.C. surpassed vase painting in quality and significance.

GUAYAS, an archaeological region on the Pacific coast of Ecuador, near the Gulf of Guayaquil. One of the richest sources of Ecuadorian antiquities, Guayas is thought to have been the meeting site of ancient Mexican and Peruvian cultures. Some scholars also conjecture contact between Guayas and the prehistoric Jomon people of Japan; pottery found at Valdivia in Guayas dates to about 3000 B.C. and closely resembles that of Jomon Japan. Most notable art objects discovered in Guayas are Guangala figurines, well-polished, hollow figures, generally about eight inches high. After 500 A.D. the Guayas people produced monolithic stone sculpture in the form of U-shaped seats supported by crouching animals and men. They also made bas-relief stelae, which depict a seated or reclining female figure.

GUMELNITSA CULTURE is named from its type site on the lower Danube River. This neolithic culture, of

Greek vases: Volute krater. Attic red-figure ware.
Painted by the Talos Painter, ca. 410–400 B.C. (Jatta
Collection, Ruvo di Puglia)

Gundestrup cauldron: Detail. Silver-plated copper. Celtic, 2nd–1st centuries B.C. (National Museum, Copenhagen)

about 2500 B.C., appears on the north (Rumanian) and south (Bulgarian) banks of the river. Incised monochrome pottery and bone and clay figurines, male and female, have been found. Most distinctive of Gumelnitsa pottery are jugs with spouts and vases with faces of human shape. The pottery shows influence from the Aegean, Anatolian, and Near Eastern regions, influences also apparent in Danubian culture sites farther north. Copper and gold objects have also been unearthed.

GUNDESTRUP, in northern Jutland, Denmark, site of a peat bog in which a great silver cauldron of the pre-Roman iron age was discovered in 1891. With a rim diameter of 27 inches, the cauldron is almost completely decorated with reliefs giving clues to early Celtic religion and art. Spoils of victory, both material and human, were frequently thrown into bogs as a ritual thank-offering to the gods. Objects both of metal and organic matter were thus preserved and provide important archaeological data. The Gundestrup cauldron may have been made in the 2nd century B.C. It is now in the National Museum, Copenhagen.

GUPTA PERIOD, the classical era in Indian art, from the 4th to the mid-7th century A.D.; also the empire control-ling northern India from 320 to 467 A.D. The revival of Hinduism, the relative peace and happiness of the period, and its luxurious aristocratic life are reflected in the perfection and balance of Gupta art, epitomized by the cave paintings at Ajanta. Gupta architecture is manifest in the Temple of Vishnu at Deogarh. This 5th-century building is 40 feet high and is embellished with ornate carvings. Gupta sculpture, found at Amaravati, Sanchi, and Mathura, is serene and has a certainty unmatched in Hindu Indian art.

GURO, an African people who live in the central Ivory Coast. Although the Guro have inhabited their homeland for hundreds of years, they have been known to Europeans only since 1892, when the French Captain Binger encountered them in his journey across western Africa. Guro artistic expression is seen largely in masks and carefully carved pulleys for looms. Guro masks can be either human or animal, though there is a preponderance of polychromed antelope heads. Typical Guro style shows a prominent forehead, an elongated and thin nose, and almond-shaped eyes. Many masks were used in ceremonies of the Guie Secret Society. The basic forms of Guro art are clearly related to those of the Baule, who are neighbors.

H

HACHA, or "axe," the name given to a thin, hatchet-faced stone profile associated with the ritual ball game in Pre-Columbian Mexico. Hachas are thought to have been markers, placed on the ball court to score the game.

HACILAR, a site in southwest Turkey excavated by James Mellaart that revealed findings comparable in importance to those of Catal Huyuk. The earliest level, with the remains of a primitive phase of settled culture, is dated (radiocarbon) to the 7th millennium B.C. Substantial houses were found constructed of stone, mud-brick, or wood. The people of Hacilar raised a kind of wheat, barley, and lentils; sheep and cattle bones were found. Pottery, painted with increasing sophistication, was found from every period but the earliest. Important terra-cotta figurines were also discovered at Hacilar.

HADDA, site near Jalalabad in Afghanistan. It is famous for its 3rd- to 5th-century A.D. stucco sculptures, which resemble 13th-century European Gothic figures at Chartres and Rheims. The site was excavated in 1922, and these plaster and stucco Greco-Buddhist sculptures were uncovered. They are akin to Gandhara art.

HADES, in Greek mythology, lord of the lower world whose name became synonymous with his realm, the abode of the dead. He is also called Pluto, the Rich One, since blessings come from beneath the earth. This name was adopted by the Romans.

HADRIAN'S VILLA, the most extravagant of all Roman country palaces. It was a vast retreat (about a square mile) built by the Emperor Hadrian from 125 to 138 A.D. at Tibur (modern Tivoli), a fashionable resort 18 miles northeast of Rome. Here this cosmopolitan lover of all things Greek collected art from throughout the empire he had so widely travelled. In the nostalgia of his old age he reproduced, on a smaller scale, the finest buildings he had seen during his tours. Much of the statuary in his villa must have been imported, and excavations there have yielded excellent copies, among them a Cnidian Aphrodite of Praxiteles. The caryatids, also unearthed, are modelled after those of the Erechtheum in Athens. A delicate mosaic of doves is a copy of a Greek original by Sosus, and a headless copy of the bronze Amazon by Phidias stood near the pool. A fantastic pavilion in the so-called Piazza d'Oro area was unique in Roman architecture both for its shape—a four-leaf clover plan surmounted by an octagonal dome—and for its method of illumination. The "Maritime Theater" is a tiny villa on an island in Hadrian's lake, surrounded by a circular canal with a vaulted colonnade.

HADRIAN'S WALL, a northern frontier wall of Roman Britain, erected in 122–126 A.D. by the Emperor Hadrian. Built of stone in the east and turf in the west, it was about 15 feet high, 10 feet thick, and stretched for about 74 miles from coast to coast, with forts and towers about every mile. After the abandonment of the Antonine Wall about 180 A.D., Hadrian's Wall once again marked the frontier against the Scots. It was finally abandoned around 400 A.D.

HAGIA TRIADA, an ancient town in southern Crete, mainly important as the site of the island's most luxurious Minoan palace, built around 1600 B.C. The site has yielded a famous painted limestome sarcophagus, dating from around 1500 B.C., and now in Crete's Herakleion Archaeological Museum. The sarcophagus painting shows a noblewoman and attendants sacrificing a bull and offering a libation while a musician plays a lyre. The above-cited palace contains several fine frescoes, including a depiction of a lady in a garden setting. Discovered here too was a stone rhyton carved in low relief, with scenes of harvesters.

Hagia Triada: Sarcophagus, detail. Painted limestone. Minoan, ca. 1500 B.C. (Herakleion Museum, Crete)

Haida: Chest, detail. Wood inlaid with shells and animal tusks. 19th century A.D. (British Museum, London)

HAIDA, a North American Indian tribe inhabiting the Queen Charlotte Islands off British Columbia, Canada. Before the 19th-century advent of European fur traders, Haida culture centered on fishing. Their highly refined wood carvings included masks, headdresses, decorated household objects, such as storage boxes and spoons, and standing family crests, known as totem poles. Of all Northwest Coast Indians, only the Haida carved in stone. The most famous of these carvings, known as the Bear-Mother, illustrates the legend of an Indian woman who bore a half-human, half-bear child. Although only six inches high, it gives the impression of great monumentality; the carving is now in the Smithsonian Institution. The Haida also made pipes and miniature totem poles in a dark slate called argillite.

HALAFIAN CULTURE, a significant stage of north Mesopotamian cultural development, dated about the 5th millennium B.C. The name is derived from the type site, a large tell at Halaf near where a tributary of the Euphrates crosses from Turkey to Syria. Pottery found here was particularly fine, with brilliant designs in black, white, and red on a dull yellow surface. The bull's head, Maltese cross, and double-axe motifs are seen. Architecture was more sophisticated than in the previous Hassuna period, with mud-brick being used. Another site of this culture was the tell at Arpachiyah on the Tigris.

HALICARNASSUS, birthplace of the 5th-century B.C. Greek historian Herodotus and the 1st-century B.C. Greek writer Dionysius. An ancient city, it stood on the southwestern coast of Asia Minor, near the island of Cos. In the 4th century B.C. Halicarnassus was one of the most spectacular cities of the ancient world and is especially famous for the funerary temple of its king Mausolus (the Mausoleum). Carved marble pieces of its superstructure remain and are in the British Museum. Its original form is unknown but much discussed.

HALL OF BULLS. See **LASCAUX**.

HALLSTATT CULTURE. The salt-mining town of Hallstatt in the Salzkammergut, Austria, is the site of a great, well-preserved, ancient cemetery discovered in 1846. The culture represented in some 3,000 graves found here stands at the end of the bronze age and the beginning of the iron age in Europe, from 1100 to 500 B.C. Most of the ornaments, pins, brooches, bracelets, and earrings are of bronze, while the majority of the weapons, swords and daggers, are of iron. The typical Hallstatt garment seems to have been somewhat like a toga, wrapped around the body, belted at the waist, and secured on shoulders and breast by brooches. Most of the bodies found were buried, while others had been cremated,

Han Dynasty: Toiletry box. Lacquer on hemp. Chinese. (British Museum, London)

indicating a cultural change and intermingling of peoples, probably brought on by Celtic invasions. Hallstatt cultural traits, as well as decorative metalwork, were spread widely in Europe. The Natural History Museum of Vienna has a great Hallstatt collection.

HAMADAN. See **ECBATANA.**

HAMITES, a much abused term for a number of North and East African peoples. Although their languages all belong to the Hamitic family, these peoples, who include the ancient Egyptians, the Berbers, Fulani, Tuaregs, Copts, Galla, Somali, and Falasha, have different racial and ethnic characteristics. It is possible that the inscriptions at the ancient Nubian cities of Napata and Meroe are

written in early forms of the Hamitic language. As a group the Hamites, named for the Biblical Ham, son of Noah, are more closely related to Semites than to African Negroes.

HAN DYNASTY, founders of the first great Chinese Empire, from 206 B.C. to 220 A.D. Its influence stretched as far west as the Caspian Sea. Culturally, the Han marked China's emergence from the bronze age into the iron age. Although Confucianism predominated, Buddhism was introduced during this period. Trade with India and the Roman Empire brought Western influences. As a result, animal silhouettes and Mediterranean realism appeared in sculpture, and painting became more naturalistic and fluid in movement. Porcelain was developed by the Han, and Yueh ware, the prototype of the famous celadon ware, was produced.

HANGING GARDENS, in ancient Babylon, one of the seven wonders of the world. According to the Greek writer Diodorus Siculus, it was an 80-foot-high ziggurat, terraced with ornamental gardens. It was built, Diodorus says, by Cyrus the Great for a Persian mistress nostalgic for the mountain meadows of her homeland.

HANIWA FIGURES, in Japanese art, terra-cotta sculptures that were set into the ground around tombs in the Great Tombs period from the 3rd to 6th centuries A.D. One of the earliest examples of Japanese terra cottas, haniwa figures were made by the coil method and shaped with bamboo tools into various animal and human forms. Haniwa subject matter demonstrates that the Japanese had bows and arrows, swords, and rode horses during this period. Haniwa are similar to *ming ch'i*, stone funerary figures placed at Chinese graves.

Haniwa figures: "Bust of an Armored Man." Terra cotta. Japanese, Kofun period. Found at Kamichujo (National Museum, Tokyo)

134

HARAPPA, a major site of the Indus Valley civilization, located largely in Pakistan. Harappa shows Mesopotamian influences of the mid-3rd to the 2nd millennium B.C. Excavations here have revealed a brick citadel 30 to 50 feet high and 460 by 215 yards in area, and a planned town, one mile square. The Harappans may have been Dravidians, and excavation of a huge granary (150 by 200 feet) indicates an economy based on agriculture and commerce. Monumental art has not been found at Harappa, but superb small naturalistic statues and carved seals, containing an undecipherable script, were discovered. Harappan culture, which was quite uniform and conservative throughout its history, began in mystery and ended with the Aryan invasions of about 1500 B.C.

HARARI. See MARI.

HASSUNA WARE, a kind of pottery that takes its name from a tell near Mosul in northern Iraq; the ware is also found elsewhere in Mesopotamia. It has been dated to the early 6th millennium B.C. After its earliest examples, a monochrome cream pottery, Hassuna ware became more elaborate, with unpainted but incised pottery, or red-on-cream painted ware, or combinations of the two. Decoration consisted largely of simple geometric patterns. Hassuna was succeeded by Samarra ware.

HATHOR, Egyptian goddess of fertility, sometimes depicted in human form, sometimes as a cow. The most important temple dedicated to Hathor was at Dendera.

HATRA, a small Arabian city-state between the Syrian desert and northern Mesopotamia. It was important as a trade center for some 300 years until its destruction by the Sassanids around 240 A.D. Investigations here have revealed remains combining Roman and Persian elements. Inscriptions indicate that Hatra's language was a form of Aramaic.

HATTUSAS. See BOGHAZKOY.

HATVAN CULTURE, so named from a site northeast of Budapest. It represents a stage in the Hungarian bronze age of about 1500 B.C. This period gives the first evidence of cheekpieces and bits for horses, a great improvement over the noserope and halter. The bronze age in central Europe achieved a blending and balance of various cultures in this epoch, which corresponds chronologically with the fall of Minoan Crete and the rise of the more distinctively European leadership of Mycenaean culture on mainland Greece.

HAVOR, a site on the island of Gotland, Sweden, which has yielded two noteworthy finds indicating far-flung trade connections in the late Roman iron age. One is a bronze vessel, with matching ladle and strainer, made in Campania, Italy. The other is a magnificent gold collar with filigree decoration from southern Russia. Thousands of Roman coins found on the same island testify to trade (through the Goths) between the eastern Mediterranean, via the River Vistula, and the Baltic seacoasts.

HAWAIIAN ISLANDS, the home of some of the most notable art of Polynesia. The culture of ancient Hawaii was distinguished by a feudal social structure, with an aristocratic ruling class and a strong priestly caste. Thus,

Hawaiian Islands: Feather cloak, detail. (Musée Ethnographique, Geneva)

most of Hawaiian art is concerned with ritual and is almost spectacular in effect. Wooden figures, both large and small, were carved to represent major gods, household deities, guardian figures, and in some cases generic portraits. Hawaiian wooden sculpture is unusual in Oceanic art for its absence of surface decoration. The most unique Hawaiian art form is featherwork. Large heads of the war god, constructed of a basketry frame covered with feathers, were carried into battle as divine protection. Elaborate feather helmets and capes were also made for persons of the highest rank. In addition, tapa cloth from Hawaii is unexcelled in the quality of its craftsmanship and design. A good deal of Hawaiian art was destroyed in 1819 during a native religious and social upheaval. The pieces that remained lost much of their ritual significance. Maraes, or elaborate stone platforms, are to be found in the Hawaiian Islands.

HAZOR, a major site in the far north of Israel; it is the largest tell yet found in Palestine. The site, including a citadel, was occupied from an early date. Destroyed when the Israelites drove out the Canaanites in the 13th century B.C., it was rebuilt by Solomon in the 10th century B.C. only to be destroyed again in the 8th century B.C. by the Assyrians. Important remains have been found here, including a series of statues in the round, steles, and animal and religious reliefs.

HEBREW CIVILIZATION, one of the world's most historic civilizations, was founded by Semitic tribes of the Arabian desert who may have been settled in Sumeria by the 3rd millennium B.C. There, it is thought, they learned the arts of civilization. From southern Mesopotamia the Hebrews migrated to Palestine, their land of milk and honey, but after a great famine they were forced to move to Egypt. Their return to Palestine forms one of the great epics of religious literature. After the exodus the Hebrews, or the Khabiru, as they are known from ancient Egyptian annals, resettled in Palestine, where they established the Israelite nation, which endured from about the 13th century B.C. to the 2nd century A.D. At the heart of Hebrew civilization was a cohesive theocratic society. The ancient Hebrews evolved a theology and an ethical code that were highly sophisticated at a very early date in world history. Their religion, which has endured to modern times as Judaism, was the first, in any important sense, to develop the fundamental idea of monotheism and the total spirituality of the god concept. As such, Judaism not only flourished in its own right but served both historically and theologically as the source for two other major world religions—Christianity and Islam. The historical record of the Hebrews is that masterpiece of world literature, the Old Testament. Traditionally, the first Hebrew patriarch was Eber—or Abraham—who came from the Sumer city of Ur. His descendants lived as tribal pastoralists in Palestine until a great famine impelled them to migrate in significant numbers into Egypt. Perhaps as early as the 16th century B.C. a prosperous Hebrew colony existed in Egypt, but a sudden shift in political climate reduced the Hebrews to serfdom and slavery. They were finally led out of Egypt in the 13th

century B.C. by the hero and patriarch Moses, who not only conducted their return to Palestine but gave them their monotheistic concept of god in the person of Yahweh and their written ethical code—the Ten Commandments. In Palestine the Hebrews of the Egyptian exodus mingled with fellow Semites, such as the Canaanites, sometimes having to fight for room to settle. A major military victory under Joshua gave them the ancient Palestinian city of Jericho on the west bank of the River Jordan. Having, in large part, subjugated the Canaanites, the Israelites during the 12th century B.C. were threatened by the advance of the Philistines from the Mediterranean coast. Hebrew opposition to the Philistines worked to unite the separate Hebrew tribal groups, and a central monarchy was forged under the leadership of Saul that was strengthened by his immediate successor, David, who defeated the Philistines. An Israelite capital was established at Jerusalem in the middle of the 11th century B.C. Solomon, the son of David, became king in 961 B.C., and during his reign the Israelite monarchy attained its zenith. However, upon Solomon's death in 922 B.C. the monarchy fell apart, and the Hebrew kingdom was split into Israel in the north, having a capital at Samaria, and the smaller and weaker state of Judah to the south, retaining Jerusalem as capital. The politically weakened Hebrews were soon attacked by stronger neighboring powers. In the 8th century B.C. the Assyrians under Sargon II conquered Israel. In the early 6th century B.C. both Judah and Jerusalem fell to the Babylonians, who transplanted many of the people of Judah to Babylon. Late in the same century the Persian Empire—which had displaced Babylon as the leading regional power—permitted the Hebrews to return to Jerusalem. The following two centuries were times of reconstruction and relative prosperity, until the armies of Alexander the Great conquered Palestine. A vigorous Hellenistic culture spread over Palestine, threatening to submerge ancient Hebrew civilization; but in the 2nd century B.C., led by the Maccabees, most notably Judas Maccabeus, the Hebrews fought against the Seleucid Greeks and won a brief independence. It ended in 63 B.C., when Palestine became a Roman province. In 70 A.D. and again in 115 A.D. there were fierce Jewish uprisings against Roman rule in Palestine. The last was ruthlessly put down by Hadrian, and national life in Palestine was annihilated. The Jews had begun their centuries-long diaspora, which ended, in part, with the establishment of the modern state of Israel.

Hebrew Art and Antiquities. Graphic images of the human or divine form were forbidden by religious law, a factor that sharply curtailed the development of Hebrew sculpture and painting. With very few exceptions, objects of Hebrew religious art (menorahs, shofars, etc.) failed to survive the ravages of Roman destruction during the first two centuries A.D. Thus, although Palestine has proved to be an area of many major archaeological finds, few of the important yields are of indisputable Hebrew origin. Those exceptions are in the realm of architecture and

136

include Saul's citadel at Gabaa, the royal palace at Samaria, and possibly the remnants of Solomon's Temple at Jerusalem. The most common form of Hebrew antiquity is the seal, having carved motifs, usually of scarabs—a design borrowed from Egypt. Discoveries at Dura-Europos in Syria have revealed startling Jewish frescoes of the Hellenistic period. By implication, it is thought there may have been ancient Hebrew paintings, long since destroyed by time and war. However, this theory is highly conjectural.

HEIAN PERIOD, in Japanese history, from 794 to 1185 A.D., the era when Japan's capital was the city of Heian (modern Kyoto). The first two centuries of Heian rule saw the disintegration of long-standing cultural links between China and Japan. This was due largely to a renaissance of Japan's ancient Shinto religion, but now much modified and influenced by Buddhism, and the collapse of the Tang Dynasty in China, which had exerted strong cultural influence in Japan. Most Heian art is religious, typical objects being Buddhist paintings, wooden sculptures, and pagodas. The Heian period often includes that of the Fujiwara.

HEI TIKI. See **MAORI.**

HELE STONE. See **STONEHENGE.**

HELIOPOLIS, ancient Egyptian city dating from the Predynastic era. Its site is about five miles northeast of modern Cairo. The city retained importance through the Old, Middle, and New Kingdoms as an important religious center, dedicated to the sun god, Ra. Notable

among its ruins is a granite obelisk, constructed about 1950 B.C. at the order of Sesostris I. It was erected before a temple to Ra, which no longer stands.

HELLENISTIC PERIOD, the final art period of Greek civilization, beginning with Greek imperialist expansion under Alexander the Great in the 4th century B.C. and ending with Roman domination of the Mediterranean in the 1st century B.C. Newly Hellenized cities developed outside Greece proper, notably at Alexandria, Egypt; Pergamon, Asia Minor; and Antioch, Syria. Hellenistic influence was widespread, appearing in the art of the Iberian peninsula and in that of Gandhara in northwestern India. Hellenistic art found its most vital expression in sculpture—both relief and free-standing. Dramatically posed subjects, depictions of scenes of intense agitation, and an almost baroque attention to detail typify much Hellenistic sculpture. Thus it departs from its Classical origins—the elegant simplicity of form, the restraint—that reached its zenith in Periclean Athens (5th century B.C.). Hellenistic painting and mosaic art were also important, notably at centers such as Antioch and Alexandria, where portraiture and love scenes in bucolic landscapes were common subjects. Major events marking the demise of Hellenistic culture included the sacking of Athens by the Roman Sulla in 86 B.C. and the burning of the library of Alexandria in 48 B.C.

HEPHAISTEION. See **THESEUM.**

HERA, sister and wife of Zeus. She was queen of heaven, the Greek goddess of wives, and the protector of marriage. In art she is a stately, majestic beauty, often enthroned in full robe with a diadem on her head, or standing with sceptre and pomegranate. The famous statue of Hera in the Louvre was found in her sanctuary on the island of Samos. The Romans identified Hera with Juno. The Farnese Juno at Naples and the Ludovisi Juno in Rome are copies of the colossal chryselephantine image of Hera by Polyclitus, made for her temple at Argos.

HERAKLES, the most popular and widely venerated of Greek heroes. Although not a god, he was often worshipped as a divinity. Called Hercules by the Romans, he was the ideal of manly strength and of prodigious deeds; he was popular in all forms of art. The classic Herakles—muscular body, short neck, small head, leaning on a great club, and wearing a lion's skin—seems to have been fixed by the 4th-century B.C. Greek sculptor Lysippus. The Farnese Hercules in the Naples Museum is probably a late Hellenistic copy by the Athenian sculptor Glycon.

HERCULANEUM, a small but wealthy town on the slopes of Vesuvius, buried along with Pompeii and Stabiae in the famous eruption of 79 A.D. Unlike Pompeii, Herculaneum was a residential town with a regular town plan and a great variety of house types. Shops are less obtrusive and the streets show no signs of heavy traffic.

Herculaneum: "The Actor." Fresco, Pompeian style. (National Museum, Naples)

Most important, this town was buried by mud-lava (not hot ashes), which hardened when cooled and provided a tight seal, preserving house furnishings, even wooden beds and doors. Eighteenth-century looters burrowed into the theater and basilica and carried off much of the sculpture. Scientific excavations have revealed notable finds: the wall mosaic of Neptune and Amphitrite, found in the court of the house given that name; a bronze herm

138

by Apollonius which helps reconstruct the Doryphoros of Polyclitus; and an indifferent bronze herm related to the bronze Amazon of Phidias. Most significant, however, are paintings in the baroque Pompeian style, which combine architectural illusion with a touch of surrealism, achieving a "stage effect" perspective of almost infinite receding depth.

HERM, a four-sided marble or bronze pillar with a head, usually of Hermes, on top and extended phallus below. Sometimes inscribed with moral precepts, herms stood along the streets of Athens and other Greek cities and recalled the god's function as protector of travellers and his association with fertility.

HERMES, messenger and herald of the gods, god of luck and wealth, patron of merchants, thieves, and associated with fertility. In art he is often shown with winged sandals, broad-brimmed hat (*petasos*), and a staff with twined serpents (*caduceus*). He was known as Mercury in Roman times. The Hermes of Praxiteles, one of the great masterpieces of Greek sculpture, is in Olympia, Greece.

Hieraconpolis: Narmer's palette. Carved slate. Egyptian, ca. 3000 B.C. (National Museum, Cairo)

HEUNEBURG, a major hilltop fort, sited on a promontory overlooking the Danube, in southwest Germany, near Sigmaringen. Occupied by a succession of peoples, it reached its height under the Celts of the 6th century B.C., when Mediterranean influence, especially that of the Greeks, was strong. Attic black-figure pottery has been found here, and in nearby barrow graves there were rich finds of gold and bronze objects. The practice of placing a corpse on a treasure-laden wagon for burial is evident here.

HIERACONPOLIS, an important site in Upper Egypt yielding finds from the 1st and 2nd Dynasties, including competently carved ivory figurines of men, women, and animals. Of greater importance is the famous slate palette of the Predynastic king Narmer; it is slightly over two feet high and depicts Narmer in relief. On one side he is killing an enemy; on the reverse he is walking processionally. The palette, probably made about 3000 B.C., is among the earliest examples of Egyptian sculpture. It is in the National Museum, Cairo.

HIERATIC, term describing an Egyptian script used roughly between 2000 B.C. and 100 A.D. It is a cursive script (i.e., its letters are linked). It was generally written with a brush on papyrus.

HIEROGLYPHIC STAIRWAY. See COPAN.

HIEROGLYPHS, picture writing of ancient Egypt. It assumed final form around 3000 B.C. and was later followed by its derivatives, hieratic and demotic scripts. Hieroglyphs usually read from right to left, exceptions often occurring when they accompany illustrations. Hieroglyphs of a different kind are found in Pre-Columbian Mexico and elsewhere.

HILDESHEIM HOARD. A rich collection of 69 pieces of Roman silver, dating from the time of Augustus at the beginning of the 1st century A.D., was discovered on a hill near Hildesheim, Germany, in 1868. It includes a wine mixing bowl (the ancients rarely drank their wine neat), decorated with figures of children; three platters with figures of Minerva, Cybele, and Hercules, respectively; and a silver folding tripod with detachable tray. The collection is now housed in the Kunstgewerbemuseum in Berlin.

HINAYANA, a major branch of Buddhism, also called the "Lesser Vehicle." It is considered southern Buddhism, having spread from its Indian origins to Ceylon, Burma, Siam, Malaya, Indonesia, and Indochina. It is the orthodox and conservative branch of Buddhism; thus, Hinayana art, as opposed to Mahayana art, tends to be relatively simple and its iconography naturalistic.

HINDU ART AND ANTIQUITIES, with minor exceptions, date from the first centuries A.D. The religion is itself much older, but early Hindu art objects failed to survive time's ravages. Oldest extant Hindu sanctuaries in India date from about 400 A.D. and include caves at

Udayagiri and Khandagiri. From 320 to 530 A.D. India experienced its golden age of Hindu art within the Gupta Dynasty, founded by Chandragupta and radiating from his capital, Pataliputra. After centuries of foreign invasion and internal troubles, the Gupta era saw the flowering of native Hindu culture, especially in sculpture and architecture. A fusion of religious and secular styles characterizes Gupta art. In sculpture, human forms often take dancelike poses, and the female figure is most sensuous. Hindu iconography became important in Gupta art, and temples to Vishnu (e.g., at Gwailor and Citorgarh) influenced much subsequent temple architecture. The Brahmanic religious revival beginning in the 8th and 9th centuries, after the fall of the Guptas, produced a corresponding revival of Hindu art. Representative examples include ornate sculpture in Chalukya temples and the intricate relief sculpture of the Pallava era. It is difficult to separate Hindu art from the temples that they were created to adorn. However, there are notable exceptions, including Pallava bronzes of deities, the Siva saint figures of 11th-century southern India, and Chola Dynasty bronze and stone figures. At its height, in the 12th century, high-quality Chola craftsmanship extended throughout southern India. Hindu antiquities are also found in Tibet, Southeast Asia, and Indonesia.

Hindu Inconography is rich and varied, as the religion's polytheistic nature might suggest. Early surviving icons from the Mauryan era (323–184 B.C.) include Siva lingam figures, in which the Hindu god is associated with a phallus-worship cult older than Indian civilization. Siva is, with Brahma and Vishnu, one of Brahmanism's three major gods, and in line with his importance he has many iconographic representations. He is often multi-armed, depicted in seated or standing poses. He is perhaps best known as a dancing figure surrounded by a fiery ring. Vishnu, the preserving god, is often shown in a regal pose, sometimes surrounded by attendants. At other times he takes an animal form, usually of a boar or a lion. Brahma, the father figure, is too vaguely conceived to take iconographic form. Lesser gods and goddesses abound in Hindu iconography and range from Parvati, sensuous wife of Siva, to Kali, the haglike goddess of death.

HITTITE CIVILIZATION, one of the most outstanding civilizations of the ancient Near East. The Hittites, an Indo-European people who probably originated north of the Black Sea, gradually infiltrated the Anatolian plateau in central Turkey in the early 2nd millennium B.C. Here they mingled with the indigenous population, eventually establishing themselves as the ruling class. In the Old Kingdom period, from about 1750 to 1450 B.C., the Hittites, with their capital at Kussara, ventured against the peoples of Syria and Mesopotamia; at one point the Hittites made an ephemeral conquest of Babylon itself. The Old Kingdom, a loose confederation of Hittite city-states,

Hindu art: Siva. Bronze. Southern India, 10th century A.D. (British Museum, London)

Hittite art: Double-headed figure. 3rd millennium B.C.

gradually became centralized and the power of the king (he was also chief priest) greatly strengthened. By the 15th century the new Hittite Empire, with its capital at Boghazkoy (Hattusas), dominated most of Anatolia, had displaced the Mitanni in northern Syria, and successfully challenged Egypt and Assyria. The inconclusive battle of Kadesh, fought against the Egyptians about 1286 B.C., seemed to signal a period of decreasing hostility between the two powers. Some 50 years later, however, the Hittite Empire came to a sudden end with the invasion of the Sea Peoples of the Mediterranean. Boghazkoy was captured and burned, as were most of the Hittite cities. Only the chain of Hittite city-states in northern Syria survived the deluge—Carchemish was the most important of these—until they too lost their independence, to the Assyrians in the 8th century B.C. The oldest recorded Indo-European language, Hittite was generally written in Akkadian cuneiform on clay tablets, although inscriptions on stone, from seals to monuments, used hieroglyphs. The identification and decipherment of Hittite writing in this century was one of the greatest feats of archaeological and philological analysis. Hittite religion, cosmopolitan in nature, had many gods taken from other peoples and featured elaborate rituals. Hittite kings seem to have ruled mildly; they did not torture defeated foes, as did the Assyrians and Medes, and the punishments provided in their legal code were fairly humane. One of the great secrets of the Hittites, which they kept until their downfall, was a practical method for smelting iron, and they enjoyed throughout antiquity the reputation of being the first iron workers.

Hittite Art and Antiquities. Few remains have been found of Hittite art and artifacts of the earliest period, although skillfully made pottery and figurines have been excavated at Kultepe. The later period of Hittite eminence, however, saw a widespread production of colossal stone and rock sculptures. The most notable of these are at Alaca Huyuk, with its Sphinx Gate, and at Boghazkoy, with its Lion Gate and reliefs of king-gods. Also remarkable are the rock carvings at Yazilikaya, with their processions of gods, kings, and queens. Hittite sculpture is very distinctive in style and has an impressive force and vigor. In the later imperial period, art styles attained a high level, although Syrian and Assyrian influences are pronounced.

HISSARLIK. See **TROY.**

HOABINH, a town approximately 50 miles west of Hanoi in modern North Vietnam and site of an archaeologically important prehistoric settlement. The Hoabinh culture did not advance beyond a stone-age technology, but there is evidence that its inhabitants developed a rice-growing economy. Recent archaeological speculation includes theories that one of the world's earliest agricultural societies may have originated in this region. The only Hoabinh artifacts of importance are polished stone tools.

HOARD, collection of precious objects, such as coins, bronzes, etc., collected or gathered together by members of a past society for reasons ranging from religious to economic. Discovered hoards may be of archaeological or artistic importance.

HOBY HOARD. Buried in a grave at Hoby on the island of Lolland in Denmark were some beautiful silver and bronze vessels from Augustan Rome of the 1st century A.D. The hoard included a bronze jug with scroll design, a large bronze dish with figures of Venus and Cupid, and a bucket. The finest pieces are two silver cups signed by a Greek craftsman, Cheirisophos, working in Rome. They bear Homeric scenes in remarkably sharp and elegant relief.

HOHOKAM CULTURE, one of the three great cultures of the American Southwest, first appeared around 100 B.C. Its center was in southern Arizona, near modern-day Phoenix. Like their contemporaries, the peoples of Anasazi and Mogollon, the Hohokam enjoyed a peaceful society, had no class system, and practiced a form of democracy. The Hohokam lived in villages in river valleys and devoted their major energies to building a massive irrigation system. These systems, which were well developed by 700 A.D., reached their maximum size by the 14th century. From 500 A.D. strong cultural influences arrived from Mexico and stimulated the construction of temple platform mounds and ritual ball courts. Hohokam art objects include carved stone palettes and vessels. Also produced was pottery, which is technically undistinguished but noted for its fanciful, lively designs. Between 1000 and 1200 A.D. the Hohokam people developed one of the world's earliest acid etching processes, which they used to decorate imported seashells. Hohokam culture died out after the 14th century. Its descendants are the present-day Pima and Papago Indians.

HOMO SAPIENS. See **CRO-MAGNON MAN.**

HOPEWELL CULTURE, a North American Woodland Indian culture that flourished in the southern Ohio region during the period from 100 B.C. to 200 A.D. The focus of Hopewell culture was on the practice of intricate burial rites, which included the construction of enormous bird and animal effigy mounds and the placement of offerings with the dead. Among the most distinctive of Hopewell grave goods are beautifully carved "monitor pipes." These stone pipes had a curved base with a bowl in the form of an animal effigy. In order to obtain exotic materials such as mica, pearls, and silver, necessary for their grave offerings, the Hopewell people maintained trade throughout large areas of what is now the United States.

HOPI. A Pueblo Indian tribe of the American Southwest, concentrated in northeastern Arizona, the Hopi trace their roots back to the prehistoric Anasazi culture. Although a farming society, the Hopi live in pueblo towns. They are famous for their woven textiles and pottery. Characteristically their ceramics have a background of orange shades with designs of naturalistic and human forms painted in red, black, or white. The kachina cult, of great importance to the Hopi, has resulted in the produc-

Hopi: Bowl. Painted earthenware. (British Museum, London)

tion of many masks and dolls. Hopi silver and turquoise jewelry is sold commercially.

HORSES OF SAN MARCO, four splendid bronze horses which stand on the façade balcony of San Marco Cathedral in Venice. Slightly larger than life size, these prancing, spirited steeds are probably of 4th or 3rd-century B.C. Greek workmanship. Their exact origin is not known, but they once decorated a triumphal arch in Rome until removed to Constantinople by the Emperor Constantine in the 4th century A.D. When that city fell to the Crusaders in the 13th century, Venetian leaders claimed them for the basilica that housed the relics of St. Mark. In 1797 Napoleon took the horses to Paris, but they were finally returned to Venice. An old tradition attributed these magnificent beasts to the Greek sculptor Lysippus, who usually worked in bronze and was famous for his statues of animals.

HORUS, Egyptian sky god, dating from the Predynastic era, usually depicted as a falcon, although sometimes having human form. In later times Horus was thought to be reincarnated in the person of each new pharaoh. He was associated with the cult of Isis and Osiris.

HORYU-JI. See NARA PERIOD.

HOUSE OF TILES, at Lerna on the Gulf of Argos in the Peloponnesus. It is a major archaeological remain of Greece of the late 3rd millennium B.C. The name comes from the mass of roof tiles (terra cotta and blue-green schist) which fell when the building burned and collapsed. This large (about 75 by 36 feet), carefully executed structure was essentially two large rooms, divided and flanked by corridors. Its purpose is unknown. The idea of a communal farm with a large, centrally defended building would agree with what is known of this period. The later inhabitants of Lerna graded down the debris of the House of Tiles but preserved the mound as sacrosanct.

HSIANGTANSHAN, a small Buddhist shrine in China's Shantung Province, dating from the Han Dynasty. The structure's smooth interior stone walls are decorated with detailed intaglio reliefs, similar to work done by skilled Han jade and ivory carvers. The shrine is roughly 14 by 7 feet, with walls about six and a half feet high.

HSIAOTUN CULTURE, a Chinese neolithic culture that existed in the 2nd millennium B.C. It is probably slightly later than the more important Yangshao (Painted Pottery) and Lungshan (Black Pottery) cultures and is known mainly from a small archaeological site in the Yellow River region near Anyang. The Hsiaotun culture is distinguished by its pottery, a finely shaped ware made of gray clay. A distinctive textured pattern was achieved on vessel surfaces by beating the pottery with cord-covered pads before baking.

HUASTEC CULTURE. Centered in the Mexican state of Veracruz, around the city of Tampico, this culture takes its name from that of a tribe who occupied the area at the time of the Spanish Conquest. While part of the mainstream of Pre-Columbian Mexican life, the Huastec people maintained a distinct regional identity. They spoke a language related to Maya, but linguistic evidence shows that the Maya and the Huastec split sometime before 300 A.D. Artistically, Huastec culture reached its climax in the centuries after 900 A.D. The most outstanding artworks created by these people are monumental limestone sculptures, believed to be representations of priests or kings. These are stiff, angular, and covered with low-relief carving in patterns resembling tattooing or textiles. Often a death image appears on the figure's back. The influence of Huastec culture was felt over a wide area. Its pottery was traded as far as southern Texas. In addition, it is speculated that beautifully carved shell ear ornaments were traded as far as the Gulf coast of the United States and served as an inspiration for similar forms created by the Indians of that area.

HUITZILOPOCHTLI, Aztec warrior god of the sun; the tutelary god of the Aztecs. One of the most fearsome of ancient deities, he was one of the very few gods in the Aztec pantheon not borrowed from earlier cultures. Great pyramidal temples were built for him at which humans were sacrificed by having their hearts cut out.

HUNS, nomads from Mongolia who swept across Asia's steppes at the dawn of the Christian era, probably impelled westward after defeats by Han Dynasty China. While some Huns settled in southern Russia, most continued westward, vanquishing the Ostrogoths and Visigoths.

Their fateful meeting with the Roman Empire came at the latter's Danube frontier in the 4th century A.D. Despite early victories, the Huns disintegrated as a people soon after Attila, their last great leader, was defeated in Gaul by a Roman-Visigoth alliance in 451. Hun art occurs over a vast region, from tomb sites on the Ordos plateau, near China's Great Wall, to a grave near Mannheim on the Rhine. The most important site is near Noin Ula in Mongolia. Objects—typically incorporating steppe animal style—include bronze plaques, ornate weapons, jewelry in precious metals, and woolen-and-leather rugs, saddles, and tent hangings.

HUNTING BATHS. See LEPCIS MAGNA.

HURRIANS, a rather mysterious people who, early in the 2nd millennium B.C., spread over northern Mesopotamia from the Zagros mountains in western Iran. The Hurrians were an element in the Mitanni kingdom, which flourished around 1500 B.C., and strongly influenced the Hittites. The distinctive Hurrian pantheon was recorded by the Hittites in rock carvings at Yazilikaya. The Hurrian language, about which a good deal is known, was apparently related to the Indo-European family of languages.

HUYUK, Turkish word for a mound or tell, the accumulated debris of a long-lived settlement. These mounds, sometimes over 100 feet high, play an important part in Near East archaeology.

HVAR, an island off the Dalmatian coast of Yugoslavia. In caves on the island there was discovered an unusual neolithic pottery of a dark ground color with painted red patterns of spiral and scroll shape.

HYDRIA, tall Greek water jar with a wide body and narrower neck. There are two horizontal handles on the sides (for lifting) and one vertical handle at the back of the neck (for holding and pouring). Hydriai of bronze have the central, or pouring, handle elaborately decorated in relief.

HYKSOS, desert nomads, probably Canaanites from Palestine, who drifted into Egypt toward the beginning of the 17th century B.C. and came to dominate that country until about 1580 B.C. They were also called the Shepherd Kings and, more properly, Rulers of a Foreign Country (*heqa-khase*, hence Hyksos). Their chief god was Set, and they ruled Egypt from Avaris in the eastern Delta. A number of scarabs and other objects bear the names of Hyksos rulers. Their expulsion was followed by the establishment of the New Kingdom of Egypt. They are usually credited with the introduction of the horse and chariot into Egypt, but this theory may be incorrect.

HYPOGEUM, term designating ancient Egyptian underground rooms or galleries, found beneath temples, pyramids, palaces, etc. It also applies to rooms dug into rock cliffs.

Huastec culture: Pectoral. Engraved mother-of-pearl. (National Museum of Anthropology, Mexico City)

I

IBEJI. See **YORUBA.**

IBERIAN PEOPLES, the earliest inhabitants of the Iberian peninsula, in what is now Spain and Portugal. A bridge between Africa and Europe, Iberia since paleolithic times has been the scene of many folk migrations and the site of many different cultures. Cave dwellers of Cro-Magnon origin appear in the north as the brilliant artists of Altamira. In the south, Capsian culture, probably derived from prehistoric Africa, arose in about 8000 B.C. In the mid-3rd millennium.B.C. a strange people, the Megalithic Builders, arrived in southeast Spain from the eastern Mediterranean; one of their major sites is Los Millares in Almeria. Some 500 years later the Beaker People occupied much of Spain, who were then followed, in the north, by the Urn People. Phoenicians, Greeks, and Romans of later times also left their imprint on the Iberian peninsula. From this commingling of diverse peoples a unique and distinct Iberian culture emerged, with a language of its own, as yet undeciphered. Beginning in the 8th century B.C. the Iberians produced an advanced art, showing all the hallmarks of a true miniature civilization, and established an autonomous political existence until annexation by Carthage during the middle of the 3rd century B.C.

Iberian Art and Antiquities. The major sites of prehistoric Iberia, such as Altamira, Los Millares, and others are treated separately in this book. The art of historic Iberia, prior to the 3rd century B.C., is known to us primarily through stone sculpture, bronzes, and ceramics. Typical early Iberian stonework can be seen in human-headed animal figurines, unearthed at several different sites; most notable of these is the Biche de Balzote, a human-headed bull figurine, discovered at Albacete and now in the Prado, Madrid. In about the 5th century B.C., however, Iberian sculpture gave way to highly naturalistic human representations. Perhaps the most important sculpture-producing center was at Elche, where a famous stone bust of a woman wearing an elaborate headdress was found. Known as the Dama de Elche, it is now in the Prado. Iberian bronzes include numerous human votive figurines; a fine bronze horse and rider, less than three inches high, is in Madrid's Museo Arquelologico Nacional. Iberian ceramics were produced in quantity from the 6th century B.C.

Ibo: Secret Society mask. Painted wood. From eastern Nigeria. (American Museum of Natural History, New York)

IBIBIO, an African people of southeastern Nigeria. Artistically, the Ibibio are noted for impressive masks, used by the Ekpo cult society to maintain social order and propitiate ancestors. The masks may be either naturalistic and painted black or extremely grotesque and remarkably polychromed. In both types of Ibibio masks emphasis is on bold sculptural statement, and typically the masks are large-scale with movable jaws. The oldest wooden art objects of the Ibibio, statuettes of bearded men, often three to four feet high, are more than 200 years old.

IBIS. See **THOTH.**

IBO, an African people living in southeastern Nigeria. The Ibo people are actually a number of tribes, differing in culture and language. Many Ibo villages developed their own separate traditions long before the British takeover

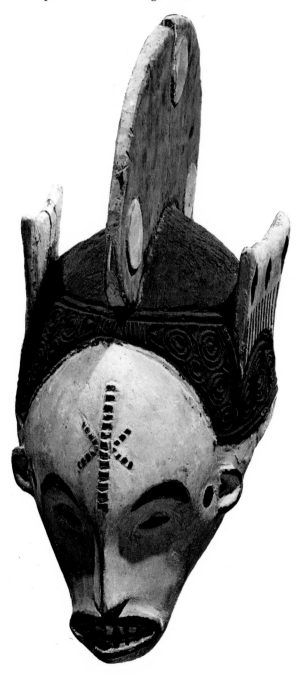

in 1900. The functions and styles of Ibo art reflected their diversity. The Ibo around the towns of Onitsha and Awka used the eerie *mmwo* mask at funerals. Its gaunt white face was topped by the attractive and elaborate hairdressing used by some Ibo women. The Ibo near Owerri created fanciful mud sculptures set in specifically built houses called *mbari*. Many of these were dedicated to the earth goddess Ala. Throughout Iboland forceful sculptures called *ikenga* were carved to ensure success for the owner in all his ventures.

ICE-AGE MAN, the types of early man dominant during the most recent of the great ice ages, a climatic sequence that began about three million years ago and ended about 8300 B.C. During this period Australopithecus and *Homo erectus* had developed and were using pebble tools, hand axes, and choppers. Neanderthal Man appeared much later, and evidence of his flake tools has been found throughout Eurasia. By the latter part of the last ice age—about 38,000 B.C.—*Homo sapiens* (modern man) arrived in the form of Cro-Magnon, replacing Neanderthal Man. Cro-Magnon Man produced the oldest surviving art: cave-wall art; art on small objects such as bone, ivory, antlers, and pebbles; and small modelled clay figures. Probably the earliest known cave art is a drawing made by fingertips on a clay wall in the Pech Merle cavern, France, dating from about 30,000 or 20,000 B.C. The best-known cave sites—Lascaux and Altamira—date from about 15,000 B.C., with African examples of animal paintings in Rhodesia and Tanzania dating from roughly the same time. Modelled prehistoric figures include clay bisons found at Tuc d'Audubert, France, and Venus figures of clay, stone, and ivory unearthed at many sites from the Ukraine to France. In general, animals are portrayed with an attempt at realism, while human figures are stylized or abstract—perhaps because of a taboo on representing man realistically. Art of ice-age man is thought to have had a magical significance, and some objects—Venus figures, for example—may even represent the earliest fertility cults.

ICONOCLAST, or "image-breaker," a term that originated with an 8th- and 9th-century struggle between Christian factions in the Byzantine Empire. Some supported and others opposed the existence of icons in churches. The iconoclasts prevailed, destroying much Byzantine church art. The term is often used to describe ancient peoples, such as the Hebrews or Arabs, who were prohibited from making images of human or divine figures.

ICONOGRAPHY, the study of art images and their meanings. The term originally described paintings on wood within the Byzantine and Russian Orthodox Christian tradition but later came to include church and temple art of all religions.

ICTINUS, a great 5th-century B.C. Greek architect who, along with Callicrates, designed the famous Parthenon on the Athenian Acropolis and wrote an account of it, now lost. Previously, Ictinus was responsible for the un-usual Temple of Apollo at Bassae, a remote site in Arcadia (Peloponnesus). Along with other architects he worked on the Telesterion at Eleusis, the hall in which the famous Eleusinian mysteries took place.

IFE CULTURE, an early African culture of western Nigeria. Even today the town of Ife is held sacred by the Yoruba-speaking people as the place where the god Oduduwa created the earth and established himself as the first divine Oni, or king. Ife is best known for its brilliant portrait terra cottas and bronzes cast by the cire-perdue method. The well-developed bronze tradition may have flourished as early as the 12th century A.D. The tradition ended abruptly, however, when, according to legend, an enraged Oni executed all members of the bronze-casting guild. Ife influenced the development of Benin civilization.

IJO, a West African people living in the Niger River delta of southern Nigeria. Most of the Ijo, who live on the banks of murky swamps and meandering streams, are fishermen, but one important sub-group—the Calabari Ijo—gave up fishing in the 18th century A.D. to become traders. Ijo riverine environment shows up dramatically in their art; many masks, horizontally worn, depict fishlike water spirits. For the Calabari Ijo an object of significance is a commemorative wood screen that shows the frontal image of an ancestor, flanked by his servants. This screen, called a *duen fobara,* may have had its genesis in the commemorative wall plaques of Benin.

IMAMKULU. See CAPPADOCIA.

IMPASTO, the use of thick layers of pigment in order to give a painting an effect resembling bas-relief sculpture. The term also describes an opaque mixture of any pigment and its base (oil, tempera, etc.).

IMPERIAL PERIOD, in Roman history, from the reign of Augustus in 27 B.C. until the fall of the Western Roman Empire in 476 A.D. This long period was most notably an era dedicated to the cult of personalities—chiefly that of the great emperors and generals. Thus sculpture, painting, and architecture dwelt upon imperial ideals and existed largely to glorify the powerful. At first, during the Augustan period, such artistic expression was generally tasteful and restrained. But as each succeeding emperor tried to outdo his predecessors, Roman art became increasingly grandiose, colossal, bombastic, and, finally, decadent. Sculpture, although based on Classical Greek aesthetics, tended from the outset to reject idealization of the human form in favor of literal depiction. Resultingly, Imperial Roman portrait sculpture ranks among the world's best. Roman artists of this era also documented history in great detail, as can be seen, for example, in the friezes on Trajan's Column (113 A.D.) in Rome.

INAU. See AINU.

Ife culture: Oni. Cast bronze. 12th–14th centuries A.D. (British Museum, London)

INCAN CIVILIZATION, one of the great empires of the world and the last Peruvian people to wear the imperial mantle before the Spanish Conquest. At its height Incan power was felt over a vast area, stretching from Ecuador and Bolivia to parts of Chile and Argentina. The Incas traced their history to the 13th century A.D., when, according to legend, their ancestors are said to have emerged from three caves located near Cuzco, the chief city of the short-lived Incan Empire. One ancestor was Manco Capoc, who became the first of the 13 Inca emperors. The successive reigns of Pachacuti and his son Topa Inca from 1438 to 1493 marked a time of great expansion and conquest. Perhaps the outstanding accomplishment of this era was the annexation and absorption of the rich and powerful Chimu Empire. The rulers of Peru governed their territory through a strong bureaucracy and a network of paved roads which crisscrossed coastal and Andean Peru, making all parts of the empire accessible. As descendants of the sun god, Inca emperors were worshipped as divine beings, and they controlled their political state with a despotic hand. The ingenuity of the Incas showed in many ways. Lacking a system of writing, they devised instead a method of keeping records with a knotted cord called a *quipu*. They constructed massive buildings and temples of dressed and carefully fitted stones and planned cities on a grid pattern with intersecting roads leading to open squares. Also they established a protective fortress near each inhabited city.

Incan Civilization: Keros, detail. Painted and lacquered wood.

An example of this scheme was the great fortress of Sacsahuaman that guarded Cuzco. Although farming was the basic economic activity, the Incas placed considerable importance on llamas not only as sacrificial animals but as beasts of burden and sources of wool for clothing. Large amounts of gold, the symbol of the sun god, and silver were mined, but these precious metals were used primarily for decorative objects and not as a medium of exchange. The empire came to an ignominious end in 1532 with the Spanish invasion led by Pizarro and the subsequent murder of the last emperor Atahualpa and the ruthless plunder of his wealth.

Incan Art and Antiquities. Incan art shows a surprising lack of creativity and inspiration. There was no stone sculpture, and architectural decoration was quite rare. Some artistic taste, however, is seen in their weaving, pottery, and precious metalwork. Incan textiles display a largely geometric ornamentation, while their pottery shapes had little modelling and were decorated with somber colors. Small figurines in stone and metal are generally static, lifeless images of llamas and humans. Of any major interest are wooden goblets with flared tops. These polychromed vessels, called *keros*, depict scenes of everyday life.

INDIAN CIVILIZATION, the rich tapestry of cultures and civilizations that arose on the Indian subcontinent prior to the 3rd millennium B.C. Earliest among these was the Indus Valley civilization, in the northwest, which had close ties to the very ancient civilizations of Mesopotamia. Complex and long-lasting, Indian civilization suffered many foreign invasions and many waves of migrants through its northwestern gateway. This flanking flow into India of Middle Eastern and Central Asian peoples was due to the Himalayas, the world's highest mountain chain, which protects the subcontinent to the north. The inpouring of peoples and cultures combined with aboriginal Indian stocks and ways of life to give rise to a civilization so intricate as almost to defy definition. Originally populated by dark-skinned Tamils or Dravidians, who probably founded the Indus Valley civilization, India was to become the birthplace of several major religions—Hinduism, or Brahmanism, Buddhism, and Jainism—whose spiritual influence was to reach out to central Asia, to China and Japan, and to Southeast Asia. For reasons of clarity the art and antiquities of these various religions are treated separately in this book. Indian cultural history, after the fall of the Indus Valley civilization, divides itself into several major periods. Earliest is the Vedic, named for the Vedas, or sacred texts— our chief source of information for an epoch extending roughly from 1500 to 800 B.C. The Vedic period began after the light-skinned Aryans of central Asia invaded and destroyed the Indus Valley civilization in about 1500 B.C. Aryan culture in India developed from tribes whose economies were based on animal herding and whose religion was a polytheistic blend of nature cults, influenced by some surviving religious beliefs from the defunct Indus Valley civilization. The Aryans gradually moved south through India, dominating native elements and, by 800 B.C., fusing indigenous cultures with their own. Hindu culture with its complex religion and social caste system was the result. The first major post-Vedic period was that of the Mauryan Dynasty, roughly from 323 to 184 B.C. Before then, parts of northern India had been annexed to the Persian Empire and subsequently conquered by Alexander the Great. Around 323 B.C. the Indian leader Chandragupta Maurya expelled the Greek forces and founded the first Indian empire. Most important among his successors was Asoka (reigned 274–232 B.C.), who extended the Mauryan empire into southern India. Asoka was largely responsible for the ascendancy of Buddhism as India's official religion, thus eclipsing Brahmanism for many centuries. The Mauryan Dynasty collapsed around 184 B.C. and was followed by 500 years of political turmoil. Among regional dynasties of this period was the Sunga, whose sphere of influence from 185 to 72 B.C. was the Ganges Valley. Farther south, roughly from Bombay to Madras, the Andhra Dynasty was more or less supreme between 32 B.C. and 320 A.D. A peripheral power that influenced Indian culture was the Kushan Dynasty. It held sway on northern India's fringes, in what is now Pakistan and Afghanistan, and bordered Gandhara, northern India's most flourishing cultural center. India's great Gupta period began in 320 A.D., when Chandragupta I was crowned supreme king at Pataliputra (modern Patna). Thus began India's golden age, a time when the many aspects of Indian art and culture expressed themselves most fully. Under Gupta leadership political rule was both unified and widespread, as it had not been since the Mauryan Dynasty, and both Buddhist and Hindu architecture flowered. The Gupta Dynasty reached its zenith under Chandragupta II (reigned 376–415), enjoying economic and cultural achievement as glorious as that of any other civilization in the world to that time. Foreign invasion from central Asia, mainly by a people called the White Huns, caused disintegration of the Gupta Empire between 530 and 647. From the 7th through the 12th centuries various regional Hindu dynasties waxed and waned—notably the Palas, Senas, and Pratiharas in the north; the Rashtrakutas, Chandelas, and Chalukyas in central India; and the Cholas and Pandyas in the south. During these centuries Brahmanism ousted Buddhism to become again India's dominant religious and cultural force. The Moghul period began gradually after 800, when the Islamic tide came down upon India from the northwest. Islamic leaders thoroughly controlled India's north by about 1100 and were dominant throughout the subcontinent from about 1500 until the 18th century. The greatest Moghul ruler was Akbar (reigned 1556–1605), who achieved partial reconciliation between Hindus and Moslems. To the present day, Moslem influence remains strongest in India's north, especially in what is modern Pakistan. Ancient Indian civilization began its decline in the 18th century with the arrival of the Europeans in force.

148

Indian Bronze and Metalwork date from the first centuries A.D. and are predominantly small Buddhist bronzes from the Ganges Valley and from Gandhara. The largest known metal Buddha of the early period is a beautiful copper statue, seven and a half feet high, from the Gupta Dynasty and currently in Birmingham, England. Artistically, the finest Indian bronzes are the work of craftsmen of southern India who flourished under the Cholas. These bronzes, which date from the 9th through 13th centuries, are typically of Hindu deities, such as Vishnu and Siva. Even after the Chola period southern India continued to produce the country's best bronzes, notable examples including the life-size statue of the reputed King of Vijayanagar, Krsna Deva Raya (reigned 1509–1529), and of his two queens.

Indian bronze: "Krishna Subduing Kaliya." South India. 16th century A.D. (Victoria and Albert Museum, London)

Indian Painting, from antiquity until the dawn of the Islamic Moghul period, was generally murallike in style. Painting began to assume importance in the Gupta period, the most typical examples of these being frescoes executed on the walls of cave temples and in freestanding temples and palaces. Hindu or Buddhist religious themes dominate, but scenes of court life, feasts, love scenes, etc., are also common. Such major repositories of Indian painting as the caves of Ajanta date from the 5th and 6th centuries A.D. India's painting changed dramatically at the height of the Moghul period, in the 16th century. Moghul Islamic culture introduced Persian influences into India's painting. This new style emphasized high detail work and, with it, miniature painting. Subject matter included birds, portraits, and illustrations of legends.

Indian Sculpture falls into two general categories—northern works from such centers of artistic activity as Gandhara and Mathura and the southern, distinctly native Indian style, found in the lower Gangetic plain and southward. Gandhara's sculpture, dating from the early centuries A.D., shows Greco-Roman influences blended with Buddhist subject matter. A differing Buddhist style arose in Mathura. Typically carved in red sandstone, Mathura figures show a harsh and unexpressive Kushan influence, although after the 4th century A.D. sculpture from this region merged with India's Gupta style and took on Gupta elegance. A characteristic mark of southern Indian sculpture is the treatment of the human figure, which is full and sensuous, although anatomically less accurate than its Greco-Roman counterparts. The earliest important southern sculpture dates from the Mauryan Dynasty and is abundantly Buddhist.

Indian Terra Cotta begins with objects from or inspired by the Indus Valley civilization. Figurines of the mother-goddess and phallic fertility symbols come mainly from Harappa and Mohenjo-Daro. Vedic, or Aryan, terra cottas have been found over a widespread area, occurring throughout the subcontinent. Many of these appear to have been trinkets and religious cult objects of India's lower classes, and some may have been simple good-luck charms without any deep religious significance. Mother-goddess figurines, more nearly naturalistic than those of Indus Valley vintage, are unmistakably Aryan and persist well into the Mauryan period. Numerous terra cottas of the Gupta period show high artistic refinement; many depict Buddha and Bodhisattvas. Most terra-cotta work of high artistic merit dates from the Mauryan through the Gupta eras, later works being of little interest to scholars or collectors.

Indian painting: "The Three Sons of Shah Jehan." Miniature. Moghul period, ca. 1637 A.D. (British Museum, London)

Indian art: "Mother Goddess." Pink terra cotta. Mauryan period, 3rd century B.C. (Musée Guimet, Paris)

INDO-EUROPEANS. The term is mainly applicable to that family of peoples who spoke Indo-European languages. Linguistic traits shared by Indian languages, notably Aryan Sanskrit, by ancient Iranian languages, by Hittite and Hurrian, by Greek, Latin, Germanic, Celtic, Romance, and Slavic languages, all point to a common regional origin. No people who spoke the original Indo-European language can as yet be identified, although their early home, most probably, lay between the Black Sea and the Caspian Sea in about 2500 B.C. Some have pointed to the Battle-Axe People, who spread out from the Russian steppes, as possibly the earliest known Indo-Europeans, but this theory is conjectural.

INDONESIAN CIVILIZATION, a little-studied but interesting civilization that once spread along the Malay Peninsula into a major chain of islands southeast of Asia. Of the 3,000 islands there, Java, Sumatra, Bali, and Borneo are the most important in the cultural history of Indonesia. The prehistory of the region possibly begins about 10,000 years ago, when, it is thought, successive waves of Malays from the north drove most of the aboriginal population into Australia and New Guinea. The Malays, who later became farmers and seafarers, were fierce fighters who worshipped animistic spirits. The Niah caves of Borneo, as well as ancient wall paintings found elsewhere, attest to the antiquity of Indonesia. Chinese historians of the 3rd century B.C. describe the wealthy cities of Indonesia, but of these very little is known. Indonesia's historic period begins around the 7th century A.D., when an Indianized, Sumatra-based empire, the Srivijaya Dynasty, became dominant. It was soon overrun by a people of apparent hill culture from Java, who were related to the Khmers and who achieved cultural maturity and power as the Shailendra Dynasty, flourishing from 778 to 864. The Shailendra Dynasty, like its predecessor, was Indian-orientated. Both the Srivijaya and Shailendra dynasties left art and architectural remains throughout Indonesia with styles very similar to those of India. By the 12th or 13th century the Java-based Singosari Empire dominated the surrounding territory; it disintegrated at about the same time that the Mongol forces of Kublai Khan forayed into Indonesia. In 1293 the Javanese Madjapahit Dynasty became strong, gradually assuming greater territorial control than any previous Indonesian power. Its kingdom extended over Java and Sumatra and touched parts of Borneo, the Moluccas, and the Philippines. The Madjapahit government was well organized and constructed many roads, public buildings, and temples. Like its major predecessors, Madjapahit culture was highly Indianized. It ruled for about 100 years, then, weakened by Islamic encroachment and

Indian sculpture: "Buddha in Meditation." Sandstone high-relief. Ca. 10th century A.D. (British Museum, London)

naval setbacks at the hands of the Japanese, it collapsed. Both politically and culturally, imported Islamic influences dominated Indonesia until the 17th century, when Moslem power began losing ground to growing Dutch colonial interests throughout Indonesia. Ultimate Dutch rule spelled an end to native Indonesian government until the 20th century.

Indonesian Art and Antiquities derive from the multiple Asian and island cultures that touched the region, although by the late 1st millennium A.D. the major art styles

were those of Indian origin. However, before Indian culture reached Indonesia, a long tradition of bronze-casting existed on many of these islands. Extant bronze ceremonial axes and kettle drums might date from as early as 1000 B.C. The earliest existing art of Indian derivation—from Java of the 7th or 8th century A.D.—are statues and monuments of Siva worshippers. Fine examples of Buddhist art in earlier Indian-inspired styles (roughly 200 A.D.) have been found in Indonesia but were almost certainly imported from the Asian mainland. The Shailendra Dynasty built outstanding Buddhist architecture. Among the world's finest Buddhist structures, the massive stupa at Borobudur on Java dates from about the 9th century. Java is the richest source of Indonesian art, its craftsmen having produced many Buddhist and Hindu statues in stone, bronze, wood, and silver.

INDRA, originally the Aryan god of war and weather, often depicted with a thunderbolt in hand. As a later Hindu deity he was somewhat demoted, becoming guardian of the eastern quarter of the universe.

INDUS VALLEY CIVILIZATION, an ancient and enigmatic civilization in and around the Indus River Valley, in what is modern Pakistan and northwestern India. Its time of origin is unknown, but by the late 3rd millennium B.C. its two major cities, Harappa and Mohenjo-Daro, were prospering. The civilization probably reached its height around 2100 B.C. Before the 1850s, when British railroad developers found remains of a settlement at Harappa, Indus Valley culture was unknown to historians. It was not until the 1920s, with discovery of Mohenjo-Daro, that this culture was recognized as one of the major ancient civilizations. Details of Indus Valley culture are sparse, although it did have some contact with Mesopotamia before the year 2000 B.C. Examples of the pictographic writing of the Indus Valley civilization have not yet yielded to translation. Thus we know of the civilization only through archaeological discovery and through slight references made by the Sumerians, with whom the Indus peoples traded, and by the Aryans, who conquered and destroyed the civilization sometime about 1500 B.C. Indus Valley inhabitants were a dark-skinned race, probably Dravidians, who worshipped fertility goddesses, as well as certain deities that ultimately, in transformed versions, were passed down to Hindu culture. Their economy was agriculturally based, but their cities show a high state of development, having streets in gridiron patterns and well-constructed buildings, mainly of brick. The largest buildings included granaries and ritual baths. Their sewerage facilities were more highly advanced than those of subsequent Indian civilizations. At its height, Indus Valley civilization extended over a wider geographic area than the Sumer or early Egyptian cultures. However, it never progressed beyond a bronze-age technology. Its culture appears to have been in a state of decline immediately prior to its destruction by the Aryans. The bulk of our knowledge of Indus Valley civilization is largely due to research by the modern British archaeologist, Sir Mortimer Wheeler.

Indus Valley Art and Antiquities include, most notably, statuettes in stone, terra cotta, and bronze, as well as some finely carved steatite seals. The stone sculpture is rare, its best examples being naturalistic human torsos and busts. The terra cottas, many of which depict female figures, are often embellished with shells, beads, or lapis-lazuli decoration. These are probably goddess figurines. Bronzes that have survived are mostly in poor condition, the best among them being a few figures of young girls, found at Mohenjo-Daro. The carved seals are considered as probably the best surviving Indus Valley art objects. Nearly all of them show animals, such as bulls, elephants, water buffalo, and mythological creatures. Pottery is relatively abundant but is generally considered inferior to that of other advanced ancient civilizations.

INFRARED RAY EXAMINATION is among several modern techniques used to help determine an art object's origins and resolve questions of authenticity. Infrared light will penetrate thin surfaces, such as paint layers and patinas, to reveal the undersurface. Thus hidden clues may present new knowledge about an art object's origins. Also a false patina can be discovered by studying the stratum of dirt that invariably accumulates between the patina and the art object.

INHUMATION, burial of the dead in a grave or chamber. The body may be extended, flexed with the knees bent less than 90°, or crouched. Containers, when used, include coffins, sarcophagi, and jars.

INSULA, literally "island," a block of houses with an open space around them in a town planned on the grid principle. The term usually is applied to ancient Roman towns or camps.

INTAGLIO, design incised, etched, or engraved into stone, gems, or metals. Intaglio produces a concave instead of a convex effect and thus is the opposite of a relief carving. Typical examples are ancient seals, like those found at the Harappa site in the Indus Valley or in ancient Mesopotamia.

IONIAN CAPITAL, the distinctive feature of the Ionic order of Greek architecture, characterized by its lateral volutes resembling rams' horns. The Ionian capital had Near Eastern affinitives, and the Ionic order prevailed in eastern Greece, Asia Minor, and the neighboring islands. The Ionic order was lighter in proportion than the Doric order and more ornate in detail. Its column had a base and above the architrave a row of small projecting blocks (dentils) instead of the Doric triglyph frieze.

IONIANS, possibly the original Indo-European Greeks who entered the Peloponnesus around 2500 B.C. from somewhere north of the Balkans. Ionian arrival in Greece is considered the transition from the early to the middle

Indus Valley Civilization: Bust. Limestone. From Mohenjo-Daro. (Central Asian Antiquities Museum, New Delhi)

Islamic art: Decorated pottery bowl. 12th–13th centuries A.D. (Museum of Fine Arts, Boston; gift of Helen Norton in memory of Harry A. Norton)

bronze age in that area. Ionians take their name from their river god, Ion. They dominated the Greek peninsula until partial displacement by other invading Indo-Europeans—the Achaeans (Mycenaeans) around 2000 B.C., Aeolians at an unknown date, and Dorians around 1200 B.C. The ultimate cultural fusion of Ionians and other Indo-European tribes produced Greek civilization and art. By the 1st millennium B.C. Ionians controlled many Aegean islands and much of coastal Asia Minor, where their towns—e.g., Miletus—were among the most advanced. They gave their name to the Ionic order of architecture. It should be noted that many scholars believe that the Achaeans, not the Ionians, were the first Greek-speakers in Greece.

IPIUTAK, an ancient Alaskan culture, named for its type site of Ipiutak, near the modern village of Point Hope. Ipiutak culture flourished in the first centuries of the Christian era and is related to Arctic cultures of Siberia. Excavations at Ipiutak have uncovered the remains of approximately 700 houses, and graves that were spread over a wide area. Burials here have yielded elaborate ivory carvings, which include small sculptures of natural and fantastic animals, especially bears, ivory chains and swivels, and composite masks made of pieces of carved ivory. By analogy with the later Northwest Coast and Eskimo cultures, these art objects are thought to have been part of a shaman's regalia. In addition to ritual objects, everyday items, such as snow goggles and har-

Ishtar Gate: Fragment of wall leading to the gate. Glazed brick. Babylonian. (Louvre, Paris)

poon heads, were also elaborately carved. Ipiutak art marks the beginning of a long tradition of intricately designed small objects in the Arctic.

IRANIANS, an Indo-European people who migrated to northwest Persia from the steppes of central Asia in the 2nd millennium B.C.; they were related to the Aryans of India, the Hurrians, and the Medes, among others. The Iranians quickly imposed their rule on the native Persian population, at that time mainly Kassites. Among the cultural attributes of these people, as evidenced by considerable Iranian remains, were metal-working (e.g., Luristan bronzes), public and royal architecture (e.g., at Susa), pottery—particularly a red-painted ware—and ornamental horse trappings. During the 2nd millennium B.C. the Iranians enjoyed cultural and artistic contact with Mesopotamia, especially with the civilizations of Sumeria, Assyria, and Babylonia. The Achaemenid Dynasty, of which many splendors remain, was Iranian in ancestry, although its cultural style had a unique Persian character. The Iranians, of course, gave their name to Iran, the modern Persia.

IRON AGE, in archaeology, the last technological stage of a sequence that includes the ages of stone, bronze, and iron. Although meteoric iron was worked from Sumerian times, it was the Hittites, between 1900 and 1400 B.C., who mastered the technique of iron smelting and were considered the chief iron-workers of the ancient world. With the fall of the Hittite Empire in 1200 B.C., the secret skill of iron-making spread westward into Europe. Among the earliest European iron-workers were the Villanovans of Italy and the peoples of Hallstatt and La Tene in central Europe. It was 500 B.C. before iron-working reached Britain and Scandinavia. In other parts of the world the iron age arrived late or not at all. In Asia, the Chinese were casting iron in the 5th century B.C., but in Pre-Columbian America iron arrived only with the Spanish Conquest.

IROQUOIS. See **WOODLAND INDIAN CULTURE.**

ISE, Shinto shrine at Ujiyamada, on Honshu Island, Japan. The most important shrine in Japan, it represents the purest style of traditional ancient Japanese architecture. The inner shrine, or Great Shrine, is dedicated to the sun goddess Amaterasu and houses the sacred mirror. The ancient Yayoi style of the shrine is characterized by a heavy thatched roof, forked timbers, and a ridge pole with a crested decorative board ending in gables. The original structure dates from about the 7th century A.D., but the shrine itself is rebuilt every 20 years according to Shinto ritual. The outer shrine at Ise commemorates the food goddess, Toyo-uke-hime.

ISHTAR, the great goddess of the Sumerian pantheon, similar in attributes to the Palestinian Astarte. She had jurisdiction over sex, love, procreation, and war. She was

Ipiutak: Seal. Carved ivory. (American Museum of Natural History, New York)

156

Islamic art: Bronze vessel. Ca. 7th century A.D. (Museum of Islamic Art, Cairo)

mystery cult involving the death and resurrection of her husband, Osiris.

ISLAMIC ART AND ANTIQUITIES. After the death of the prophet Mohammed in the 7th century A.D., his Arab followers conquered lands east to Persia and west to Spain. Many nationalities came under Islam, and an international art style developed. Because of the paucity of art traditions among Arabs and their puritanical beliefs, natural representation of the human figure was forbidden to Islamic artists. Instead, Islamic creativity flowed toward architecture and the decorative arts. Among the most notable of early Islamic monuments are: the 7th-century Dome of the Rock in Jerusalem, the 8th-century desert palace Khirbat al-Mafjar in Jordan, and the 9th-century Mosque of Kairouan in Egypt. In later times Islamic architecture became eclectic, and from this period are such buildings as the Mosque of Selim in Turkey, the Mausoleum of Tamerlane in Samarkand, the Alhambra of Granada in Spain, and the Taj Mahal in India. Despite the almost breathtaking success of Islamic architecture, the true genius of Moslem art is revealed in the so-called minor arts: decorative Korans, finely carved wood, stone, and ivory, calligraphy, ceramics, furniture, metalwork, miniatures (essentially Persian in origin), and textiles and rugs. Ornament, pure ornament, pattern and decoration, is the essence of Islamic art.

ISRAEL. See HEBREW CIVILIZATION.

ISTANBUL. See BYZANTIUM.

ITALIC PEOPLES. The term covers a variety of peoples in Italy who emerged at dates roughly between the transition from the bronze to the iron ages, about 1000 to 500 B.C. It generally excludes, however, peoples with quite distinct origins outside Italy, such as the inhabitants of the Greek colonies and the Carthaginians in Sicily. The Etruscans, whose home was in Italy north of Rome, are a special case, for they ascribed their own origin to Lydia in Asia Minor, and their culture and language, still largely undeciphered, are quite distinct from those of other Italic peoples. The early Romans, who were ruled for about a century by Etruscan kings, owed many elements in their religion, political system, and mastery of civil engineering to the Etruscans. The Italic peoples properly so called comprise in the main the following groups: Raetians in the foothills of the Alps and Ligurians on the coast near Genoa; iron-age cultures, such as the Comacine-Golaseccan in the north, the Atestine near Venice, and the Villanovan in north-central Italy; the peoples inheriting the Apennine culture and speaking the Sabellian language in its northern, or Umbrian, and its southern, or Oscan, forms. Among these peoples are those who, in historic times, were the founders or the allies and fellow soldiers of Rome—namely, the Latins, Aequi, Sabines, Volscians, Samnites, and Apulians.

often represented seated on a lion and carrying a weapon. Ritual prostitution was part of her cult. Her husband was Tammuz. She was also known as Inanna.

ISHTAR GATE, one of the few monumental remains of ancient Babylon, located about 50 miles south of modern Baghdad. A magnificent structure, more than 35 feet high, it is built of brick, covered with blue-glazed tiles, and decorated with bulls and dragons in low relief. The bulls were painted yellow; the dragons (sacred to Marduk) were white with details in yellow. The Ishtar Gate was one of the splendors of the city.

ISIS, ancient Egyptian goddess, legendary daughter of Geb and Nut, wife of Osiris, and mother of Horus. Isis is goddess of the moon and bears some relationship to the Near Eastern love and fertility goddesses, Astarte and Ishtar. She is often depicted as a cow or as a woman with cow's horns. In Roman times Isis was the center of a

J

JADE, a hard semiprecious mineral found mainly in Burma and Turkestan and in Middle America. It is a silicate of aluminum or calcium with sodium or magnesium. The two types—jadeite and nephrite—range in color from white to green and have been superbly carved by Chinese and Pre-Columbian American artisans.

JAGUAR-GOD. The worship of the jaguar-god was one of the great unifying themes of most of the early cultures of Pre-Columbian America. This deity is especially prominent in the art of the two earliest civilizations of the New World, the Olmec of Mexico and the Chavin of Peru; he also appears in the San Agustin culture of Colombia, which is sometimes considered the link between the two civilizations. The iconography of the jaguar is not completely clear. At various times he seems to be a rain god, the night sun as it passes through the underworld, an emblem of royal lineage, and a symbol associated with shamanism and sorcery. In Aztec and Toltec times the jaguar was the most important emblem of the warrior class. Representations of the jaguar-god are widespread in the pottery, sculpture, painting, and weaving of the earliest New World civilizations. Some scholars believe the jaguar-god was derived from ancient China.

Jade: Plaque. Mayan, ca. 750 A.D. From Nebaj, Guatemala. (La Aurora Museum, Guatemala City)

Jaina figure: Painted terra cotta. Mayan, 600–800 A.D. (National Museum of Anthropology, Mexico City)

JAINA FIGURES, highly prized Mayan statuettes, first found on the island of Jaina, off the Mexican coast of Campeche. These extremely elegant figurines, among the greatest in Pre-Columbian art, were used as burial offerings in the centuries before and after 900 A.D. Though of different styles, Jaina figures generally offer sophisticated portrayals of Mayan nobles, warriors, priests, and old matrons. The only deity represented with frequency was the so-called Fat God, a divinity whose function is still unknown but who was popular among Mexican peoples of the era. Jaina faces were made from molds with details added by hand. After firing, the whole figurine was painted in bright polychrome colors.

JAIN ART AND ANTIQUITIES, the sculpture, paintings, and temples of the Jains, an ascetic sect founded by Mahavira in the 6th century B.C. in India. The stupa, chaitya hall, and rock-cut caves are early architectural forms. Typical Jain architecture is the elaborately carved white marble sanctuaries of Mount Abu at Rajputana; the temples have a courtyard-enclosed sanctuary surrounded by 24 smaller sanctuary niches. Temples built during the 15th century A.D. and later show Islamic influences. Early Jain sculpture was quite similar to Buddhist art, and statues of Mahavira emphasized abstract treatment of the body. A distinct Jainist iconography developed during the Gupta period, and icons of the 24 *tirthankaras* were intricately carved and often inlaid. However, their modelling was often conventional and lifeless. Jainist painting developed quite an individual style, as illustrated in the 13th-century Gujarat illuminations; but while the color and linear quality of these paintings are truly elegant, the composition is mechanical.

Jain Iconography. The main images of Jainist veneration are the *tirthankaras*, men who already have attained perfection in earlier cycles of life. Early Jainist art often depicts these saints completely nude in accordance with the ascetic example set by the founder, Mahavira. The *tirthankaras* are portrayed either standing rigidly or in *yogasana*, with a jewel on their chest and a Wheel of Law on their thrones. In the 5th century A.D. Jainist sects produced two different kinds of images. The "clothed in white" images were dressed in loincloths, while the "clothed in space" images remained nude. Also depicted in Jain art are Hindu deities, sacred mountain cities, world diagrams, mandalas, and legends of the *tirthankaras*.

JAPANESE CIVILIZATION, one of the great civilizations of the Orient, took root on the large Asian islands of Hokkaido, Honshu, Shikoku, and Kyushu, and smaller adjacent islands, off the coast of China. The first evidence of human burial here appears in Jomon culture, which

Jain art: "The Consecration of Mahavira." Miniature illustrating the *Kalpasutra* manuscript. 1404 A.D. From Gujarat. (British Museum, London)

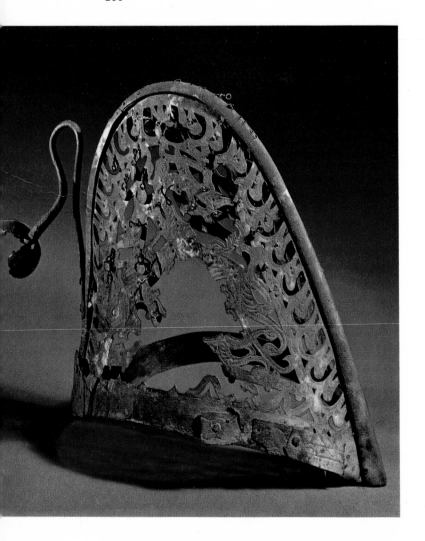

Japanese bronze: Head ornament. Gilt bronze. Kofun period, 5th century A.D. (National Museum, Tokyo)

Chinese system of writing was adopted, and in 604 Prince Shotoku issued a constitution setting forth the rights of the major clans. The Nara period (710–794) saw the beginning of Japan's written body of history with the appearance of the *Kojiki* and the *Nihon Shoki*. Both Buddhism and Shinto took firm root in Japanese soil. With the removal of the royal capital from Nara to Heian (now Kyoto), the Heian period (784–1184) began, and a culture that was truly distinct from its mainland ancestry developed in Japan. Powerful clans took control of local government, and at the end of the period the Minamoto clan established a military government at Kamakura. The Kamakura period (1185–1333) was the beginning of the Japanese feudal age, when the emperor was only a figurehead and military shoguns were the true rulers. During this time the Mongols twice invaded Japan but were repelled. The government returned to Kyoto in 1338, amid the continuation of civil strife among the clans. In the 16th century Spanish Jesuit missionaries and Portuguese traders entered Japan. The Momoyama period (1573–1600) saw the clans finally subjugated by Nobunaga and Hideyoshi, military leaders who were subservient to the Imperial Court. During this era class lines became fixed, and foreigners were banished from Japan. In 1595, with the ascension of the Tokugawa shogun, which began the Edo (or Tokyo) period, the country's feudal lords took their places in a system that fully accepted centralized leadership and remained virtually unchanged until 1868. Clan lands were redistributed, and the four class lines—samurai, or warriors, peasants, artisans, and merchants—became rigid. In 1853 a U.S. naval fleet under Matthew Perry entered Tokyo Bay and virtually forced a treaty between the United States and Japan. Thus ended Japan's centuries-long isolation from the rest of the world.

Japanese Bronze and Metalwork. Bronze was known as early as the 3rd or 2nd centuries B.C. in Japan. Early decorative bronze mirrors were influenced by Chinese counterparts, but the more indigenous *dotaku*, or bronze bells, were characterized by distinctive linear decoration. The arrival of Buddhism in Japan in 552 saw the first casting of bronze statues; the Sakyamuni Triad, at Nara, made by Tori in 623, is a particularly fine example. Other fine Nara period bronzes include the Amida Triad, a Buddhist bronze altar now in the Tokyo Museum; and the famous Great Buddha of Nara, which is 53 feet high and one of the largest bronze figures in the world. From a later period but nearly as large is the 52-foot Great Buddha of Kamakura, cast in the mid-13th century. After that time bronze sculpture declined, but Japanese metal craftsmen continued producing such notable works as relief-decorated cast-iron tea kettles for the country's tradi-

Japanese painting: "The Kabuki," detail. Painted paper screen. Edo period, 17th century A.D. (National Museum, Tokyo)

marked the start of the Japanese neolithic period around 6000 B.C. The Jomon people appear to have been northern Asiatics, similar to the modern Ainu rather than to Mongoloids. Between the 5th and 3rd centuries B.C. there gradually dawned the Yayoi period, when Mongoloid types migrated to Kyushu from coastal China and Korea. They brought with them rice cultivation, the pottery wheel, and the use of iron and bronze. Yayoi houses were built on ground level and resembled Japanese country dwellings of today. The subsequent Great Tombs, or Kofun, period, which emerged in the 3rd century A.D., was characterized by a highly aristocratic society that built huge mound tombs and established a ruling clan headed by an emperor believed to have descended from the heavens. From this time onward the Japanese emperor, more a priest than a ruler, was recognized as the leader of the national religion—which came to be called Shinto and deified nature spirits—while his secular leadership was often to become merely nominal. Japan's second major religion, Buddhism, was introduced to the country in 552, at the start of the Asuka period, a time of cultural borrowing from China and Korea and a period during which learning and the arts flourished. The

Japanese painting: In colors on silk. Heian period, 12th century A.D. (National Museum, Tokyo)

tional tea ceremony and the exquisitely designed and inlaid *tsuba*, or sword jewelry, of the Tokugawa period.

Japanese Painting. Early Japanese tomb and temple murals followed Chinese models, and a true Japanese style did not evolve until the 11th century, in the form of *yamato-e*. *Yamato-e* painters preferred the narrative scroll, although they typically subordinated narrative elements to the abstract patterns of their forms. The Kamakura period saw the refinement of portrait painting, with favored subjects being Buddhist saints and monks and Japan's traditional 36 Immortal Poets. During the Muromachi period in the 14th century the dominant painting style became *sumi-e*—ink-painted landscapes influenced by Sung Chinese works and Zen Buddhism. Masters of *sumi-e* included Josetsu, Shubun, Sesshu, and Sesson. The Kano family school, a major offshoot of *sumi-e* painting, began to flourish in the 14th century, while the Tosa family carried on the *yamato-e* tradition. Genre painting appeared in the Momoyama era and later developed in a style called *ukiyo-e,* which means "floating world." These paintings and prints of everyday life—which attempted to capture a moment of reality before it floated away forever—were popular during the Edo period. At about the same time, the Korin school produced some of the greatest Japanese paintings.

Japanese Porcelain. Despite Japan's proximity to China— the birthplace of porcelain—the industry did not achieve artistic importance until the late 1600s, in the early Tokugawa period. At that time, deposits of the proper clays were found on Kyushu, and the craft began flowering in surrounding towns. Among the best is procelain from Kutani—designated Old Kutani ware—and, after 1722, porcelain from Nabishima. Also of generally fine quality are Imari and Kakiemon wares. Designs on early pieces are typically bright and loosely drawn, lacking the delicacy and precision of Chinese porcelains. Slightly later, a tradition of artist-potters arose around Kyoto, the most famous figure being Kenzan (1664–1743), who made magnificently decorated porcelains in unusual shapes. Many 19th-century porcelains from Daishoji (a town near Kutani) have been incorrectly labeled and wrongly attributed as Old Kutani. Also, some pieces until recently believed to be Kakiemon have proved to be copies.

Japanese Sculpture. Although most surviving early Japanese sculpture is in bronze or clay, Japanese sculptors excelled at the working of wood. Buddhist figures of the Asuka period are quite plastic and have faces exhibiting the perfect expression of Buddhist inner harmony. The Nara period felt influence from Gupta India, with a resulting increase in naturalism; but by the

OVERLEAF—Japanese art: *Page 164*: Kimono. Silk. Momoyama period. (National Museum, Tokyo) *Page 165*: Statue of Sogyo Hachiman. Wood. Kamakura period. (Museum of Fine Arts, Boston; contribution of the Maria Antoinette Evans Fund)

Japanese porcelain: Kakiemon ware (*above*) and Kutani ware (*below*). Edo period, late 17th century A.D. (Museum of Fine Arts, Boston; Edward S. Morse Foundation)

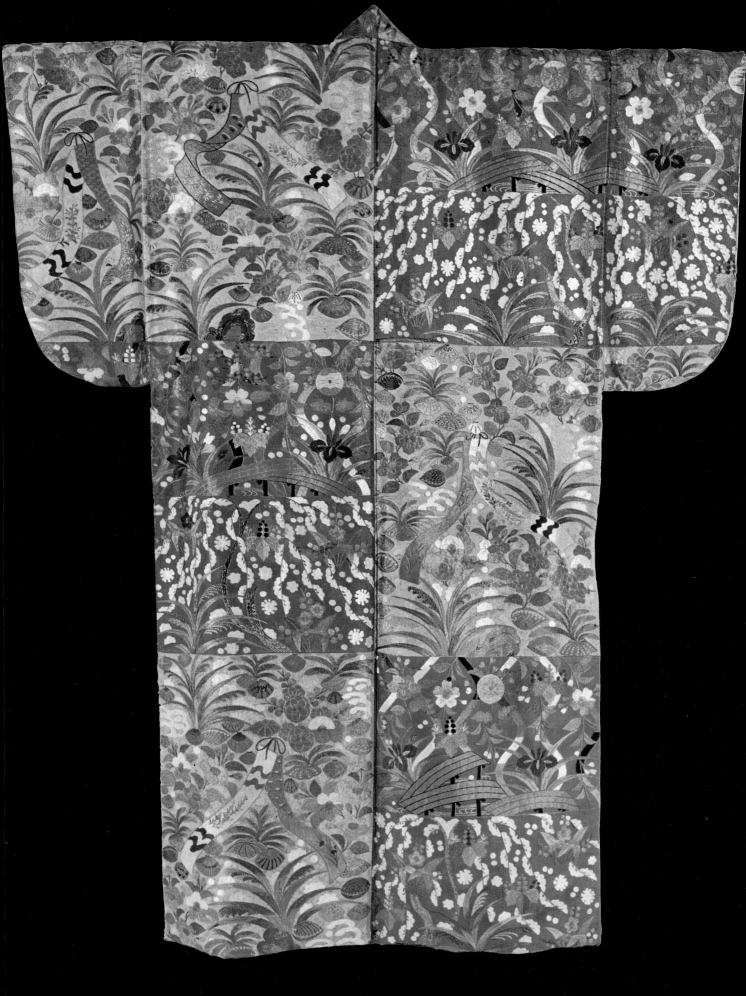

early Heian era, sculpture had become manneristic and heavy. By this time sculptors were becoming less anonymous, and probably the period's greatest artist was the monk-sculptor Jocho. His great wooden Buddha Amida at Byodo-in was carved in 1053. The Kamakura period saw the last flowering of Japanese sculpture, with the Buddhist religious establishment remaining the art's major patron. The pieces produced at that time, particularly the portrait sculpture, have vigor and realism as their chief attributes.

Japanese Terra Cotta. The earliest Japanese terra cotta appears in the Jomon culture in the form of primitive female figurines and in skillful and imaginative pottery. The Kofun *haniwa* figures, which were coil-made and modelled with bamboo sticks, show a remarkable plasticity for so early a period. Clay was a popular medium for several imposing Buddhist sculptures of the Nara period. Early Japanese pottery follows Chinese types and techniques, but toward the end of the Fujiwara period the kilns established at Seto began producing subtle Japanese designs. The Momoyama period was well known for sculptural Oribe ware, decorated with abstract designs, and for Raku, a ware considered ideal for the tea ceremony.

JARMO, a village site in the Kurdish mountains of northeastern Iraq, about 35 miles east of Kirkuk. Some 16 levels of this very early agricultural community have been excavated, dating from around 6500 B.C. No pottery was found in the first 11 levels, but there was a considerable quantity of chipped and polished stone implements and vessels. Houses were built of clay (bricks were still unknown), and primitive grains were grown. The goat, and perhaps the dog, had been domesticated; wild pigs, sheep, gazelles, and cattle were hunted. The pottery that appeared at the higher levels here and at similar sites is known as Jarmo ware. Bone jewelry has been excavated, as well as figures of animals and the Mother Goddess.

JATAKAS. See SHUNGA DYNASTY.

JEHOVAH. See YAHWEH.

JELLING STONE. See NORDIC PEOPLES.

JERICHO, one of the oldest, continuously occupied sites in the world, now known as Tell es-Sultan, at the north end of the Dead Sea. Jericho was apparently first inhabited around 8000 B.C. A millennium later it had developed into a town defended by massive stone walls surrounding solid mud-brick houses; its inhabitants had a thriving agricultural economy. A number of plastered human skulls have been found dating from this period. A series of fortified towns followed, occupied by various peoples, carrying down to around 1600 B.C., when the Egyptians destroyed a Hyksos settlement here. From this period notable tombs have been excavated, with pottery, bronzes, and well-preserved woodwork. The town was again conquered, and its walls destroyed, by the Israelites under Joshua in the 13th century B.C.

JERUSALEM, one of the world's holiest of cities, is sacred to Jews, Christians, and Moslems. Now situated in Israel, ancient Jerusalem was founded in the mid-3rd millennium B.C. but became a true town only in the 19th century B.C., when the Jebusites, a Canaanite people, settled here. Jebusite Jerusalem was sacked by Joshua in the 13th century B.C. and captured in about 1000 B.C. by the Hebrews under King David, who established his capital here. Solomon expanded the city in the 10th century B.C. and built his great temple here. Soon after his death the union of northern and southern Hebrew kingdoms dissolved, and Jerusalem became the capital of the southern kingdom of Judah. In 597 B.C. Nebuchadnezzar of Babylonia captured the city and carried off much of its population to captivity in Babylon. About ten years later, following a Jewish rebellion, he completely destroyed the city and Solomon's Temple. Later in the 6th century B.C., when the Persians became the new masters of the Near East, Jerusalem and Solomon's Temple were rebuilt under their patronage, and Jews were allowed to return to the sacred city. In the late 1st century B.C. Herod the Great built his temple near the ancient temple site. The Jews revolted against Roman rule in 70 A.D., and Titus captured and destroyed Jerusalem. It soon after became a Roman city, to which Jews were forbidden entry. The city fell to the Moslems in the 7th century A.D. and remained in Moslem hands until 1967, when it was recaptured by the Israelis. The Islamic Dome of the Rock is said to be built on the original site of Solomon's Temple.

JOMON CULTURE, prehistoric Japanese culture lasting from about 6000 B.C. until the 3rd century B.C. Considered the first Japanese culture, its people made a characteristic cord-impressed pottery and lived in thatched houses built over two- to three-foot-deep pits about 15 feet in diameter. There was no agriculture until perhaps 4000 B.C.; the hunting and gathering, particularly of shellfish, left identifying shell mounds. Jomon skeletons are not distinctly Mongoloid and indicate that the Jomons may have migrated from northern Asia. Jomon culture thrived in eastern and northern Japan.

JORDANOVA, a neolithic settlement and large cemetery in Polish Silesia near Nimptsch. The pottery found here is incised or painted. Some metal objects of copper were discovered, indicating the beginning of copper-founding. Jordanova has given its name, as a type site, to the most northerly of sub-cultures belonging to the Lengyel, that great Danubian blend of cultures formed after 2500 B.C. The others were the Wolfsbach of Lower Austria and the Munchshofen of Upper Austria and Bavaria.

JUDAISM. See HEBREW CIVILIZATION.

JUNO. See HERA.

JUPITER. See ZEUS.

JUTES, a Germanic tribe whose name is perpetuated in the peninsula of Denmark known as Jutland. Not very much is known about this people. The region of their settlements probably extended to the mouths of the Rhine. They took part in the Anglo-Saxon invasions of England in the 5th century A.D., when a power vacuum had been created by the fall of the Roman Empire. The part of England conquered and settled by the Jutes was mainly the county of Kent and the Isle of Wight. Exquisite Jute jewelry has been discovered in Kent.

K

KA, an Egyptian hieroglyph designating a man's soul; similar terms—*Ba* and *Akh*—have slightly different connotations. Ka was used chiefly in funeral texts, and it was represented by two extended arms.

KACHINAS. A prominent part of the mythology of the Pueblo Indians of the American Southwest, kachinas may themselves be beneficent divinities, or merely messengers who carry man's prayers to the gods. The kachinas, of which 300 types have been identified, are represented by the masked and costumed dancers of the kachina cult who usually perform their ceremonies in underground chambers known as kivas. In order to instruct children in their religion, the Pueblo people made kachina dolls which faithfully reproduced the characteristics of each kachina. The older, traditional dolls are very stiff, with little bodily detail. However, due to the great demand by collectors for kachina dolls, with its ensuing commercial advantages, the dolls have become more naturalistic in style. Kachina face masks, used by the sacred kachina dancers, are made of wood, and their features may range from simple stylized forms to fantastic but artistic distortions.

KAILASANATHA TEMPLE. See ELLORA.

KALI, Hindu goddess of death and destruction. She is the terrible form of Parvati, the consort of Siva. Kali is represented as an emaciated black hag with enormous eyes, dripping blood, and carrying skulls.

KALYX KRATER, one type of a large wide-mouthed vessel used by the Greeks for mixing water with wine. It was named for the two scroll-like handles rising above the rim, shaped like the calyx of a flower.

KAMAKURA PERIOD, a time of warrior rule in Japan begun in 1185 A.D. by Minamoto Yoritomo. He moved the government from Kyoto to Kamakura and established himself as the shogun, or hereditary military dictator, and thus instituted the first stage of the feudalism that would dominate Japan for the next several centuries. Relations with China were resumed, and Zen Buddhism, *sumi-e* painting, and salvation Buddhist sects like the Amida made their appearance. Although the artistic center remained at Kyoto, military virtues were now combined with traditional Japanese elegance to form new artistic standards. The period ended with the rise of the *daimyo*, or territorial lords.

KAMARES WARE, an elegant painted pottery with very thin sides produced at the Cretan centers of Knossos and Phaestos between 2000 and 1500 B.C. The painter-potters used white, red, and yellow on a dark ground, and motifs included delicate spirals, scrolls, stars, suns, leaves, and flowers in a rich, imaginative manner. This was the first time in early Aegean civilization that such pains were taken with the humble pottery of everyday life.

KAMI. See SHINTO ART AND ANTIQUITIES.

KANESH. See KULTEPE.

KANCHI, also Kanchipuram, a coastal city in southern India, sacred to Hindus. It is the site of several 6th-to-8th-century A.D. temples of Dravidian origin. The capital of the Pallava kings and a center of learning, the city is best known for a Kailasanatha temple built around 700 A.D. by Rajasimhavarman and dedicated to Siva and Parvati. The temple is basically a pyramidal tower built of small barrel vaults with a stupalike cupola at the top. Another notable temple here is Vaikuntha Perumal.

KANG HSI PERIOD, in Chinese history, an epoch named after the early Ching (Manchu) Dynasty emperor who reigned in Peking between A.D. 1661 and 1772. The period saw an abundance of extremely fine porcelain in an incredible variety of colors and bearing designs of unsurpassed draftsmanship. The major porcelain center was the city of Chingtechen, in Kiangsi. Kang Hsi porcelain falls into several categories. Notable are the *famille verte*, decorated mainly in greens and yellows; the *famille noir*, bright colors against a black background; and the *famille rose*, a late development incorporating shades of red.

KANO, a school of Japanese painters who based their style on Chinese-inspired *sumi-e* landscapes; they reached their height of popularity as professional court painters during the Momoyama and Edo periods. The Kano painters were descendants, adopted or real, of Kano Masanoba (1434–1530), a warrior-class painter. The characteristic Kano style is boldly decorative and brilliant in color and effect. Among the best known of the Kano painters are Eitoku, Tanyu, Sanraku, and Sansetsu.

KANSU, northwestern province of China and a center of neolithic Chinese culture before 2000 B.C. Several early cultural groups in the area include the Pan Shan, whose buff paste, painted pottery with clay relief was similar to Caucasian pottery, and the Ma-ch'ang, who produced a coarser type of pottery. The region remained important to Chinese cultural development because it served as a link to central Asia and the Russian steppes.

KANTHAROS, a Greek wine cup with two high handles rising well above the lip. The kantharos is deeper and on a higher stem than the kylix. Early versions of the kantharos (8th century B.C.) have a flat base and no stem.

KAOLIN, a well-decayed feldspar, one of the essential ingredients, along with petuntse, of Chinese porcelain. Also called china clay, kaolin is found in Kiangsi Province and elsewhere.

KARANOVO, an ancient village site in eastern Bulgaria with a tell, or mound, which revealed a valuable series of occupation levels in 40 feet of earth. The first level is of the neolithic and dates from 5000 B.C., or earlier, when farming had just begun in the region. The last level is of the bronze age about 1300–1200 B.C. During this long period the wattle and daub huts of the villagers show a development from scattered square huts to larger and more elaborate rectangular ones, with porches, plaster, and paint. A clay seal of about 4000 B.C. found at Karanovo has symbols which may be an early form of writing related to that of Tartaria.

KARASUK CULTURE flourished on the central Asian steppes during the late 2nd and early 1st millennium B.C. By about 1100 B.C. the Karasuk people, of Mongoloid racial stock, began displacing the Andronovo people in the eastern steppe region. At about this time the Karasuks were also migrating into Mongolia and establishing some contacts with China's Chou Dynasty. The art of the Karasuk people marks the first unmistakable manifestation of steppe animal-style bronzes. Their metalwork, especially their bronze knives, shows some Chinese influence, mainly in the use of animal heads for handle decoration. The economic well-being of the Karasuks was largely based on their success as animal herdsmen; they apparently attached religious significance to their animals, which comes forth in their art. Karasuk influence in metalworking spread across Asia and is seen as far west as in early South Russian art objects.

KARATEPE, a fortress-settlement on the west bank of the Ceyhan River in southern Turkey. Discovered and excavated in the 1940s, it appears to be the remains of a Sea People's town dating from the 8th century B.C. Its builder, a local ruler named Asitawandas, left bilingual inscriptions on the gateway in Hittite and Phoenician. These have been enormously useful in the decipherment of the Hittite language. In addition, a series of stone reliefs was found, quite unsophisticated in workmanship and design but informative of the period and place. The short-lived fortress-town appears to have been destroyed by fire.

KARNAK, an Upper Egyptian site, famous for its temple to Amon, patron god of Thebes, which was situated directly across the Nile from the temple. This massive and complex temple originated around 2000 B.C.—during the 12th Dynasty—as a simple structure. During the 18th Dynasty, when Karnak became the capital of the New Kingdom, the temple assumed vast proportions, ultimately covering an area of about 200,000 square yards. Its largest component, the Great Hypostyle Hall (i.e., the hall resting on pillars), dates from Seti I and Ramses II (14th century B.C.) and contains 134 pillars, decorated with relief figures and hieroglyphics. Among the last important structures built at Karnak was a huge entry gate, dating from the 8th century B.C., during the reign of the Nubian king Taharqa. Near to Karnak is Luxor.

KASSEL APOLLO, a Roman copy of a Greek bronze believed to have been the work of the 5th-century B.C. Greek master Phidias. It is in Kassel, Germany.

KASSITES, a people, possibly Elamite horsemen, from the Zagros mountains between Iran and Mesopotamia. They descended onto the Mesopotamian plain and attacked Babylonia early in the 2nd millennium B.C. Although at first repulsed, they later took advantage of the abortive Hittite raid on Babylon around 1600 B.C. to occupy that city, which they held for more than four centuries. In the 12th century B.C. Babylon was taken by Assyria and Elam, and the Kassites withdrew to the Zagros mountains. Few antiquities have come down from the Kassite occupation period of Babylon. Among these are the renovations to the city of Ur; a building at Warka, which for the first time known used molded brick to form relief figures; and a large number of sculptured boundary stones.

KAVAKAVA. See EASTER ISLAND.

KERAMEIKOS CEMETERY, a large and ancient necropolis near the Athenian Agora and the Dipylon gate. It probably originated as a burial ground in the 12th century B.C., and excavations here have revealed magnificent examples of Geometric-style pottery and grave goods. Enormous vessels of the Geometric period, known as Dipylon vases, have been unearthed; they often are decorated with black silhouettes of mourners, chariots, and animals, painted within the lines of geometric pattern. Kerameikos has also yielded early free-standing Greek statues, among them the famous "Dipylon statue," which once stood more than eight feet high; it depicts a male and probably served as his funerary monument. Other finds from various periods of Greek art include a stone sphinx, richly carved gravestones, and sculptured column bases. Most of the antiquities of Kerameikos can be seen at the Kerameikos Museum, Athens.

KEROS. See INCAN CIVILIZATION.

KHAJURAHO, site in north Madhya Pradesh, India, of magnificent Hindu and Jain temples built by the Chandela Rajputs from 950 to 1050 A.D. The site, which covers about eight square miles, contains 28 of the original 85 temples representing the high point of Indo-Aryan architectural genius. Typical temple structures here emphasize the vertical with a mass of domes and turrets culminating in a crowning finial. The Khajuraho temples are adorned inside and out with ornate carvings and sculptured figures famous for their grace and vitality.

KHAMSA. See PERSIAN MINIATURES.

KHIROKITIA CULTURE, a neolithic culture on Cyprus of exceptional originality, first excavated and studied in the 1950s. Unearthed were more than 1,000 densely clustered round and vaulted stone dwellings and paved streets dating from about 5500 B.C. Characteristic of Khirokitia are stone artifacts of high quality, especially large stone bowls, some with incised decorations, fiddle-shaped idols, and pottery of geometric design in red on white ground.

KHITANS, a nomadic central Asian people who, in the 10th century A.D., settled in southern Manchuria, thus making contact with Chinese civilization. They soon established a Manchurian dynasty of their own—the Liao Dynasty—which lasted until about 1125 and adopted Buddhism. They built numerous octagonal pagodas, usually seven to 13 stories high. Their glazed pottery resembles Chinese Tang ware but has distinctive shapes, most notable being the so-called cockscomb vase, derived from the shape of a nomad's leather flagon.

KHMER CIVILIZATION, native Cambodian civilization that lasted for more than 1,000 years. It reached its zenith during the 9th to 12th centuries A.D., when it centered at Angkor and controlled the area of modern Cambodia and parts of Thailand, Laos, and Vietnam. The Khmers were present in Cambodia as early as the 1st century A.D., along with the Funanese and the Chams. They were Hinduized and used the Indian alphabet. When the Chenla kingdom disintegrated in the 8th century, the Khmers filled the vacuum. King Jayavarman II returned to Cambodia in 790, and in 802 he founded his capital 20 miles from Angkor. He originated the Khmer Dynasty by establishing himself as a "divine mountain" king. The dynasty removed to Angkor under the rule of Indravarman (877–889), and here the great irrigation system, which became the source of prosperity and strength for Khmer civilization, was engineered. The first *baray*, or reservoir, for this system was a vast monumental undertaking. Suryavarman II built Angkor Wat, one of the largest of the Angkor temples, during his reign (1112–1152). The god-king dynasty was ended by the invading Chams in 1177, but the empire continued. The Chams were driven from Angkor by Jayavarman VII in 1181. He extended Khmer power to its farthest borders and introduced Buddhism. During his reign (1181–1201) the temple of Angkor Thom was begun. In order to build this colossal structure many of the earlier buildings were torn down. His death marked the decline of the Khmers. The kingdom had been weakened by massive royal building programs; the irrigation system had been neglected; and people were diverted from rice cultivation to building. Successive incursions by the Thais again drove the Khmer kings from Angkor, and 15th-century Siamese invasions eliminated the Khmer nobility and priesthood. Although the Khmers retook Angkor in the 16th century and rebuilt it, Khmer civilization was at an end.

Khmer Art and Antiquities. Early Khmer art was influenced by Indian Gupta styles; the sculpture was elegant and had a native Khmer quality in its simple surfaces and precisely engraved details. Architecture was based on the diminishing tier style—square towers rising in smaller stories with outstandingly carved lintels. During the classic Khmer period (800–1000) temples became a physical symbol of the universe. The earliest of the temple "mountains" is the Bakong built by Indravarman in 881. Essentially, these temples were tiered levels of small shrines combined to form a complicated mass. Supple and natural sculptured panels decorated these temples. By

Khajuraho: Detail of decoration on the Temple of Kandariya Mahadeva.

Khmer art: "March of the Champa Army," detail. Relief, early 13th century A.D. Bayon Temple, Angkor Thom, Cambodia.

the 10th century a definite Khmer style was established; faces were structured by incised eyebrows and stylized hair styles, and clothing was rigidly depicted. In the last phase (1000–1450) Khmer art was flamboyant, with exuberant carvings covering the entire surface of temples and huge face masks appearing on their towers. Sculptured faces assumed the characteristic lowered eyelids and beatific smile of high Khmer art.

KHORSABAD, a village in Iraq about 12 miles north of Mosul. It is the site of the ancient Dur Sharrukin, or Fort of Sargon. Built by Sargon II as his capital of Assyria, it was dedicated in 706 B.C., the year before the king's death, and was deserted shortly thereafter. Excavations of Dur Sharrukin have revealed a magnificent palace in a mile-square city. The palace was protected by Lamassu, the winged, human-headed bulls of Assyrian mythology, carved in low relief. In the palace complex was a ziggurat. Among the other buildings found was the temple of Nabu, with its mysterious carved figures. Many reliefs celebrating Assyrian military prowess were discovered, as were domestic wall paintings, bronze figurines, and ivory inlays. Many Khorsabad antiquities are now in the Louvre.

KHUFU PYRAMID. See GREAT PYRAMID.

KIEV, an ancient city in the Soviet Ukraine, located on the River Dnieper. An early center of Slavic culture, with settlement sites dating from the 1st millennium B.C., Kiev was destined to become the cradle of Russian civilization. It was originally occupied by the Rus, a Slavic people, but in 882 A.D. the city was annexed by Oleg, a Varangian prince of Scandinavian ancestry. At that time it was a major settlement on the great trade route between Scandinavia and Constantinople. In the late 10th century Vladimir, great prince of Kiev and a descendant of the Varangian ruling house, converted to Christianity. Early Slavic artists in Kiev, prior to the Christian period, remained unaffected by Varangian art and, in the ancient manner, continued to erect wooden temples and innumerable idols of wood, and worked metals, such as silver, bronze, and copper, in the nomadic styles of the Eurasian steppes. Unfortunately, Vladimir, after his conversion, ordered all pagan Slavic art destroyed.

KIMON, Greek painter of the late 6th century B.C. An almost legendary figure, he is the first Greek artist who is not merely a name. Kimon is said to have introduced movement to the traditionally rigid poses of Greek art and to have carefully rendered the fall and folds of drapery garments. His innovations are reflected in the red-figure vase painting of his time.

KIRKUK, a large town in northeastern Iraq and the site of the ancient city of Nuzi. It has yielded up antiquities

Khmer Civilization: The Bayon Temple, early 13th century A.D. Angkor Thom, Cambodia.

which are believed to show the influence of the Mitanni, dating from around the mid-2nd millennium B.C. Among these are two pairs of large glazed-clay lions, which may have guarded a temple gate; a small green faience head of a boar; fragments of wall painting from private houses; and painted pottery believed typical of Mitanni ware.

KISH, ancient Sumerian city-state near Babylon, about 50 miles south of modern Baghdad, Iraq. Occupied from the 4th millennium B.C., Kish became an important center of Sumerian civilization around 3200 B.C., but by 2600 B.C. it was overshadowed by the rival city of Ur. Occupation of Kish continued until the early centuries A.D. Excavations in 1912, and continued between 1923 and 1933, uncovered a Sumerian palace, a temple showing early use of columns, the remains of a large ziggurat, and cuneiform tablets inscribed with fragments of a Creation epic.

KITCHEN-MIDDEN PEOPLE. On the coasts of northern Europe, from about 5000 to 2000 B.C., the so-called Kitchen-Midden People lived in small settlements on top of heaps of mollusk shells, bones, and other refuse, called middens. They lived not only on shellfish but on fish,

Knossos: The Great Palace (partially reconstructed).

fowl, and big game from the forests, including deer and aurochs. They used small axes made of deer antlers, bows and flint-tipped arrows, very fine flint tools, and simple pottery. The neolithic agricultural revolution, though contemporary, had not yet reached them from the Near East. Their only domesticated animal was the dog. The discovery of these kitchen-middens in north Jutland, Denmark, was made in 1849.

KIVA, a sacred underground chamber used by Pueblo Indians of the American Southwest. The construction of kivas reached its height between 1000 and 1200 A.D. when they were incorporated into the great cliff towns of the region. The kiva is a circular structure, although it may be rectangular, and is entered through a hole in its roof, which symbolizes the entry of man into the underworld. Kivas served as a center for the kachina cult and were often decorated with wall paintings of a ceremonial·nature.

KIVIK, in southern Sweden, is the site of a decorated stone slab, a funerary monument from the bronze age, approximately 1000 B.C., on which is depicted a group of women gathered round a cauldron while lines of captives are being slaughtered. Strabo in the 1st century B.C. mentions a similar ceremony of the Cimbri, whose original

home was on the Jutland peninsula of Denmark. Kivik is also the site of one of the largest grave mounds in Scandinavia.

KLEIN-ASPERGLE, the site of a large Celtic grave mound near Ludwigsburg in Wurttemberg, Germany. Excavations of the mound revealed gold and silver ornaments, bronze vessels, and two bowls with handles, which were of Greek origin of the 5th century B.C. The contents of this grave and of the Hildesheim site indicate the considerable wealth of many German tribal chieftains, acquired either by trading or as booty in war.

KNOSSOS, a major Minoan archaeological site, on the north coast of Crete, near Herakleion. Discovered and excavated, from 1900 to 1935, by the great British archaeologist Sir Arthur Evans, Knossos proved to be one of the most brilliant cities of its age. Here were rich villas and a vast palace, said to have been that of the legendary King Minos, who gave his name to Minoan civilization. Destroyed and rebuilt several times, the great stone palace, with its large paved courtyard, its pillared halls, and its numerous chambers and shrines, was originally constructed about 2000 B.C. It rose to four or five stories, and its labyrinthine passages gave birth to the myth of Theseus, the Labyrinth, and the Minotaur. Palace decorations, including magnificent frescoes and large terra-cotta reliefs, many of which were imaginatively reconstructed by Evans, reveal an attractive, luxurious, and lively Mediterranean culture. The murals are numerous and depict delightful scenes of royalty, ceremonial processions, and bull-leaping, probably a religious ritual. There are many painted landscapes, with charming birds, animals, and plants, and seascapes with dolphins. Vase painting, done with delicacy, usually had floral or sea-life designs. Figurines of high artistic quality have been recovered from the shrines of Knossos. The city of Knossos reached its zenith between 1550 and 1400 B.C., when it fell under Mycenaean rule.

KOBAN CULTURE prospered in what is now Soviet Georgia from the late 2nd millennium B.C. until about 500 A.D. A mounted nomadic culture, it is known mainly from several burial sites around the modern village of Koban, in the Caucasian foothills, where interesting bronze and iron objects have been found. Perhaps most notable are artfully shaped axe handles having geometric decoration and which probably served some ritualistic purpose. These "ritual axes" date from no later than about 200 B.C. Other distinctive finds include ornate bronze belts and buckles bearing animal-style ornamentation. A recurring Koban motif on these objects is a doglike figure usually appearing with some larger animal (e.g., stag, horse, etc.). Koban craftsmanship shows some Scythian and Greek influence.

KOFUN CULTURE, a protohistoric culture that flourished in central and southern Japan from 250 to 710 A.D. and is characterized by huge mound tombs, often covering as much as 80 acres. This culture, which imposed itself on the Yayoi, was highly aristocratic and maintained close contacts with Korea. At some time during this period one of the Kofun clans managed to establish its leader as the first emperor Jimmu Tenno, who claimed descent from the Sun Goddess. Kofun culture is often considered as an expression of the Japanese Great, or Old, Tombs period.

KOGURYO, a northern Korean kingdom, one of the so-called Three Kingdoms; it was founded in 37 B.C. and lasted until 668 A.D., when the other two Korean kingdoms overthrew it. At first based on a hunting economy, by the 3rd century A.D. the kingdom was ruled by aristocratic tribal warriors. The introduction of Buddhism and Chinese laws in the 4th century led to the disintegration of the tribal system.

KOLN-LINDENTHAL, a neolithic village site outside the city of Cologne on the Rhine. A major farm settlement of about 3000 B.C., it probably developed from two migrations: the Michelsberg people, originating in North Africa, and the Danubian people, whose culture and knowledge of farming came from the Near East via the Balkans and the fertile Danube Valley. The site, occupied several times, was fortified in its latest phase. Large gabled houses, 90 feet by 20, built on posts once existed in this neolithic village. Bandkeramik ware is the typical pottery of Koln-Lindenthal. It is one of the very few neolithic sites of Europe that has been completely excavated.

KOM, a small African kingdom on the grassy plateau of central Cameroons. A hereditary king, called a Fon, ruled the country from his capital at Laakom. The art heritage of the Kom received worldwide attention in 1973 when a large carved figure called the Afo-a-Kom, which embodied the symbolic unity of the Kom people, was spirited away by overzealous entrepreneurs. It turned up in New York City and was subsequently returned to its rightful owners.

KONARAK, site of a well-known Hindu temple to the sun god Surya, in India's Orissa State. Built in the 13th century A.D., the temple was dominated by a 200-foot-high tower, which collapsed soon after construction. The temple is among the world's more famous sites of erotic art. Much of the shrine's exterior is decorated with friezes depicting couples in various, often unusual, sexual poses. Inside, a stone statue of Surya, in a sober regal pose, is dominant. The temple is often called the "Black Pagoda."

KONDE, a fearsome African carving used widely in Zaire to bring harm to an enemy. The konde was an animal or human figure replete with an assemblage of feathers, metallic objects, and cowries, and pierced with many nails or pieces of iron. A small hollow, carved usually in the stomach, contained magical substances. The konde is sometimes known by the more general term *nkisi.*

KONGO, the name of a once glorious African kingdom in southwestern Zaire and of the people who comprised the kingdom. Kongo developed strong ties to Portugal during the 15th century, and the relationship reached a milestone in 1491 when King Nzinga-a-Nkuwu was baptized and renamed John I. The lasting importance of this contact with Christianity and Europe has been a subject of endless debate. Some scholars have argued inconclusively that the naturalistic quality in Kongo art resulted from early European influence. Commemorative mother-and-child figures best display Kongo naturalism. These statuettes carved from wood normally consist of a woman sitting cross-legged and holding a child in her lap.

KORE, a term used in the study of Greek sculpture to designate the female standing figure of the 7th century B.C., which, unlike the kouros, was usually shown fully clothed.

KOREAN CIVILIZATION, although a distinct cultural entity, is often considered a derivative of Chinese civilization and the bridge that served to transmit Chinese cultural influences to Japan during the early centuries A.D. Racially, the Koreans share a common ancestry with the northern Chinese. Ancient writings tell of migrations from China into the Korean peninsula during China's late Shang era (about 1200 B.C.) and again during the Ch'in Dynasty (3rd century B.C.). However, centuries of Korean isolation led to the creation of a distinctive culture, about which little reliable documentation exists until roughly the 1st century B.C., when Korea's recorded history begins. At that time Han Dynasty China made enduring colonial inroads into the Korean peninsula's northwestern region. The resulting Korean-Chinese culture had its center in the city of Lolang, located a few miles from modern Pyongyang, North Korea. Lolang flourished as a Han Dynasty colony between 108 B.C. and 313 A.D. Objects of gold, silver, and lacquer found at Lolang tomb sites are considered among the finest extant examples of Han Dynasty art. From the 1st through the 7th centuries A.D. most of the Korean peninsula was ruled by three regional kingdoms. Initially, the most vigorous was the Koguryo kingdom, which controlled the north and lasted until 668. The Paekche kingdom held

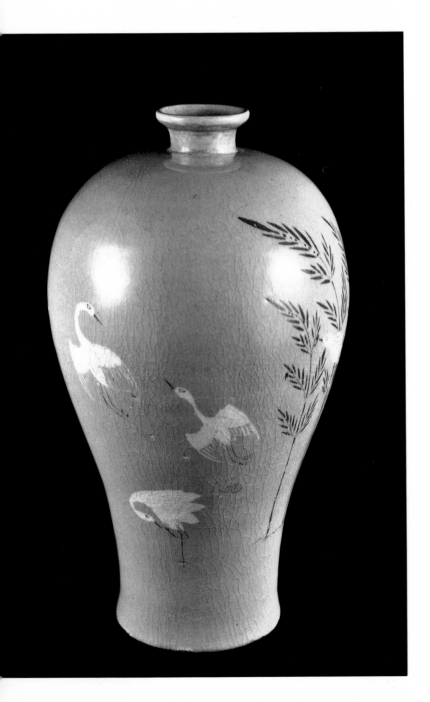

sway in Korea's southwest during approximately the same years. Southeastern Korea was long ruled by the Buddhist Silla Dynasty, which in 668 defeated its rival kingdoms and established rule over virtually the whole peninsula. Silla rule prevailed until 918, when a bloodless coup, prompted by descendants of the old Koguryo rulers, left the Silla king a figurehead. The Silla Dynasty soon gave way to the Koryo Dynasty, which lasted until 1392. Under Koryo rule Buddhism reached its zenith in Korea. In 1392 the Yi Dynasty seized political control and set up a strongly centralized government in Seoul. Influenced by Ming rulers in neighboring China, the Yi Dynasty governed as a Confucian state and suppressed Buddhism. Yi rule survived a catastrophic Japanese invasion that ravaged large parts of Korea between 1592 and 1599. In 1627 an invasion by Manchu armies from China relegated Yi rulers to the position of vassals; in effect, the Yi became servants to China. Korea's Yi Dynasty disappeared in 1910, the year of the country's annexation by Japan.

Korean Art and Antiquities, excluding architecture, had their main expression in the areas of sculpture, painting, and ceramics. Important Korean sculpture is Buddhist-inspired, dating from the 4th century A.D. and reaching its peak of excellence under the Silla kingdom in the 6th century. A typical and famous Silla work is the gilt-bronze seated Maitreya Buddha, now in Seoul's Palace Museum. Representative Korean stone Buddhas are found in the Sukkulam caves, near modern Kyongju, South Korea. Painting flourished during the Silla and Yi periods. Both regimes kept an official register of major painters, many of whom were commissioned to do portraits of notable personages. Animals, landscapes, and genre scenes were also common subjects in Korean painting. By the 10th century Korean ceramics ranked among the world's finest, retaining their peak of quality throughout the Koryo period (10th through 14th centuries). Porcelain-making was profoundly influenced by techniques developed in Sung China. In turn, Koryo potters invented a method of inlaying different types of clay in a single vessel to produce a two-colored finished product—a technique that subsequently influenced China's porcelain masters.

KORWAR, a wooden ancestor figure formerly used in the Geelvink Bay region of New Guinea. The object typically had an oversized head that was sometimes replaced by the skull of a deceased relative.

KORYO, a Korean kingdom that flourished from 918 to 1392 A.D. Its founder, Wang Kon, was initially the military leader of the Koguryo Dynasty, which had held power over central Korea. Many Buddhist pagodas and stupas survive from the Koryo period, perhaps the finest being the Pusoksa Temple in northern Kyongsang Prov-

Korean art: Vase. Porcelaneous stoneware with celadon glaze and inlaid decoration. Koryo period, 12th century A.D. (Museum of Fine Arts, Boston; Charles B. Hoyt Collection)

Korwar: Painted wood with glass eyes. New Guinea, early 20th century A.D. (British Museum, London)

ince. Ceramics of Koryo Korea, especially fine porcelains, rank among the world's best.

KOSZIDER BRONZES, three hoards of important bronze objects found at Dunapataj-Koszider, Hungary, near modern Budapest, and dating from the mid-2nd millennium B.C. They are attributed to the Tumulus peoples—eastern and central European bronze-age cultures—and consist of weapons, tools, and jewelry. They bear a similarity to many objects found throughout eastern Europe from the Black Sea to the Baltic. These objects, often embellished with geometric or spiral designs, include long decorative pins, spiral arm and ankle jewelry, bracelets, belt plates, swords, and daggers.

KOTA, an African people living in eastern Gabon and parts of the Congo (Brazzaville). Although they have a reputation for being bloodthirsty, the Kota were not as aggressive as their neighbors. Their history in the 19th century was that of continual flight in the face of Fang invaders who eventually split the Kota into two major groups. The ancestral cult adhered to by the Kota has led to remarkable works of art. Known as the *mbulu ngulu,* these ancestor figures were carved of wood with overlaid strips of copper or brass. Frightening, yet beautiful, they had large oval heads and symbolic arms joined in an abstract diamond shape. These figures guarded the remains of ancestors in much the same way as the *bieri* of the Fang.

Korean art: "The Nine Dragons," detail. Dated 1244 A.D. Scroll. (Museum of Fine Arts, Boston; Francis Gardner Curtis Fund)

Kuba: "King Shamba Bolongongo." Carved wood. (British Museum, London)

KOUROS, in Greek sculpture, a term for the statue of a male nude standing in a strictly frontal pose, a posture the Greeks borrowed from the Egyptians when they began to carve large stone statues in the mid-7th century B.C. Older reference books use the term "Apollo" for this kind of figure.

KRISHNA, a celebrated Hindu deity and mythological hero. As a divine lover he had thousands of wives, although only one principal wife, Rukmini. Many of his boyhood pranks are recounted in Vedic literature. He is often represented as a dark, erotic youth playing the flute in a rustic setting.

KUBA, an African people living in central Zaire who reached their greatest political expansion in the 17th century A.D. under the leadership of one Kuba group—the Bushong—and its Nyimi, or divine king, Shyaam aMbul aNgoong. During this period began the famous tradition of carving a dignified commemorative portrait of Kuba kings. These statues depict the king in a cross-legged position. Many Kuba arts, such as boxes with incised geometric designs, effigy cups for palm wine, and lush raffia pile cloths, were of a prestige nature. The Kuba used masks made of beads and wood.

KUBAN ROYAL TOMBS, major graves of various Scythian-related tribal leaders in the Soviet Caucasus, found mainly in or near the Kuban River valley. They date from the 3rd millennium through the 7th or 6th centuries B.C. Probably the earliest of these is the pre-Scythian Maikop site (around 2300 B.C.). Others of importance include Ulski, Kostromskaya, and Kalermes. These timbered barrow tombs have yielded fine animal-style art in bronze and precious metals. A few among many examples include a golden griffin and several wild-bird figurines found at Kalermes, bronze figures that had adorned a chariot at Ulski, and a famous Scythian gold stag plaque from Kostromskaya, all dating from the mid-1st millennium B.C. They are housed in the Hermitage, Leningrad.

KUDARA KANNON. See PAEKCHE CULTURE.

KUEI, type of bronze vessel dating from China's Chou era (1122–400 B.C.). These round, deep food bowls had ritualistic uses. Unlike the *chia*, which they resemble, they have no tripod base.

KUKULCAN, the Maya name for Quetzalcoatl, the Mexican god of life and fertility, depicted in art as a feathered serpent. Although early representations of feathered serpents appear at Mayan sites such as Tikal, the cult of Kukulcan did not reach its peak until the 10th century A.D. Maya legend holds that a Mexican leader named Quetzalcoatl conquered the Yucatan peninsula at that

Kota: "Mbulu ngulu" ancestor figure. Brass-plated wood. (British Museum, London)

time. This supports the contention that the Toltecs, whose chief god was Quetzalcoatl, invaded the Yucatan. The image of Kukulcan appears on a great number of buildings in the Yucatan, but the center of his cult seems to have been the city of Chichen Itza.

KUL OBA, a 4th-century B.C. Scythian burial site in Russia's Crimea, located between the Black Sea and the Sea of Azov. The site is unusually rich in art objects showing Greek influence; thus it ranks with Chertomlyk as one of the two most important sources of Greco-Scythian art. Major art objects from Kul Oba include vases in gold, silver, and electrum, having highly realistic depictions of Scythians at their daily activities. Stylized leaf-and-scroll borders and backgrounds are pure Greek in style. Similarly, a gold scabbard is covered with animal decorations, but the style is naturalistic and Greek, showing little of the contortion that characterizes Scythian animal-style art. Objects cited here are housed in the Hermitage, Leningrad.

KULTEPE, a tell in Cappadocia, central Turkey, covering the very ancient city of Kanesh. Its importance to archaeology lies in the extensive correspondence in Assy-

Kwakiutl: Ceremonial cape. (Horniman Museum, London)

rian cuneiform tablets found at the foot of the tell and dating to the beginning of the 2nd millennium B.C. These, the oldest written records found in Turkey, were left by Assyrian merchants who established Kanesh as an important *karum*, a way station on the caravan trade route between Anatolia and Mesopotamia. They shed much light on the period just before the rise of the Hittites.

KURGAN CULTURE, general name for the various South Russian tribes of the 3rd millennium B.C. who buried their dead in pit chambers beneath earthen mounds. From about 2500 B.C. the Kurgan peoples were copper-using agriculturalists who raised grain and bred pigs, cattle, and sheep and probably domesticated horses. Kurgan culture includes, notably, the Kuban and Maikop peoples. Objects found in Kurgan graves are copper, gold, and silver vessels, animal figurines, stone and copper axe heads, and pottery having corded surfaces. These peoples apparently migrated into eastern Europe by the late 2nd millennium B.C., bringing with them Indo-European languages.

KUSHAN KINGDOM, a short-lived but artistically important Asian kingdom. Founded in the 1st century A.D., it soon held sway over much of modern Afghanistan, Pakistan, and northern India. The Kushans entered this region from the northwest and ruled here until the mid-3rd century. Kushan patronage prompted artistic development, especially in India's Gandhara and Mathura regions. Under such Kushan rulers as Emperor Kanishka, Gandharan sculptors produced the finest art of that district's entire history. Styles are often more akin to Greco-Roman than to Indian art, although subject matter is predominantly Buddhist.

KVALSUND, on the west coast of Norway, is the site of a bog in which were found the remains of two ships of the 7th century A.D., thus predating known Viking ships by almost 200 years. The ships were placed in the bog as a sacrifice or thank-offering to the gods. Their sleek shape and clinker-built construction of oak planks, along with the use of a steering oar, are features approximately the same as those of the Viking age. The larger ship is over 50 feet long. It was propelled by oars and probably did not have a mast or sail.

KWAKIUTL. The most flamboyant tribe of the American Northwest Coast Indians, they live in the Vancouver Islands of southern British Columbia. The Kwakiutl were noted for their extremely well-developed secret societies and ritual, which included the use of enormous wooden masks with movable parts. These masks, along with other characteristic carvings, such as totem poles, are remarkable for their powerful design and strong colors. Kwakiutl wood sculptures can sometimes be identified from their facial features, especially by the presence of a rounded or projecting eye with a flattened pupil.

KYATHOS, a Greek vessel, with a single long, high handle, used for ladling wine and as a drinking cup.

KYLIX, a two-handled Greek drinking cup, resembling a deep saucer or shallow soup bowl. The handles were high on the rim, and sometimes a narrow stem was attached. The major decoration was on the inside of a kylix.

KYONGJU, a city in southeastern Korea, once the capital of the Silla kingdom, which reached its peak of power between the 7th and 10th centuries A.D. The Silla kings were Buddhist, and Kyongju became the site of several Buddhist monasteries and many temples. The Pulguksa monastery, just outside Kyongju, contains many fine relics of Buddhist sculpture, showing Chinese Tang Dynasty inspiration.

L

LABYRINTH, the legendary maze devised for King Minos of Knossos in Crete by Daedalus. Inside dwelt the fierce Minotaur (half man, half bull), slain by the Greek hero Theseus. The Labyrinth appears on coins of Knossos, Greek vases, Roman mosaics, and, roughly drawn, on the walls of a Pompeian villa with the inscription "here dwells the Minotaur." The legend may be more fact than fiction, since the symbol of ancient royal power in Crete was a double-headed axe, called a *labrys*; thus, archaeologists have suggested that the complex Minoan palace at Knossos was in fact called the "labyrinth," the place of the double-headed axe.

LACHISH, a city important in Biblical times, located about 25 miles southwest of Jerusalem. Its site consists of the mound Tell ed-Duweir, which occupies about 18 acres. Lachish was first settled by cave dwellers in the early 3rd millennium B.C. and subsequently occupied by the Hyksos, Canaanites, Israelites, and Babylonians. It was excavated from 1932 to 1938 and found to be important because of several groups of inscriptions discovered here. They include an 18th- or 17th-century B.C. dagger bearing four symbols—one of the earliest known examples of alphabetic letters; four inscriptions on vessels from a temple (destroyed by Joshua around 1220 B.C. and rebuilt several times) showing the alphabet in a relatively late stage of development; shards of inscribed tablets found beneath the Babylonian levels and proving to be documents in a court-martial case; and tablet fragments having 100 lines of readable Hebrew dating from the time of Jeremiah (late 7th century B.C.). Lachish was partially destroyed by the Babylonian Nebuchadnezzar in 598 B.C. and permanently demolished in 589 B.C.

LA COLOMBIERE, in southeastern France, a prehistoric site whose engraved stones and drawings on pebbles give clues to the hunting magic of man in the last ice age. On one pebble a wooly rhinoceros is shown pierced by arrows, the drawing standing for the hope and prayer that the real animal in the ensuing hunt will be so pierced. On another stone the lines of the drawings are very confused, because many pictures were superimposed, one upon another, representing repeated drawings executed on this one magic stone before each of many hunting expeditions.

Lacquer: Ogata Korin, writing box. Japanese. Edo period, early 17th century A.D. (National Museum, Tokyo)

LACQUER, a combination of pigment and the processed sap from certain trees, notably the lac tree. After application to an art object, the sap hardens into a solid coat. Lacquer finishes are high gloss, perfectly smooth, and waterproof. Lacquer was first identified with the Han Dynasty Chinese.

LAGASH, a major city of Sumeria whose tell is at the modern village of Telloh in southeastern Iraq. Lagash flourished in the 3rd millennium B.C., but fell to Larsa at the end of that period. Eannatum, around 2500 B.C., and Gudea, around 2100 B.C., were its most notable rulers. Excavations at Lagash since the last century have revealed some 30,000 cuneiform tablets giving much information on the city. In addition, a score of extraordinary statues of Gudea, carved from diorite stone, have been found, as well as the famous Stele of the Vultures, a silver vase, and stone and bronze art objects. Lagash was contemporary with the 3rd Dynasty of Ur.

LAKE DWELLERS. See **PILE DWELLERS.**

LAKSHMI, Hindu goddess and the wife of Vishnu. Legend depicts her as having sprung into existence from a churning ocean. Hindu artists have often portrayed her as seated on a lotus, while attending elephants shower her with water from their trunks.

LAMAIST ART AND ANTIQUITIES, the art and religious objects originating in Tibet, home of Lamaist Buddhism. Lamaism fuses Buddhism, imported from India in the 7th century A.D., with Tibet's indigenous shamanistic religions, mainly Bonpo, which dealt with magical nature spirits. Accordingly, the art shows the mixture of influences. The form of Buddhism entering Tibet was Mahayana, which emphasizes a social-religious hierarchy, giving a special place to monastic life, and embellishes complex rituals with an ornate religious art. Although Lamaism and its art are primarily Tibetan, they also exist, somewhat diluted, in Nepal and Mongolia. Lamaist painting occurs as frescoes; as *tanka*, which are

Laocoön: Marble. (Vatican Museum, Rome)

paintings on banners of canvas or silk; and as miniatures in holy manuscripts. The earliest paintings leave no part of their surfaces unadorned, and this density of images produces a monotonous effect, placing Lamaist painting in an inferior position to that of its Chinese and Indian counterparts. After about the 13th century, however, Lamaist painting began reflecting a new Chinese influence, with a central figure—often a Buddhist saint—standing out against a landscape background. Typical sculpture includes cast bronzes of the Buddha, often gilded or painted. A uniquely Lamaist form of sculpture is the *bzo sku*, a rendition of a demonic deity in painted plaster, molded on a wooden armature. *Papier-mâché* is also a common medium for images or fantastic facial masks of such deities. Lamaist sculpture is usually executed in gigantic dimensions.

Lamaist Iconography is never the expression of an individual artist but the strict visual interpretation of sacred literature. Thus, if the artist is not himself a monk, all details of his work, including colors, are rendered according to specific instructions of a monk versed in the literature and its symbolism. As a result, Buddha images are highly conventionalized and usually lacking in expression. The only color that may be used with some freedom is gold, which represents all colors. It is applied on some types of *tanka*, where figures outlined in black stand vividly against a gold background. The *mandala* is the most important abstract religious design, constituting a geometric pattern representing the world, with Buddha at its center. Lamaist theology includes numerous demonic deities, and some freedom of coloring and adornment is allowed the artist in depicting such figures. Among the best known is *Span ras gzigs*, a four-armed, multiheaded apparition who is considered the patron and protector of Tibet.

LANZON. See **CHAVIN CIVILIZATION.**

LAOCOON, Trojan prince and priest of Apollo, crushed with his two sons by serpents after protesting the dragging of the Greek Wooden Horse into Troy. The story is immortalized in Vergil's *Aeneid* and is the subject of one of the most famous marble sculptures of antiquity. A masterpiece of the Pergamene school and probably created by Hagesandros, Polydoros, and Athanodoros in the 2nd century B.C., it was exhibited in Roman times in the palace of the Emperor Titus. It was rediscovered in 1506 and now stands in the Belvedere courtyard of the Vatican.

LAPIS LAZULI, a dark-blue semiprecious stone, used since ancient times for decorating jewelry, as well as for carving and inlaying. It takes a high gloss. When pulverized it was used as paint pigment (ultramarine).

Larsa: Statuette. Bronze with gold. 18th century B.C. (Louvre, Paris)

LAPP CULTURE. The Lapps, concentrated north of the Arctic Circle in Norway, Sweden, Finland, and the Kola peninsula of Russia, are a unique and ancient people who arrived in this area around 2000 B.C. They follow the seasonal migrations of the reindeer herds on which they are completely dependent for survival, thus leading a way of life thought to be almost identical with that of European paleolithic man of almost 38,000 years ago. The Lapps are skilled in many crafts, including braiding and weaving, tin filigree work, and bone and horn carving. Along with other nomadic Arctic peoples they have a bear cult in which they ritually kill this animal, which they believe shares a mystical relationship with their tribe. Their most distinctive art object is a shaman's drum, made from the skin of a young reindeer and painted with signs and figures that represent the forces of nature, hunting scenes, divinities, and aspects of daily life. As the shaman, or priest, beats the drum, small dice bounce across these painted images. The spot where they finally come to rest aids him in predicting the future.

LARA JONGGRANG. See **SHAILENDRA DYNASTY.**

LARSA, a tell at the modern site of Senkera between the ancient locations of Ur and Uruk in southern Iraq. Larsa was one of the great city-states of Sumer and contested for supremacy with such cities as Assur, Eshnunna, and Isin. Larsa's greatest period was in the early 2nd millennium B.C. under its king, Rim Sin, who was overthrown by Hammurabi of Babylon around 1760 B.C. Larsa has as

Laughing heads: "Laughing Man," detail. Terra cotta. 300–800 A.D. From Remojadas, Veracruz. (National Museum of Anthropology, Mexico City)

yet not been extensively excavated, although preliminary investigations have been most promising, revealing a ziggurat, a royal palace, many small art objects, and clay-tablet documents.

LASCAUX, a world-famous painted cave site in the Perigord, France, near Montignac. It ranks with Altamira in the richness of its upper paleolithic art and dates from about 15,000 B.C. Lascaux was accidentally discovered in 1940, and since then superb paintings have been revealed on the rock faces of the cavern, particularly those of four bulls in jet black, three times life size, covering the ceiling of the Hall of Bulls. In all some 2,000 drawings were found, a few in compositions 20 feet long. They include a string of shaggy ponies, two wild goats attacking each other, and a herd of stags swimming across a lake. One scene shows a supine human figure with the head of a bird, about to be attacked by a bison, possibly the first known action picture. The lines of these rock engravings and of the paintings, in black, red, yellow, and brown, show the complete certainty and consummate skill of Cro-Magnon artists. In contrast to the more colorful but less dynamic paintings of the Altamira cave, those at Lascaux portray violent and magnificent movement and exultation in the chase and in life itself. Lascaux was probably a secret underground religious shrine for ice-age man. The fact that a large number of the beasts shown are pregnant would indicate the practice of fertility magic. Access to the caves is now severely restricted, owing to damage caused to the paintings by changes of atmosphere and temperature and by fungus disease.

LA TENE, a major iron-age culture that spread widely over central and western Europe prior to the 5th century B.C. It takes its name from a type site on Lake Neuchatel in Switzerland, where in 1857 a rich find of wood, bronze, and iron objects was discovered in the shallow offshore waters. Weapons, horse trappings, parts of a wooden chariot, as well as imports from the Classical world of the Mediterranean were found. Of Celtic origin, La Tene objects, with their beautiful ornamentation of curved and interwoven tendrils and animal forms, correspond exactly with other finds as far afield as Britain and Ireland, thus indicating the widespread migration of Celtic warrior tribes. The La Tene hoard, probably of votive offerings thrown into the lake, was the largest find of immediately pre-Roman Celtic culture. La Tene culture followed that of Hallstatt.

LATIUM, an ancient lowland region of west-central Italy, extending southward from the Tiber River Valley. It was occupied from about the 3rd millennium B.C. by migrants probably from central Europe; sites in Latium indicate the presence of an Urn people. By about 900 B.C.,

Lascaux: Cave painting, ca. 15,000 B.C.

while Etruscan culture flourished to the north, this relatively backward region contained about 50 loosely federated pastoral tribes who were gradually infiltrated by a people from the mountains to the east—the Sabines. The Latins and the Sabines assimilated, the most important of their towns ultimately becoming Rome.

LAUGHING HEADS, in Pre-Columbian Mexican archaeology, among the most charming of pottery figurines. They are best known from the site of Remojadas in Veracruz and are generally associated with the Totonacs. However, "laughing heads" may have been produced as early as the first centuries A.D. Characteristically they exhibit a distinctive openmouthed "smile" seen on the faces of thousands of mold-made figurines. A wealth of ethnographic data has been obtained from these exuberant figures, which depict ball players, lovers, and warriors. All are clothed in appropriate attire and wear elaborately decorated headdresses.

LA VENTA, the greatest of Olmec sites, on a small swampy island in the state of Tabasco, Mexico. The first major ceremonial center of Pre-Columbian Mexico, it was probably occupied by 1000 B.C. It covered an area of more than a mile and reached its peak between 800 and 400 B.C. Its most imposing feature is a large round earthen pyramid, thought to be modelled after the shape of a nearby volcano. Rich offerings of carved jade, as well as

Lekythos: Detail of a white-ground lekythos by the Achilles Painter. Greek, 440–435 B.C. From Eritrea. (National Museum, Athens)

lekythos usually described as "squat." The oil was shaken rather than poured out, and the incurving rim prevented dripping. Decorated and painted lekythoi were often used as funerary offerings.

LENGYEL CULTURE is named from a site in central Hungary west of the Danube. A settlement and a great cemetery of neolithic times discovered here have yielded black polished pottery of bowl, beaker, and bottle forms. These represent a later development of Tisza culture objects. The same site also contained vessels with handles and several pottery pedestals reminiscent of metal types found at Troy and others similar to early Minoan pottery of about the same date, approximately 2800 B.C. In addition to Hungary, Lengyel culture sites have been found in Austria, Czechoslovakia, and Poland.

LEOCHARES. See GANYMEDE.

LEPCIS MAGNA, a Roman colony on the coast of North Africa, in Libya. It was founded by the Emperor Augustus on the site of a much older 7th-century B.C. Phoenician settlement. Lepcis Magna was given a regular chessboard town plan and furnished with a forum, basilica, market, and theater. Hadrian added large baths, but it was the Emperor Septimius Severus (193–211 A.D.), a native of Lepcis, who beautified the city to a splendor rivalling that of Rome. A new forum, with basilica and temple, a beautiful colonnaded street leading to a new harbor, a lighthouse, and especially a great four-way triumphal arch bearing four large historical reliefs were built. The reliefs were executed by Greek artists from Aphrodisias, and their sharply drilled and incised carving are in the Near Eastern manner. The full frontal pose of the Emperor Severus in his chariot symbolizes the complete merging of the cult of emperor-worship with the idolatry of the East. On the western fringe of Lepcis Magna are the "Hunting Baths," named for a fresco in its barrel-vaulted main hall, and several small structures of great architectural interest, since the sand cover of centuries has left their domes and vaults virtually intact. Lepcis Magna is without doubt the greatest surviving example of Roman transitional art and architecture of the Severan period.

LEPENSKI VIR, a mesolithic village site of about 6000 B.C. on the banks of the Danube above the Iron Gate, in Yugoslavia. A fishing settlement, the site is noted for its carved stone heads, which seem to have been used for worship or for funerary purposes. Since some of them have fishlike features with open, turned-down mouths, it is thought fish may have figured in the religion of the period.

LERNA. See HOUSE OF TILES.

LES EYZIES is the name of a village from which the archaeological investigation of the Vezere Valley region of the Dordogne in France was undertaken. This is the district in which the greatest concentration of prehistoric

serpentine pavements, have been found. La Venta is most famous for its monumental stone stelae, altars, and "colossal heads."

LEGA, a central African people living in eastern Zaire. Although the Lega did not have hereditary chiefs, they were held together by the powerful Bwami Association, a secret male society. Art works of the Lega were created for the needs of this association. Carved wooden and ivory maskettes and figurines served as emblems of rank within the Bwami or aided in the instruction of male initiates. The Lega (sometimes called the Warega) have been known to Europeans only since the 1890s.

LEKYTHOS, a pitcher with a single handle and narrow neck, used by the Greeks to hold oil. Though they are usually tall and thin, there is another broader-shaped

cave sites in the world is to be found. It enjoys to the present day a peculiarly warm and healthful climate, a factor that must have been of paramount importance in the ice age. Close to Les Eyzies are the significant sites of Cro-Magnon, La Mouthe, and Font-de-Gaume.

LESSER VEHICLE. See **HINAYANA**.

LEUBINGEN, in Saxony, Germany, is an early bronze-age site where a grave mound was found to contain a complete house with entrance, oak beams, and paved floors. It was evidently used for the burial of a chief, and the bodies of an old man and a young girl had been interred in a chamber of stone slabs roofed with oak. Ornaments and rings of gold and bronze daggers found in the tomb are now in the Museum of Prehistory in Halle.

LEVALLOISIAN, a paleolithic period in Europe. In contrast to stone tools made in earlier epochs from rock lumps, called cores, the tools of Levalloisian man consisted of flakes struck off from a previously prepared core. The type site is Levallois outside Paris, but similar tools have been found in the Thames Valley in England, near Leipzig in Germany, and elsewhere. The period was a temperate one in Europe and possibly dates from 125,000 B.C. Tools made from cores, however, coexisted with the newer flake-type blades.

LI, an ancient Chinese vessel shape. It is a small jar with its base divided into three hollow legs. The li, which may have developed from pots fused together over a fire, later evolved into the famous Chinese bronze tripods.

LIBATION BOWL, a vessel used in offering libations— for the Greeks the phiale, for the Romans the patera. The liquid poured from the libation bowl might be wine, milk, or honey.

LIGURIANS, inhabitants of a region extending through northwest Italy and southern France during the late 1st millennium B.C. They were of mixed Celtic and Germanic ethnic origin. From around 200 B.C. they battled the Romans sporadically, until finally overwhelmed and absorbed into the empire during the reign of Augustus. The archaeology of the Ligurians is but little studied.

LINEAR A AND B, modern designations for scripts used by inhabitants of Greece and Crete roughly between 2000 and 1100 B.C. The older script, Linear A, was used by the Minoans of Crete and remains undeciphered today. Linear B—which has been found inscribed on clay tablets at Knossos on Crete and Pylos on the Greek mainland— appears unrelated to Linear A and was used by the Mycenaeans. In 1952–53 Linear B was finally deciphered by an English architect and military code expert, Michael Ventris. It proved to be a written form of early Greek, having 59 known symbols, each designating a syllabic sound. The writing disappeared from use during the chaotic period of Dorian invasions in the 12th century B.C.

LINGAM, a phallic figure, the chief worship symbol of the Hindu god Siva. Carved ritual lingams were used as early as the 2nd millennium B.C. in India and were later employed by various Asian kings as a symbol of their divine power.

LION GATE, the monumental entrance to the citadel of Mycenae in the northwestern Peloponnesus, Greece. The doorway itself is about 20 feet high, with a massive lintel stone weighing about 20 tons, supported by two slightly smaller monoliths. This is topped by the triangular relief which gives the gate its name—two lions (actually lionesses) with forepaws resting on the base of a column which stands between them. Their heads are missing and were carved separately. The symbolism of this noble and majestic relief is uncertain; some suggest a religious meaning, others a secular or heraldic one. The relief slab is relatively thin and light to reduce the weight on the lintel stone. This technique is called "the relieving triangle" and occurs in the doorways of older Mycenaean tholos tombs. The Lion Gate dates from about 1300 B.C., when the cyclopean circuit walls of the citadel were expanded.

LION MOUNTAIN. See **SIGIRIYA**.

LIPARI, the largest of the volcanic Aeolian (or Lipari) Islands, located off the northeast coast of Sicily. In antiquity the islands were thought to be the mythical residence of the wind god, Aeolus. Lipari is best known for its rich stratigraphical sequence of ancient cultures; some archaeological levels are 30 feet deep. Continuously occupied from about 4000 B.C., Lipari held great deposits of obsidian (volcanic glass), much valued in antiquity. Finds

Lion Gate, Mycenae.

on the island include a wide variety of implements and pottery types, most distinctive of which are the ornamented and polychromatic Centuripe vases of the 3rd century B.C. Named for the town in Sicily where they were first discovered, Centuripe vases, with their mural-like paintings, often offer insights into the development of Greco-Roman wall frescoes. Greek and Roman sculptural remains are in the form of inscribed stelae, terra cottas, and statuettes of comedic actors.

LITTLE-MASTER CUPS, in Greek art, a series of delicate drinking bowls with two handles set on slender stems. They were so named because they were usually painted with graceful, precise black-figured miniatures. Many are signed by the potter, and the best of a large number of miniaturists is the "Tleson Painter," who decorated over 60 cups signed "Tleson, son of Nearchos, made me."

LOGGIA, a Roman architectural term designating a roofed portico or gallery that projects from the wall of a building. A loggia was typically ornate, and its walls were often adorned with paintings and sculpture.

LOKI. Originally a fire demon and not one of the old Nordic gods, Loki was admitted to the company of the gods and indeed became blood brother to Odin. He was an evil personality, attractive to the goddesses, sometimes helping the gods, but often working for his own ends. Finally, after he killed Baldr, Loki led the giants and demons against the gods in the cataclysmic struggle known as "The Twilight of the Gods." After the coming of Christianity he was more and more invested with the characteristics of the devil.

LOLANG, a Han Chinese military district established in northern Korea in 108 B.C. One of several Han commanderies, Lolang, with its capital at Pyongyang, was the longest lasting. Lolang became rich and had extensive trade with China, Japan, and Korea. Superb Han objects have been found in Lolang tombs, including lacquer ware and gold filigree. Koreans took possession of Lolang in 313 A.D.

LOPBURI, site of a large Khmer city on the Menam River in Thailand. Prehistoric tools have been found here, although the site was continuously occupied only from the 6th century A.D. It is one of the greatest Khmer cities outside Cambodia. Both Khmer and Dvaravati (Mon) cultures were represented at Lopburi. The earliest Mon inscriptions, dating from the 7th to 8th centuries, were discovered here. Buildings and palaces built by the later Thai kings in the Khmer style remain at the site. One example is the 12th-century Phra Prang Sam Yot of brick and stucco. Many Lopburi terra cottas as well as statuary show evidence of an early non-Indian art style.

LOS MILLARES, a fortified copper-age site, near the coast in southeast Spain and part of Almeria. The period when rich Spanish metal ores were beginning to be worked was about 2500 B.C. The metal workers of Los Millares were also traders, and the wealth of their culture, just emerging from the earlier neolithic era, is attested to by the many elaborate stone passage graves they erected for their dead. Their pottery is engraved with designs of stags and of human beings as well as with geometric patterns. Interesting "idols" of pottery, bone, and stone were produced by the ancient people of Los Millares.

LOST-WAX PROCESS. See CIRE PERDUE.

LOUGH GUR, a site of the early iron age, of about 1800 B.C., on the west side of a small lake in County Limerick, Ireland. Standing stones, or menhirs, are placed edge to edge in a circle of 150 feet diameter. The center area is formed of packed clay to a depth of two feet and may have been used for religious ceremonies. The pottery found in the neighboring lake was probably offered as votive gifts to a deity.

LOYANG, northern Chinese city on the south bank of the Yellow River in Honan province and the capital of the Chou Dynasty from 771 B.C. until 256 B.C. The city had a population of 600,000 when it was sacked by northern nomads in 311 B.C. Loyang has rammed earth walls and pit-grave cemeteries. Extremely attractive bronzes, decorated with interlacing designs of dragons and snakes, were produced here during the Chou occupation. The city fell to the Ch'in in 256 B.C.

LUBA, an African people of east-central Zaire. From the 16th to 19th centuries A.D. the Luba had vital kingdoms in what is now the country of Zaire. Because their settle-

Loyang: Gilded bronze inlaid with gold and silver. Chinese. Chou Dynasty, 4th century B.C. (British Museum, London)

Ludovisi Sarcophagus: "Girl Playing the Flute." Marble relief. Side panel from the sarcophagus. (Terme Museum, Rome)

ments extended over great distances, the Luba developed many distinct art styles. One such style, that of the "master of Buli," was noted for its arrestingly long and attenuated hands and faces in contrast to the usual round and supple forms of other Luba sculpture. Images of women were important in the corpus of Luba art work. Female figures are seen in caryatid stools, neck rests, and ancestral statuary.

LUCANIA, a predominantly mountainous region of southern Italy, bound on west and east respectively by the Tyrrhenian Sea and Gulf of Tarentum; the plains of Campania lie to Lucania's north. Earliest known native Lucanians were peasants, a southern branch of the Samnite peoples. In the early 1st millennium B.C. coastal cities were established here by Greek colonists—the first city being Sybaris, around 720 B.C.—and Lucania thus comprised a large part of Magna Graecia.

LUDOVISI SARCOPHAGUS. Considered by some as the remains of either a throne or an altar, it is a three-panel relief sculpture in marble, dating from about 460 B.C. Although the so-called sarcophagus was found among Roman ruins, its sculptural style is Classical Greek. The marble was undoubtedly imported to Italy, where it was sculpted by an artist of Magna Graecia. The front section—about 55 inches wide and originally about 40 inches high—depicts the birth of Persephone or Aphrodite from the sea, assisted by nymphs. Slightly smaller side panels portray a seated nude girl playing a flute and a robed woman burning incense. A magnificent work, it is housed in the Terme Museum, Rome.

LULUA, or Bena Lulua, an African people living in southern Zaire. The Lulua, a splinter group of the Luba, migrated to their present homeland 200 to 300 years ago. Lulua wood figurines stand out in the corpus of African art because of their elaborate hairdressings and concern with detailed scarification. Some of these scarification patterns, often grotesquely incised, covered the face, hands, neck, legs, arms, and torso of the carving. Many Lulua objects depict warriors carrying their emblems of rank. Some were used as fertility fetishes and hunting amulets. Lulua masks were polychromed and adorned with beads, cowries, and raffia.

LUNDA, an African people of southern Zaire. Beginning about 1600 A.D. and for some 250 years afterwards, the Lunda people built an empire that covered parts of Angola, Zaire, and Zambia. Their highly advanced woodcarving tradition, found throughout the empire, was once attributed to the Lunda themselves, but now it seems that the real artists were the Chokwe, a people living within the borders of the Lunda Empire.

LUNGMEN, site of a series of decorated Buddhist cave shrines located ten miles south of Loyang in northern Honan, China. Begun in 494 A.D., these limestone caves reflect influences of central Asian Buddhism. Much of the sculpture is austere, although reliefs at the site show more naturalism. One of the finest shrines is that of Pin-Yang, which dates from the 6th century A.D. Here, Buddhist trinities and monsters adorn the walls while flying figures and jataka scenes cover the ceiling around a central lotus. The giant guardian deities at the site are early Tang (672–676).

LUNGSHAN CULTURE, a late neolithic culture in northeast China, precursor to the Shang Dynasty. Lungshan sites have been found in Manchuria, Shantung, Honan, Shansi, and Anhwei. The Lungshan people had pounded-earth walls 30 feet thick and one mile long, oracle bones, jade objects, sheep and horses, and the pottery wheel. They produced a paper-thin, burnished black pottery in 30 or so shapes—perhaps the finest neolithic earthenware of any time.

LUR, a long bronze trumpet in the form of an S or snake shape, used by the inhabitants of Denmark from about 1300 B.C. These horns exhibit some of the finest craftsmanship of the north European bronze age. Many lurer have been found in ancient peat bogs. The lur has become something of a national symbol in Denmark.

LURISTAN, an ancient region in the Zagros Mountains between Iran and Iraq. Here have been found the remains of a bronze-working culture that flourished from about 1100 to 700 B.C. and influenced the later civilizations of

188

the Medes and Persians. The sophisticated bronzes discovered include implements, weapons, adornments, and horse trappings, using animal, human, and demonic motifs. The bronze workers of Luristan were probably horsemen from the Caucasus who merged with the indigenous Kassites, to whom bronze working had been known as early as before 2000 B.C. Luristan bronzes are eagerly sought by collectors, but many are modern forgeries.

LUSATIAN CULTURE. This bronze-age culture, named from Lausitz in East Germany, extended into Silesia and Brandenburg. Dating from about 1500 B.C., it was linked with Unetice culture but had its own traditions of fine bronzework, of knob ornament on dark pottery, of the use of barrows for graves, and of the increasing practice of cremation instead of burial of the dead. It was a dynamic culture affected by a mixture of warrior peoples, and it spread into central and western Europe and into Illyria in later times as the forerunner of Urnfield cultures. Biskupin, a site in Poland, is often considered a classic example of late Lusatian culture.

LUXOR, an Upper Egyptian temple site, near ancient Thebes and about two miles from Karnak. The Luxor temple, dedicated to Amon, was built mainly during the

reign of Amenhotep III and is nearly 300 yards long. An adjacent court, added by Ramses II, contains large statues of him, as well as numerous reliefs depicting scenes from Ramses' military victories and varied representations of religious festivities. An obelisk from this court was removed to France in the 19th century and now stands in the Place de la Concorde, Paris.

LYCIA, an ancient kingdom in southwestern Asia Minor that flourished during much of the 1st millennium B.C., until its conquest by Alexander the Great in the 4th century B.C. Lycians had a written language bearing some

Luristan: Bit plate from horse harness. Bronze. Ca. 1100 B.C.

Luxor: Portico (west side) enclosing the Courtyard of Amenhotep III, the Temple of Amon. Egyptian, 18th Dynasty.

relationship to early Greek. Lycia's main city, Xanthus, was situated on two low hills adjacent to the Xanthus River. This site has yielded remains of a large rectangular building—known as the Lycian Parthenon—and an altar to Artemis, dating from the 5th century B.C. Also unearthed at Xanthus are remains of distinctive Lycian tombs, which were set up on pillars. A famous collection of Lycian antiquities is in the British Museum.

LYDIA, a wealthy kingdom of west-central Asia Minor that prospered during the 1st millennium B.C., with Sardis as its capital. The Lydians were influenced by both Greek and Near Eastern cultures. They made fine textiles, rugs, and gold and silver jewelry and apparently initiated the coinage of money—a custom they quickly introduced to the Greeks. The earliest known design on Lydian coins is the head of a lion, signifying the authority of the then reigning king, Ardys (mid-7th century B.C.). Croesus was Lydia's last king. Lydia may have been the original homeland of the Etruscans of Italy.

LYSIPPUS, the favorite sculptor of Alexander the Great and one of the most prolific and famous of 4th-century B.C. Greek artists. He worked chiefly in bronze and is said to have produced over 1,500 works, mostly portraits. He studied the canon of Polyclitus but created a new ideal, characterized by slender proportions, precision of detail, and harmony of form. These are exemplified by a Roman copy in the Vatican of his Apoxyomenos—an athlete scraping oil from his body with a strigil. Lysippus was also well known for his sculptures of animals, especially horses.

M

MAAT, an ancient Egyptian term for world order, as created by the sun god, Ra, and often cited in sacred texts. Maat was also conceived of as the goddess of truth and natural order and was symbolized by an ostrich feather.

MACHU PICCHU, a well-preserved ancient Incan city, located northwest of Cuzco on an Andean promontory nearly 9,000 feet above sea level. Probably the most spectacular of all ancient Peruvian cities, Machu Picchu was forgotten until its rediscovery by Hiram Bingham in 1911. Although its massive architecture, consisting of fitted and dressed stones, was typical of other Incan cities, its city plan was unique. The different levels of buildings here conformed to the mountain-top topography, and a maze of stairways allowed access from one level to another. The city was divided into sectors probably to accommodate different social classes. Although the exact function of the city is conjectural, it is apparent from the numerous terraces that agriculture was of prime importance. Machu Picchu may have been the ancestral home of the Incas prior to their migration to Cuzco.

MADAGASCAR, or Malagasy, the fourth-largest island in the world, is located off the coast of southeast Africa in the Indian Ocean. Its elaborate and ancient tombs, standing menhirs, and fortified hill villages, as well as the Malagasy language, which is said to be a branch of the Polynesian linguistic family, tend to indicate that the island was first settled by peoples from Asia, probably between 300 B.C. and 200 A.D. Later migrations brought African and Arab influences. Malagasy culture was distinguished by a preoccupation with death, and a complex burial cult was developed. Tombs were large and contained the remains of entire families. Bodies were disinterred every five years, amid joyous ceremonies, and rewrapped in new funerary garments. Still to be seen on the island are sculptures associated with cemeteries. These may be flat wooden panels, placed on the roofs of tombs and carved in the form of stylized human beings, crescent moons, or octagonal suns. Other funerary sculpture found here are wood shafts, bearing several bands of scenes carved in the round. The early people of Malagasy also erected engraved stone dolmens as memorials to those who could not be buried in ancestral tombs.

Machu Picchu.

MADJAPAHIT, the Javanese empire that controlled Sumatra, Molucca, the Borneo coast, and part of the Philippines from A.D. 1293 to the end of the 14th century. Javanese culture took its form under Madjapahit rule. Its characteristic brick and stone architecture can be seen in the great temple complex of Panataran. Fine Hindu and Buddhist statuary was made, and stone reliefs bear a striking kinship to the cutout figures of the modern *wayang.*

MAES HOWE, the site in the Orkney Isles of the finest prehistoric tomb in Britain. Built about 2000 B.C. in the style of the Megalithic Builders and closely resembling the great tombs at Los Millares and elsewhere in Spain, it has a chamber in the form of a cross with three small niches and a high corbelled roof. It is approached by a 54-foot passage, the inner part of which is formed in floor, walls, and roof by four immense stone slabs each 18 feet long. The whole is covered by a cairn of loose stones. The treasure within the tomb was probably looted by Vikings in the 12th century A.D.

MAGDALENIAN, the well-known upper-paleolithic culture, famous for its cave art and named for its type site at La Madeleine in the Dordogne, France. It superseded the Aurignacian period in western Europe and lasted from about 15,000 B.C. to 10,000 B.C. Magdalenian artifacts reflect communities of Cro-Magnon fishermen and reindeer hunters. As the reindeer moved north with the retreating ice, Magdalenian men turned to hunting bison and horses, which were moving into Europe from the Russian steppes. The tools, weapons, ornaments, and art of the Magdalenians were derived from the earlier Aurignacian culture. Superb cave murals, some superimposed several times over earlier paintings, are the hallmark of the era. Magdalenian art can be seen in the caves of Altamira, Lascaux, Font-de-Gaume, and Trois Freres. Other features of Magdalenian culture were decorative bone and ivory carvings, ornamented throwing-sticks for increasing the velocity of spear-casting, and magic staves thought to be for bewitching game.

MAGHREB, a region of North Africa bordering the Mediterranean Sea on the north and the Sahara desert on the south. It contains parts of modern-day Morocco, Algeria, Tunisia, and western Libya. The Maghreb has long been famous as a source of antiquities, which include the remains of Phoenician, Carthaginian, Roman, and Islamic civilizations, as well as prehistoric rock paintings.

MAGLEMOSIAN CULTURE, a widespread mesolithic culture of the north European plain, roughly contemporaneous with that of the Azilian of southern Europe. At that time, from about 7000 to 5000 B.C., north Europe consisted of one large land mass that included Britain in

Magdalenian: Cave painting, detail. Peche-Merle, France.

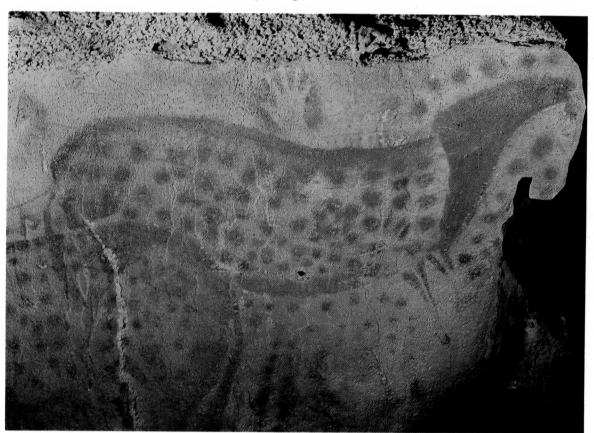

the west to Poland, Russia, and southern Sweden in the east. The culture is named for its type site in Zealand, Denmark. Maglemosian man hunted and fished in the forests and lakes of north Europe. He made tools of tiny flints, or microliths, set in wood or bone. Maglemosian objects, often decorated with geometric designs, include animal and fish spears, axes and adzes, and paddles and dugout canoes.

MAGNA GRAECIA, a Latin name designating the Greek colonies of Sicily, southern Italy, and Asia Minor, which reached their cultural peak from the 5th through the 3rd centuries B.C. They included Syracuse, Taras, Pyrgoi, Sybaris, and Poseidonia, among numerous others. The sculpture and architecture of these towns ultimately became a major factor in the Hellenization of Roman art.

MAHAYANA, a major branch of Buddhism, also called the "Greater Vehicle." It is considered northern Bud-

dhism, having become dominant in China, Korea, and Japan and, in its Lamaist form, in Tibet, Nepal, and Mongolia. Mahayana art tends to be highly ornate. At its Lamaist extreme, art objects are often fantastic and exotic, reflecting northern Buddhism's concern with magic and complex ritual. Southern Buddhism, as expressed in Hinayana art, is essentially fundamental and conservative.

MAIDEN CASTLE, site in Dorset, England, whose earliest remains show an unfortified hilltop village of about 2000 B.C. Later it was succeeded by a barrow tomb 600 yards long. A fortification of a single rampart and ditch was erected around 350 B.C. When the Romans were on the attack in Britain during the 1st century B.C. the 15-acre site was greatly strengthened with three and four lines of ramparts and winding, defensible entrances. Vespasian's 2nd Legion captured the fort in 44 A.D. Hastily buried casualties from this last stand have been unearthed near the gates, along with simple pottery and piles of sling stones stored beside the ramparts.

MAIDEN STONE. See **PICTS.**

MAIKOP, southern Russian site of a Kuban tomb, dating from around 2300 B.C. It contained some of the finest copper-age objects ever discovered in the Caucasus region. A wooden multichambered structure buried beneath an earthen mound held remains of a chieftain and two probable attendants. Art objects included a silver goblet with a landscape frieze showing numerous animals—one of the earliest known depictions of this kind in the world. Also found were two gold bull figurines, originally attached to pole tops supporting a canopy over the mound grave. Copper axe heads and various ornaments were also in the tomb. Jewelry of lapis lazuli, turquoise, and carnelian probably came from contact with central Asian peoples. Most Maikop art objects are in the Hermitage, Leningrad.

MALACHITE, a green carbonate of copper used as a pigment and for encrusted ornamentation. It is seen on ancient art objects, especially those of the Egyptians.

MALANGGAN, on the western Pacific island of New Ireland, a term used for funerary ceremonies and for the art objects associated with those rituals. Brightly colored malanggan masks and figures were carved from a single piece of wood in open-work style.

MALAYS, a Mongoloid peoples who occupied the Malay Peninsula and Archipelago, the Philippines, and other islands near southeastern Asia, probably between 2500 and 1500 B.C. They were boat builders, fishermen, and farmers; their early religion was animistic. Malayan culture was profoundly influenced by India, especially with the foundation of two powerful and Indian-orientated kingdoms—the Sumatran Srivijaya (5th century A.D.)

Malanggan: Detail of a malanggan pole. From New Ireland. (British Museum, London)

and the Javanese Shailendra Dynasty (9th century A.D.). Islam became dominant from the 13th century. Early Malayan art objects include a large variety of carved wooden sculpture, notably anthropomorphic ancestor figures.

MALI, an ancient West African empire. This wealthy state, the political successor to Ghana, grew from the small kingdom of Kangaba (founded about 1000 A.D.). Its economic power derived largely from control of the lucrative gold trade. The best-known ruler of Mali was Mansa Kankan Musa, who from 1312 to 1337 governed the empire from its capital of Niani. At that time Mali was one of the large empires of Africa. Mansa is said to have made a pilgrimage to Mecca in 1325. Along the way he spent and gave away so much gold that he upset the economy of Egypt. Mali fell to Tuareg invaders in the mid-17th century.

MALLIA, ancient Minoan port site on the northeastern coast of Crete, dating from perhaps 2000 B.C. It had a few narrow streets and closely packed two-story houses, constructed of timber and stone. It was damaged, either by invaders or natural disaster, around 1700 B.C. and again before 1400 B.C.—this time, perhaps, by the rival king of Knossos. Mallia's major ruin is a palace built around a large central courtyard. Its necropolis has yielded fine golden pendants and necklaces and gold and ivory decorated weapons.

MALTA, an island in the Mediterranean, south of Sicily, which, including the smaller islands of Gozo and Comino, is only 122 square miles in extent. It is very important in European prehistory as the site of some of the oldest stone temples in the world, which date from about 3000 B.C. First settled about 4000 B.C., Malta witnessed invasions from Sicily in about 3000 B.C., from the Aegean several centuries later, and by 800 B.C. it was under Phoenician control. In the earliest prehistory of Malta the main influences came direct from the Near East, not to any great degree mediated through the early Minoan civilization of Crete. Evidence for this stems from Maltese antiquities, including the form of temples and an apparently complex ritual with phallic and mother-goddess worship alien to Crete; the fine finish and decoration of pottery; and the absence of all metal from sacred sites, probably as being taboo. When, in later times, sea traffic from Minoan Crete declined, Malta's culture seems to have become stagnant and died. Malta may have played a major role in the development of European Megalithic culture.

MALTA TEMPLES. A series of great stone temples of about 3000 B.C. on this island may be the oldest extant stone temples in the world. They are built with oval, open courts, entrance, passages, and one or more apses, or roofed chambers, leading off the inner court. The construction is megalithic, of huge stone slabs set on end or on edge, and roofed in part with capstones or domed corbelling. The buildings resemble the rock-cut tombs found in the Near East and also in Sardinia and in Malta itself. But they are clearly temples and not primarily tombs, though later burials are found in them. The religion of Malta man is necessarily hard to ascertain, but it appears to have been a worship of the gods of death and the underworld. Female figurines and male sexual symbols indicate a Near Eastern mother-goddess cult. Among major Maltese temple sites are Gigantija, Mnajdra, and Tarxien.

MAMALLAPURAM. See PALLAVA PERIOD.

MAMMOTH-BONE CULTURE, a recently discovered ice-age hunting culture of the Soviet Ukraine. Sites there date from 20,000 to 75,000 years ago. In settlements along the Dniester, Dnieper, and Don rivers, Mammoth-Bone man lived in large heated dwellings built of mammoth bone and wood and covered with animal hide. Bone and stone carvings of Venus figures and animals, especially the mammoth, have been found.

MANA, the Polynesian term for the innate power or spiritual force possessed to a varying degree by men, animals, or inanimate objects. Extraordinary qualities of men, including leadership or artistic ability, and things—for example, the curing power of a carved mask—are attributed to the power of mana. Since mana can be obtained by transfer, in many world areas it is

Mana: Mask. Oceanic. Carved wood. (Pigorini Ethnological Museum, Rome)

Maori: Headman's cloak. (Musée Ethnographique, Geneva)

closely associated with the practice of cannibalism. By consuming parts of a human being, one could absorb some of his vital force. Taboo, a set of special prohibitions, is designed to protect one's own mana from danger. Art objects from primitive or prehistoric worlds are sometimes taboo but, much more often, are the embodiment of mana.

MANCHU. See CHING DYNASTY.

MANDALA, a circular and magical diagram in Hindu and Buddhist art. It depicts the spiritual plan of the universe and the cosmological arrangements of deities.

Temples were laid out according to mandalas, and mandalas are often seen painted on cloth or walls.

MANGBETU, central African people living principally in northeastern Zaire. Before the 19th-century arrival of Europeans, the aristocratic Mangbetu had formed kingdoms. A long, cylindrical hairdress was their distinguishing mark. Elegant harps carved from wood or ivory and effigy pottery displayed humans with this characteristic hairdressing. The custom of wrapping an infant's head in a band to achieve the desired elongated head complemented the unusual hair style.

Mari: "Superintendent Ebihil," detail. Alabaster. 3rd millennium B.C. From the temple of Ishtar. (Louvre, Paris)

MAORI, a Polynesian people inhabiting the islands of New Zealand. An aggressive people who waged incessant warfare, the Maori arrived in their present homeland about 1350 A.D. as immigrants from central Polynesia. The colder climate of New Zealand led the Maori to develop a material culture quite different from the rest of Polynesia. In need of warm clothing, they alone of all Polynesians devised a way of weaving fibers. Their fortified villages contained sturdy houses constructed from hewn logs. In every village the central meetinghouse, lavishly decorated, was a source of pride. The front gable, door, and window frame were carved and adorned with ancestor figures. On the inside of the meetinghouse carved and woven panels alternated, and rafters were painted with floral scroll patterns. Useful objects such as bowls, war clubs, and canoe prows bore the unique and distinctive Maori decorative patterns of spirals, concentric circles, and rich open work. The most prized of all possessions was a *hei tiki*, a small grotesque human figure carved from emerald-hued jade. High-ranking Maori men tattooed their faces profusely with curvilinear designs, and the women tattooed their lips.

MARAE, a type of religious structure found throughout eastern Polynesia and on Easter Island. Their exact age is uncertain, but they were still being built when the first European explorers arrived. The marae consists of a stone platform of varying dimensions and detail, which in most cases is located at the far end of a paved court. Sometimes stone phallic figures are found in connection with a marae. Maraes reach their greatest elaboration in Tahiti and Hawaii. The most famous of these, at Mahiatea, Tahiti, consists of a ten-stepped stone platform that rises to a height of 50 feet. In most locations the marae site was used for social gatherings, important funerals, ancestral worship, and political meetings. On Tahiti and Hawaii, however, the marae was regarded primarily as a monument to the family that built it, as well as a sign of prestige and rank.

MARDUK, the chief god of Babylon and Babylonia, also known as Bel. He superseded Enlil around the 13th century B.C. He ruled nature, kingdoms, and man and was the source of civilization. His primary mission was to conquer the god of primeval chaos, Tiamat.

MARI, an ancient city in Syria, now the site of Tell Harari, on the right bank of the Euphrates near the Iraq border. Mari was, in the period just before 1760 B.C., the most prosperous city of the middle Euphrates, particularly under the reign of Zimri-Lim, its last king. It was destroyed by the Babylonians under Hammurabi. Zimri-Lim's palace, covering about six acres and the best preserved of its period and place, is the most remarkable of the many discoveries made at the site. Numerous temples, as well as statuettes, bronze lions and vessels,

and painted frescoes, have been excavated here. Also found were some 25,000 cuneiform tablets shedding much light on the politics and economics of the period.

MARIB, the capital of the Sabaean kingdom in what is now Yemen in the southwestern part of the Arabian peninsula. It was fixed as the leading Sabaean city around 400 B.C. and was the center of an enormous system of irrigation dikes. The collapse of this system in 542 A.D. was a crucial event in the history of the area. Most impressive of the many antiquities found here is the great temple attached to an elliptical precinct wall.

MARS. See ARES.

MASADA, a natural rock fortress on the western coast of the Dead Sea in Israel. A stronghold of Herod the Great, it was later held by a garrison of Roman troops, who were massacred by a band of Jewish Zealots in the revolt (70 A.D.) against Rome. The Zealots, who had occupied Masada, were the last survivors of the Jewish uprising, and when it failed they committed suicide rather than surrender to the Romans. Excavations at the site have uncovered the remains of Herod's palace, 12 scrolls inscribed with passages from Genesis, Leviticus, and apocryphal books, and a large piece of scroll belonging to the Hebrew original of the Book of Jubilees.

MASTABA, in Egyptian archaeology, a burial structure built aboveground; forerunner to the pyramids. It was characteristic of the Old Kingdom (2800–2200 B.C.) and developed as an elaboration of the prehistoric burial pit and mound. The typical mastaba was rectangular, with a flat roof and inward-sloping walls, and built of brick, faced with limestone.

MATHURA, an ancient Indian city, sacred to Krishna, on the river Jamuna in Uttar Pradesh and the center of a famous school of sculpture that flourished under the Saka and Kushan kings from the end of the 1st century B.C. until the 5th century A.D. It is here that some of the earliest images of the Buddha were produced. These Buddhas, influenced by Greco-Roman art via Gandhara, are characterized by massive proportions and subtle, rounded modelling. Hindu and Jain icons also came from Mathura. The Mathura art style later developed into that of the Gupta.

MAURYAN EMPIRE, in Indian history, the first empire to join the various regions of the Indian subcontinent into one political unit. This brilliant epoch began when Chandragupta Maurya expelled the Greeks from the Ganges area in 323 B.C. His grandson Asoka, who ruled from 269 to 232 B.C. and extended Mauryan conquests from the Hindu Kush mountains in the far north deep into south India, is revered as the greatest of all Indian leaders. He inaugurated Buddhist art by founding many stupas. After his death the empire began to disintegrate until it was overtaken by the Sunga in 184 B.C. Art of the period, heavily influenced by the Achaemenids of Persia, was imperial, as characterized by the Mauryan Palace at Pataliputra (modern Patna) and the finely sculpted pillars of Asoka. These highly polished stone pillars marked a major departure from traditional Indian carving in wood.

MAUSOLEUM. See HALICARNASSUS.

MAYAN CIVILIZATION, the best-studied and most admired civilization of the New World, where it represents the highest intellectual and artistic peaks ever achieved by indigenous Americans. At their height, the brilliant Maya people controlled a vast area, stretching from northwest Honduras, through most of Guatemala, to the southern Mexican states of Chiapas, Campeche, and Yucatan, a mixed geographic region of highlands and jungle lowlands. Among their major ceremonial cities were Tikal, Copan, Chichen Itza, Uxmal, Palenque, Piedras Negras, and Bonampak. Although parts of the Mayan area were settled as early as 1500 B.C., the earliest Mayan pyramids date from about 200 B.C. and the oldest

Mayan stele from 292 A.D., when the hallmarks of Mayan civilization first appear—hieroglyphic writing, a calendar more accurate than that used in Europe of the period, the carving and dating of stone stele, the use of the corbelled arch, and a rich and distinctive art style. The origins of Mayan civilization can be traced in great part to the ancient Olmecs of the Mexican gulf coast, who possessed early forms of the calendar and a system of hieroglyphic writing. Mayan society, largely settled in and around ceremonial centers, was divided into several classes, the most important of which were the priest-kings, who asserted royal rule. Other classes included musicians, artists, highly skilled artisans, and merchants, whose trade with other Mexican peoples brought constant stimuli to the development of Mayan life and art. However, the overwhelming majority of Maya were simple farmers who spent much of their adult life building ceremonial centers and religious structures and satisfying the needs of the powerful priestly class. All aspects of Mayan life were pervaded by religion, a religion obsessed with the ordering of time, thus the ritual significance of the Mayan calendar, and with a pantheon of Mayan gods, who demanded grandiose religious centers. Elaborate religious ceremonies were conducted from temples built atop pyramids. Human sacrifice was practiced, but sparingly, as contrasted with other Mexican civilizations. Formerly it was thought that Mayan ceremonial cities were largely independent city-states and only loosely confederated. However, recent research points to the collaboration of the priestly classes, from the various cities, in matters concerning ritual, technology, and a common culture. In the 9th or early 10th century A.D. Mayan civilization suddenly collapsed, and dozens of religious centers were mysteriously abandoned. It is suggested that a widespread revolt of Mayan farmers against the priestly hierarchy brought this about. In the Yucatan, of about a century later, Mayan culture enjoyed a brief resurgence, especially in its chief city, Chichen Itza. This rebirth may have been due to Toltec invasions from central Mexico. However, with the infusion of a fresh and vigorous blood into the stream of Mayan life, a new militarism, as well as a great artistic decline, finally occurred. Toltec-Mayan times are characterized by the worship of Kukulcan, said to be the Toltec god Quetzalcoatl. By the time of the Spanish Conquest in the mid-16th century the great Maya people had degenerated into small, warring chiefdoms.

Mayan Metalwork is extremely scarce due to the lack of natural ore deposits in ancient Mayan lands. An object of gold, discovered beneath a stele at Copan, dates from before 1000 A.D. but is probably a trade piece. Metalwork seems to have been introduced by the Toltec invaders during the 10th century A.D. Spectacular examples of this art have been retrieved from the Sacred Cenote at Chichen Itza, into which they were thrown as votive

Mayan Civilization: Governor's Palace, Uxmal, Yucatan.

Mayan sculpture: "Lady Making an Offering." Stone bas-relief. 600–900 A.D. From Yaxchilan. (National Museum of Anthropology, Mexico City)

offerings to the gods. Characteristic of these are large hammered disks of gold which usually depict Toltec warriors or motifs. Another group of metal objects from the Sacred Cenote reveals the influence of lower Central America.

Mayan Painting. Examples of Mayan painting survive in codices, on pottery, and in the form of large-scale wall paintings. In addition, evidence shows that most Mayan sculpture was painted. The oldest Mayan murals are at the site of Uaxactun and are dated earlier than 633 A.D. Wall paintings are also found at the cities of Tikal, Palenque, and Chichen Itza, but the most famous come from the site of Bonampak in the Mexican state of Chiapas. Here, paintings, covering three rooms, have miraculously survived the effects of centuries of jungle dampness; they date from before 800 A.D. The stylistic canons of Mayan painting are the same for both large murals and small pottery. The subject matter usually consists of events from Mayan ceremonial life, arranged in narrative form. The murals at Bonampak depict musicians, dancers, priests, soldiers, and prisoners. The silhouette of the figure is stressed by the use of a heavy black outline, which is filled with bright unshaded color. Although the human body is shown from different angles, the head is always seen in profile. Depth is created by overlapping figures or placing them at different levels in the composition. A great variety of polychrome colors is used, including the mysterious "Maya blue," a pigment that until recently modern investigators were unable to duplicate. The Bonampak murals are considered unique in all of Mayan art for their energy and emphasis on the individuality of each figure. Of the three surviving Mayan codices—the Madrid codex, the Paris codex, and the Dresden codex—the strong color contrasts and the animation of its figures makes the Dresden codex the most artistic. The Mayans also created elaborately designed mosaics, as can be seen at Uxmal.

Mayan Sculpture. Considered by many to be the best expression of Mayan artistic genius, sculpture exists in jade, wood, stucco, flint, and stone. The Mayan artist excelled in relief carving, famous examples of which are on stele. These are large stone monuments erected at regular time intervals in Mayan cities between the years 328 and 880 A.D. Often they were associated with carved altars. All of the stele follow the same basic formula of a central figure surrounded by decorative elements. It is possible to follow a stylistic evolution from the earliest stele, with simple carvings, to the late period of excessive flamboyance. The great portion of Mayan sculpture, however, was created for the purpose of architectural embellishment. Low-relief limestone panels decorated both the inside and outside walls of buildings. Carved lintels of wood

and stone cover doorways, and elaborate stucco work can be seen in reliefs, masks, and life-size sculpture attached to buildings. On a smaller scale, Mayan artists produced exquisite jade masks, figurines, jewelry, and stone plaques carved in low relief.

Mayan Terra Cotta. Figurines created in this medium rank among the masterpieces of Mayan sculpture. Terra-cotta art reached its high point from the 7th to 10th centuries A.D., when the production of pottery figurines increased enormously. Most of these small figures were mold-made, with details added by hand. Their bodily proportions are lifelike, and facial features are portrayed with a minimum of stylization. They depict diverse human, animal, mythological, and grotesque subjects and range in size from a few inches to approximately two feet. Many of the figurines are actually whistles and probably had a ceremonial function still unknown to us. The finest of Maya terra-cotta figurines come from the cemeteries on the island of Jaina off the Campeche coast. These are well noted for their realism, elegance, and refinement. The city of Palenque also produced highly artistic figurines but is best known for an unusual type of decorated incense burner. It consists of a tall hollow tube, modelled with anthropomorphic heads or figures. Vertical flanges are attached to the side of the tube, thus giving the appearance of wings. After firing, most Maya terra cottas were painted in bright polychrome colors.

Mayan terra cotta: Painted vase. 400–800 A.D. (La Aurora Museum, Guatemala City)

Mayan sculpture: Urn. Polychrome terra cotta. 13th century A.D. From Mayapan. (National Museum of Anthropology, Mexico City)

MAZAPAN WARE, a characteristic orange-on-buff pottery of the Toltecs of Tula, Mexico. It made its appearance with their rise to power around 1000 A.D. The pottery is usually in the form of a simple bowl. The distinctive design element of Mazapan ware is a multiple, parallel, wavy line painted on the bowl's interior.

MBULU NGULU. See KOTA.

MEDES, the Indo-European inhabitants of northwestern Iran, closely related to the Persians. They arrived in the area, probably from northern India, around the 17th century B.C. From the 9th to the 7th centuries B.C. they were dominated by the Assyrians. Medes were the leading force in the destruction of the Assyrian Empire, under their king Cyaxares, in 612 B.C. In this period the Persian kings were vassals of the Medes, who had their capital at Ecbatana. In the mid-6th century B.C., however, the then Median king was defeated by his son-in-law, Cyrus the Great of Persia, who established the Achaemenid Empire in which, in theory, the Medes were equal partners. Little is known of early Median history, but in later times, as inscriptions and monuments attest, they had become highly Assyrianized.

MEDUSA, the best known of the Gorgons, the three terrifying sisters of Greek myth, but, unlike the others, mortal. Also called Gorgo, she is a popular subject in Greek art, variously depicted as being beheaded by Perseus, running alone, or, later, as having a snake-wreathed face of touching beauty.

MEGALITHIC CULTURE, a term derived from the Greek for "great stone" and now used to describe some of the most impressive monuments of European prehistory, including the circles or lines of massive standing stones, such as those of Stonehenge in England or Carnac in Brittany. Archaeologists attribute these remarkable engineering feats—some stones weigh as much as 100 tons—to a seafaring people who, it is said, brought the idea of vast megalithic ceremonial centers, sepulchres, and temples from the eastern Mediterranean. These Megalithic Builders arrived in Spain and on nearby islands, then gradually made their way by sea round the coasts of western and northern Europe. Megalithic monuments and, in still greater numbers, chambered stone tombs, buried under a mound or cairn and containing many bodies, extend from Spain and Portugal through Brittany, Ireland, the west coast of Wales, England, and Scotland, through the Shetland Isles and into Norway, Sweden, Denmark, and Holland. The dates of this stupendous activity range from 2400 to about 1500 B.C. Weapons have not been found on megalithic sites in northern coastal Europe. On the other hand, the objects found correspond exactly to those of the local culture of the nearby hinterland. It is thus supposed that the Megalithic Builders came not as invaders or conquerors but as missionaries of a new religion, with new ideas about burial and perhaps about an afterlife. Seemingly, these ideas were peacefully adopted by the various local, pre-existent peoples of coastal Europe.

MEGARON, the central room of a Mycenaean palace. Megarons from the 13th century B.C. at Mycenae, Tiryns, and especially Pylos, in the southwestern Peloponnesus, show it had two porches, was roughly square in shape, and featured a round hearth centered between four columns. The king's throne was placed along one wall. The megaron's design may have influenced the architectural evolution of the later Greek temple.

MEGIDDO, site of ancient fortifications in northern Palestine, about 15 miles southeast of Mount Carmel, dating from about 3500 B.C. Early historical inhabitants were the Canaanites; and among the most important finds at Megiddo is a collection of some 200 carved ivory and stone vessels dating from about the 13th century B.C. Israelite remains date from roughly 1000 B.C. and include horse stables built by Solomon and other Israelite kings. These stable ruins show evidence of good planning and sturdy construction and were quite extensive, accommodating perhaps 450 horses. Megiddo was destroyed by the Assyrians in the 8th century B.C., then rebuilt as an Assyrian provincial capital. Major modern excavations were conducted here by a German team in 1903–05 and by the University of Chicago from 1925 to 1939.

MEIDUM, an Old Kingdom site in Egypt, most notable for the 4th Dynasty tomb of Atet, dating from about 2600 B.C. The famous Geese Fresco was painted for that tomb. There are many private tombs at Meidum having reliefs carved in a distinctive sunken style, the resulting depressions originally having been filled with colored paste or plaster, which fell out years after they were applied. Also at Meidum is the pyramid of the 3rd Dynasty pharaoh Huni.

MELANESIAN CULTURE, a culture spread over several large islands in the western Pacific Ocean. Melanesia, coined from the Greek words meaning "black islands," was so named because of its dark-skinned inhabitants who, in the very distant past, migrated from southern Asia. Unlike the small coral islands of Polynesia and Micronesia, many islands of Melanesia, such as New Guinea, New Caledonia, and the principal islands of the Bismarck Archipelago, have a large land mass. This has led to a difference in culture between Melanesian farmers of the interior and fishermen of the coast. Men's houses—the meeting places for the governing males—were dominant features in all Melanesian villages. A belief in the existence of *mana*, or vital force, in all living and non-living things, formed the basis of Melanesian religious thought. Many aspects of life were devoted to the unending quest for increasing one's mana. Head-hunting and human sacrifice were customary, often as revenge for the murder of relatives. These ritual practices, often viewed badly by outsiders, were in fact ways of enhancing one's mana. The Melanesians were artists of the first order. They carved canoe prows and sterns, elaborate war clubs, masks, ancestor figures, and funerary images. Houses and household objects were often richly adorned with painting. Although arts varied considerably from tribe to tribe, they created forms that were,

202

in general, active, colorful, and bold. Since wood was the main medium—highly perishable in tropical climates—nearly all extant Melanesian art dates from no earlier than the late 19th century.

MEMPHIS, a major city of ancient Egypt, on the west bank of the Nile near the Delta region, said to date from the 1st Dynasty reign of Menes in the late 3rd millennium B.C. It was the most important political center of the Old Kingdom but was finally eclipsed by Thebes in the 21st century B.C. Little of importance remains at the site of Memphis, although nearby burial sites at Saqqarah and Giza contain much art and architecture of the Memphis-based Old Kingdom rulers. The patron god of Memphis was Ptah, considered creator of the world and of other gods.

MENDE, a West African people living in Sierra Leone. Organized into small chiefdoms, they have occupied this area as settled farmers for more than four hundred years. The Mende have the distinction of being the only African people whose women wear and control the use of ritual masks. The magnificent conical black mask used by the Bundu Society, a secret women's organization, depicts a woman with elaborate hairdressing, a large curving

forehead, and rings of fat around the neck. Other sculpture such as the elongated figurines of the Yassi, a curing society, have a graceful quality. Stone heads, called *nomoli,* are found in the area inhabited by the Mende. These objects may have been made by a people who predated Mende settlement.

MENHIR, in European prehistory, a single upright stone, in natural form or roughly shaped. It is the simplest form of megalithic monument and was usually set up beside a grave. Some menhirs are small, some as high as 30 feet, as at Carnac in Brittany.

MENORAH, originally the seven-branched golden candlestick of the Hebrew Tabernacle, cited in Exodus (25:31). Its treelike shape and floral decoration may have been derived from the ancient "tree of life" motif. The earliest extant representation of a menorah is on the Arch of Titus, built in Rome by Domitian in the 1st century A.D. This relief-carving was based on the menorah from the Temple of Herod in Jerusalem, which was lost in the Jewish-Roman war of 70 A.D. The oldest existing menorah is a carved limestone candlestick, 24 inches wide and 18½ inches high, with floral decoration. It dates from the early centuries of the Christian era and is in the synagogue of Hammath, near Tiberias, in Israel. A variant type of menorah, having eight branches, is used in the Jewish festival of Hanukah to celebrate each of the feast's eight days and the victory of the Maccabees over

Menorah: Detail from Titus' Arch, Rome. 1st century A.D.

Mescala figurine: Funerary mask. Mosaic. 400–600 A.D. From Guerrero. (National Museum of Anthropology, Mexico City)

the Greeks in the 2nd century B.C. Some of the most ornate eight-branched menorahs are silver pieces of 17th-century European origin, almost invariably marked with the initials of Christian silversmiths. Brass versions from approximately the same era are assumed to be of East European origin. Important menorah collections include those in the Jewish Museum, New York City; the Prague Museum; and the Israel Museum in Jerusalem.

MERCURY. See **HERMES.**

MEROE, the capital city, from the 8th century B.C. to 300 A.D., of the ancient kingdom of Kush in Nubia. It succeeded Napata as the chief city of the region. Stretching for miles along the Nile above modern Khartoum, in the Sudan, the remains of Meroe, showing heavy Egyptian influence, include great walled enclosures, temples, palaces, royal baths, and pyramids. The site is still scarcely explored. Vast iron-ore slag heaps at Meroe testify to the city's importance as a center for the working and smelting of iron. The Chinese-inspired bronzes, Greek head of Dionysus, as well as a Roman head of Augustus, now in the British Museum but unearthed at Meroe, indicate a far-flung trade. Other finds here were fine graphite pottery and stone stelae and votive plaques, deeply engraved with representations of Meroitic kings and glyphs of an undeciphered language. Large stone rams guard what was once a temple of the sun. Iron technology was probably introduced to central and western Africa through Meroe.

MERSIN, the site of a tell (Yumuk-tepe) on the Mediterranean coast of Turkey, southwest of Tarsus. Excavations here go back to a level dated about 6000 B.C. Monochrome pottery from this era has been found. A considerable series of levels follow which can be correlated with the sequence of early Mesopotamian cultural development. The site was later occupied by the Hittites and early Greeks.

MESA VERDE, a region of southwestern Colorado, famous for its great apartment-type pueblo villages built in the shelter of overhanging cliffs. Cliff dwellings in Mesa Verde reached their height from the 11th to the end of the 13th centuries A.D. The largest of these pueblos, the so-called Cliff Palace, had over 200 rooms and 35 sacred kivas. The rooms, which are less than five feet high, were probably used only for sleeping and storage, while most daily activities were carried out on the terraced roofs. An odd and distinctive feature of Mesa Verde architecture is the several-story tower. Their function is still unclear, but it is speculated that they might have been defensive structures, ceremonial buildings, or primitive solar observatories.

MESCALA FIGURINES, in Pre-Columbian art, highly abstract, small-scale stone sculpture found in burials near the town of Mescala in Guerrero, Mexico. Although the figurines cannot be dated with certainty, it seems likely that the bulk were made between 300 and 600 A.D. Their subject matter is limited to human and animal effigies, masks, and representations of temples. The most distinctive and highly unusual characteristic of the style is the reduction of the figure's features into planes and the depiction of details by means of grooved lines. The overall shape of the figures resembles that of a hand axe, an extremely important implement to prehistoric peoples and frequently associated with supernatural power. Mescala figurines were traded as far as the city of Teohuatihucan, in central Mexico, and probably influenced some of the stone carving produced there. The great appeal of these abstract figures to the modern eye has made them highly desired by collectors.

MESOLITHIC. See **STONE AGE.**

MESOPOTAMIA, a very ancient and historic region along and between the Tigris and Euphrates rivers in modern Iraq. It was the forcing-ground of the world's earliest civilizations. The word "Mesopotamia" comes from the Greek and means "between the rivers."

METAPONTUM, ancient Greek seaport in southern Italy, founded about 680 B.C. It was one of several secondary colonies of the then rapidly growing Magna Graecia and was actually a subsidiary port to the larger nearby city of Sybaris, which had been founded some 50 years earlier.

METATE, a flat or grooved stone, widely used in Pre-Columbian Mexico for grinding corn. Often the metate was decorated with carving or elaborated into a zoomorphic form for ceremonial use, thus transforming a simple utilitarian object into a work of art. In European archaeology a metate is called a quern.

METOPE, the rectangular panel between the triglyphs of the frieze of a Greek Doric temple. It is usually blank but could be painted or carved in relief.

MICRONESIAN CULTURE, an island culture spread over the northwestern Pacific Ocean. Micronesia consists of several far-flung archipelagoes (the most important being the Carolines, Pelew, Marianas, Gilberts, and Marshalls), with a total land area of only 1,400 square miles. Its name, aptly coined from the Greek, means "small islands." Ferdinand Magellan brought Micronesia into European annals with his trans-Pacific voyage in 1521. By the end of the 17th century the Spanish, through a variety of barbarisms, had nearly destroyed the native population. Living primarily as fishermen, the Micronesians were influenced by the surrounding seas. They were expert builders of canoes and boats, and they made numerous household articles from the abundant seashells. The inhabitants of Yap had a distinctive currency, large stone discs with a hole in the center. As for art, figurative sculpture was rare, occurring only on ceremonial bowls and painted house murals. A few extant carved figures show the human body elegantly reduced to abstract geometric forms.

MIDDLE KINGDOM, a period in ancient Egyptian history from roughly 2100 to 1786 B.C., encompassing the 11th and 12th dynasties, during which royal power was transferred from Memphis to the Upper Egyptian capital of Thebes. The period saw unprecedented amounts of sculpture in the round, rendered in more nearly naturalistic style than the stiff and blocklike works of previous eras. Tomb paintings and reliefs show something of a departure from older magical and religious themes in favor of historical scenes. The Middle Kingdom came to an end in the late 18th century B.C. with the Hyksos invasions.

Melanesian culture: Decorative shield. Polychrome relief and vegetable fibers. From New Guinea. (Musée Ethnographique, Geneva)

Middle Kingdom: "Soldiers," detail. Painted wood. Egyptian. From Asyut. (National Museum, Cairo)

Ming Dynasty: Dish. Blue and white porcelain. Chinese, early 15th century A.D. (National Museum, Tokyo)

MILDENHALL. See **ROMAN CIVILIZATION.**

MILETUS, ancient Greek town in western Asia Minor, founded around 1500 B.C. and predominantly Ionian in ethnic and cultural flavor. It was located on an inlet from the Aegean Sea (now silted over) and had three-story-high houses, contained within a city wall. It was a thriving commercial town that reached its height of prosperity around the 6th century B.C. A cultural center, it produced

some of the earliest Greek philosophers. Miletus was sacked by the Persians in the early 5th century B.C.

MIMBRES WARE. Considered to be the outstanding aesthetic accomplishment of the American Southwest, Mimbres ceramics were produced by the people of the Mogollon culture between 1000 and 1300 A.D. They are distinctive for their life-form motifs, which, although highly stylized, are also lively and charming. The designs were painted on the interior of otherwise shallow, sparely decorated mortuary bowls. Subjects include frogs, insects, birds, various animals, and human beings in naturalistic poses. Authentic Mimbres ceramics characteristically have a hole punched through the center of the design. This was done to "kill" the spirit of the bowl before it was placed in the grave with its former owner.

MINERVA. See **ATHENA.**

MING CH'I. See **HANIWA FIGURES.**

MING DYNASTY, in Chinese history, a brilliant period, 1368–1644 A.D., during which peace and prosperity reigned and the Chinese aesthetic was brought to new peaks of perfection. The dynasty began when a former Buddhist monk, Chu Yuan-chang, seized Peking from the Mongols after four centuries of occupation and unified all of China by 1382. In all, there were 17 Ming emperors, ending with the Manchu capture of Peking in 1644. Painting in the Ming era was practiced by the scholarly class, with Sunglike landscapes predominating. Ming porcelain, perhaps the greatest in Chinese art, featured a brilliant white base with cobalt blue or polychrome decoration. In general, Ming arts were bold, vigorous, and assured.

MINOAN CIVILIZATION, a highly sophisticated and often dazzling civilization that arose on the Aegean island of Crete in the 3rd millennium B.C. It had long disappeared from history when Sir Arthur Evans, the great British archaeologist, rediscovered it in the early 1900s. He named this earliest of Aegean civilizations Minoan, after Minos, a legendary king of Crete. Although they are often termed the first civilized Europeans, especially by European authorities, the Minoans were an ethnically mixed people with roots in Asia Minor, the Near East, and in Egypt. In short, they were non-European in genesis and spoke a language unrelated to those of the Indo-European family. Their earliest script, called Linear A, is yet to be deciphered. At its height, from about 2000 to 1400 B.C., Minoan civilization rivaled the contemporary civilizations of Egypt and the Near East. The island of Crete, which is situated in the eastern Mediterranean, perhaps 100 miles south of the Greek mainland, enjoys a coastline with many natural harbors, harbors which provided the Minoans with an extensive maritime trade, the source of their wealth and prosperity, and served as havens for their large navy. Although Cretan culture may date back to the 5th millennium B.C., it was not until the mid-3rd millennium B.C. that Minoan civilization began to take shape: a written language was developed; royal palaces, such as those at Knossos, Mallia, and Phaistos, were built; large and well-populated towns sprang up around the royal complexes; and urban centers were connected by paved roads. By about 2000 B.C. Minoan

civilization, after a meteoric rise, was flourishing. More than 100 cities and towns had been founded, royal palaces were lavishly appointed, and townspeople lived in storied houses constructed of stones or sun-dried brick. Town sites, always artistic in conception, were laid out on terraced slopes to accommodate the landscape. This period, the so-called Middle Minoan, came to a sudden and violent end in about 1650 B.C., when, it is thought, a catastrophic earthquake struck Crete. For some 50 years after the disastrous event the Minoans rebuilt their towns and cities and their royal palaces, and by 1600 B.C. a new and more glittering era of Minoan history was ushered in. Sometimes termed the Late Minoan period, it remained in flower until about 1450 B.C. During these golden 150 years power became centralized in the palace of Knossos, the home of the double axe.

Minoan Civilization: "Young Prince," detail of a restored fresco from the Palace of Knossos. (Herakleion Museum, Crete)

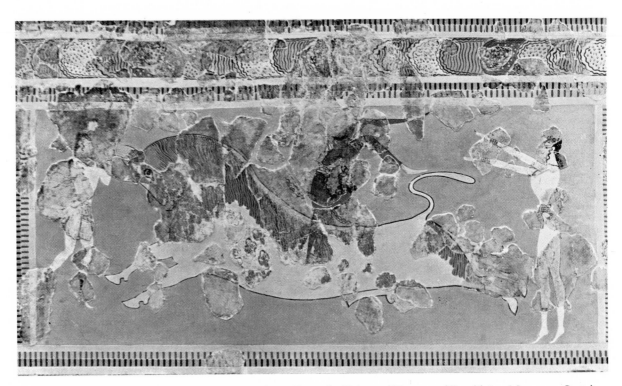

Minoan art: "Bull-leaping." Fresco. Ca. 1500 B.C. From the Palace of Knossos. (Herakleion Museum, Crete)

While Linear A awaits translation, modern Minoan studies center on architectural remains as the chief source of archaeological reconstruction. Minoan palaces, for example, were vast and unfortified building complexes, quite different in style and design from those of contemporary Egypt and the Near East. Instead of having a unified architectural design, built around a royal throne room, Minoan palaces had a bewildering array of rooms (storerooms, workshops, living quarters, council chambers, etc.) within a multilevel royal compound, which surrounded a large open courtyard. Inside the palaces were many staircases, light wells, and an ingenious system for the running of water and drainage. Brilliant frescoes decorated palace walls, and their spirit and content reflect a Minoan love of surprise and a penchant for gaiety and vividness. Although the great palaces at Knossos and at Hagia Triada obviously housed kings who were probably priest-kings, little is as yet known about the Minoan monarchy or its political systems, religion, and social composition. Minoan religion, as surmised from surviving art objects, played a limited role in the life of the people, and unlike the ancient religionists of Egypt and the Near East, the Minoans raised no temples, made no images of priests, nor used cosmic or astral symbols. Worship seems to have taken place at outdoor altars, near mountain tops, groves of trees, or caves. Central to the Minoan pantheon was a female deity, who probably derived from the prehistoric mother-goddess cult of Anatolia. In sculpture and painting she often appears holding snakes and wearing a Cretan gown that exposes her large breasts. Also depicted in Minoan art is the well-known religious rite in which a dancer vaults over the back of a bull; its meaning remains a mystery. This singular and fascinating civilization neared its end in about 1450 B.C. after the eruption of nearby Thera and with the arrival on Crete of the warlike and aggressive Mycenaeans. These invaders from the Greek mainland pillaged Minoan towns and palaces and quickly gained control of the entire island. Evidence of Mycenaean rule over Crete comes from the appearance of a new written script, called Linear B by modern scholars. Now deciphered, the script proved to be archaic Greek written with Minoan characters. Under Greek-speaking foreigners, Minoan culture and art lost its own character and vitality, and by 1200 B.C. Minoan civilization had disappeared. Crete soon became a forgotten backwater in the Aegean world.

Minoan Art and Antiquities. Unique and easily recognizable, Minoan art, as with Minoan lifestyle, was free, inventive, dynamic, and naturalistic. Although Egyptian influence is evident in the earliest phase of Minoan civilization, by 2000 B.C. the island of Crete had a developed art tradition of its own. From the Middle Minoan period, which lasted to about 1650 B.C., came finely sculptured reliefs in terra cotta and faience, an artistic Kamares ware, and engraved gems and seals. Typical of this epoch are depictions of the mother-goddess; the bull-and-dancer

Minoan art: "Snake Goddess," restored. Ivory and gold. Ca. 1500 B.C. Found near the Palace of Knossos. (Museum of Fine Arts, Boston; gift of W. Scott Fitz)

religious ritual; simple genre scenes, such as cows, goats, etc., suckling their young; and representations of house facades. Sculptured relief panels were probably used to decorate palace, as well as house, interiors. By 1600 B.C. and the start of the Late Minoan era, art enjoyed its greatest flowering. Fresco painting, especially those at Knossos and at Hagia Triada, became the hallmark of Minoan art. In astonishing profusion the Minoans painted their palace walls with landscapes, seascapes, fish and marine life, animals and birds, scenes of everyday life and of religious festivals. Painted pottery, formerly bearing abstract designs, now portrayed naturalistic marine motifs: fish, seashells, octopuses, etc. Small statues and carved ivory figurines were also produced, but large-scale sculpture was shunned by the Minoans. The Minoan genius for richly composed but delicately colored frescoes was equalled only by the quality of Minoan metalwork. Of simple and elegant form are bronze, gold, and silver bowls and vases, drinking cups, and other objects. Bands of reliefs often enhanced the beauty of Minoan metalwork. The famous smiths and painters of ancient Crete strongly influenced the artisans of later Mycenaean civilization. A major collection of Minoan art is in the Herakleion Museum, Crete.

MINOS, a legendary king of Crete, around whom centered the oldest tales of the island. (Historically, Minos may have been the name of a dynasty.) Minoan civilization takes its name from him. Considered a just ruler by Minoans, he became one of the judges in Hades, but Greek myth shows him as a cruel tyrant demanding annual sacrifice of Athenian youths and maidens. His wife, Pasiphae, mated with a bull at the instigation of the god Poseidon and bore the Minotaur, a monster, half man and half bull, who was hidden in the Labyrinth of Knossos, where, it was said, he devoured human flesh.

MIRAN. See SERINDIA.

MISSISSIPPIAN CULTURE, a way of life that spread over what is now the southern and eastern United States between 900 A.D. and 1700 A.D. The Mississippian people, possibly from Mexico or under Mexican influence, took possession of the central Mississippi Valley through migration and conquest and built ceremonial centers, which consisted of large plazas, temple platforms, and fortifications. The most outstanding artistic products of the Mississippians appear after 1400 A.D., when the Southern Death Cult, with its repertoire of strange art motifs, took hold in the area. Art objects include heavy stone pipes carved with human and animal effigy figures; shell pendants; and squatting male statues, engraved palettes, and carved bowls, all of stone.

MITANNI, a short-lived kingdom in northern Mesopotamia·that arose in the mid-2nd millennium B.C. Composed of a mixed population, the kingdom was probably ruled by Hurrians, a steppe people of central Asia, related to the Aryans of India. The Mitanni kingdom came to dominate Assyria and dealt favorably with Egypt; Mitanni princesses married successive pharaohs. Mitanni was overthrown by the Hittites early in the 14th century B.C. The Mitannians left a variety of painted pottery, usually with white decoration on a dark ground, and apparently introduced to Mesopotamian art the motifs of elaborate "sacred trees," as well as crested griffins.

MITHRA, the Persian god of light and truth, eventually identified with the sun god who conquers the demons of darkness. He is represented as a young man, with the peaked cap and flowing robes of the Near East, usually in the act of slaying a bull. Frescoes of Mithra are found on the end walls of numerous *mithraea* all over the Roman Empire. Mithra was a special favorite of the Roman armies, and his worship competed with that of Jesus in early Christian times.

MITHRAEUM, a temple of Mithra, the Persian god of light and truth. Either a natural or artificial cave, a mithraeum was small and oblong with a central nave and side benches where devotees reclined at sacred banquets. Mithra slaying a bull (*tauroctony*) was painted or sculpted on an end wall. Mithraea dating from the first three centuries A.D. have been found throughout the Roman Empire, especially in the northern and western frontier provinces, the Rhine and Danube regions, and along Hadrian's Wall in Britain.

MITLA, sacred city of the Zapotecs and Mixtecs and burial place for kings and high priests, located about 20 miles southwest of Oaxaca, Mexico. Probably founded prior to 600 B.C., it was related to nearby Monte Alban. Mitla thrived as a small but important city until the Spanish Conquest under Francisco de Orozco in 1521. Built in gently rolling terrain, the city consisted of five widely separated architectural complexes. It is unknown how the broad spaces between the buildings were used, but they were probably ceremonial plazas. Major interest in Mitla lies in its fine temples and palaces, embellished with mosaic panels of small, carefully fitted inlaid stones. These mosaics, as well as frescoes in Mixtec style, gave the entire city an aura of grace and beauty.

MIXTEC CIVILIZATION. At first confined to the hilly country of the Mexican state of Oaxaca, the Mixtecs, by 1300 A.D., had spread over a vast area, including parts of the states of Veracruz, Puebla, Tlaxcala, Guerrero, and Morelos. The singular character of Mixtec civilization, as contrasted with other Mexican civilizations, was Mixtec concern with the secular affairs of men rather than with religion. The wide range of their conquests as well as their history are known to us from beautifully painted codices that still survive. The oldest written records in Mexico, the codices trace the Mixtec people back to the 7th century A.D. Among the historic people who appear in these

Mixtec Civilization: Ceremonial brazier. Terra cotta. 15th century A.D. From Veracruz. (National Museum of Anthropology, Mexico City)

212

Mixtec art: Cup. Painted terra cotta. From Tanayuca. (National Museum of Anthropology, Mexico City)

records was the famous Mixtec leader Eight-Deer, who was born in 1011 A.D., conquered neighboring peoples, such as the Zapotecs, visited the Toltec city of Tula, enjoyed eight marriages but was put to death in 1063 A.D. Since the worship of the gods was not preeminent in Mixtec society, there is an absence of great Mixtec ceremonial sites. They used the old Zapotec cities of Monte Alban and Mitla as burial grounds. The Mixtecs consolidated their conquests by marriages which established rule by aristocratic dynasties. Redoubtable warriors as well as artists, they were one of the few peoples to resist conquest by the Aztec nation. Surviving groups of Mixtec people still retain a distinct cultural identity in modern-day Mexico.

Mixtec Art and Antiquities. Although lacking in examples of large-scale sculpture and poorly represented in architecture, the Mixtecs excelled in painting and mosaic-making and in the production of small-scale objects of exquisite refinement. Their great artistic range is best seen in the contents of the so-called Tomb 7 from Monte Alban, one of the few Pre-Columbian burials to remain intact until modern times. Here amid the bodies of a Mixtec ruler and his seven retainers, archaeologists found a wealth of gold and silver ornaments, richly carved animal bones, lapidary work, thousands of pearls, copper objects, and turquoise mosaic. Outstanding Mixtec frescoes and wall mosaics embellish the old city of

Mixtec art: Cup. Painted terra cotta. From Tanayuca. (National Museum of Anthropology, Mexico City)

Mitla. The Mixtecs seem to have introduced a new form of pottery, in which a sculptural element is incorporated with the pot shape. One of the most important regional centers of Mixtec art was in the state of Puebla, where a mixture, known as the Mixteca-Puebla style, developed. This style became extremely widespread and had a major influence on Aztec art.

MNAJDRA, on the south coast of Malta, is the site of a temple of ancient date, built between 3000 and 2000 B.C. A characteristic plan shows an entrance, an oval court, and apses, or small roofed chambers, at the rear, which were probably the most holy places. The whole is surrounded by a wall of large stone slabs, similar to the rest of the building and forming a convex forecourt.

MNESIKLES See **PROPYLAEA.**

MOABITES, a Semitic people who, toward the end of the 2nd millennium B.C., settled in Palestine in the highlands east of the Dead Sea. They played an active part in Palestinian power struggles and are frequently mentioned in the Old Testament. The only significant written record left by the Moabites is the Moabite Stone, a stele of black basalt left by the Moabite king Mesha in the 9th century B.C. This—in an inscription very close to contemporary Hebrew—records a Moabite defeat by the Israelites.

MOCHICA CULTURE, an ancient Peruvian culture that flourished from the 1st century B.C. to the 8th century A.D. The Mochica people had great irrigation works. Centered in the Moche River valley of coastal Peru, they are best known for their prolific production of effigy pottery. These handsome vessels depict birds, animals, fruits, vegetables, and startlingly realistic portraits of humans. Mochica craftsmen also fashioned objects in gold, silver, and copper. Mochica arts influenced the later styles of Peruvian civilizations.

MOGHUL PERIOD, in India, extended from the 16th through the 18th centuries A.D. It is named for India's Moghul conquerors, Islamic Persians, who unified the subcontinent, infusing fresh cultural life and initiating a period of Indian artistic splendor, especially in painting and architecture. Leader of the invaders was Babur (1494–1530), whose successor, Humayun (1530–40), appointed Persian artists Mir Sayyid Ali and Abdus Samad to the imperial court, thus establishing Moghul painting. During the reign of Akbar (1556–1605) genuinely native schools of Moghul architecture and painting developed.

Mixtec art: Sacrificial knife. Turquoise, jade, shells, and coral. 15th century A.D. (British Museum, London)

Akbar had a strong personal interest in painting, and beginning with his rule the Persian-inspired miniature became the dominant painting genre. Miniature painting flourished at his academy, where native artists worked under Persian tutors. Moghul architecture reached its peak of splendor under Shah Jehan (1628–58), whose important edifices include the palaces at Agra, Lahore, and Delhi and the famous mausoleum for his consort, the Taj Mahal.

MOGOLLON CULTURE, along with the Hohokam and Anasazi, one of the great cultural traditions of the American Southwest. Its characteristic traits appear around 100 B.C., and the Mogollon are believed to be the earliest people in the region to produce ceramics and practice agriculture. Their early pottery decoration consisted of highly complex arrangements of triangles, frets, and scrolls. The most distinctive of their ceramics is Mimbres ware, which appeared around 1000 A.D. and introduced life motifs for the first time in the Southwest. The Mogollon people also carved a great many stone objects, including paint palettes, disks, and smoking pipes. Although Mogollon culture lasted until 1700 A.D., its later stages were strongly influenced by the Hohokam and Anasazi cultures and can hardly be distinguished from them.

MOHENJO-DARO, one of the two main cities of the mysterious Indus Valley civilization. It is located in Pakistan on the west bank of the river Indus, 400 miles southwest of Harappa. The site was discovered in 1922. Larger and better preserved than Harappa, the city was about one mile square and dates from about 2300 to 1750 B.C. Its buildings were of burnt brick and reveal a high degree of architectural skill. The citadel contains the public buildings, including an 80-foot-square pillared hall and a great ritual bath (39 by 23 feet). Mohenjo-Daro carried on an international trade, and seals produced here have been found in Mesopotamia. The final collapse of the city came with the Aryan invasions.

MOLOCH. See PHOENICIAN CIVILIZATION.

MOMOYAMA PERIOD, an era of rule in Japan by the military commanders Nobunaga and Hideyoshi from 1573 to 1603 and a time of splendor in Japanese arts. In 1573 Nobunaga drove the last Ashikaga shogun from Kyoto. Nobunaga was murdered in 1582, and Hideyoshi reunited all of Japan, controlling it through vassalage. The break with Chinese artistic tradition came during this period, and the foundations of Japanese art were laid. The Kano school dominated painting, and the famous Seto kilns were established.

MONGOLS, a central Asian people who were nomadic horsemen and marauders of Asia's steppes and deserts from China to Iran and into eastern Europe, especially in the 12th through the 14th centuries A.D. Their vast empire began assuming shape under Genghis Khan (1162–1227).

In 1258 they established a capital at Baghdad, and two years later, under Kublai Khan, they overran China. Their native religion, shamanism, involves worship of nature spirits (e.g., forests, wind, rocks) but cross-cultural influences generally occurred in places that they conquered; most notable was a Buddhist-Lamaist counterinfluence. Nomadic existence discouraged artistic development, but the working of precious metals and stones into jewelry prevailed for centuries as a distinct Mongol art. Mongol sculpture, mainly of the 16th century and later, is commonly in wood or gilded copper and shows Tibetan influence.

MONOTHEISM, in religion, the belief in one god, as opposed to polytheism, the belief in many. Judaism, Christianity, and Islam are monotheistic, while most other religions are polytheistic. The ancient Mesopotamians, Egyptians, Greeks, Romans, Hindus, and Chinese are some of the many peoples who worshipped a pantheon of gods and spirits.

MONS, a people who occupied Burma's Irrawaddy Valley from the early 1st millennium A.D. During the 5th and 6th centuries they became Indianized, assimilating both Hindu and Buddhist cultures. Major Mon cities were located in the Irrawaddy delta region, although physical traces have all but vanished and practically nothing is known about Mon art. However, the most important monuments in the ancient Burmese city of Pagan are considered to be Mon-inspired.

Mochica culture: Jar. Painted terra cotta. (Private collection, Paris)

Monte Alban: "Mask of Murcielago." Jade. 15th century A.D. (National Museum of Anthropology, Mexico City)

MONTE ALBAN, the major Zapotec ceremonial center, near Mitla, in Oaxaca, Mexico. Originally a hilltop site, it was settled about 700 B.C. and flourished for more than 1,000 years. In its early periods Monte Alban shows Mayan and Teohuatihucan influences; there are hieroglyphic inscriptions and stone calendars. The Great Plaza in the center of the city is one of the most splendid public spaces ever created in the New World. Four large struc-

Monte Alban: "Jaguar with Collar." Painted, plaster-coated clay. 200 B.C.–200 A.D. (National Museum of Anthropology, Mexico City)

tures stood in the center of the plaza, where the Zapotecs came to take part in religious or civic ceremonies. Buildings of Monte Alban were painted but were not extensively decorated with sculptures or reliefs. One set of reliefs, however, has survived to be popularly known as *los danzantes*, or the dancers. There are Zapotec tombs, one of which, the so-called Tomb 7, has yielded a treasure of gold and silver objects, probably Mixtec in origin. In the 11th century Monte Alban was occupied by the Mixtecs.

MOORS, a mixed Arab and Berber people, predominantly nomadic, inhabiting northwestern Africa from Mauritania to Tunisia. They were an integral part of the Islamic world by the 8th century A.D. and invaders of western Europe. The term "Moor" is too imprecise to serve as an ethnic identification, but "Moorish style" is a universally recognized term that applies to much architecture and structural ornamentation in northwest Africa and parts of Spain. Cordoba, Spain, contains probably the most and best of Moorish-style architecture, the distinguishing features of which include extremely varied arch forms, often in a single structure; minarets; bays;

Monte Alban: Ring. Gold. Mixtec, 1300–1521 A.D. From Tomb 7. (National Museum of Anthropology, Mexico City)

216

Mossi: Mask. Carved wood. From Upper Volta.
(Museum of African and Oceanic Art, Paris)

MOSSI, a West African people living for the most part in Upper Volta.. The Mossi were founders of five imperial states, all of which achieved importance before 1500 A.D. Two of these—Yatenga and Ouagadougou—were the most prominent. The Mossi were essentially organizers who imposed their authority on many diverse peoples. Their arts showed little variety and may have been borrowed in the main from the less advanced peoples, such as the Kurumba and Gurunsi, over whom they ruled. One distinct type of Mossi mask, however, had a small oval head with two large triangular eyes and topped either by a human figure or by a long and narrow superstructure. The Mossi also carved small, abstract dolls, the use of which has not yet been determined.

MOTHER-GODDESS CULT, a prehistoric religious cult that arose in the 7th or 6th millennium B.C., possibly in Anatolia, and spread widely over the Near and Middle East, the eastern and central Mediterranean, and elsewhere in Europe and Asia. Its advent coincides with the neolithic agricultural revolution, when farming and the making of pottery first appeared in history. As farmers, the people of the neolithic conceived of the earth—Mother Earth—as the creator, the nurturer, and, at times, the destroyer of life. Mother Earth, or the Great Mother, was often depicted in the ancient arts of Anatolia, Mesopotamia, and the Mediterranean. The earliest evidence of the cult appeared at Hacilar, in Anatolia, where several baked-clay female figurines, dating from about 5600 B.C., were unearthed. Of several centuries later is the mother-goddess vase from Uruk in Sumeria. Around 4000 B.C. the mother-goddess cult reached Crete and from there, in the ensuing centuries, to the Greek mainland. In the 4th or 3rd millennium B.C. stone reliefs of the Great Mother were carved in Troy; elegant and abstract mother figures were sculpted in the Cycladic Islands; and, in Malta, voluptuous cult statues were erected in her honor. By the mid-3rd millennium B.C. the mother-goddess cult, perhaps transported by the mysterious Megalithic Builders, made its appearance in Spain and perhaps even in France and Britain. It is thought that the worship of the mother goddess was associated with orgiastic rites, as well as ritual castration and prostitution.

MOUNT CARMEL, mountainous ridge in modern Israel and the site of the Wadi el Mugharah—Valley of the Caves—inhabited from paleolithic times by men having both Neanderthal and *Homo sapiens* characteristics. Mount Carmel is also the site where comparatively advanced peoples, such as the Natufians, entered the Palestinian area around 8500 B.C. and occupied the caves there.

MOUSTERIAN, a mid-paleolithic period, roughly between 70,000 B.C. and 35,000 B.C., which includes the last ice age. The period was first identified from tools found in a small rock shelter at Le Moustier in the Perigord,

ceramic-tile wall decoration; and ornate column capitals, heavily adorned with palmettes and similar motifs.

MOSAIC, the art of arranging small, colored fragments of stone, glass, tile, or enamel to produce a surface design. Mosaics appear in Egypt and Mesopotamia, in Greece, and in Rome. Well-known Roman floor and wall mosaics were probably based on Greek examples. Mosaics have also been found in Pre-Columbian Mexico.

Mummies: Human-shaped sarcophagus. Painted wood. Egyptian. Ca. 9th–8th centuries B.C. From Thebes. (British Museum, London)

France. The tools included small hand axes, flint knives, scrapers and awls, and some crude bone implements. Mousterian culture was that belonging to Neanderthal man and is found in sites all the way from the Soviet Ukraine to Spain and in Asia and Africa. The animals whose bones were unearthed in association with the remains of this early human culture include the mammoth and woolly rhinoceros.

MUDRAS. See **BUDDHIST ART AND ANTIQUITIES.**

MUMMIES, ancient Egyptian embalmed animal or human corpses, a religious practice connected with belief in life after death. Mummification was a complex process and accompanied by much ritual. Internal organs were removed and placed in canopic jars, later entombed with the mummy. The brain was also removed, via a nostril. The body was treated with preservatives, dried, then tightly wrapped in linen. Papyrus funerary texts as well as art objects and jewelry usually accompanied the body into a decorated wood, stone, or gold casket of vaguely human shape. Mummies of a different kind are found in ancient Andean cultures.

MUNSINGEN. Near this Swiss village in the canton of Bern is a large cemetery dating from the iron age in the last centuries before Christ and belonging to the Helvetii, the redoubtable opponents of Julius Caesar in his conquest of Gaul. Swords and weapons, with Celtic designs, from this site are similar to those discovered at La Tene on Lake Neuchatel. They may be seen in the Basel Museum.

MUREX, the ancient purple dye of Phoenician origin, produced from the murex shellfish, which lives in the Mediterranean Sea. The coloring was widely used for textiles and also by the Minoans of Crete to decorate pottery.

MUROMACHI PERIOD. See **ASHIKAGA PERIOD.**

MUSES, the nine Greek goddesses of literature, science, and the arts, daughters of Zeus and Mnemosyne (memory). Their association with specific arts developed in Roman times. Their attributes are usually given as follows: *Calliope* (epic poetry), shown with wax tablet and stylus; *Clio* (history) with a scroll; *Euterpe* (lyric song) with flutes; *Terpsichore* (dancing) with a lyre; *Erato* (lyric poetry and hymns) with a smaller lyre; *Polyhymnia* (mimic art or sacred song), veiled and pensive; *Melpomene* (tragedy) with tragic mask, ivy wreath, or attributes of individual heroes; *Thalia* (comedy) with comic mask or ivy wreath; *Urania* (astronomy) with a celestial globe. The Muses are generally depicted in flowing garments; the word *museum* is derived from the Muses.

MYCENAE, chief city of Mycenaean civilization, located on a hill overlooking the plains of Argos in the northeast Peloponnesus of Greece. One of the most powerful cities of the Aegean world, Mycenae attained its era of great-

Mycenaean Civilization: Pendant. Gold. 17th century B.C. From the Chrysolakkos necropolis. (Herakleion Museum, Crete)

ness between 1500 and 1200 B.C. At that time it was a strongly fortified citadel, stoutly encircled with massive stone walls, some 16 feet in thickness, with houses and villas inside and outside the walls. A paved highway led to the citadel's entrance, an entrance defended by two large bastions. Deep within the flanking bastions stood the famed Lion Gate, its lintel crowned by an enormous relief of facing lionesses. In the center of the hill fortress were palaces and a circular terrace, probably an early form of the Greek agora, or marketplace. In 1874, under this circular terrace, Heinrich Schliemann, the pioneer German archaeologist, unearthed the royal shaft graves of Mycenae; their fabulous contents can be seen in the National Museum, Athens. Large tholos tombs were also discovered, but outside the walls of the city. One of these, the so-called Treasury of Atreus, has the largest vault ceiling ever built in the ancient world, prior to the Roman Pantheon. The power and splendor of Mycenae declined after 1200 B.C., and in about 1100 B.C. the once great city fell to invading Dorians.

MYCENAEAN CIVILIZATION, the first true civilization of Europe, arose in Greece, particularly in the Peloponnesus, in the 2nd millennium B.C. The Mycenaeans, who called themselves Achaeans, were the successors to the Minoans of Crete as the leading seafarers and traders of the Aegean, or Achaean, world. Unlike the gifted Minoans, however, the Mycenaeans were redoubtable Indo-European warriors who by force of arms established heavily fortified towns at Mycenae, their chief center of power, and at Tiryns, Pylos, Argos, Thebes, and Athens. Probably invaders from the north and the first Greek-speakers to enter Greece, the Mycenaeans were settled on the peninsula by about 2000 B.C. After 500 years of tribal strife, wars, and other hardships, what is now termed Mycenaean culture emerged. By 1500 B.C. and following the lead of Minoan Crete, the Achaeans had become a major land and sea power in the Aegean. They lived in large citadel towns, had a complex social system based on "lord and vassal" relationships, a written script, now called Linear B, and a government of kings and nobles who directed a highly organized military bureaucracy. Artisans, masons, metalworkers, tailors, etc., serviced the rich upper class. All in all, archaeological data, Hittite and Egyptian annals, and readings from Linear B give the impression of a somber, even grim, society bent on combat, quite decidedly non-Minoan in nature. Soon after 1500 B.C. the Mycenaeans launched a series of trade wars, which ultimately led to their conquest of Crete, Rhodes, Cyprus, and the Cycladic Islands; by 1450 B.C. the Aegean was a Mycenaean lake. From their holdings in the Aegean Mycenaean maritime power was felt throughout the Mediterranean. A great trade empire, which was to reach as far north as the Baltic, had been born. In about 1200 B.C. the Mycenaeans engaged in war with Troy for control of Black Sea trade; this, the immortal Trojan War, was epically embellished by Homer some 400 years after the event. At its earliest, Mycenaean religion centered on a mother-goddess cult, probably borrowed from the Minoans. However, by the end of the Mycenaean era the

Mycenaean Civilization: Mask. Gold. 16th century B.C. (National Museum, Athens)

Myron: "Lancellotti Discobolus." Marble. Roman copy of Myron's bronze original. (Terme Museum, Rome)

Olympian male pantheon was fully established; the female goddess had waned in power as such gods as Zeus, Poseidon, Hermes, Apollo, and Ares attained widespread veneration. Offerings to the Olympians, who were to become the chief gods of later Greek civilization, included the sacrifice of animals. The early Mycenaeans buried their royalty in shaft graves, which they filled with great treasures of art, gold and silver vessels and weapons, carved ivory and amber, and ornate jewelry. Some shaft-grave corpses appear to have been mummified, and many had their faces covered with splendid gold death masks; this burial practice may have emanated from ancient Egypt. In later times, Mycenaean kings and nobles were interred in large tholos tombs, the greatest of which, the so-called Treasury of Atreus, was unearthed at Mycenae. After 1200 B.C. and exhausted by the Trojan War, Mycenaean power, once a terrific force in the Aegean, began its decline. Within a century new conquerors from the north, the Dorians, invaded Greece. The worn Mycenaean armies, with their bronze weapons, proved no match against the iron-sworded Dorians, and by about 1100 B.C. all the major Mycenaean cities had been put to the torch. The Dorian conquest of mainland Greece marks a dark age of Aegean history.

Mycenaean Art and Antiquities. While Mycenaean art, especially as expressed in portable objects and painting,

seems to be a provincial imitation of a much finer Minoan art, Mycenaean architecture is unique in the Aegean world. Unlike Minoan palaces, with their wild maze of rooms, the Mycenaean royal citadel was well planned, carefully laid out, and centrally organized around a megaron, a large throne room with a central hearth; the megaron was destined to play a leading role in the later development of Greek temple architecture. In the use of stone the Mycenaeans excelled, and their massive cyclopean walls rival those of Egypt and the masonry of Incan Peru. Large-scale stone sculpture, unknown to the Minoans, was also enjoyed by the Mycenaeans. From the earliest period, stele, with scenes of combat and war, were carved, and towards the end of their era Mycenaean sculptors produced the famous Lion Gate at Mycenae, the first monumental stone sculpture in Europe. In painting, metalwork, and ceramics, the civilizing hand of Minoan Crete is clearly evident. Frescoes from the citadels at Mycenae, Pylos, and Tiryns show techniques and subject matter borrowed from Crete but handled in a distinctly Mycenaean manner; scenes of warfare, of the hunt predominate. In metalwork too, such as can be seen in the gold death masks and the cups and vessels from Mycenae, Minoan craftsmanship was emulated, or perhaps even imported from Crete. Ceramic vases, manufactured in great quantity by the Mycenaeans, are crude and primitive when contrasted with their Minoan counterparts. Mycenaean art, apart from architecture and monumental sculpture, took the spontaneity and naturalism of Crete, the line and movement of the island of Minos, and directed it into more formal, more rigid, and more schematic channels. One of the world's greatest collections of Mycenaean art is in the National Museum, Athens.

MYRINA FIGURES, molded terra-cotta statuettes found at Myrina in Greek Asia Minor. Similar to the better-known Tanagra figurines but later in date (late 3rd to early 1st century B.C.), Myrina figures reflect the sculpture style of the later period. Poses are livelier, deities become popular subjects, and there is a restlessness of technique.

MYRON, a 5th-century B.C. Greek sculptor who worked largely in Athens. A master of bronzework, Myron is known to us only through ancient writings and from Roman copies, in marble, of his masterpieces, among which is the famous Discobolus, the discus thrower. Many of his works decorated the Athenian Acropolis and were justly appreciated for their dynamic symmetry. Exquisite Roman copies of Myron's Herakles are in the Museum of Fine Arts, Boston, and in the Ashmolean Museum, Oxford.

N

NABATAEANS, a pre-Islamic Arab people who settled on the border areas between Arabia and Palestine. Their major city, Petra, lay in the mountains south of the Dead Sea. In the 4th century B.C. the Nabataeans dominated trade from the Arabian interior to the Red Sea and thence to Egypt. They became allies of Rome, and their dominions stretched from the outskirts of Damascus to the Red Sea. Their lands were annexed by Rome in the 2nd century A.D. The Nabataeans developed a unique architectural and sculptural style, and their pottery was among the finest ever produced.

NABU, a major god of the Assyro-Babylonian pantheon, second only to Ashur and, later, Marduk. He was the secretary of the gods and patron of the art of writing. His symbols were the clay tablet and the stylus.

NAGA, a Dravidian Indian spirit of water, depicted in earliest Indian art as a serpent or cobra. In later representations nagas assume human form while wearing a cobra hood behind their shoulders. Nagas also appear in some early Buddhist art of India.

NAGA, primitive tribes that inhabit the Naga Hills, Assam, India, and the Upper Chindwin River area in northern Burma. Racially the tribes are mainly Mongoloid and they speak a Tibeto-Burmese language. In ancient times the Naga were pushed aside by the invading Aryans of the 2nd millennium B.C. However, as head-hunters they remained a threat to the civilized areas throughout much of Indian history. The Naga created highly decorated log drums, carved funerary statues, and almost life-sized human and animal figures for the center posts of their dwellings.

NAGADA, a large Predynastic cemetery in Upper Egypt, near the modern village of the same name. More than 2,000 burials were uncovered here, dating to the period between 3800 and 3200 B.C. The first people of Nagada lavished great care on their burials, and the contents of the earliest graves include stone palettes in geometric and animal forms, ivory pins, armlets, and combs, as well as female figurines and symbols of a fertility goddess. Around 3600 B.C. a new people, bearing Near Eastern influences, settled in Nagada. Beautifully polished stone vessels, in a variety of shapes, were their most distinctive grave offerings. They also designed pottery painted with pictures of ships, religious ceremonies, and sacred ob-

jects such as trees. Clay and ivory figurines of falcons, animals, and humans were modelled by the new people of Nagada.

NANNAR'S ZIGGURAT. See **UR.**

NAPATA, the ancient capital of Kush, in Nubia, the Sudan. Founded sometime prior to the 8th century B.C., the city was famous for its dedication to Amon, the Egyptian sun god; at nearby Gebel Barkal was a great temple to Amon. In 750 B.C. Napatan kings conquered Egypt and there established the 25th Dynasty. With this military success the Napatans undertook the restoration of the Temple of Amon. Stone reliefs, altars, and statues adorned the new temple, in a style characterized by firm modelling and a new, almost brutal, realism. In 550 B.C. the capital of Kush was moved to Meroe, where iron-working had developed into a major industry. A well-known stele in the Cairo Museum has an account of the Napatan victory over the Egyptians.

NAPIRASU STATUE. See **SUSA.**

NARA PERIOD, in Japanese history, a short period (710–794 A.D.) that saw the first permanent Japanese capital established at Nara and the first Japanese histories—the *Kojiki* in 712 and the *Nihon Shoki* in 720—

Nara period: Yakushiji pagoda, Kyoto.

written. Buddhism, along with Chinese Tang ideals, spread throughout Japan and strongly influenced Japanese art. Sculpture was realistic, well modelled, and covered with draperies. Large Buddha images such as the 18½-foot-high Vairocana in the Todai-ji of Nara were common. The Daibutsu of Nara, a colossal bronze Buddha, measures almost 53 feet in height. The Horyu-ji, probably the oldest complex of wooden temple structures in the world, contain important wall paintings. Many other Buddhist temples were built in Japan during this period.

NARMER'S PALETTE. See **HIERACONPOLIS**.

NASCA CULTURE, an ancient culture that straddled the Ica and Nasca valleys of coastal Peru. Although little is known about the culture, which flourished for a period of 400 years beginning about 200 A.D., the general picture is that the people were a democratic group without great distinctions of class. Considerable work went into preparation of funeral offerings for the dead, as textiles and pottery are found abundantly in Nasca graves. Pottery shapes are few and simple, but their gleaming polychromed surfaces radiate an extraordinary beauty. Themes generally include plants and animals, both naturalistic and mythological.

NATARJA. See **SIVA**.

NAT FIGURES, images of Burmese forest and nature spirits who were the original deities of Burma before the advent of Buddhism. Traditionally there are 37 Nats, the 37th and most recent addition being Buddha himself. Typical Nat figures are expressively carved wooden statues, often in teak and having a somewhat doll-like appearance. Nats often have been incorporated into Burmese Buddhist art.

NATUFIAN CULTURE, an early Palestinian culture dating from the 9th to the mid-5th millennium B.C., identified from cave sites at Wadi-en Natuf, which is northwest of Jerusalem. The Natufians, a small-boned, long-skulled people averaging about five feet tall, settled in Palestine from the north. They made no pottery, nor did they domesticate animals. However, they did have seeds of emmer wheat, and the presence of straight bone sickles at Natufian sites in Palestine suggests that they sowed and harvested the wheat. These people later migrated to the Egyptian Delta, bringing wheat cultivation to the early Egyptians. Natufian art ranges from naturalistic sculptures in bone and antler to abstract representations of human heads in stone. Important Natufian sites include burials at Mount Carmel, an early shrine at the base of the tell at Jericho, and an open-air village of 50 stone round-houses at Enyan on Lake Huleh.

NAVAHO CULTURE, the way of life shared by a peaceful, sheepherding people who live scattered across parts of Arizona, New Mexico, and Utah. Archaeological finds suggest that they entered the American Southwest in about 1300 A.D. The outstanding characteristic of the Navaho is their ability to borrow the cultural elements of other peoples and transform and refine them into their own unique style. In this way they acquired their best-known arts from their Pueblo Indian neighbors. These

Nasca culture: Double-spout jar. Painted clay. South coast of Peru. (British Museum, London)

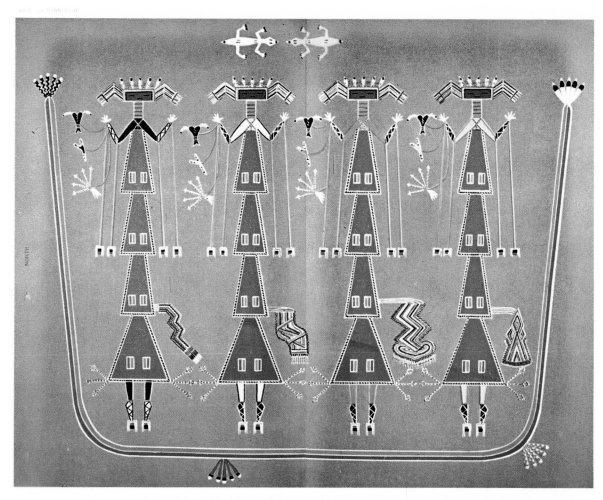

Navaho culture: Painting on sand. (Private collection, Paris)

include sand painting and the weaving of distinctive rugs with geometric designs, still much in demand today. They are also noted for their silverwork, set with native turquoise and cast by original techniques, one of which is the use of sandstone molds, developed by the Navaho themselves.

NAXOS, a Greek island in the Aegean, site of ancient marble quarries, and a center of sculpture from about the 7th century B.C. Thus, Naxos is among the earliest important Greek centers for the production of marble sculpture in the round. At least one of the island's sculptors is known by name—Euthykartides (7th century B.C.). Typical Naxian works are life-size or colossal human figures; the largest known is a standing man—left unfinished in its quarry—measuring roughly 36 feet high.

NAYARIT CULTURE, a Pre-Columbian Mexican culture, in the western state of the same name, which flourished from 300 A.D. to 900 A.D. It is famous for its amazingly naturalistic figurines. These are made of polished redware and frequently represent male and female couples and grotesqueries of bodily deformations and illnesses. The most charming are group portrayals of people sitting in houses or watching ritual ball games.

The presence of shaft tombs, typical of Andean cultures, has led to speculation about direct contact between Nayarit and Peru.

NEANDERTHAL MAN, an early man of the Mousterian period, not a true *Homo sapiens*. His remains were first unearthed in 1856 in the Neanderthal Valley near Dusseldorf, Germany. Since then evidence of Neanderthal has been found widely in Europe, Africa, and Asia. Neanderthal man was little more than five feet in height, heavy-set, with legs slightly bowed. He had a receding chin and forehead, a prominent bony ridge above the eyes, a low skull, but still with considerable brain capacity. He appeared in the last ice age, about 40,000 B.C., used fire and tools of both stone and bone, and lived in cave dwellings. The first traces of planned burial, and hence perhaps of religion, are to be noted here in that Neanderthal buried his dead with weapons and funerary goods under the cave floor.

NEAPOLIS, Latin name for the Greek port settlement on Italy's west coast, dating from the 6th century B.C. (The modern city is Napoli, or Naples.) The original Greek city was laid out on a grid pattern, with three major avenues intersected by about 20 small streets. Traces of the ancient

Nefertiti's portrait: Thutmose, bust. Painted limestone. Egyptian, 14th century B.C. (State Museum, West Berlin)

NEGATIVE PAINTING. Also known as resist-dye painting, this technique of pottery decoration was used widely throughout Pre-Columbian America. The process consists of covering the design area of the vessel with wax or clay and then dipping the pot into a vat of dye, usually black in color. When the wax is removed, the design stands out in its original ground color. Although two-color negative painting is more common, ceramics were also produced in three-color negative designs.

NEOLITHIC. See **STONE AGE**.

NEPTUNE. See **POSEIDON**.

NETSUKES, buttonlike objects or toggles used in Japanese dress to hold the sash for the *inro* (box) firmly under the belt. The earliest netsukes, merely bamboo rings, were made in the 16th century A.D., but by the mid-18th century they were exquisitely carved miniatures of people, animals, and landscapes in ivory and wood. Because there was little demand for sculpture at that time, these buttons provided one of the few creative outlets for Japanese sculptors. Among the most important netsuke-makers were Yoshimura Shuzan, Tachibana Minko, and Nagai Rantei. Today, netsukes are eagerly sought by collectors.

NEW GRANGE, on the bank of the river Boyne, about 25 miles north of Dublin, the site of one of the most outstanding passage graves of Europe. It has a central chamber, passages, and smaller cells formed by great stone slabs, some of which are richly engraved with spiral designs. The whole is surmounted by a vast cairn of loose stones, 265 feet in diameter and 45 feet high. The Megalithic Builders responsible for this and other tombs and places of worship flourished in the bronze age of about 2000 B.C.

NEW GUINEA CULTURE, the way of life shared by the many villages and tribes scattered over this remote and huge island, the second largest in the world, located in the western Pacific. With an area of more than 300,000 square miles and fewer than three million inhabitants, sparsely populated New Guinea was, until the most recent times, one of the world's greatest primitive art-producing regions. Bisected by soaring snow-capped mountains, the land divides itself into several hostile and forbidding regions: the central highlands, steamy rain forest, large and dangerous rivers, and endless coastal swamps. Vast areas of the island still remain unexplored. Although scarce, existing archaeological evidence, especially that of the central highlands, where ancient stone carvings and rock paintings have been discovered, suggests that New Guinea was first settled about 8000 B.C. by immigrants from Southeast Asia and Indonesia. The present-day inhabitants are Papuans, and their resemblance to the dark-skinned peoples of the Guinea coast of Africa led 16th-century explorers to give the island its lasting name. The people of New Guinea speak

city wall have been identified. Also standing are remains of several ancient Greek structures, including a temple and a theater. The city has numerous remains from the Roman era. Nearby was Cumae, the home of the famous Roman Sibyl.

NECROPOLIS, or "city of the dead," an ancient burial ground, usually of major archaeological importance. A necropolis is quite often near the ruins of the city that used it—e.g., Egypt's Valley of the Kings adjacent to the city of Thebes. Rich treasures are often discovered buried in a necropolis.

NEFERTITI'S PORTRAIT. Among the several known portraits of the wife of the Egyptian pharaoh Akhenaten, the most famous is the exquisite limestone bust carved by the sculptor Thutmose and painted in light red. This elegantly executed work, done in the mid-14th century B.C., emphasizes the queen's delicate beauty. It is in the State Museum, West Berlin.

New Guinea culture: Ritual stool. Painted carved wood.

over 700 different languages and can be divided into at least 11 different culture areas, among them the Asmat, Sepik River, and Fly River. In spite of this great cultural diversity, a certain homogeneity does exist. Yams and pigs in the highlands and fish and sago in the lowlands provide the staple diet. Religion is the dominant force in New Guinea life and the major impetus behind its art. Papuans share a belief in a creative god or gods, the veneration of ancestral dead, and a strong faith in the spirit world which exists alongside the real world and can be manipulated by magic. Although both sexes shared in food-gathering and certain crafts, only the men had custody of sacred cult objects and could perform ritual acts. Villages were governed by a men's society, and a large, often elaborately decorated house, the cult center, was constructed for them. Head-hunting and cannibalism, which in some isolated areas still exist today, have a religious significance connected with fertility. The abundance of artistic wealth from New Guinea includes startling masks, painted and modelled skulls, bark paintings, and carved ancestral figures, canoe prows, bisj poles, and animal representations, particularly that of the crocodile.

NEW KINGDOM, a golden age in ancient Egyptian history from roughly the 16th through the 11th centuries B.C. (18th through 21st dynasties), when Egypt, after expel-

New Guinea culture: Panel. Painted wood. (Museum of African and Oceanic Art, Paris)

225

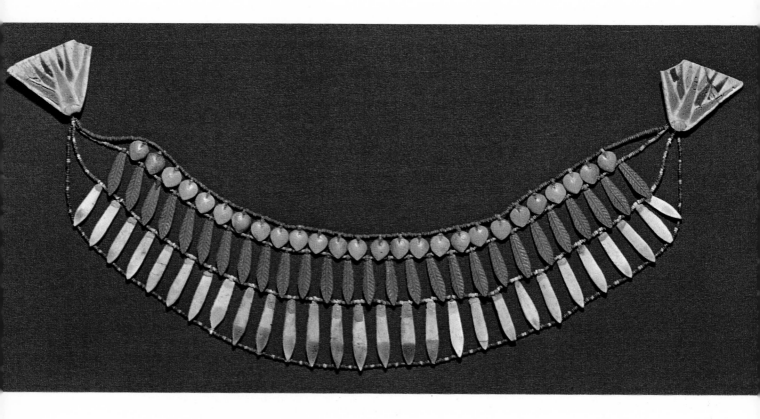

New Kingdom: Necklace. Colored glass paste. Egyptian, 18th Dynasty. From Amarna. (British Museum, London)

ling the Hyksos, experienced its height of power and influence. Under numerous pharaohs named Amenhotep, Seti, Ramses, etc., culture flowered and temple and palace architecture, as well as sculpture and painting, attained high levels of achievement. Karnak became the main religious center and Amon-Ra the major god. It was an era of military might and material prosperity, based partially on imperial expansion into Palestine and Nubia.

NIAH CAVES, an extensive network of limestone caves in Sarawak, Borneo, where relics of several prehistoric cultures have been found. Earliest evidence of human habitation dates to the paleolithic period (perhaps 38,000 B.C.). However, Niah's main site, the so-called Great Cave, contains Buddhist and Hindu ceramic figures dating from as recently as the 10th or 12th centuries A.D.

NIAUX, a very deep cave in the Ariege department of France with paintings on its walls and engravings in clay soil of bison, horses, ibex, and other animals. The mid-Magdalenian period, about 12,000 B.C., to which this art is assigned, is the high point of cave art. The drawings at Font-de-Gaume, Trois Freres, and Altamira belong to the same period. At Niaux the drawings are half a mile from the entrance, and some form of lighting, such as a wick in fat or oil, must have been used to execute them.

NICOYA, a major archaeological region of Costa Rica. From 500 to 750 A.D. the native people of Nicoya created elaborate grave offerings, including effigy metates and "axe-god" jadite pendants, with birdlike heads. After 800 A.D. the region came under the strong influence of Mexico, and a distinctive sculptural style appeared in the "Isthmus of Rivas" area of Nicoya. Statues in this new Mexican style characteristically depict human males with animal guardians on their backs.

NIELLO, a process of decorating gold or silver, said to have originated in Egypt. A design cut into the metal is filled with an alloy paste which, when hardened, leaves the design in permanent black outline.

NIKE, Greek goddess of victory, usually represented as a draped, winged woman holding a palm branch and wreath. She is often represented as a small figure held in the hand of another god—e.g., Zeus or Athena. However, she may also be depicted as a large, free-standing "Winged Victory," such as the Nike of Samothrace, now in the Louvre. Nike was called Victoria by the Romans.

NIKE OF SAMOTHRACE, one of the greatest and most striking sculptural achievements of Hellenistic art. Displayed in the Louvre in a dramatic setting at the top of a long flight of stairs, the winged goddess is posed as though alighting on the prow of a ship, bringing naval victory—perhaps that of Rhodes over Syria in the 3rd

New Kingdom: Coffin of Queen Merit Amon, detail. Painted and gilded wood. Egyptian, 18th Dynasty. From Deir el Bahari. (National Museum, Cairo)

Nike of Samothrace: Parian marble. Greek, ca. 200 B.C. (Louvre, Paris)

century B.C. It was carved by an unknown masterful sculptor from a single block of Parian marble and stands eight feet high. The statue, also called the "Winged Victory," was originally erected on the Aegean island of Samothrace and discovered there in 1863.

NIKKO TEMPLE, located in the town of Nikko, in central Honshu, Japan, a Shinto memorial shrine and mausoleum dedicated to Ieyasu, a shogun who established a united Japanese government in 1603. The shrine was constructed in 1615 in a grandiose manner typical of Japan's Tokugawa period (1600–1867). Its ornate style is not representative of the best qualities in Japanese architecture, but its splendor is indicative of the great wealth that pervaded Tokugawa Japan. The temple's interior is decorated with numerous carvings and wall paintings.

NIKOPOL, a city in northern Bulgaria, located on the Danube River. It was founded by the Byzantine Emperor Heraclius in 629 A.D. and subsequently became a flourishing trade, military, and cultural center. Since medieval times Nikopol has been mistakenly confused with the ancient city of Nicopolis ad Istrum, the site of which is several miles down river. Nicopolis ad Istrum may prove to be an important archaeological site.

NIMRUD, along with Nineveh and Assur, one of three great capitals of the Assyrian Empire, sited about 20 miles southeast of Mosul, Iraq. Known anciently as Kalhu, or Calah, in the Old Testament, this vast city was encircled by a five-mile wall and contained royal palaces, temples, and a ziggurat. Founded by Shalmaneser I in the 13th century B.C., it was rebuilt, after its decay, by Ashurnasirpal II in the 9th century B.C. Nimrud was conquered and burned by the Medes in 612 B.C. Its excavation, begun by Sir Austen Henry Layard in 1845, has unearthed many rich finds, including several huge stone winged-bulls, the Black Obelisk, sculptured reliefs, bronzes, and one of the world's finest collections of carved ivories. Cuneiform inscriptions abound. Most of Nimrud's portable art objects are in the British Museum.

NINEVEH, one of the greatest of ancient Mesopotamian cities and, with Assur and Nimrud, a capital of the Assyrian Empire. Its site, Kuyunjik, is on the east bank of the Tigris across from Mosul in modern Iraq. Nineveh was occupied from prehistoric times, and Hassuna ware has been found there. With the rise of Assyrian power at the beginning of the 1st millennium B.C., Nineveh came into its glory. Excavation has revealed three spectacular royal palaces—those of Sennacherib, Ashurbanipal, and Ashurnasirpal II—and two temples, one to Ishtar, the other to Nabu. In addition, the richest trove of cuneiform tablets ever found and many superb sculptures, including a noble bronze head, have been discovered here. The palace and temple walls were richly decorated with outstanding Assyrian reliefs. Nineveh was destroyed by the joint attack of the Medes and Babylonians in 612 B.C. It never rose again as a city. Many art objects from Nineveh are now in the British Museum.

229

NIPPUR. Now a ruined city southeast of Baghdad in Iraq, Nippur was once the chief religious center of Sumer, dating back to the time when urban civilization in Mesopotamia was beginning. By the 14th century B.C., when Babylonian hegemony had been established, Nippur became the seat of the worship of Enlil, the storm god. Thereafter it gradually declined. The excavation of its tell has brought to light some 40,000 cuneiform tablets, including thousands of literary texts from the first half of the 2nd millennium B.C. These have been the major source of information on Sumerian literature.

NJORD, the Nordic god of wealth and fertility. With his son, Freyr, and the great gods Odin and Thor, he is sometimes accounted one of the principal Nordic deities. He and his son were admitted to Asgard, the dwelling of the warlike Aesir race of divinities, but belonged originally to the more peaceful group of fertility deities, the Vanir.

NOIN ULA, ancient Mongolian burial ground near Lake Baikal and the most important known repository of Hun art and artifacts. The tombs here date from the 1st century A.D., and their grave goods show similarity in art style

Nineveh: "Ashurbanipal's Lion Hunt," detail. Alabaster relief, originally painted. Assyrian, 7th century B.C. From the North Palace. (British Museum, London)

Nootka: Ceremonial cape. Pre-1850 A.D. From Vancouver, British Columbia. (British Museum, London)

(and in burial customs) to both Scythian and Pazyryk peoples. Hun chieftains were buried at Noin Ula with their horses. Their coffins were of lacquered wood, probably of Chinese origin, as were many other items in the tombs, including furniture and bronze cauldrons. The burial chambers' floors and ceilings were covered with woolen fabrics having animal designs and sometimes mounted on leather backing.

NOK CULTURE, a remarkable but enigmatic culture formerly centered in northern Nigeria. It is one of the earliest yet found in West Africa. Nok, whose name derives from a Nigerian mining village where the first archaeological remains were found, spanned a period from about 500 B.C. to 200 A.D. Although much research remains to be done, it is possible that the art of Nok was ancestral to most other art in West Africa. The beautiful and arresting portrait terra cottas, which characterize Nok, have been discovered at many sites across northern Nigeria. Nearly life-size sculptures, depicting animals and richly adorned humans, have also been unearthed. The Nok people also made a coarse, heavy but well-fired pottery, much of which has been found along with sculpture. The Nok were evidently interested in personal adornment, as they wore many beads and possibly nose, ear, and lip plugs.

NOOTKA, a North American Indian tribe of the southern part of the Northwest Coast cultural area. They shared many of the art traits of the neighboring Bella Coola and Kwakiutl, including skillful wood carving and the use of strong colors. Their most notable sculptures are wolf masks in an angular, geometric style. They also made a unique swordlike club from whale bone that was widely traded on the coast and in the interior.

NORDIC PEOPLES, Indo-Europeans who came to occupy Denmark, Norway, and Sweden no later than the 1st millennium B.C. They established a vigorous albeit barbaric culture based on maritime trade and conquest of neighboring peoples. Their so-called Viking period dates from about 800 A.D., when the spirit of adventure and desire for trade drew their sea-warriors to attack Britain and the coasts of Europe; to found the dukedom of Normandy along the coast of France; to settle Orkney, Shetland, Iceland, and Greenland; to share in the foundation of the early Russian state; and even to explore the coast of North America. They travelled in narrow, shallow-draught ships, usually powered by a large single sail and oars. They could be fierce and cruel warriors whose appearance struck terror into the hearts of their more sedentary prey. Nordics were predominantly tall, blond, and blue-eyed and worshipped a variety of gods, including Thor and Odin. They were among the last of the Europeans to be Christianized but by about 1100 A.D. were finally absorbed into Western civilization.

Nordic Art and Antiquities. Early Nordic, or Scandinavian, art is derived at least in part from La Tene culture of the 6th century B.C. It shows heavy Celtic influence, as can be seen in the Gundestrup cauldron. Viking art, a late development of pre-civilized north European culture, reached its zenith from about the 8th through the 11th centuries A.D. Highly advanced artisans, the Vikings produced various types of sculpture—in metal, wood, and stone—and built beautiful and distinctive sailing ships, called *drakkars*. Favored motifs in Nordic art were animals, birds, dragons, and abstract interlacing designs, derived from the spiral and coil motifs of their Celtic La Tene ancestors. Floral and leaf-pattern motifs were almost unknown in Nordic art, and human figures occur but only with relative rarity. Metal sculpture was mainly used for items of personal adornment, such as belts, helmets, weapons, and bracteate—the last being thin metal disks, often of gold or silver, decorated with runic symbols or abstract patterns and worn as ornaments on clothing. Among Nordic stone reliefs are fine carvings on irregular blocks of granite or sandstone, consisting of elaborate runic inscriptions and sometimes of human or ship figures. A notable example is the Jelling Stone, dating from 958 A.D. and carved as a memorial to the royal ancestors of Harold Bluetooth; it is in the National Museum, Copenhagen. The *drakkars* were typically embellished with intricate wood carvings, usually in abstract patterns. Prows were adorned with ornate bowsprits, often depicting the head of a dragon. These ships had religious as well as practical significance and were often used for funerary purposes. Finds of ancient ship burials, such as those of Oseberg and Gokstad, have been recovered in modern times, with enough of their hulls intact to display extremely fine carving. The shores of Oslo Fjord in Norway have yielded the major examples.

NORTHWEST COAST CULTURE, the way of life shared by several large tribal groups, such as the Tlingit, Haida, Kwakiutl, Bella Coola, Nootka, and Tsimshian, settled along the Canadian Pacific coast of North America from southern Alaska and its offshore islands to the state of Oregon. The culture was probably well developed long before the arrival of European explorers and traders, but the dampness of the region has left few archaeological remains. Several social and economic factors contributed to the high level of artistic accomplishment and distinctive styles of Northwest Coast Indians. Among these were the abundance of fish and a reasonably pleasant climate, which brought forth an easy life with much leisure time; the vast cedar forests, which provided raw materials; and the existence of rich and elaborate ceremonies that inspired artworks and motifs. Northwest Coast art was primarily of wood, with motifs concerned with legends and social status. The most characteristic art objects of the region were totem poles and masks, although large-scale sculpture and other beautifully carved wooden objects were also produced. The Northwest Coast Indians created the most significant art of the American continent north of Mexico.

NUBIA, a historical region of northeast Africa, which covers the southern reaches of modern Egypt, from the first cataract of the Nile to the city of Khartoum in the Sudan. In ancient Egyptian times it was known as the Kingdom of Kush; the Greeks and Romans called it Ethiopia, and at the time of the great medieval Christian kingdoms of the Sudan it became known as Nubia. The earliest known inhabitants of Nubia were hunting and food-gathering peoples who arrived about 3900 B.C. Always strongly shaped by Egyptian influence and at times

under direct Egyptian control, the people of Kush nonetheless maintained a distinct identity and finally became an independent state in 1050 B.C. By 750 B.C. Nubian kings were powerful enough to invade Egypt and ruled there, as the 25th Dynasty, until they were expelled in 663 B.C. However, they continued to rule Kush, first from their capital at Napata and, after 550 B.C., from the splendid city of Meroe. Although much remains to be learned about Nubia, it is clear that Kush was a great trading center with contacts as far away as China. The Nubians developed their own script, which has yet to be deciphered. Pottery painting reached a high state of excellence, with thin-sided bowls bearing stylized plants and animals. Art objects unearthed in Nubia include bronze and copper vessels with Chinese motifs, stone stelae, large granite rams which stood as temple guardians, and a variety of artworks of Greco-Roman origin or influence. It is likely that the concept of "divine kingship," as well as the art of metal-casting, were introduced to central and west Africa through Nubia. The region was conquered by the Hamito-Semitic Kingdom of Axum in 350 A.D. At Dendur, a village beyond Aswan in Nubia, there stood a small 1st-century B.C. temple built by the Romans. This temple, more Roman than Egyptian in conception, was given as a gift to the American people by the government of Egypt in 1967. The temple of Dendur was to be reconstructed on the grounds of the Metropolitan Museum of Art, in New York, by the late 1970s.

NURAGHE, a term used for a type of prehistoric tower found only in Sardinia, though somewhat similar types exist in Corsica. The towers date from about 1600 B.C. They are built of massive masonry and consist of two or more stories, with walls slightly sloping inwards. There is only one corbelled-roofed room to each floor. It is probable that Sardinian architecture played a role in the Megalithic culture of European prehistory.

NUZI. See **KIRKUK**.

Nubia: Ring. Semi-precious stones set in metal. (National Museum, Cairo)

O

OBELISKS, tall, thin, tapering stone columns with pointed tops, probably originating in ancient Egypt. They were usually decorated with hieroglyphics and served religious purposes, typically honoring the sun god, Ra. Some were erected to commemorate royalty. Obelisks have been erected by other civilizations such as those of the ancient Near East and in Ethiopia. Cleopatra's Needles are well-known obelisks.

OBSIDIAN, a glasslike volcanic stone, usually gray or black in color, found in many parts of the world. Stone-age cultures used obsidian for weapons and tool-making or for art objects. It is a common material in Pre-Columbian Mexican and Mediterranean antiquities.

Old Kingdom: "Salt Head." Painted limestone. Egyptian. (Louvre, Paris)

OBSIDIAN DATING is accomplished by examining the surface of an object made of obsidian. From the time that the mineral's surface is cut and exposed to air, it absorbs water from the atmosphere at a constant rate. Thus, by scientific analysis of its water content archaeologists can determine how many centuries have elapsed since the obsidian object was originally carved.

OCEANIC, a term used to describe artworks from the islands of the Pacific. It includes objects from Melanesia (and New Guinea), Micronesia, and Polynesia.

OCEO, site of a Funan royal port in South Vietnam's Mekong Delta. The town, although of undetermined size, appears to have reached its peak of importance around the 5th century A.D. Its site contains ruins of Indian-style temples from that era, built of brick and stone. The international flavor of Oceo is evidenced by discovery of coins and other objects originating from as far away as the Roman Empire.

OCULUS, a design motif found especially on prehistoric European art objects and dating from the 2nd millennium B.C. or earlier. The design, resembling a pair of eyes, appears on pottery and carvings and on tomb walls; it probably had religious significance.

ODIN, the chief god of the Nordic pantheon, husband to Frigg. Also known as Woden (compare Woden's day, Wednesday), he was the god of poetry and a master of wisdom and magic. So great were his powers he could even hear the grass grow. He was also the god of war and welcomed dead heroes to feast with him forever in his great hall of Valhalla. Odin was the father of Thor and Baldr.

OINOCHOE, a Greek wine vessel. Flat-bottomed and oval, it had a single handle and a round or trefoil mouth.

OLD KINGDOM, an early and culturally isolated period of ancient Egyptian history, thought to have begun around 2700 B.C. with the establishment of the 3rd Dynasty at Memphis under King Zoser. It lasted until about 2170 B.C., which marks the end of the 7th Dynasty and the temporary dissolution of Egyptian national unity. The Old Kingdom was the era of great pyramid and obelisk construction. Major examples of Old Kingdom sculpture and wall painting were found in the pyramid-tomb complexes at Saqqarah and Giza. Heliopolis, near modern Cairo, was the Old Kingdom's chief center of religion, and worship of the sun god Ra reigned supreme. The Old Kingdom was followed by the rise of the Middle Kingdom.

OLMEC CIVILIZATION, probably the earliest civilization of the New World. The only other culture in the Americas that can claim parallel age and preeminence may be the Chavin of Peru. The ultimate origins of the Olmec are still shrouded in mystery. However, by 1200 B.C. they had permanently settled in and around the

Olmec art: "Colossal Head." Stone. (Park of the Museum of La Venta)

swampy lowlands of Veracruz, along the Mexican gulf coast. Some three centuries later they had established a powerful trading empire, ruled by an aristocracy whose influence was felt as far west as the Pacific coast and south to Guatemala and El Salvador. Underlying Olmec expansion was their need for such raw materials as basalt, serpentine, and the highly prized jade from which they carved so many of their artworks. The Olmec, a people of outstanding cultural achievement, also developed a system of hieroglyphic writing, still undeciphered, and may have invented the so-called Long Count system of calculating dates, later elaborated by the Maya. In the 3rd century B.C. the Olmec were absorbed by the Maya of Yucatan. Often referred to as the "mother culture" of ancient Mexico, Olmec lifestyle profoundly influenced the later civilizations of the Maya, Zapotec, Toltec, Mixtec, Aztec, and others.

Olmec Art and Antiquities. Olmec sculpture is of superb quality, ranging from small, elegant jade figurines to massive "colossal heads," carved from basalt and often weighing as much as 18 tons. Their art appears even more remarkable when contrasted with that of neighboring Mexicans of the same era. Typical of Olmec iconography are the many representations of the jaguar-god, the chief deity in the Olmec pantheon. With slanted eyes, animal-like mouth, and elongated heads, jaguar-god sculpture is often awesome in its effect. A highly gifted people, the Olmec introduced the technique of bas-relief into ancient Mexico, as can be seen in the very early stone altars and stelae at San Lorenzo, La Venta, and Tres Zapotes. Olmec art is uncluttered and, with the exception of a great but abstract mosaic of the jaguar-god at La Venta, essentially realistic. Although Olmec architecture is confined to just a few ceremonial centers, elements of their style are found widely in ancient Mexico. Olmec cave murals, painted in polychrome color, have been discovered as far west as Guerrero, and in Morelos there are large-scale Olmec rock reliefs. Olmec influence is especially evident in the jade figurines and ceramic sculpture unearthed at Tlatilco, near modern Mexico City.

OLYMPIA, a major Greek religious site in the western Peloponnesus, near the river Alpheus. A sacred place from about 1000 B.C., Olympia was by the 8th century B.C. the great national sanctuary of the god Zeus and the site of the Olympic Games, the most important festival in the ancient Greek world. In the 7th century B.C. a temple to Hera was built of wood here. Its wood columns were replaced over many decades by those of stone, which vary in design and proportion and thus present the viewer with a visual chronology of the development of the Doric architectural style. Statues were erected within the temple, among which was the masterful Hermes of Praxiteles; unearthed in the 19th century, it is still in Olympia. The 5th-century B.C. temple to Zeus here was, after the Parthenon, the largest on the Greek mainland. It housed the colossal chryselephantine statue of Zeus by Phidias, said to have been one of the seven wonders of the world. The stadium at Olympia dates from the 4th century B.C.

OMPHALOS. See **DELPHI.**

OPHIR, legendary lost city that may have been on the Red Sea coast of Arabia, or possibly as far east as Ceylon. It is cited in the Old Testament as a source of the fabulous wealth of King Solomon. He used the fleet of Hiram to import gold, musical instruments, and precious stones from Ophir.

ORACLE BONES, relics of China's prehistoric Black Pottery culture and of its bronze-age Shang era. These fragments of animal bones were inscribed with symbols and engravings and used for fortunetelling. Archaeologists have learned much about Yellow River cultures by studying these bone fragments. Relatively modern discovery of oracle bones at Anyang gave researchers the first evidence that the Shang culture was historical.

Olmec art: Group of figures. Light green and white jade. From La Venta. (National Museum of Anthropology, Mexico City)

Oxus Treasure: Bracelet. Gold, originally inlaid. Persian, Achaemenid Dynasty. From the Amu Darya basin. (British Museum, London)

ORCHOMENOS, an ancient Boeotian town on the Greek mainland, occupied from before the 2nd millennium B.C. Orchomenos was a prosperous export center for a distinctive pottery during this period. Important Mycenaean ruins include a large domed tomb, called the Treasury of Minyas, with an interior having relief carving in stone. Orchomenos was destroyed by Thebans in 365 B.C. and later reconstructed—in part by Philip of Macedon and Alexander the Great. An acropolis here dates from the latter period.

ORDOS BRONZES were products of craftsmen working in the Ordos region of north-central China, roughly from the 3rd through the 1st centuries B.C. Important among Ordos bronze artworks are plaques illustrating scenes from a mythology shared in common with Siberian and central Asian cultures. The plaques show warriors in fierce combat, with even their horses struggling against enemy horses. This cultural link between Caucasian and Oriental peoples apparently survived until the Arab invasions of central Asia in the 7th century A.D.

OSEBERG SHIP BURIAL. At Oseberg in southern Norway a ship used for the burial of a princess of the early Viking age (about the 9th century A.D.) was discovered. The ship-grave contained, among many other magnificent carved objects, a ceremonial wagon, pieces of furniture, and sleds. The wood carving, at this high point of Viking art, is characterized by intricate designs of animals interwoven with each other and with plant tendrils in repeating curves, in a style shared with Celtic art.

OSIRIS, a major god of the Egyptian pantheon, profoundly identified with the idea of death and resurrection. Son of Nut and Geb, the deities of sky and earth, and the husband of the fertility goddess Isis, Osiris was the great benefactor of mankind. He brought fertile lands with the rise and fall of the Nile River. Legend has Osiris murdered by his evil brother Seth, god of the desert, only to be resurrected miraculously by his wife, Isis. Osiris is often depicted in mummy wrappings and as wearing the crown of Upper Egypt. Abydos was his chief center of worship. In Roman times Osiris and Isis became the major figures of a miracle cult.

OSTIA, an ancient coastal city at the mouth of the Tiber, dating from the 4th century B.C. and constructed as the seaport for the city of Rome. Ruins of Ostia's fort date from approximately the city's founding and have stone walls about 20 feet high and five and a half feet thick. The town had straight, regular streets, and major structures included a bath, forum, theater, and commercial buildings, some of which still retain their mosaic floors. Most of these ruins date from the 2nd century B.C., by which time Ostia's military importance had become secondary to its commercial significance. The remains of the oldest Jewish synagogue in Europe are in Ostia.

OSTRAKON, a fragment of pottery. In Athens in the 5th century B.C. each citizen wrote or scratched the name of the man he wished to be banished (ostracized) on such a fragment. Six thousand votes meant ostracism for ten years. Ostraka have value for the study of ancient writing, history, and vase decoration and were used widely in the ancient Greek world.

OXUS TREASURE, a hoard of central Asian art objects found in 1877, buried near the bank of the Oxus River (modern name, Amu Darya) in the Soviet Union near Afghanistan. The hoard is believed to date from about 200 B.C. but includes objects from as early as the 7th century B.C. Among the treasures are some of the finest known examples of Bactrian and Achaemenid Persian metalwork, as well as Scythian and Greek jewelry. A ten-inch Bactrian bronze griffin, now in the British Museum, is one of several unusually interesting objects that show a blending of Persian influence with that of the remote Siberian animal style.

OXYRHYNCUS, an Egyptian city from the Roman era, its ruins located about 120 miles south of Cairo. Rubbish mounds have yielded the largest single accumulation of papyrus manuscripts ever found. Most are Greek; others are Latin, Coptic, hieratic, and demotic. While most are of a business and legal nature, those of artistic interest include previously unknown works by Euripides, Pindar, Sappho, and others, as well as early texts of known literary works of Classical antiquity.

P

PAEKCHE CULTURE dominated southwestern Korea from about the 1st century A.D. to 663. Cultural ties between the Paekche kingdom and Japan were fairly strong. A gilt bronze Buddha, made by Paekche artists and presented to the Japanese court in the 6th century, marks the traditional introduction of Buddhism to Japan. Much extant Paekche art is now in Japan, notably the famous painted wood Bodhisattva figure, the Kudara Kannon. Paekche culture lost importance after 663, when the Silla Dynasty came to power in Korea.

PAESTUM, the Roman name for Poseidonia, a Greek colony, founded from Sybaris around 600 B.C. Set in a coastal plain about 20 miles south of Naples, Paestum has a fine museum and three magnificent Doric temples. The "Basilica" (mid-6th century B.C.) and "Temple of Poseidon" (mid-5th century B.C.) were actually dedicated to Hera, while the "Temple of Ceres" (late 6th century B.C.) was really a temple to Athena. They give a graphic illustration of the rapid evolution of Greek temple architecture. The "Poseidon" temple is the finest example of the Doric order outside Athens. Important 6th-century metopes from another temple to Hera (at modern Sele, five miles away) are effectively displayed in the museum, as are rare examples of 4th to 3rd-century B.C. frescoes from local tombs.

PAGAN. An ancient capital of Burma, Pagan is one of the archaeological gems of Asia. It was founded in A.D. 849 and in the 11th century became the capital of King Anawratha, who introduced Buddhism into upper Burma. During his reign thousands of Buddhist shrines and temples were built at Pagan, mostly of stone and brick, and adorned with magnificent stone sculpture. The surviving ruins, covering 40 square miles and extending for several miles along the shore of the Irrawaddy River, show influences of architectural styles from China and India.

PAGODA, primarily a Chinese or Japanese Buddhist religious structure. The term is of Portuguese origin, its Chinese equivalent being *ta*, a tapered tower. Chinese pagodas date back to the Tang Dynasty and often consist of superimposed stories, sometimes as many as 15; from each story projects an upwards-curving tiled roof. Japanese pagodas, rarely more than five stories high, were generally made of wood. Originally, the word *pagoda* described Indian and Indonesian shrines seen by Portuguese traders before European exploration of China and Japan.

PAHARI ART describes the work of a school of north Indian painters, mainly from Kangra, Jammu, and several other centers in the Himalayan foothills. The group, which flourished in the 18th century A.D., represented a resurgence of Hindu styles at a time when Moghul art was in decline. Typical works include richly colored manuscript illustrations.

PALA PERIOD, in Indian history, extended from the 8th through the 10th centuries A.D. in northeastern India's Bengal regions. Pala kings, who were Buddhist, built many temples and monasteries; the most important Pala monastery is at Nalandra. Buddhist sculpture also flourished, and Pala bronze icons are so numerous that they appear to have been mass-produced. Pala stone sculpture is quite distinctive, typical works being executed in black stone and polished to an extremely glossy finish.

PALATINE, one of the seven hills of ancient Rome, traditionally the hill associated with the mythology of Romulus and Remus, legendary founders of Rome. Dominating the Roman Forum from the south, the Palatine was a fashionable residential district during the late Republican era and the site of the imperial residence of Augustus.

Paestum: Fresco. 4th–3rd century B.C.

Palenque: The Temple of the Hill. Mayan, 7th century A.D.

PALENQUE, a Mayan site in the state of Chiapas, Mexico. It reached its height from the 4th to the 8th centuries A.D. Although comparatively small, Palenque is often considered the most beautiful of all Mayan cities. Prominent buildings here include a palace complex with a three-story tower and five temple pyramids. Palenque is remarkable for the absence of stelae. Its sculptural style is expressed in the elaborate stucco work and limestone relief panels which decorate its buildings. Hundreds of motifs are depicted, including butterflies and foliated crosses. However, the central theme of Palenque art is the human figure, which is treated with such sensitivity that representations approach true portraiture. A hidden tomb, discovered beneath the so-called Temple of the Inscriptions here, yielded a treasury of vessels, carved jade, and two human heads realistically carved in stucco.

PALEOLITHIC. See STONE AGE.

PALERMO STONE, an inscribed black-basalt stone dating from Egypt's 5th Dynasty (about 2400 B.C.), the largest fragment of which has, since the 19th century, been housed in the Palermo Museum, Sicily. The stone is a royal record of all pharaohs from the 1st through the 5th dynasties and contains descriptions of their various accomplishments.

PALESTINE, the historic Mediterranean coastal region of the Near East, bounded on the east by the river Jordan and the Dead Sea and on the south by the Sinai desert. Palestine has been occupied by man for about 100,000 years. Excavations at Jericho indicate that around 7000 B.C. Palestine led the world in cultural development. However, by 4000 to 2000 B.C. agricultural problems and the absence of natural resources slowed the pace of Palestine's development. Semitic peoples began occupying the region toward the end of the 4th millennium B.C., and the area came under Egyptian control in the mid-2nd millennium B.C. Semitic dominance in Palestine reached its climax with the arrival of Moses and his Hebrews around the 13th century B.C. From the 8th century B.C. onward, the region was occupied and, in varying degrees, controlled by Assyrians, Babylonians, Persians, Macedonians, Seleucids, Romans, Arabs, Turks, and, most recently, Israelis.

PALLAVA PERIOD, in India, was at its height between the 4th and the 9th centuries A.D. Territory ruled by Pallava kings extended along much of India's eastern Deccan. Notable among Pallava cultural achievements was their construction of many Hindu temples, the most unusual of which were those carved from a single huge block of stone. Good examples of this monolithic temple construction are the 17 structures, dating from the 7th century, located at Mamallapuram, near Madras.

PALMETTE, a decorative leaf motif probably originating in Egypt but which found its way to Minoan Crete, the Near East, and Greece.

Pantheon: View of the interior. Rome.

PALMYRA, an ancient city, still extant, in the Syrian desert northeast of Damascus. Formerly called Tadmor, it was mentioned in an Akkadian tablet of the 19th century B.C. It became the center of an Arabic city-state with language and culture adopted from the Aramaeans. By the 1st century B.C. it was an important commercial way station for the commerce between the Roman and Persian empires. In 272 A.D. it and its Queen Zenobia were captured by the Romans. Much Greco-Roman building still stands in Palmyra, as well as funerary monuments and reliefs. Most imposing of the city's ruins are the temple to Baal and the tower-tombs, structures several stories high and adorned with sculptured figures in high relief.

PAN, the amorous and occasionally formidable (he caused panic) Greek god of flocks and shepherds. Inventor of the seven-reeded pan pipe (*syrinx*), he is shown on vases and reliefs of the 5th and 4th centuries B.C. with a man's body and arms and goatish head, legs, and tail. The Romans called him Faunus.

PANAGURISHTE, a town in central Bulgaria and the site of Thracian burial mounds dating from the 4th and 3rd centuries B.C. Objects from these tombs reveal the large extent of commercial contact then existing between Thracians and Greeks and also show evidence of cultural kinship between Thracians and Scythians. The objects include Greek vases and golden animal figures classified as Greco-Scythian.

PANATARAN. See MADJAPAHIT.

PANATHENAIC AMPHORA. See AMPHORA.

PAN SHAN, site of a neolithic culture near China's Wei River, in Kansu province. The Pan Shan people are considered an offshoot of the more extensive Yang Shao, or Painted Pottery, culture. Pan Shan culture is known mainly through pottery finds discovered in the 1920s at burial sites. The pottery pieces are urns painted in red and black, with abstract, curving, or spiral designs. They occur in two general shapes, being either short jars with broad mouths or tall, high-necked jars with narrow mouths. Similar pottery has been found as far west as the Ukraine.

PANTHEON, the greatest of all existing Roman temples, said to be the architectural embodiment of the Roman cosmic view, of which the Roman Empire was its political expression. It ranks with the Parthenon and Hagia Sophia as one of the great architectural landmarks of Western civilization. Dedicated to the seven planetary deities, it was built by the Emperor Hadrian on the Campus Martius of Rome in about 126 A.D. It took its name from two earlier temples on the same site, which were, in fact, dedicated to "all the gods"; one of these was the Pantheon built by the Emperor Augustus in the late 1st century B.C. The surviving Pantheon is a vast cylinder of coated brick (about 130 feet in diameter), covered by a dome (about 130 feet high) and joined to a pedimented portico with eight Corinthian columns of granite in front and two groups of four behind. In antiquity, the exterior porchlike façade of the Pantheon rose in five steps above a colonnaded forecourt, which is now four feet lower than modern street level. The decorative design of the lower interior can be seen almost intact. Seven niches are hollowed deeply into the walls at equal intervals, and the entire lower interior is covered with subtle purple and yellow marble revetments, an architectural element fully developed by the Romans. Decoration above the first cornice was radically altered in 1747, and an exact recon-

Paracas culture: Woven textile. Ca. 400 B.C. From the Paraca necropolis.

struction is uncertain. However, the interior of the Pantheon, with its thick walls lightened by recesses, its strong lines of coffered dome, and its bold dome opening (27 feet in diameter) directed to the heavens, remains a superb expression of imperial pride in dominion. No longer in use as a church, it now houses several tombs, including that of Raphael.

PAPUANS, a negroid people whose language and culture appear only in New Guinea and in some isolated Melanesian islands. Their origins are still uncertain. It is speculated that they came to New Guinea from Asia sometime after 10,000 B.C. or that their culture grew from an intermingling of Australian and Tasmanian aborigines already on the island. The Papuans developed a primitive form of agriculture and believed in a celestial father deity. By 3500 B.C. they were being pushed back into the interior by new waves of immigrants. Papuan culture survives today in the southern area of New Guinea, particularly around the Gulf of Papua, parts of the Sepik district, and with the Baining and Sulka peoples of New Britain. Papuan influence on the art of these cultures can be seen in the presence of spectacular cult objects, especially masks, which are usually made of rattan or bark cloth rather than wood, and in the importance of curvilinear and two-dimensional surface decoration.

PAPYRUS, a reed growing some 20 feet high, once abundant in the Nile River region. The Egyptians made a paperlike writing material from its fibers. The oldest extant inscribed papyrus dates from Egypt's 5th Dynasty (about 2500 B.C.). From about the 7th century B.C. papyrus paper was exported for use in Greece.

PARACAS CULTURE, a unique culture of arid south coastal Peru, located in the Nasca and Ica valleys and the Paracas peninsula. It flourished from about 700 B.C. to 400 B.C. Paracas culture is distinguished by exceptional accomplishments in the arts of pottery and textile. Paracas pottery is decorated with vivid, polychrome painting. Designs, including human and feline faces, as well as geometric forms, are emphasized by heavy incised black lines. Excavations in the area uncovered more than four hundred mummies, most wrapped in layers of beautiful textiles; the designs on the textiles are extremely imaginative. Common motifs include monsters, mythological beings, trophy heads, birds, and fishes, all woven in rich and varied colors.

PARIETAL, a Latin term meaning "on the wall." In European prehistory it refers to the rock art of the last ice age as executed by paleolithic man on the walls, and sometimes the ceilings, of caves, such as those at Altamira in Spain and Lascaux in France.

PARIAN MARBLE, a very fine creamy white marble that, in ancient times, was quarried on the Greek island of

Parthenon: Front view of the west facade. Athenian Acropolis.

Paros, in the Aegean Sea. It took an extremely high polish and was easily cut. This was the marble that became the medium for some of the finest sculpture and architecture of Classical Greece. Since the Romans preferred Carrara marble for their sculpture, while the Greeks enjoyed Parian or Pentelic marble for their works, a close examination of the marble used may determine a Roman copy from a Greek original.

PARSIS. See **ZOROASTRIAN ART AND ANTIQUITIES.**

PARTHENON, the most elaborate Doric temple ever built by the Greeks, the crowning jewel of the Athenian Acropolis, and one of great architectural landmarks of

Western civilization. Dedicated to Athena the Virgin (*Parthenos*), patron deity of Athens, it was built of Pentelic marble from 447 to 438 B.C. by the Greek architect Ictinus during the Periclean age. In later centuries it became a Christian church; an Islamic mosque, with minaret; and in 1687 served as an ammunition store during the Turkish-Venetian war, when a stray shell partially destroyed it. Drawings rendered in 1674, some years before the explosion, have been used to reconstruct the temple; its exterior colonnade is now almost completely restored. A temple of magnificent scale, the largest on the Greek mainland, it had 46 columns, a spacious cella, and an inner chamber. Sculptured friezes of almost 525 feet formed a continuous band around the Parthenon. The

Parthenon: Detail of the west frieze. Athenian Acropolis.

harmonious proportions and subtle refinements of the Parthenon are matched only by its sculptural decoration, unequalled on any other Greek temple, and imbued with the artistic genius of Phidias. Its two pedimental groups, superb works of sculpture, featured the contest between Poseidon and Athena for domination of Athens, on the west, and the birth of Athena, on the east. Its 92 carved metopes showed combat scenes: Greeks against Amazons, Lapiths versus Centaurs, gods and giants, and depictions of the Trojan War; few of the metopes survive. The Panathenaic Festival procession frieze ran around the cella wall, too high for all but the gods to enjoy. Inside the Parthenon stood the colossal chryselephantine statue of Athena Parthenos, a masterpiece by Phidias and the focus of Athenian religious awe. The statue, lost forever, depicted a standing and helmeted Athena holding a spear and shield. Much of the sculptural decoration from the Parthenon was removed in 1806 by Lord Elgin and is now in the British Museum.

PARTHIANS, a nomadic people from central Asia who entered northeastern Iran in the 3rd century B.C. Under their first king, Arsaces I, they won independence from the Seleucids and in the 2nd century B.C., under Mithridates I, expanded into an empire. At its height the Parthian Empire controlled modern Iran, Iraq, and most of Afghanistan, and for about 350 years it was in almost continuous war with the Seleucids and, later, the Romans. Parthian cavalry was world-famous. They were finally conquered by the Sassanians in 224 A.D. The town of Nisa was the site of the necropolis of the early Parthian kings, and excavations here have unearthed many statues and ivory and other materials and Parthian inscriptions. Hatra in Iraq and Darabgerd in Iran are other Parthian sites.

PASARGADAE, the dynastic capital of the Achaemenids before the construction of Persepolis. Situated some 60 miles northeast of Shiraz in modern Iran, it was built by Cyrus the Great around the middle of the 6th century B.C. It contains Cyrus' residence, an audience hall, and a massive gatehouse guarded by winged bulls and bearing the inscription, "I, Cyrus, the King, the Achaemenid." The tomb of Cyrus is here also, a strong and simple building of white limestone.

PASSAGE GRAVES OF IBERIA. These megalithic tombs are found in many parts of Spain and Portugal, especially in Almeria, Granada, Malaga, and Seville. They date from the mid-3rd millennium B.C. and are related to the stone tombs of early Crete and the Cyclades and the rock-cut tombs of Sardinia. Typically, a passage grave consists of a chamber made of large upright stone slabs covered by flat stones. From this chamber emerges a passage, similarly constructed, leading to the outside air.

The whole may be covered by a mound of earth or may be dug into a hillside. A stone slab with a hole large enough to have a body passed through is sometimes interposed between the chamber and the passage. Some tombs bear traces of a circular floor outside the entrance for the celebration of funeral rituals.

PASTICCIO, or "hodgepodge" in Italian, the conscious imitation of the artistic style of another individual, era, or culture, while making use of new subject matter or decorative devices. It is a technique often used by art forgers.

PATINA, frequently a glossy green or blue film found on ancient bronzes. Patina is not immediately evident when an antiquity is first excavated but reveals itself after careful cleaning of the thick outer layer of oxidation. Patinas are affected by the chemical composition of the bronze, by location, and by time. Thus a bronze exposed to volcanic (sulphuric) winds could turn black or if buried in alkaline soil, free of carbonic acid, could become red. It was common in the ancient East to mix lead with bronze, which resulted in a deep black patina. Chemical examination of patina may determine age and origin of a bronze antiquity.

PAZYRYK, a well-preserved multi-tomb site in the Altai Mountains of western Siberia, dating from the 5th through the 3rd centuries B.C. and used by chieftains of a Scythian-related nomadic people. The region's permafrost preserved the tomb's corpses and other perishable items, which were in an excellent state of preservation when this royal burial was discovered during the 20th century. Embalmed corpses of two men and a woman survived almost intact. The men were heavily tattooed with animal-style designs in patterns similar to those reportedly adorning the body of Scyths from south Russia's steppes. The bodies were buried with their horses

Pazyryk: "Pazyryk Carpet," detail. Scythian, ca. 5th century B.C. (Hermitage, Leningrad)

and carriages, with at least one chariot closely resembling a vehicle of China's Han era. Fine rugs and hangings, certainly originating from Achaemenid Persia, were also found here. Graves of Pazyryk also yielded much clothing, saddles, jewelry, etc. Many objects bear the distinctive animal-style decoration of central Asia; but the abundance of gold and silver antiquities for which Scythian tombs are famous have not been found at Pazyryk as yet.

PEACOCK THRONE, an ornate, unusually spacious throne of probable 17th- or 18th-century origin, first used by the Moslem rulers of Delhi, India, but since 1739 possessed by the Shah of Iran. It was looted during a military expedition against Delhi by the 18th-century Iranian ruler Nadir Shah. The throne is heavily studded with precious stones and rests on a pedestal having silver steps. Still used in Iranian coronation ceremonies, it is the most highly regarded possession in the Palace of Roses, Teheran.

PECTORAL, an ornament worn on the breast (Latin, *pectus, pectoris*). In prehistoric and ancient times pectoral ornaments were mainly of bronze, though precious metals were also used.

PEDIMENT, the triangular space above the front and back columns of a Greek or Roman temple. The Greeks usually filled the pediment with a large and elaborately sculptured composition depicting a mythological or religious scene.

PELLA, a Macedonian Greek city and capital for Philip and his son, Alexander the Great. During Hellenistic times a then navigable river emptying into the Aegean made Pella a port city. Archaeologists have found sections of a town wall some six feet thick and ruins of large houses with Ionic colonnades and floors of pebble mosaic. Probably the best of these mosaics dates from about 300 B.C. and depicts two hunters and a dog slaying a stag. It bears its artist's signature—Gnosis—and remains in the house for which it was made.

PENDE, an African people inhabiting southwestern Zaire. Unlike many of the other peoples in southern Zaire who had strong kingdoms, the Pende were organized into small chiefdoms. Male initiation ceremonies stimulated the production of many masks. Abstract raffia masks, with large cylindrical eyes, and naturalistic anthropomorphic masks with heavy-lidded, half-closed eyes were common. The Pende also carved maskettes and figurines in the latter style.

PENTELIC MARBLE. Though this type of marble is occasionally found in 6th-century B.C. Greek monuments, it was not until the early 5th century, when Athens fully exploited the quarries of nearby Mount Pentelikon, that this superb marble came into wide use. This close-grained, milky white marble was used for the Parthenon. Exposure gradually turns it a golden brown when the iron in it oxidizes.

PEOPLES OF THE SEA. See SEA PEOPLES.

PERGAMON, a Hellenistic city in Asia Minor, built by Macedonian kings, which flourished in the 3rd and 2nd centuries B.C., especially under King Attalus. A brilliant center of Hellenistic civilization, it was the source of Pergamene sculpture, a distinctive school of art that emphasized realism and dramatic composition. Thus a style evolved diametrically opposed to the Classical symmetry of ancestral Greece. Representative works include the Dying Gaul, the Altar of Zeus frieze, depicting a battle between gods and giants (Pergamon Museum, East Berlin), and the Laocoön, created in Pergamene style. Pergamon was also the seat of a great library; the word *parchment* takes its name from Pergamon. The city was annexed to Rome in 133 B.C.

PERIGORDIAN, belonging to an area of the Dordogne in southwest France in which a number of important discoveries in prehistory were made from 1863 onwards. In the limestone hills of the Vezere Valley, which flows into the Dordogne near Bergerac, is to be found the greatest concentration of paleolithic sites in the world, among them Lascaux, Le Moustier, La Madeleine, Laugerie Haute, Laugerie Basse, Cro-Magnon, Les Eyzies, Les Combarelles, and Font-de-Gaume. The cultures found in the Perigord date from the Mousterian to the Michelsberg culture of neolithic farmers, among the first in Europe, about 3000 B.C.

PERISTYLE, one or more rows of columns surrounding a building or open space. In Greek architecture the term most often refers to the columns of a temple. The Romans used peristyles to enclose gymnasia and courtyards of private houses.

PERSEPOLIS, the cosmopolitan capital of the Achaemenid Dynasty, the ruins of which are located about 40 miles northeast of Shiraz in modern Iran. Founded by Darius I about 520 B.C. and completed by his Achaemenid successors some 60 years later, this city was the showplace of the Persian Empire. There were great palace-fortresses, treasuries, princely homes, and other monumental architecture, all mounted on a vast limestone platform butting against a mountain. The palace compound of Persepolis is the high point of Achaemenid art. It is approached by a noble stairway and contains pillared audience halls, a throne room, royal apartments, a harem, and other appurtenances of an imperial court; some remaining columns are more than 60 feet tall. Monumental bas-reliefs, often depicting processions of tribute-bearers, decorated Persepolis. The city was looted and burned by Alexander the Great in 330 B.C. A few miles distant from the magnificent ruins of Persepolis are the rock-hewn tombs of Persian kings, Sassanian remains, and a 3,000-year-old Elamite rock inscription.

PERSIAN CIVILIZATION, one of the most unique civilizations of the ancient world, arose on the Iranian

Persepolis: Detail of relief on the external side of the staircase to the Apadana. Persian, Achaemenid Dynasty.

Persian art: Bowl. Islamic polychrome enamel ware. 12th–13th centuries A.D. (British Museum, London)

plateau, to the east of Mesopotamia, in the 2nd millennium B.C. Despite reports to the contrary, especially from Greek historians, the Persians were a liberal and gifted people who established a well-administered empire, built great cities and roads, and left spectacular art and architectural remains. Persian civilization, a singular blend of eastern and western cultural styles, begins with the people of Siyalk, who settled on the Iranian plateau in the 5th millennium B.C. Susa, perhaps the earliest city of Iran, was founded in the 3rd millennium B.C. and probably by Mesopotamians; it ultimately became the capital of the Elamites. Strategically situated between the ancient cities of the Near East and the Eurasian steppes, Iran, throughout its long history, absorbed successive waves of nomadic horsemen from central Asia. Among these were the Medes, of whom little is known other than that they established a capital at Ecbatana, and their tribal cousins, the Persians. An Indo-European people, related to the Aryans of India and, like them, sun worshippers, the Persians settled in and around Parsa, now called Fars, in the mid-2nd millennium B.C. However, it was the Medes, not the Persians, who became dominant on the plateau. They set up a kingdom, which became so powerful that the Assyrians, in the 9th and 8th centuries B.C., attempted to conquer Median Iran. Meanwhile, to the northwest, the Persians still led a more or less pastoral life, as evidenced by Luristan bronzes of the 8th and 7th centuries B.C. By 600 B.C. the Median kingdom had become so weakened that Persian incursions were suffered, and, in 553 B.C., it finally fell to the Persian Cyrus the Great. A man of noble vision, Cyrus established a vast empire, ruled by his dynasty, the Achaemenids. From their capital at Pasargadae, the Achaemenids promoted trade throughout the conquered lands, laid roads and fostered communications, emphasized rule by law, and, although Zoroastrians, practiced religious tolerance. After 518 B.C. they built a magnificent capital at Persepolis, the so-called city of the Persians. In the 5th century B.C. the Achaemenids suffered major defeats at the hands of the Greeks. Exhausted and torn by internal power struggles, the Persian Empire went into decline, and in 331 B.C. Alexander the Great, at the Battle of the Issus, delivered the final blow to the Achaemenids, thus ending the history of this once glorious Persian dynasty. After Alexander's death in 323 B.C. the Persian Empire was ruled by Greek Seleucids, who introduced Hellenistic culture to the Iranian plateau. Within a century the Seleucids were ousted by the Parthians, a barbaric con-

Persian art: "Hawk Attacking Dove." Stucco relief. 10th–11th centuries A.D. From Rayy. (Museum of Fine Arts, Boston)

Persian art: Head of ibex. 6th–5th centuries B.C. (Metropolitan Museum of Art, New York)

when the Sassanians came to power in the 3rd century A.D. The Sassanids revived Achaemenid forms, such as large rock reliefs, with scenes of the royal hunt, the king and his court, and the celebration of victories. They also made fine and famous sculptured textiles.

PERSIAN MINIATURES, in Islamic art, the exquisite, jewellike manuscript illustrations that developed in Persia after the 7th century A.D., when the forces of Islam swept the Iranian plateau. Among the masterpieces of world art, Persian miniatures in the earliest stages probably decorated the Koran. In later times, especially after the Mongol invasions of the 13th century, when Chinese painting techniques arrived in Persia, miniatures flowered as an art form, reaching their full blossom in the 15th century. At Shiraz and Herat, miniature painters, including the famous Kamal ad-Din Bihzad, created a highly decorative, richly colored art, meticulous in detail, magnificent in setting, and displaying a varied subject matter that included tales of adventure, of heroism, and of romance. At the beginning of the 16th century the Safavid

federation of nomadic horsemen, who quickly adopted Hellenistic ways. It was not until the advent of the Sassanians, in about 224 A.D., that Persia enjoyed its second brilliant period of history. Under the Sassanian dynasty, with its capital at Ctesiphon, a revival of Achaemenid art and culture was undertaken, Zoroastrianism became the state religion, and many palaces were built. A major factor in the rich silk trade between China and Rome, Sassanid Persia grew prosperous, even though in frequent conflict with the legions of Rome. In the mid-7th century A.D. the winds of Islam swept the Sassanians from power, an event that marks the conclusion of ancient Persian civilization.

Persian Art and Antiquities. Despite its long history of racial and ethnic mixture, ancient Persia maintained a distinctive art style. From the earliest finds of unglazed painted pottery from Siyalk and Susa to the fantastic metalwork of Luristan and Ziwiye, decoration predominates over representation. This tendency was encouraged by Zoroastrian priests, who forbade the making of statues and the building of temples. However, in later imperial times, under the Achaemenids, the Persian genius for assimilation asserted itself. Babylonian, Assyrian, and Egyptian influences can be seen in the royal buildings at Pasargadae, Persepolis, and Susa, but the architecture is harmonious, elegant, and, above all, decorative. The spectacular rows of stone reliefs at Persepolis, as well as the colossal rock reliefs, cut into living rock, at Behistun, are typically Achaemenid—eclectic but recognizably Persian. Under the Seleucids and the Parthians Persian art was thoroughly Hellenized, but it regained a new vitality

Persian art: Rhyton. Silver with gold foil. Achaemenid Dynasty, 5th century B.C. From Erzincan. (British Museum, London)

Persian art: "Polonaise" carpet. (Austrian Museum of Applied Arts, Vienna)

Persian art: Jug. Brass, inlaid with copper and silver. From Mosul. (British Museum, London)

250

Persian miniatures: "Genghis Khan Addressing the People." Miniature on parchment. 1397–1398 A.D. From Shiraz. (British Museum, London)

Dynasty of Persia led a great national art revival, and the illustrated manuscripts created for its kings are among the most sumptuous ever made. Celebrated painters of this era—Sultan Muhammad, Mirak, Mazaffer 'Ali, Mir Sayyid 'Ali, and Mirza 'Ali—are represented in a copy of the *Khamsa*, now in the British Museum. The Safavid period also produced the brilliant miniaturist Riza-i-Abbasi (1598–1643), who worked in Isfahan and is best known for his love scenes and realistic portraits. His style was widely imitated by later masters of the 17th and 18th centuries, although they lacked his originality. In the 18th century the richness of Safavid style degenerated into affectation, thus ending the great age of Persian miniature painting.

PETERBOROUGH WARE, an elaborately decorated pottery bearing impressions of stones, bones, and pits. It was first discovered at Peterborough, England, and identified with British neolithic hunters. These hunters moved across England to Wales and the Irish Sea. Of an enterprising turn, they made stone axes in west-coast "factories" and traded them to neighboring farm peoples.

PETRA, once the capital of the powerful Nabataean kingdom, an Arabic domain; its ruins lie in a large deep valley of modern Jordan. By the 5th century B.C. it was a wealthy and flourishing trading center on the caravan route between Arabia and Syria. An almost impregnable site, Petra was surrounded by high redstone cliffs whose vividly colored stone was quarried for temples, tombs, and shrines. There are innumerable rock caves, probably used as living quarters. The architecture of this "rock city" features ornately carved façades. Petra came under Roman influence in the 1st century B.C. Its remains, including a "treasure house," amphitheater, and palace, are largely in late Greek style, but there are traces of Egyptian and Near Eastern influence. The fabulous ruins of Petra were rediscovered in 1812.

PETRENY, in Bessarabia, a site at which fine painted pottery of about 2200 B.C. has been recovered, with stylized patterns in abstract form. There are panels of design in different colors, alternating with spiral patterns. This pottery corresponds to that of a middle stage of the Cucuteni culture of Rumania.

PETROGLYPHS, an image or series of images etched or painted on stone. This form of expression dates from earliest antiquity and from many prehistoric cultures. Very early European petroglyphs, found in Spain, date from around 6000 B.C.

PETUNTSE. See KAOLIN.

PHALLIC FIGURE, any symbol or image of the male reproductive organ. The phallic figure has meanings beyond its shape. It is connected with fertility, the power to avoid evil, and cosmic energy. Found almost worldwide, phallic figures are among the earliest objects of art created by man. They are especially prominent in the sculpture and painting of ancient Greece. The herm, a stone pillar with a prominent phallus, was considered an emblem of fertility and placed before homes and public buildings and along roads in Athens. In India a stone phallus, or lingam, is the traditional and sacred way of representing the power of the god Siva. Ancestral images with erect phalli from Africa are considered symbols of immortality and the continuation of the line of life in the face of individual death.

PHIALE, a wide shallow bowl used by the Greeks for libations. Without handles or base, it had a raised boss in the center into which the fingers were inserted while pouring the libation.

PHIDIAS, the 5th-century B.C. Athenian considered the greatest sculptor of antiquity. He made three statues of Athena for the Acropolis, two in bronze and one, the colossal cult statue for the Parthenon, in gold and ivory (chryselephantine). His masterpiece was the majestic seated Zeus (also chryselephantine) for the temple at Olympia, acclaimed as one of the seven wonders of the ancient world. The other sculptures of the Parthenon—metopes, frieze, and pedimental figures—were done under his direction and are the only surviving "originals" we have to judge the influential Phidian style.

PHILAE, island in the Nile River, site of an ancient Nubian town, the remains of which were virtually submerged by modern flooding from the Aswan Dam. The island, a mere 500 by 160 yards, retains many stone structures, including a large temple dedicated to Isis. However, traces of numerous mud-brick houses (excavated in 1893) have been obliterated by the island's periodic, dam-controlled submersion in Nile waters. An obelisk at Philae, inscribed both in Greek and hieroglyphics, has aided scholars in deciphering ancient Egyptian texts.

PHILISTINES, one of the Sea Peoples who, after unsuccessfully attacking Egypt, occupied parts of the coastal plain of Palestine, displacing the Canaanites around 1200 B.C. The five cities of the Philistine confederacy were Askelon, Gath, Gaza, Ashdod, and Ekron. The Philistines came in conflict with the Israelites; Samson the Israelite was the great hero of that struggle. The Philistines were finally subdued by King David about 1000 B.C., although border battles continued. They have left a distinctive pottery in Aegean styles, and their original homeland may have been Crete or Cyprus. The name Palestine comes from Philistine.

PHOENICIAN CIVILIZATION, a little-studied but famous seafaring civilization which, by the early 2nd millennium B.C., was well established along the eastern Mediterranean coast in present-day Lebanon and Syria. A Semitic people who derived from the Canaanites, the Phoenicians were merchants of the first magnitude who lived in commercial city-states, such as Ugarit, Byblos, Sidon, and Tyre. The name Phoenician comes from the Greek and refers to their famous purple dye, also called

Tyrian purple, extracted from seashells. Prosperous and the envy of neighboring nations, Phoenicia suffered much foreign control, first the Egyptians in the 17th century B.C., then the Hyksos in the mid-15th century B.C., and in the 14th century B.C. the Hittites and the Amorites. The Sea Peoples invaded Phoenician coasts in about 1200 B.C. After throwing off the yoke of the Sea Peoples and until 900 B.C., Phoenicia reached the height of its power and influence. Phoenician fleets sailed the length of the Mediterranean, making it a Phoenician lake. They traded in finished metals, ores, grain, timber, ivory, and slaves. Their ships, large craft propelled by galley slaves and sail, ventured as far west as Cornwall, England, for tin ore and may even have circumnavigated Africa. Phoenician colonies were established widely on the shores of the Mediterranean: Carthage in North Africa, Cadiz in Spain, and many others in Sicily, Greece, and France. With the rise of the Assyrian Empire in the Near East in the 9th century B.C., Phoenicia once again fell under foreign domination; in the 6th century B.C. it was absorbed by the Babylonians. As power ebbed and flowed in the Near East, the Persians, the Greeks, and, finally, the Romans won control of Phoenician cities. A people of limited originality in the visual arts, the Phoenicians made their greatest contribution to world culture with the development and diffusion of the alphabet. Little Phoenician literature remains, especially from the earliest period when perishable papyrus was in use. The clay tablets discovered at Ugarit, however, dating from the 14th century B.C., show striking parallels of language and thought to portions of the Old Testament. In religion, each Phoenician city had its own Baal, or supreme god, as well as a Baalat, or female consort. One of the most repugnant of Phoenician deities was Moloch, in whose honor children were burned alive.

Phoenician Art and Antiquities. In motifs and techniques Phoenician art was derivative, as might be expected from a people who were the great traders of their world. Egyptian, Assyrian, and Babylonian influences are clear. However, the Phoenicians did excel in their metalwork, especially in copper and bronze, in their glassware, in their textiles, and in the making of carved ivories, many of which were found at Nimrud. In addition, a large number of stone sarcophagi with carved human faces, as well as a few vividly painted burial chambers, have survived.

PHRYGIANS, a people, related to the Armenians, who migrated from the eastern Balkans to Anatolia around the 11th century B.C. There they established a kingdom which, although of short duration, was highly prosperous (as evidenced by the legend of King Midas, said to have been the second king of the Phrygians). They were overwhelmed by the Cimmerians early in the 7th century B.C. Among the antiquities left by the Phrygians in Anatolia are monuments to their early kings, including Midas, elaborately carved in rock; painted pottery related to that of the early Greeks; probably a group of rock reliefs near Ankara showing animals and a bearded human-headed lion; and, possibly, a large rock relief near Ivriz depicting a king standing before a god. Gordion was the chief city of Phrygia.

PICTS, literally "the painted people," referring to the use of the blue dye, woad, on the bodies of these Scottish tribesmen. The Picts may have come from the continent of Europe in about 1000 B.C., before the arrival of the Celts in Scotland. Some Picts moved to Ireland in the 2nd century A.D. The Romans mention the Picts and Scots as being the "barbarians" who attacked Hadrian's Wall in the 4th century A.D. A few Pictish carved stones are scattered over Scotland, one good example being the Maiden Stone near Aberdeen. It is of red granite and has carvings in relief of fish, monsters, and human beings.

PIEDRAS NEGRAS, an ancient Mayan site, located in Guatemala near the Mexican border. Until the 7th century A.D. the architecture of this city remained relatively simple. After that time, masonry vaults, and the only sweat baths found at a Mayan site, appear. Piedras Negras is most famous for its large number of finely carved stelae, limestone wall panels, and stone lintels. Piedras Negras sculptural style skillfully combines low and high

Phoenician art: Inlay. Carved ivory with gold foil and inlaid gold, lapis-lazuli, and carnelian. 721–705 B.C. From Nimrud. (British Museum, London)

Plains Indian culture: Robe. Painted buffalo hide. (Private collection, Paris)

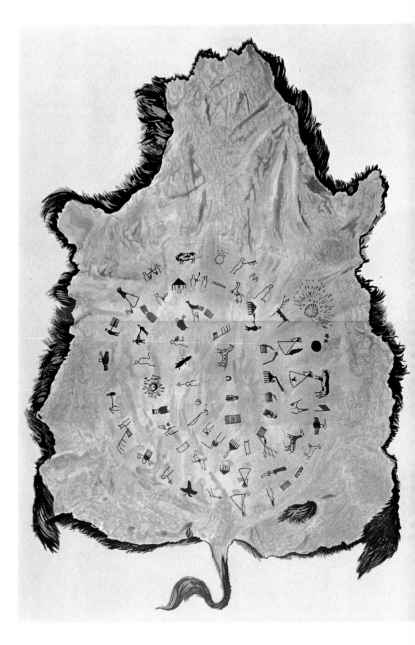

relief, the latter only rarely found in Mayan sculpture. Along with the painted murals from the nearby site of Bonampak, Piedras Negras sculpture introduced martial motifs for the first time in Mayan art.

PILE DWELLERS. In the 19th century discoveries were made in Switzerland at Obermeilen on Lake Zurich and at Robenhausen of villages built on piles driven into the lake shores. When these discoveries became known, hundreds of other lake sites were brought to light in Switzerland, Germany, Italy, Britain, and elsewhere. Most sites were occupied in the neolithic but many continued into the bronze age, beyond 2000 B.C. Since the marshy water and peat have preserved perishable objects such as wood, matting, and even some textiles, it has been possible to reconstruct the life of the pile dwellers with some accuracy. Platforms were erected on tree-trunk piles, which supported wattle huts with rush roofs and clay-packed floors. Crops were grown on the fertile shores and stock raised, although some of the meat supply came from wild game. Wild fowl and fish were an important part of the diet. Archaeologists sometime refer to the pile dwellers as the lakeside dwellers.

PILTDOWN MAN. See **FLUORINE TEST.**

PINAX, a small Cretan terra-cotta relief, pierced at the top and made to be hung. Pinakes often depict standing female figures with tall headdresses, naked youths and warriors, as well as male heads and busts. They show the triangular faces and low foreheads characteristic of the "Daedalic" period of the later 7th century B.C. Pinakes were also popular in Classical times.

PIN-YANG. See **LUNGMEN.**

PIPAL, a fig tree held sacred by Hindu cults. Many Indian villages had their own special sacred tree, which became a site for worship. Its roots and branches usually had some symbolic significance.

PISE, clay, sometimes mixed with gravel and used as material for construction, especially by ancient Near East cultures. Pise is not made into bricks but is molded as a single solid surface.

PLAINS INDIAN CULTURE, the way of life shared by the tribal peoples who once inhabited the Great Plains of the American Midwest. Originally foot nomads or semi-settled farmers, the Plains Indians developed their typical culture after the 16th century, when the Spanish of Mexico introduced the horse to the Plains. Although the many tribes here possessed widely differing customs and levels of material culture, the so-called Horse Indians, such as the Sioux, Cheyenne, and Blackfeet, shared several cultural traits in common, among which was a semi-nomadic existence, trailing the buffalo herds on which they depended for most of life's necessities. Warfare, among themselves or against the Village Indians, especially the Pawnee and Mandan, was a commonplace that established tribal prestige. The Indians of the Plains had few material possessions, and art consisted mostly in the decoration of utilitarian and small portable objects. They excelled in elaborate bead work and porcupine-quill embroidery, which were applied to hide garments, moccasins, and horse trappings. Painting was also well used by the Plains Indians and can be seen on parfleches, a rawhide carrying bag, as well as on tepee covers, buffalo robes, and ceremonial shields, which were painted with war chronicles. Sculpture, however, was deficient and confined only to the production of stone-headed war clubs and ceremonial pipes.

PLUMBATE WARE, a fine pottery made of a special clay, which, when fired, resulted in a surface with metal-

lic luster. It is one of the few true glazed potteries of Pre-Columbian Mexico. The widespread presence of Plumbate ware in the Yucatan peninsula after the 10th century A.D. is thought to indicate the occupation of that area by the Toltecs. Plumbate was a major trade ware at Tula, Mexico, the Toltec capital, and may have been imported from the Guatemalan border. Some of the pottery is modelled in the form of Toltec warriors, but the majority consists of simple pear-shaped vessels.

Polynesian culture: Urn cover. Carved and incised wood. Maori, 19th–20th centuries A.D. From New Zealand. (British Museum, London)

PLUTO. See HADES.

POBLICIUS TOMB, an outstanding 1st-century A.D. tomb for the Roman legionnaire Poblicius, who was stationed in what is now Cologne, Germany. Discovered after the Second World War, the tomb, which is more than three stories high, was reconstructed from many fragments. The upper part of the tomb simulates a miniature Roman temple with four Corinthian columns, fronted by a statue of Poblicius. The monument is the centerpiece of the Roman-German Museum in Cologne.

POLLEN ANALYSIS, method of determining types of vegetation and changes of climate for periods in the ancient or prehistoric past. Earth samples are studied for yields of fossilized pollen to shed light on the kinds and abundance of plant life at a given location. Archaeologists can thus determine something about how man and nature affected each other during the life span of a culture. Radiocarbon dating, made in conjunction with pollen analysis, will provide fairly specific dates to coincide with the sequence of vegetation growths.

POLONNARUWA, capital of Ceylon between 781 and 1290 A.D. The city's ruins hold some of the finest examples of Singhalese art and architecture. Its height of creative activity occurred during the reign of Ceylon's King Prakrama Baha I (1164–97). Influences are mainly Buddhist, but some fine Chola-style Hindu monuments also exist. The most impressive sculpture includes a nearly 50-foot-long reclining Buddha figure and a 25-foot-high standing Buddha, both in stone. Polonnaruwa also has numerous beautiful temples and monastery buildings, set against a lush rain-forest background.

POLYCLITUS, a 5th-century B.C. Greek sculptor, second only to Phidias in reputation. His best-known works, known only through Roman copies, are the Doryphoros (a young athlete carrying a spear), which became the standard of Greek excellence; the Diadoumenos, a powerful youth tying a ribbon around his head; and, most famous of all, a chryselephantine Hera for her shrine at Argos in the Peloponnesus, said to have compared favorably with Phidias' Olympian Zeus.

POLYGNOTOS, celebrated Greek painter of the mid-5th century B.C., regarded as the real "inventor" of painting. Nothing of his work survives, but ancient descriptions of his murals at Delphi and Athens indicate he created large and dignified representations of mythological scenes. Aristotle praised him for the lively expression he gave to the faces of his figures.

POLYNESIAN CULTURE, a homogenous culture spread over a vast area of the Pacific Ocean. Polynesia, coined from the Greek words meaning "many islands," was first reached by Europeans in 1595. Extensive exploration, however, did not begin until the 18th century, notably with the great voyages of Captain Cook. Many

18th-century myths about Polynesia—as a paradise of free love, idyllic life, and abundant food, in short, the home of "the noble savage"—persisted until recent times and tended to obscure the harsh realities of warfare, starvation, infanticide, and human sacrifice. Polynesia covers a large triangle of islands with corners at New Zealand, Hawaii, and Easter Island; fabled Tahiti is at the geographic center. The similarity of culture, however, remained fairly consistent throughout this wide area. Highly stratified societies of nobles, commoners, and slaves produced many prestige art objects, which tended to delineate and emphasize rank. Belief in two basic spiritual forces, *mana* (power) and *tabu* (the forbidden), permeated Polynesian culture. Religion, based on the existence of numerous gods and dominated by priests, inspired Polynesian art. Many wood and stone figure sculptures represented such gods as Tane, Tu, Rongo, and Tangaroa. However, relatively few such sculptures survive; sadly, a vast quantity of Polynesian art was destroyed by 19th-century missionaries. The style and scale of art was uniform throughout Polynesia, though environmental variation led to such anomalies as the mammoth stone works on Easter Island and the large intricate wood sculptures of New Zealand. Although most scholars agree that the Polynesians gradually settled their islands as migrants from southeastern Asia about 500 B.C., other tantalizing theories of settlement have been proposed. One, espoused by Thor Heyerdahl, suggests that the Polynesians came from South America. Another rests on the highly questionable belief that the Polynesians are the mountaintop survivors of a huge continent now submerged beneath the Pacific Ocean. The most common Polynesian artifacts seen today are elaborately carved utilitarian objects.

POLYTHEISM, belief in many gods. Religions of early cultures are commonly polytheistic, and some sophisticated theologies—Brahmanism, for example—retain polytheistic features from their primitive origins. Efforts to depict gods in iconographic form greatly enriched the sculpture of several polytheistic cultures—among them, Indian and Greek. Polytheism is opposed to monotheism, the belief in one god.

POMPEII, in southern Italy, near Naples and at the foot of Mt. Vesuvius. One of the great archaeological treasures of the world, Pompeii, along with Herculaneum and Stabiae, was buried in the epic eruption of Vesuvius in 79 A.D. Pompeii, before its catastrophic demise, was a bustling Roman resort and commercial center, with a population of more than 20,000. Its public architecture included statue-lined streets, a typical Roman forum and basilica, large temples, two theaters, and a Roman amphitheater, built in 80 B.C. and the oldest yet unearthed in Italy. More important than the public buildings, however, are the sumptuous villas and gardens, decorated with wall paintings and mosaics, that made the city a showplace for the wealthy. Founded by Italic peoples and briefly occupied by the Etruscans, Pompeii reached its zenith from the 3rd century B.C. to the 1st century A.D., while under Samnite and Roman rule. Covered by more than 20 feet of volcanic ash, Pompeii disappeared from memory in the centuries following the disaster, and only in the late 1500s was it rediscovered. In 1748 the excavation of Pompeii began in earnest and continues, often intermittently, to the present day; by the 1970s more than three-quarters of this once prosperous city had been excavated. Because of its well-preserved archaeological record and its propinquity to the Greek colonies of southern Italy, Pompeii is a mine of precious data of Roman life, town planning, architecture, and, above all, of Greco-Roman art. Thousands of wall paintings and mosaics have been unearthed, and close analysis and study of these Pompeian frescoes and mosaics have

Pompeii: Wall painting, detail. House of the Mysteries.

served as a basis for the fundamental classification of Roman art generally, as well as a source for tantalizing glimpses into the lost world of Greek mural painting. Among the most noted of decorated Pompeian villas—and they are myriad—are the House of the Faun, which occupies a whole city block; the House of the Silver Wedding; the House of the Vetii, with its superb murals; and the House of the Mysteries, with its puzzling but important series of religious murals celebrating the Dionysian mysteries. While most Pompeian art can be seen at its site, the nearby Naples Museum has a large Pompeian collection, which includes a famous mosaic, the Battle of the Issus, and an outstanding silverwork hoard from the House of Menander.

PORCELAIN, extremely hard, glazed earthenware, sometimes translucent, made from kaolin, a white clay. Developed in Tang Dynasty China and becoming high art by the Sung era, porcelain making was successfully imitated by Europeans from the 16th century A.D.

PORCH OF THE MAIDENS. See ERECHTHEUM.

PORTLAND VASE, an elegant and refined example of the cameo-type Roman glass vase. About ten inches high, the vase is adorned with decorative figures (perhaps Apollo and Atia, mother of the Emperor Augustus), which are etched in delicate relief—opaque white against the rich violet-blue background of the glass underneath. It was made about 30 B.C., discovered in an ancient sarcophagus near Rome in 1644, and bought for the Duchess of Portland in the 18th century. It was completely shattered by a madman in 1845, then skillfully reconstructed, and is now in the British Museum.

POSEIDON, violent and powerful Greek god of the seas and waters, earthquakes, and horses. Called Neptune by the Romans, Poseidon dwelt at the bottom of the sea. His famous contest with Athena for domination of Athens was the subject of the Parthenon's west pediment. Poseidon is depicted as strongly built and bearded, much like his brother Zeus. His attributes are the trident, dolphins, and other creatures of the sea. Poseidon is often seen in a chariot drawn by horses with fishtails. A magnificent seven-foot bronze, found off Cape Artemision and now in the Athens Museum, may be a 5th-century B.C. statue of Poseidon.

POSEIDONIA. See PAESTUM.

POST-AND-LINTEL, an ancient form of building construction, based on the concept of a pair of vertical members, or posts, extending from a fixed base and supporting a horizontal beam, or lintel, placed across their tops.

POTALA, the massive Tibetan palace of the Dalai Lama, situated on a hill overlooking the city of Lhasa. The original structure dates from the 7th century A.D., but most of the present palace was constructed during the 17th century. It consists of two major sections. One is the residential buildings for the reigning Dalai Lama; the other includes memorial halls and funerary pagodas. The largest of the pagodas is over 30 feet high, decorated with elaborate carvings and inlaid with precious stones. The memorial halls contain frescoes based on historical events.

POTTERY, mainly denotes baked clay containers. Pottery making was developed by virtually all neolithic cultures. However, marked stylistic differences in pottery design and decoration serve as important evidence in efforts to distinguish among cultures. Earliest pottery was hand-molded, although most cultures ultimately developed the potter's wheel.

POU, type of Chinese bronze vessel, bowllike in shape, dating from the Shang and Chou eras. It has a contracted, plain-rimmed top and a slightly splayed base.

PRATIHARA PERIOD, in Indian history, prevailed in northern India from 725 to 1019 A.D. It is named for the Pratihara Dynasty, whose chief contribution to India's art and culture rests in the fact that, through military strength, it temporarily held back Islamic advances into India. Founded by Nagabhata I, it reached its peak of strength under his 9th-century successors, Nagabhata II and Bhoja I. In 1019 its king, Rajyapal, fled before Islamic invaders, turning his Hindu allies against him and thus causing the dynasty's fall.

PRAXITELES, a supreme and enormously influential Greek sculptor of the 4th century B.C. His Hermes carrying the infant Dionysus, discovered in the ruins of the Temple of Hera at Olympia in 1877, is almost certainly an original—among the very few original works of any of the great Greek sculptors to reach us. Praxiteles' reputation, however, does not rest on this statue but rather on his lost Aphrodite of Cnidos, which subsequent sculptors adopted as their model of feminine grace and beauty; the Aphrodite of Capua, the Townley Aphrodite, the Ostia, Capitoline, and Medici Aphrodites are all variations of his masterpiece. Influential also were his Apollo Sauroctonos (lizard-slayer) and his statue of Eros. Characteristic of his graceful and sensuous style are the supple languor of the "Praxitilean curve," the oval head, and the dreamy, far-off look in the eyes. The majesty and grandeur of Phidias ultimately gave way to the Praxitilean style: less grand, more intimate, a celebration of the body's physical beauty. The head from Chios in Boston, the Aberdeen head in the British Museum, and the Bronze Boy from Marathon in Athens are not original Praxitilean works, as is sometimes implied, but directly derive from his creations.

PRE-COLUMBIAN, a term frequently used to describe cultures, civilizations, and antiquities of the New World prior to the arrival of Christopher Columbus in 1492. More specifically, the term applies to those civilizations centered in Mexico before the Spanish Conquest in 1519 and those of Peru prior to 1532.

PREDMOST, a prehistoric site near Prerov in Moravia, where remains of ice-age mammoth-hunters were found, dating from about 20,000 B.C. A communal grave of 20

Poseidon: "Artemision Poseidon," detail. Bronze. Greek, ca. 5th century B.C. Found off Cape Artemision. (National Museum, Athens)

Q

QUERN. See **METATE**.

QUETTA, site of an ancient town in the northwest of modern Pakistan. Its earliest habitation dates from about 3700 B.C. The town was along the Baluchistan overland trade route between the Indus Valley and Mesopotamia. By the early 3rd millennium B.C. buildings were being constructed of mud brick, and a white pottery was being made. Terra-cotta figures from the site include those of a fertility goddess and also phallic emblems.

QUETZALCOATL, one of the major gods of Pre-Columbian Mexico. In art he is represented as a feathered serpent. The "culture-hero" of the ancient Mexicans, he was the god of life and fertility who introduced learning and the calendar and taught men how to farm. He is also associated with the east and with light, twins, and the planet Venus. Representations of Quetzalcoatl abound in all media. Round temples were dedicated to him in his manifestation as the wind god. The name Quetzalcoatl was often given to high priests. In legend Quetzalcoatl was the light-skinned, bearded, priest-king of Tula who was forced to leave his Toltec kingdom in disgrace. In one version he sets off on a raft towards the east, vowing to return. Montezuma II, the Aztec emperor, mistook the Spaniard Cortez for the returning Quetzalcoatl and offered little resistance to the man he believed was a god returning to claim his kingdom. Among the Maya, Quetzalcoatl was known as Kukulcan.

QUIMBAYA, a people living in Colombia at the time of the Spanish Conquest. The term "Quimbaya" is also applied indiscriminately to a wide variety of ceramic and gold artifacts that come from tombs in the Cauca Valley, near the city of Medellin. The Quimbaya gold style is one of the most advanced of the New World, as well as one of the most pleasing to the modern eye. Quimbaya ceramic style does not correspond at all with the quality of their goldwork.

QUIRINAL, northernmost of the seven hills of Rome and site of an ancient settlement, perhaps that of the Sabines. The western slope was radically altered to make room for Trajan's Forum. Terraces buttressed the hill and were used to support tiers of shops, storehouses, and government offices. An inscription on the base of Trajan's Column says the column's height (about 130 feet) corresponds to the depth of the earth that had to be removed from the Quirinal.

QUMRAN. See **DEAD SEA SCROLLS**.

QUTB-MINAR. See **DELHI SULTANATE**.

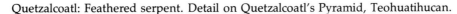

Quetzalcoatl: Feathered serpent. Detail on Quetzalcoatl's Pyramid, Teohuatihucan.

R

RA, also called Re; Egyptian sun god, patron of Heliopolis, and originally the highest among Egypt's deities. Egyptian obelisks were often monuments to Ra and were gilded to glitter in sunlight. He was depicted in human form wearing a sun disk and was later equated with Amon, god of Thebes.

RADIOCARBON DATING, a laboratory test used to determine the approximate ages of very old organic material and thus an aid to the archaeologist attempting to place a site (and its relics) within a time frame. All living matter contains a measurable amount of carbon, a very small part of which begins changing at the time of death. Specifically, it is the radioactive carbon isotope (C14) which, at death, starts decomposing at a determinable rate into more stable nitrogen atoms. After 5,568 years there are only half the C14 atoms that are present in an equal amount of living organic matter. This figure is halved again for every additional 5,568 years, with an error factor estimated at ± 30 years for each of these so-called half-life periods.

RAJPUT MINIATURES, paintings of an Indian school dating from the 15th century A.D. to about 1825 and representing a rebirth of Hindu art following dominance by the Islamic Moghuls. Rajput miniatures were done on paper, thus departing from the large wall murals that typify earlier Hindu painting. They originated with a popular renewal of interest in ritual and legend dealing particularly with the heroic figures Rama and Krishna. Thus their subjects are often legendary scenes, delicately drawn and brightly colored. During the 18th and 19th centuries the painting of Rajput miniatures attained unsurpassed heights at the Pahari capital, Kangra, under the patronage of Rajah Samsar Cand.

RAKNEHAUGEN, the site in Romerike, Norway, of a great burial mound of a Norse chieftain. Dating from about the 5th or 6th century A.D., this is one of the most massive burial mounds in Scandinavia.

RAM'S HORN, in Hebrew, a shofar, the ancient ritual horn of the Jews. It was used in religious ceremonies and, in Biblical times, as the signal horn of war. The shofar is the oldest form of wind instrument—next to reeds—still in use. It is usually made from the curved horn of a ram, although it may be the horn of any other ritually clean animal, except that of a cow or calf (bovines are associated with the incident of the "golden calf" mentioned in the Old Testament). According to Talmudic law, the shofar may not be painted, though it can be gilded or carved with geometric designs or inscriptions so long as the mouthpiece remains natural. A large collection of shofars can be seen in the Israel Museum, Jerusalem.

RASHTRAKUTA PERIOD, in India, extended from 753 to 973 A.D. Dantidurga Rashtrakuta overthrew dominant Chalukya rule in 753 and founded his own feudal dynasty which, at its height, governed much of India's Deccan. The major Rashtrakuta contribution to India's cultural heritage is the great Kailasanatha Temple at Ellora, built by Emperor Krisna I in the 8th century. Unlike most cave temples, the Kailasanatha complex was carved as a free-standing structure and is considered the finest among Ellora's many rock temples.

RAS SHAMRA. See **UGARIT.**

RECLINING BUDDHA. See **POLONNARUWA.**

RECUAY CULTURE, one of the local cultures that flourished in northern Peru during the first centuries of the Christian era. Recuay pottery is distinctive for its two- and three-color negative painting, a technique that left the design area unpainted but stained the background. The designs on the pots include birds, fish, and animals arranged in interlocking patterns. Although the Recuay style is thought to be one of the sources of the Mochica, its modelling does not approach Mochica naturalism. Monumental stone carving in the form of stiff columnar statues is also found in the Recuay area.

Recuay culture: Ceremonial jar. (British Museum, London)

RED-FIGURE VASES. See GREEK CIVILIZATION.

REMOJADAS, an archaeological site in the Mexican state of Veracruz, with ceramic finds dating back to Olmec times, of the 7th century B.C. It is especially well known, however, for its "laughing head" figurines, which date from 600 to 900 A.D. They were found here in such abundance that "laughing heads" are often referred to simply as "Remojadas" figures. Often the name "Remojadas," like the overused attribution "Totonac," is mistakenly applied to all of the art objects to come from the Mexican gulf coast area.

REPOUSSE, a design made on a sheet of metal by hammering it from the back side. Thus, the finished design appears in relief on the front surface.

REPUBLICAN PERIOD, in Roman history, extends from about the 5th century B.C. and the first written Roman legal code to the Sulla and Caesar dictatorships of the 1st century B.C. During this era Rome emerged from the position of a minor Italian city to become the greatest single world power of the time. Republican art style was eclectic, although the two most important influences it absorbed were Etruscan and Greek—the latter emanating from the many Greek-founded cities in Italy and Sicily. Portraiture in sculpture and painting displayed unprecedented realism in Republican Rome, then went on to achieve still greater importance in subsequent Roman epochs. Rome's adherence to realism—as opposed to Greek idealization—was at least partly connected with the ancient Italian custom of making wax death masks.

RESISTIVITY EXPLORATION, a method used by archaeologists to chart potential buried finds before having to dig. The device used in this technique is a set of four earth probes, one of which is connected to a source of electricity. The other probes are attached to meters that take readings of electrical current. The probes are inserted into the ground around a suspected site, and current is passed into the earth. Since materials denser than the soil (for example, brick used for construction of an ancient building) will offer differing resistance from the already-known resistance of the soil itself, an abnormal current reading implies that something is probably buried in the area being explored.

RHODES, ancient Greek port city on the Aegean island of the same name. The city dates from about 408 B.C. and reached its peak of importance during the 3rd and 2nd centuries B.C. A colossal bronze statue of the sun god, Helios, was the city's most important monument. Approximately 105 feet high, it was considered one of the so-called seven wonders of the ancient world but was destroyed by an earthquake in 227 B.C. No trace of the statue remains. The ancient city comprised perhaps one-third of the modern city of Rhodes; its earliest main streets measured roughly 15 feet wide. Extant ruins include temples to Zeus, Apollo, Dionysus, and tombs from the Hellenistic period.

RHONE CULTURE, an early bronze-age culture (about 1800 B.C.) of the Rhone Valley in France, which had ties to Italy and to Swiss lake-dwelling peoples. It also shows influences from even farther east in Bohemia. Typical of Rhone culture is a bronze-hilted dagger with broad, sharply tapering blade and decorated handle found at La Guillotiere.

RHYTON, an ancient Greek drinking horn with a single handle and a body molded in the form of an animal's head (wolf, ram, snake, griffin, stag). Minoan bull-rhytons were libation vessels designed so that liquid could pour through the animal's mouth.

RILLATON CUP. This magnificent cup, four inches high, now in the British Museum, was found in a barrow grave in Cornwall, England. Dating from the bronze age in 1600 B.C., it was beaten out from a single piece of gold. The shape is akin to pottery cups of the Beaker People, but the horizontal ribs and the attachment of the handle by gold rivets recall the gold cups of Mycenae in Greece.

ROMAN CIVILIZATION, centered on the city Rome, was the emanation of the far-flung Roman Empire, perhaps the most successful empire in world history. At its height, in about 200 A.D., the empire held sway over much of Europe and the British Isles and most of North Africa and the Near East; the Mediterranean Sea was a Roman lake. While the Greeks excelled as artists, poets, and intellectuals, the Romans were practical men of the world, organizers and administrators, soldiers, engineers, lawyers, artisans, etc. Roman civilization, which lasted from about the mid-1st millennium B.C. to the 5th century A.D., was to become the nuclear source of early Western civilization, the supreme giver of laws, of political sophistication, religion, and technology. From humble, even barbaric, beginnings, the Latin tribes of Rome, destined to be the Romans of history, ultimately founded the most powerful nation of its time, an imperial nation, proud, rich, acquisitive, and, at times, exceedingly vulgar. In the 6th century B.C., after the Latins had overthrown their Etruscan rulers, the city of Rome came into its own as a semi-democratic republic, a republic influenced by the Etruscans to the north and the Greek colonists to the south. Republican Rome, despite internal strife, soon embarked on a series of conquests and by about 250 B.C. controlled almost the entire Italian peninsula. While military campaigns were continuing in Italy, Rome, ever-expansionist, engaged its first foreign adversary, the Carthaginians of North Africa, in 264 B.C. These Punic Wars against Carthage lasted for more than a century, and Rome, the final victor, emerged as a major naval power, with new landholdings in North Africa and Spain. In the following years, especially under the dictatorship of Sulla, Rome conquered and occupied Greece, became an international power of the first magnitude and a participant in the Hellenistic world. Meanwhile, a new plutocracy of wealth, battened on conquest, was undermining the foundations of Republican Rome. Family, home, and hearth, the traditional values of the republic, had seen their last days under the rising sun of riches. Warring factions, each supported by a strong military leader, tore at the social fabric of the waning republic. In 46 B.C. Julius Caesar became the first autocratic ruler of Rome. His popular regime, marked by endeavors to still the political turmoil that had become the city of Rome, finally ended the republic. With the ascent of Augustus to power in 27 B.C. the Roman Empire began. Under his rule, law and public safety were the order of the day, and tranquillity was established throughout the realm. The Augustan period saw an unprecedented flowering of Roman culture, the growth of great imperial cities, and the acceptance of the Greek aesthetic in Roman art. After the death of Augustus in the early 1st century A.D. a succession of disastrous emperors came to rule Rome. However, by the 2nd century A.D. Imperial Rome had attained its period of grandeur, especially with the strong and able leadership of Trajan, Hadrian, Antoninus Pius, and Marcus Aurelius. Roman society of the imperial era was composed of four major classes: a wealthy aristocracy, a well-to-do merchant class, a poor laboring class, and slaves. The upper classes enjoyed luxuries unmatched in the ancient world and, in many instances, not to be seen again in Europe until the 19th century. The rich owned townhouses and summer villas, with hot and cold running water and steam heat. Private art collections, with paintings, statuary, and mosaics, were a commonplace. The poorer classes lived on farms or in city tenements, their poverty somewhat alleviated by public-assistance programs. The Roman genius for engineering asserted itself in a vast network of highways and bridges and a system of aqueducts that joined their cities and provided the sources of pure water. The far reaches of their road system also served for military transport when provinces revolted or when slaves rose against their masters, a chronic fear among upper-class Romans. Architecture, closer to the profession of engineering than to that of the architect, was colossal in scale, largeness being the ultimate essence of the Roman character. One of the most complex, if superficial, aspects of Roman life was religion. In the Republican period it centered on Italic and Etruscan household gods, but as Rome entered the Hellenistic world the old gods vanished, and the Greek pantheon was officially adopted. Cosmopolitan, affluent, and materialistic, upper-class Rome paid little attention to its own gods or to those borrowed from other countries. Instead, the wealthy Roman, for obvious reasons, offered divine obeisance to his emperor, a genuflection which in later times developed into the full-blown deification and worship of the emperor. Closer to the heart of the poorer classes, and nearer to their vision of a heavenly afterlife, were the cults of Mithra, of Osiris and Isis, and that of Jesus, brought to Rome by returning legions. During the disturbances, chaos, and excesses of the 3rd century A.D., and while the energetic pleasure-seekers of Rome grew more decadent, these salvation-cults attracted greater and greater popularity. The empire was in decline. Military overextension, barbarian inroads, and incompetent leadership had brought the once dynamic empire to the brink of disaster. In the late 3rd century A.D. the Emperor Diocletian administratively divided the empire into East and West,

which for a short time halted the erosion of Roman power. In 313 A.D. Constantine the Great accepted Christianity as a state religion and soon after moved his capital to Byzantium, renamed Constantinople. Although the Roman Empire of the West, with its capital at Rome, lingered on until 476 A.D., when Romulus Augustulus, the last emperor of Rome, was forced to abdicate, the golden years of imperial power, wealth, and supremacy had long since disappeared into history.

Roman Bronze and Metalwork. Of the greatest imaginable variety, Roman metalwork, at its finest, surpassed even that of the Greeks. Although bronze was frequently used for vessels, it was more commonly employed for chariot mounts, furniture finials, and the armor of gladiators. Bronze statuettes were very popular, and many examples of animals, human heads, human figures, etc., have survived the ravages of time. From the late Republican period onward silver, the status symbol of the rich, was the major art metal of the Roman world. The aristocracy of Rome and its large middle class were essentially a *nouveau riche* society with a passion for acquisition, and exquisitely worked silver vessels—at first imported from Roman colonies in Greece—were actively sought for every well-appointed home. This attraction to silver persisted throughout the Imperial period. Among a number of surviving silver treasures is the hoard found at Mildenhall, England (goblets, dishes, etc.), dating from the 4th century A.D. and now housed in the British Museum. Other great hoards of Roman silver include those from Boscoreale, Pompeii, Hoby, and Hildesheim. Silversmiths, rather than goldsmiths or bronze-workers, enjoyed great renown in Roman times and often signed their work. Finely designed reliefs, many bearing mythological subjects, decorated the work of the Roman smith.

Roman Copies. The very large number of extant Roman copies of Greek statuary is another indication of the wealth of the Roman upper classes and of their passion for acquiring art objects. The earliest Greek statues appeared in the Roman world around 200 B.C. as war booty. This importation established a fashion that flourished quickly, but since the collection of originals was limited, a new commercial enterprise, based on the exact duplication of art, developed and prospered; by 150 B.C. copying studios were established throughout the Mediterranean world, notably on the Asia Minor coast. The copyist used a set of compasslike pointers or dividers, measuring off points from an original statue and transferring them to the new stone. Although some Roman copies are more accurate than others, modern knowledge of ancient Greek sculpture would be extremely fragmentary if it were not for the avid Roman art collector. Such objects may be seen in quantity in many museums throughout the world, including the Metropolitan Museum of Art,

Roman bronze: Head of Hadrian. Found in the Thames River under London Bridge. (British Museum, London)

266

Roman copies: "Venus of Cnidos." Marble. 1st–2nd centuries A.D. Copy of Greek original, ca. 350 B.C., by Praxiteles. (Vatican Museum, Rome)

aqueducts, and triumphal arches. Extending the arch in depth, they created the barrel vault, which became a basic unit, either as part of a house or as the major structural element of an amphitheater, like the Colosseum. From the simple barrel vault came another innovation—two intersecting barrel vaults, called a groin vault—which eliminated masonry because it rested on four columns, not on a solid wall. Groin and barrel vaults, in combination, made possible the large interior spaces which became the hallmark of public buildings in Imperial Rome, as for example in the Basilica Maxentius and the Baths of Caracalla in Rome or the Sanctuary of Fortuna in Palestrina. One of the most brilliant feats of Roman engineering was the development of the true dome built of concrete, as can be seen in the Pantheon. In transportation, the Romans invented new road construction techniques that served later Europeans for many centuries after the empire's demise. Probably the best ever built anywhere on earth to their time, Roman roads were flanked by drainage ditches and were composed of layers of rock, gravel, and sometimes mortar.

Roman Mosaics, one of the most spectacular forms of Roman art, were probably first based on Greek models during the Republican period, then improved upon during the centuries that followed. Roman mosaic work at its most typical shows a fondness for naturalism and narrative. Among the very famous examples of narrative mosaics is the huge and almost photographic Battle of the Issus, from the House of the Faun in Pompeii. Throughout the empire, mosaics of marble were built into the floors of fine private homes and public baths, with scenes of myths and legends, athletic contests, the chase, and of everyday genre subjects. Just a few examples include the

New York. The art of copying also served to foster skills—as well as establishing a tradition and creating a demand—that by the Augustan period contributed to the new and distinctly Roman form of portrait sculpture.

Roman Engineering, rather than architecture, expresses the quintessence of the Roman spirit. The principles of physics and mathematics developed by Greek philosophers during the mid-1st millennium B.C. did not receive large-scale application until they were taken over by the innovative engineers of Republican Rome. The Romans, whose chief building materials were stone, brick, and terra cotta, were the first to use concrete, which they invented. Their passion to enclose vast interior spaces, bearing the fewest possible supports, led them to pioneer many technological advances. The first constructional form explored by the Romans was the round arch, which they had inherited from the Etruscans. They put it to many new uses, making it the basis for bridges,

Roman architecture: Temple of Vesta, Rome

Roman engineering: Coffered vault of Titus' Arch, Rome. 1st century A.D.

pastoral mosaics from Hadrian's Villa at Tivoli (around 130 A.D.), now housed in the Vatican Museum; and the Street Musicians scene, from the Villa of Cicero at Pompeii, signed by the Greek artist Dioscurides of Samos, now in the Naples Museum. The largest works were obviously made on the site of installation. However, the master mosaicist frequently prepared an *emblema* in his own studio. This was the central illustration of the mosaic, which was then shipped to its site of installation and placed in a less expertly worked mosaic frame. An original Roman invention in mosaic art was work in glass for wall, rather than floor, designs. The first of these was found on the interior walls of fountains at Pompeii and Herculaneum, and scenes included the same wide variety of subjects as in floor mosaics.

Roman Painting, once considered the mere duplication of earlier Greek painting, is of such extraordinary range in subject matter and in technique, especially in the fine and vivid use of light and color, that it now demands consideration as a distinct and important phase of world art.

Most modern knowledge of Roman painting comes from the wall paintings at Pompeii and Herculaneum, which date from before 79 A.D., the year of the great eruption of Mount Vesuvius. Entire walls within villas were covered with the widest possible variety of subject matter, including portraiture, still lifes, landscapes, seascapes, genre scenes, etc. There are four generally recognized styles of art from Pompeii and Herculaneum. The earliest dates from the 2nd century B.C. and consists of simple painted decoration on stucco panels. The second style, from the early 1st century B.C., shows wall paintings with strong Hellenistic influence; some illusion of depth is attained, in a manner that resembles stage scenery of today. The third style emphasizes foreground detail, reducing backgrounds to more or less flat fields of one color. The fourth style, of the 1st century A.D., is the most complex, often including both foreground detail and intriguing illusions of background depth. It should be noted that while the ancient Greeks decorated public buildings with wall paintings, it was the Romans who brought this splendid art into their own homes.

Roman Sculpture, apart from its devotion to replicas of Greek statues, had a life and style of its own, realistic and thus quite un-Greek. Antithetical to Greek art are marble sculptures of the Republican period, such as the statue of the Patrician Carrying Busts of His Ancestors, now in the Barberini Museum, Rome, as well as detailed portrait busts of many Roman notables. During the Augustan era a new Imperial style appeared, which was to evolve during the course of future centuries. It combined a more conscious desire to emulate the ideals of Greek classicism with concentration on historical subject matter, usually glorifying to the emperor. Examples of Augustan sculpture include the masterful Ara Pacis in Rome, dedicated to Augustus, and the Arch of Titus. An emphasis on factual detail—abhorrent to the Greeks—appears in all the commemorative reliefs of the later empire, such as those on the columns of Trajan and Marcus Aurelius, with their wealth of detail of dress, arms, and customs of the conquered barbarian tribes. Portrait sculpture, from the almost brutal realism of Republican times, grew more idealized in the Imperial era, and flattering busts of the

Roman mosaics: The "House of the Mosaic Atrium," Herculaneum.

Roman painting: "Bacchus Near Vesuvius."

Roman sculpture: Bust of Philip the Arabian. Marble. 3rd century A.D. (Vatican Museum, Rome)

emperors were sent far and wide through the realm. In the 3rd century A.D. Roman sculpture, under the influence of Near Eastern art forms, suffered a drastic change. Classical ideals were abandoned, while poor craftsmanship, rigidity, and expressionism reflected the social chaos of the times.

Roman Terra Cotta achieved its greatest importance during the early Republican period, when it was used extensively to make votive statues. Roman terra cotta derived directly from Etruscan civilization, whose artists made the greatest imaginable use of terra cotta in their statuary. However, with the Hellenization of the Romans, which came around 200 B.C., Greek styles and materials—notably stone—rapidly eclipsed the older terra-cotta tradition. The Romans clearly preferred sculpture of stone and objects of precious metals to those of baked clay. Even decorated pottery failed to achieve importance in the history of Roman art, with the single exception of red-gloss Arretine ware, made in Arezzo between roughly 30 B.C. and 30 A.D. and embellished by relief figures that seem copies of metalwork designs.

ROME, in central Italy, one of the great, historic cities of the world and for centuries the capital of the Roman Empire. From the lowliest of beginnings, and despite the scorn of its neighbors, Rome rose to become the most powerful city of its time and at its zenith, in about 200 A.D., the most magnificent on the face of the earth. Its statue-lined streets, embellished with splendid public monuments, temples, theaters, sports arenas, and elegant townhouses, served the pleasure of more than a million Romans. Outside this teeming city were the fashionable suburbs, where palatial villas, often decorated with sculpture gardens and art collections, graced the countryside. An incredible complex of bridges and roads linked the city to the farthest reaches of its European empire, while massive aqueducts dotted the Roman landscape. Rome enjoyed the first public baths and hospitals and a system of sanitation not to be equalled until the 19th century. One tradition, promoted by Vergil, attributes the founding of Rome to the Trojan prince Aeneas in about 1000 B.C.; another offers the legendary twins Romulus and Remus as the true founders of Rome in 753 B.C. Alba Longa, the birthplace of the fated twins, is often called the mother of Rome in ancient annals; its site, somewhere in the Alban Hills south of Rome, has yet to be discovered. While the legends are conflicting, it is certain that the site of the future city of Rome was first settled by Italic peoples in about 1500 B.C. The original settlement was on the Palatine Hill on the east bank of the Tiber River, and over the years villages appeared on the

Roman sculpture: "The Belvedere Torso." (Vatican Museum, Rome)

other hills of Rome: the Capitoline, to the northwest of the Palatine, and the Quirinal, Viminal, Esquiline, Caelian, and Aventine in an outlying north to southwest curve. These seven hills of Rome, which were free from the malaria that afflicted the marshy plains below, attracted many peoples from neighboring areas. In the early 1st millennium B.C. the Etruscans, an advanced, non-Italic people with domains to the north and west of Italic Rome, conquered the hill pastoralists there, probably the Latins, a remarkable group of tribes destined to become the Romans of history. The Etruscans unified the hilltop towns of Rome as a city-state and by the 7th century B.C. had built a protective wall around the city, drained the malarial swamps, and laid out a sewerage system. However, in the 6th century B.C. the Latins overthrew their foreign kings and established a Roman Republic, whose genesis was profoundly affected by former Etruscan rule and by the advent of Greek colonies to the

Rome: The Golden House of Nero.

south of Rome. The Roman Republic, despite incessant civil strife and the Gaulish sack of Rome in 390 B.C., not only survived but prospered; by 250 B.C. the city controlled almost the entire Italian peninsula. Under the republic the seven hills of Rome were enclosed by the so-called Servian Wall, part of which can still be seen near the modern railroad station; the Appian Way was opened; and aqueducts, bridges, basilicas, and forums were built. However, it was only with the dictatorships of Sulla and Caesar in the 1st century B.C., which marked the end of the republic, that the great age of building began, an age that lasted for about 400 years. In 78 B.C. Sulla linked the Capitoline Hill and the Roman Forum, the center of ancient Roman life, with the Tabularium, or record office, whose foundations are still visible today under the modern Senate building. Pompey, the Roman general, built the first stone theater in Rome in 55 B.C., while his rival,

Julius Caesar, rebuilt the Circus Maximus, a structure whose foundation may have dated from Etruscan times. With the ascent of Augustus to power in 27 B.C. the Roman Empire, one of the greatest the world has ever known, began. The Emperor Augustus added another forum to an already congested city; built a modest palace on the Palatine, which was enlarged by subsequent emperors; constructed a Pantheon temple; and left many monuments, including the famous Ara Pacis, or Altar of Augustan Peace. Nero, the last of the Augustan line, built his imperial palace, the fabulous Golden House, near the southern end of the Roman Forum. During his rule, one of the most notorious in all history, the great fire of 64 A.D. destroyed almost half of Rome. In the following decades Rome was rebuilt in a more grandiose, imperial style: Titus completed the Colosseum; Trajan radically changed the Roman Forum and set up his well-known column;

and Hadrian erected the Temple of Venus, on the site of Nero's Golden House, built the famous Pantheon, and laid out his mausoleum, now called the Castel Sant' Angelo, beside the Tiber. In the 2nd century A.D. the pace of monumental building slackened. A brief rebirth of Roman architecture and engineering occurred under the Severians of the 3rd century A.D., who made daring use of concrete and of architectural elements, such as the vault, the dome, and the arch. The triumphal arch of Septimus Severus, as well as the baths of Caracalla and Diocletian, are fine examples of Severian style. In 284 A.D. another great fire struck Rome, burning much of the city. Constantine, the last great Roman emperor, came to power in the early 4th century A.D. He left many monuments, especially his triumphal arch, but history remembers him best for the Edict of Milan, which established Christianity as a state religion. In 330 A.D. he moved the capital of the disintegrating Roman Empire from Rome to Byzantium, which was rebuilt and renamed Constantinople, or the city of Constantine. From that time on the city of Rome, exhausted by more than 1,000 years of vigorous history, declined in political importance; in 410 A.D. the weakened and vulnerable city fell to invading Goths. In the ensuing centuries Rome, the Eternal City, emerged as the center of Christianity, shorn of political or military power.

ROSETTA STONE, an inscribed basalt slab, about 45 inches high and 28 inches wide, discovered in 1799 in the Nile Delta region by troops of Napoleon. It is a decree dating from 196 B.C., inscribed in Greek and in two Egyptian scripts—a cursive script called demotic and in ancient hieroglyphics. It was first translated by the great French Egyptologist Champollion. The stone was thus a key to the deciphering of hieroglyphics, which had resisted all previous modern efforts at translation. It is now in the British Museum.

ROSSEN, a neolithic cemetery site near Merseburg, in central Germany, which gives its name to a culture centered in the Elbe-Saale region. Of mixed origin, the culture dates from the mid-4th millennium B.C. Basketweaving decoration on Rossen pottery shows influence from the north, while the practice of burying corpses in a crouched position comes from the south, the region of the Danube. Rossen sites have been found in southern Bavaria and in Switzerland.

RUNES, the ancient Scandinavian form of writing, consisting of an alphabet of 24 symbols and employing only straight lines, since they are easier to scratch or carve on wood, metal, or stone. This alphabet, and hence literacy, appeared in Scandinavia in the 3rd or 2nd centuries B.C., possibly coming in from the eastern Mediterranean via Russia. Runic characters first appeared on weapons from Moos in Gotland and from Stabu north of Oslo. A secondary meaning of runes, which has come to dominate the use of the word, is that of inscriptions with magical or religious meaning.

RUS, an eastern Slavic people who dominated the Soviet Ukraine by the 9th century A.D., establishing there the most important of the early Slavic kingdoms—the Kievan State. Although Slavs, the Rus were ruled by a Scandinavian dynasty, beginning with Rurik the Dane in 862. Kiev, their main commercial and cultural center, flourished between the 9th and 12th centuries. The Kievan State was destroyed in 1240 when it was invaded by the Tartars, Turkic nomads from central Asia.

Rosetta Stone: Detail. (British Museum, London)

S

SABAEANS, a Semitic people of southwestern Arabia, in what is now Yemen, who formed a highly prosperous and civilized kingdom, called Saba, in the early 1st millennium B.C. They built the famous dikes and irrigation system centered at their capital, Marib. Saba, the Biblical Sheba, was the homeland of a famous queen. Sabaeans may have colonized ancient Ethiopia. The Sabaeans were noted for their gold and silver vases (very few of which survive) and produced fine jewelry, as well as small bronze reliefs. The kingdom of Saba fell about the 1st century B.C.

SABBATH. See **SIN.**

SABINES, a tribe identifiable on the Italian peninsula, northeast of Rome, from about the end of the 2nd millennium B.C. By the 8th century B.C. they had begun settling the Tiber Valley, establishing villages near those of their neighboring peoples, the Latins, with whom they ultimately merged to found the city of Rome. Ancient legend has the Latins taking Sabine women into bondage, the resultant offspring being Rome's early citizens.

SACRED TREE. See **TREE OF LIFE.**

SACSAHUAMAN. See **CUZCO.**

SAHARAN ROCK DRAWINGS. The earliest known examples of African art, rock engravings and paintings, are found in almost all of the mountainous regions of the Sahara. To date, over 30,000 have been discovered, more than half of them being the Tassili frescoes. At the time of their creation, between the 6th and 2nd millenniums B.C., the Sahara was open grassland, supporting animals no longer there but who survive in Saharan rock art. Changing subject matter as well as differing Saharan art styles have enabled scholars to divide the many centuries of rock art into four major periods. The earliest Saharan engravings belong to the Bubalus period and reflect a hunting economy with mostly wild animals depicted. These are portrayed in a naturalistic manner and on a large scale. Drawings of humans, for example, are often 11 feet tall. The Bubalus is followed by the Cattle period, in the 4th millennium B.C., when domesticated cattle first appeared along with wild animals. The Cattle style, however, is less naturalistic than that of the Bubalus, poses are stiffer, and engravings become smaller in scale. The Horse period, following that of the Cattle era, appears in about 1200 B.C. Newly tamed animals are portrayed, such as camels, dogs, and horses; chariots are also shown. The drawings are greatly reduced in size, and representations become more conventionalized. The last Saharan rock-art period, the Camel period, persists until the present day. Desert nomads still paint and engrave the rocks with highly schematic but very small images. The nature of the many peoples who created ancient Saharan rock art remains a mystery.

SAKAS, a nomadic central Asian steppe tribe, flourishing from about the 8th through the 2nd centuries B.C., having originated in eastern Turkestan and Tibet. Defeated by Cyrus the Great in the 6th century, they later allied with Persia to fight the Greeks. Saka arts and crafts were acquired from other cultures: Scythian-style vessels and spears; Chinese silks, lacquers, jades; and Greco-Bactrian bronzes and gold objects. Saka influence exerted itself in India as late as the 1st century A.D.

SALINAR CULTURE, one of the small ancient cultures that prospered on the northern coast of Peru from about 200 B.C. to 200 A.D. The Salinar people led a simple life; little evidence remains of class distinctions. The only outstanding artistic accomplishment of the culture lies in the production of oxidized pottery. When fired, this type of pottery turns to a red color, which the Salinar people then painted with simple white designs. The emphasis of the pottery decoration was on life-figure modelling. Animals, birds, houses, humans, and an occasional erotic scene are all portrayed. Salinar pottery represents a transition between the earlier Cupisnique and later Mochica styles.

SAMARIA, a city and region in the center of ancient Palestine. The city, whose site is near Nablus, was founded in the 9th century B.C. by the Israelite king Omri after the defeat of the Canaanites of the region. It became the capital of the northern kingdom of Israel, and because Ahab, Omri's son, married the Phoenician princess Jezebel, Samaria was considered a place of iniquity by the Hebrew prophets. From the time of Omri and Ahab date some excellent buildings showing Phoenician influence and a remarkable collection of carved ivories. Slightly later in date are a number of inscribed pottery fragments highly informative of political developments. The city was destroyed by the Assyrians in the late 8th century B.C., but the site remained occupied and was later under Roman control.

SAMARRA WARE, a distinctive and very early painted pottery of upper Mesopotamia dating from the 6th millennium B.C. An advance on Hassuna ware, which it replaced, it depicted animals and humans together with geometric designs. The most common motif of Samarra ware was a whirllike composition, whether exemplified in the streaming hair of women or in stylized leaping goats. This ware was first discovered in northern Iraq about 60 miles above Baghdad. Halaf pottery styles succeeded that of Samarra around 5000 B.C.

SAMIAN WARE, a type of fine red pottery, often lavishly decorated, in common use all over the Roman Empire in the form of jars, plates, and bowls. Many articles of Samian ware have been found in Gaul. Although Classical Greek pottery was manufactured on Samos, an island in the Aegean Sea, there is no connection with the Samian ware of the Romans, the name being due solely to a chance reference in Pliny's *Natural History*. True Samian ware (*terra sigillata*) was ultimately derived from earlier Roman Arretine ware.

SAMNITES, warlike peasants of Italy's fertile Campania plain and possibly related to the Sabines. By about 400 B.C. the Samnites had superseded the Etruscans in the Campania region, having conquered the major Etruscan center of Capua and the Greek colonial city of Cumae. They subsequently fought the Romans, enjoying initial victories but finally falling to superior Roman military tactics around 290 B.C.

SAN AGUSTIN, a large and rich archaeological region in the Department of Huila, Colombia, surrounding a modern village of the same name. The 30 sites so far discovered in the area have yielded no traces of monumental architecture. However, the largest and most spectacular sculptures in northern South America have been found here. Most of these are free-standing stone slabs, resembling stele. The San Agustin people also carved monolithic sarcophagi, stone altars, boulders, and the bedrock of streams to produce channels and pools that may have been used as sacred baths. Since the carving on the statues ranges from high to low relief and the images from human to non-human, they are thought to cover a time span of up to a thousand years. The only reliable date from the site is 500 B.C., but it is still uncertain whether this is the earliest date. A frequent figure in sculpture is that of a jaguar-god, holding a baby. This and other similarities of style connect with Olmec civilization of Mexico and that of the Chavin of Peru. Speculation therefore grows that San Agustin was either a point of contact between these two great Pre-Columbian civilizations or even the cultural watershed for both.

SANCHI, a well-preserved hill site in central India, near modern Bhilsa, offering some of the country's finest examples of Buddhist sculpture and architecture. Sanchi flourished as a religious and cultural center in the last few centuries B.C. It was abandoned at some later time and forgotten until its rediscovery in 1818. Sanchi's most important structure is the largest of several hemispherical stupas, the Great Stupa. It is roughly 120 feet in diameter, surrounded by walls having ornate gateways. Exuberant carvings at Sanchi are probably the most important sculptural remains of post-Mauryan India, the best examples dating from about the 1st century B.C.

SANTA LUCIA, an ancient site near Ljubljana in northwest Yugoslavia where a large cemetery provides evidence both of cremation and of inhumation, or regular burial in the ground. Over 6,000 graves here have been studied, and the objects found in them show cultural connections with Italy and central Europe. The site is important in part because of its long history of burial, ranging from the 9th to the 2nd century B.C.

Sanchi: Detail of the North Gate of the Great Stupa.

SANTORINI. See **THERA**.

SAQQARAH, famed Egyptian necropolis at Memphis, about 20 miles from modern Cairo. This site extends more than four miles along the Nile, encompassing numerous mastaba tombs, probably the burial places of the royal families of the 1st Dynasty. Dominating Saqqarah is Egypt's oldest pyramid, the Step Pyramid of Zoser, dating from about 2800 B.C. Study of this structure shows that it was first conceived as another rectangle-shaped mastaba, then subsequently was enlarged in several stages until assuming its pyramid shape. Original pyramid dimensions were 204 feet in height and 411 by 368 feet at the base. Numerous archaeological finds have been made at Saqqarah.

SARCOPHAGUS, from the Greek for "flesh-eater," a stone casket. It was so named because the ancients used a special limestone which was said to have dissolved the flesh of corpses in about a month. In antiquity they were also extensively used by Etruscans and Romans but were made of terra cotta, lead, marble, or porphyry. The most impressive sarcophagi are those decorated with high reliefs, or fully rounded figures, on their lids.

SARDINIA. See ANGHELU RUJU.

SARDIS, chief city of Lydia in western Asia Minor and capital of the famed King Croesus; it was a wealthy trade center. In the 7th century B.C. Lydian kings were the first to mint gold and silver coins. Excavations here are currently being carried on, and the mint of Croesus has recently been found, as well as numerous Lydian inscriptions, a language not well understood.

SARGON'S PALACE, the great building at Khorsabad, the Assyrian capital founded in northern Iraq by Sargon II towards the close of the 8th century B.C. The palace included living quarters, temples, offices, state rooms, and the great throne room in which Sargon would receive visitors. The entrances to the palace and the throne room were guarded by huge and winged human-headed bulls, and the walls were decorated with more than life-size reliefs of the king and his courtiers. The palace was destroyed in about 705 B.C. Much sculpture from Sargon's Palace is now in the Louvre.

SARMATIANS, nomadic horsemen of probable Siberian origin who, from the 4th century B.C., began displacing the Scythians in the northern Caucasus and southern steppe regions of Russia. Early Sarmatian art, found in many parts of Siberia, includes gold animal figures used for personal adornment; they are sometimes decorated with inset stones and cloisonné. Later Sarmatian works include gold and bronze plaques of stylized animal forms that show strong Scythian influence, although never equalling Scythian art in excellence. In turn, Sarmatian influence is clear in the work of the Chinese bronze craftsmen of the Ordos plateau, whose animal plaques date from about the 1st century B.C.

SARNATH, holy Buddhist site, location of the famous Deer Park, and now part of the Indian city Benares. Buddha's first sermon was at Sarnath, and the often photographed stone statue of the seated, preaching Buddha is located here. It is but one of many fine Buddhas at Sarnath, dating from Gupta India. The traditional sermon site (the Deer Park) is marked by ruins of a cylindrical stupa. Notable architecture at Sarnath spans the long period from the Mauryan through the Moghul eras. India's national seal, the lion, was taken from the capital of an inscribed pillar of Emperor Asoka, at Sarnath.

SASSANIANS, a cosmopolitan and illustrious Persian dynasty founded in 224 A.D. by Ardashir I after the demise of the last Parthian king. Great town planners, the Sassanians established a strong central government and carried out large-scale public works. Persia under the Sassanians enjoyed a rich prosperity, an artistic renaissance, and a political and military power that inevitably led to formidable confrontations with Rome and later the Byzantine Empire. The most impressive and best-known Sassanian works of art are colossal reliefs carved into cliffs. The best of these, those near Persepolis, depict the military victories of Ardashir over the Romans. The Sassanians also excelled in architecture, as can be seen at Ctesiphon. The rough masonry of their buildings was faced with distinctive plaques of carved and molded stucco. Metalwork reached a high level of artistry, and precious metals were crafted for use as bowls and plateware. Their interiors were generally decorated with royal hunting scenes executed in high relief. Some fine examples of Sassanian metalwork can be seen at the Metropolitan Museum of Art, New York, and the British Museum, London. Sassanian craftsmen also produced brilliantly colored and patterned textiles whose designs influenced European, Byzantine, and Islamic artists for centuries to come. In 651 A.D. invading Moslem Arabs destroyed the Sassanian kingdom.

SATAVAHANA PERIOD, an era that began in the 2nd century B.C. in India's Deccan and lasted for about 300 years. It was a time of some of India's greatest art, including the building of the earliest cave temples at Ajanta and Karle. Also dating from this time is the stupa at Amaravati, which contained much beautiful sculpture. Many of these objects, now housed in the British Museum, are marble and sandstone reliefs depicting scenes from Buddha's life. Satavahana dominance of the Deccan originated when its feudal leader, Simuka, overwhelmed faltering remnants of the Sunga Dynasty.

SCARAB, name for a Mediterranean beetle venerated in ancient Egypt. The scarab's periodic recurrence in great numbers in the Nile mud led to its association with the worship of the Egyptian sun god. Representations of the sacred scarab, or beetle, were made in precious and semiprecious stone, metal, and faience. In the 3rd millennium B.C. finely carved scarabs came into use as seals. Many scarabs sold today are forgeries.

SCARLET WARE, a distinctive and attractive type of early Iranian pottery from the 3rd millennium B.C. It is found particularly in southwest Iran and in the Diyala River valley bordering Iraq. It featured progressively more dense and elaborate ornamentation, usually in geometric designs, with black on buff separated by a red wash. In its later periods the painted composition included human and animal figures.

SCHIST, a stratum of rock formation, visible as a ribbon-like layer when a vertical cut is made into the earth. Such formations are the result of geologic heat and pressure. Schist has been used in the making of antiquities.

SCOPAS, Greek architect and sculptor, a contemporary of Praxiteles and, like him, a representative of the new, realistic spirit of the 4th century B.C. None of his work

Sassanians: Horse's head. Silver gilt with mercury. Persian, 4th–5th centuries A.D. From Kirman. (Louvre, Paris)

survives with certainty, although many believe two impressive heads from the pediment of the temple of Athena at Tegea (Peloponnesus) are his. The many subsequent attributions are based on this identification. He worked on the temple of Artemis at Ephesus, and the carved column drum from that building, in the British Museum, may be his. He also sculpted the east side of the Mausoleum in Halicarnassus (southwest Asia Minor), and three of the four slabs of the east frieze (also in the British Museum) are attributed to him. Scopas' expressive style of pathos, of violent force and movement, paved the way for Hellenistic sculpture.

SCYTHIANS, mounted nomads of the south Russian steppes whose earliest archaeological and historical records date from around the 9th century B.C. The Scythians left no remains of communities, but as a mound-burial culture they left many important tomb sites, the best being near the Black Sea, from the Kuban to the Dnieper valleys. Scythian art, which has been found only at tomb sites, is the finest expression of the so-called animal style—or steppe art—the major aesthetic flowering of the Eurasian nomads. Scythian craftsmen fused earlier steppe and Caucasian art traditions, using motifs of birds, horses, stags, and similar woodland animals, into a totally new art, characterized by dynamic and often powerful designs. Scythian influence affected related animal-art traditions east to Mongolia and south to the Iranian plateau. The Scythians had contact with several high cultures, most notably that of the Greeks; thus their art, especially in finds from the Crimea westward, shows visible Greek influence. The Scythians were displaced on the steppe by the Sarmatians in the 3rd century B.C. and subsequently vanished from history. Probably the finest Scythian art collection in the world is in the Hermitage, Leningrad.

SEALS, small, hard objects with intaglio designs that can be transferred to clay or wax by rolling or pressing to signify ownership, authenticity, or authority. Derived from amulets, seals were first used in the Near East during the 6th millennium B.C. The many forms of seals include the famous Egyptian scarab-beetle seals of semiprecious stones and faience, Chinese porcelain seals, and ancient Roman portrait seals.

SEA PEOPLES, an enigmatic group of sea raiders, principally of Aegean origin but possibly including ancient Sardinians, Sicilians, and even Etruscans, who quite suddenly, in the 13th and 12th centuries B.C., invaded the lands of the Near East. They destroyed the Hittite Empire and attempted to occupy Egypt but were finally driven off by Ramses III around 1200 B.C. Some of the Sea Peoples occupied portions of Palestine and became known as the Philistines. The eruption of the Sea Peoples was an outcome of the crumbling of Mycenaean civilization, and it is believed to have been an aftermath of the Trojan War. In the Palestinian area the onslaught and subsequent withdrawal of certain of the Sea Peoples created a power vacuum that was soon filled by such Semitic peoples as the Hebrews.

SECCO, a method of painting a mural on a dry plaster wall, as differentiated from the more usual method of fresco painting, which is to allow pigments to permeate wet plaster.

SEINE-OISE-MARNE. The valleys of these three rivers in the region surrounding Paris were the home of a culture in early neolithic times that arose when a forest people—hunters and stock breeders—adopted the faith of the Megalithic Builders, which was at this time spreading over northern Europe. Beginning about 2400 B.C., the new culture, known as Seine-Oise-Marne, was marked by collective graves holding from 40 to 80 bodies, which were either natural burial places or artificial caves dug into the chalk, called "Paris cists," a form of gallery grave.

SELEUCIDS, a Greek dynasty, based in Syria, which lasted from around 312 B.C. to 64 B.C. and comprised some 26 rulers. It was founded by Seleucus I, an able general of Alexander the Great, who succeeded to much of Alexander's Near Eastern empire. Seleucus built Antioch in northern Syria and Seleucia near modern Baghdad. The main linguistic and artistic thrust of the

Senufo: Lo Society ceremonial bird. Carved wood. From the Ivory Coast. (Museum of African and Oceanic Art, Paris)

dynasty was Greek, while politically it was a mixture of Greek elements with Near Eastern despotism and mysticism. The Seleucid Empire was absorbed by the Romans.

SEMITES, a generic term for those Near Eastern groups of nomadic herdsmen who in ancient times spoke related Semitic languages. Their earliest records indicate that they came from the fringes of the Arabian desert to Mesopotamia in the 3rd millennium B.C., where they had contact with Sumerian civilization. Major Semitic peoples include the Akkadians, the Amorites, the Canaanites, the Hebrews, the Aramaeans, the Phoenicians, and the Arabs. Their cultural legacies include the Jewish, Christian, and Islamic religions.

SENUFO. An African people living principally in the Ivory Coast, the Senufo migrated from the north to their present homeland several centuries ago. The Senufo are governed by the Lo Society, a secret organization to which every male eventually belongs. The Lo Society, while providing the basic social and political framework, also stimulates the arts, as ritual masks are required in its ceremonies. Among the most striking masks is the so-called fire-spitter—a fearsome composite mask of crocodile, warthog, antelope, and human features, designed to seek out and exorcise witches. The wearer blew hot coals through the jaws of the mask, which, during his nighttime appearance, seemed to spit fire. The Senufo also used ancestor figures and other masks, both human and animal in form.

SEPIK RIVER, a river flowing from the central highlands of New Guinea northeast to the Pacific Ocean. The tortuous path of the Sepik runs through the homeland of many art-producing New Guinea peoples. Each of these groups has a distinctive art style. But, in common, there are colorful figurines, masks, dance shields, and musical instruments, richly decorated in relief with emphasis on curvilinear designs. The human form in Sepik River art has an unusually large head, a body with an unbalanced or slightly bent pose, and a unique nose shaped either as a bulbous figure 6 or as an elongated imitation of a bird's beak. Animals are frequently depicted.

SERAPIS, an Egyptian god who combined the features of the sacred bull Apis and those of Osiris. His cult originated in Memphis, Egypt, where a huge Serapeum, or underground necropolis, was excavated for the burial of mummified bulls. However, the cult reached its high point in Alexandria during the Ptolemaic period, after Ptolemy I chose Serapis as a unifying divinity between Greek settlers in Egypt and native Egyptians. Serapis cults subsequently appeared throughout the Greek and Roman worlds. Serapis is usually depicted as a seated bearded figure with horns.

SERINDIA, ancient central Asian region in Chinese Turkestan, located along the silk trade route. It was important as an area of artistic exchange between Iran, Greece, Rome, China, and India. Serindia was continually disputed, but even so, art developed to a high level from the 1st century A.D., under Chinese influence, until about the 10th century when the Moslems invaded. Many of the cities of Serindia—Miran, Niya, Endere, and Khotan—were excavated by Sir Aurel Stein in the 19th century. The ruins of Miran (south of Lop Nor) are decorated with Hellenistic-influenced wall paintings believed to be the oldest in Turkestan, and the shrine of Rawak in Khotan is embellished with magnificent Greco-Indian reliefs.

SERPENTINE, a hydrated magnesium silicate that occurs in a variety of forms. Precious serpentine is a translucent green stone (marble) used for art objects and for ornamental details on ancient buildings.

SERVIAN WALL. See **ROME.**

SESKLO, a term that came into use about 70 years ago to describe the then oldest known neolithic culture in Greece. Sesklo takes its name from a 5th-millennium B.C. mound found in eastern Thessaly. Sesklo culture is characterized by roomy houses and especially by geometric red-on-cream vases of high technical quality, decorated with flame and triangle designs.

SETH, also called Set, Egyptian god who was the son of Osiris and the brother of Horus. Because he murdered Osiris he usually represents the darker side of life. Seth was worshipped in the form of a composite animal by the 19th Dynasty Egyptian pharaohs and by the Hyksos.

SETHI TOMB, or the Tomb of Seti I, a magnificent monument of a 19th Dynasty pharaoh, discovered in the Valley of the Kings by Giovanni Belzoni in 1819. Considered the largest and most impressive of ancient Egyptian royal tombs, it is cut 100 yards into a limestone mountain and is profusely decorated throughout with brilliantly painted reliefs. The tomb contains a series of large halls, each about 28 by 26 feet; a burial chamber, which contained a nine-by-four-foot solid alabaster sarcophagus, carved inside and out and covered with a blue paste inlay; and five additional rooms surrounding the burial chamber. At discovery, the royal mummy was not in the tomb.

SEVEN HILLS OF ROME. See **ROME.**

SEVEN WONDERS OF THE WORLD, monumental creations of ancient civilizations considered particularly awe-inspiring. The generally accepted wonders are the following: The Colossus of Rhodes, a 100-foot-high statue of the sun god Helios, by Chares of Lindus. It was built between 292 and 280 B.C. at the harbor entrance and was destroyed by an earthquake in 224 B.C. The Pharos of Alexandria, a 400-foot-tall lighthouse, was built in 270 B.C. The Mausoleum at Halicarnassus in Asia Minor, designed by Pythius and containing sculptures by Praxiteles and Scopas, was built around 353 B.C. and was destroyed by an earthquake before the 15th century. The Statue of Zeus at Olympia, carved by Phidias between 437 and 425 B.C., was over 40 feet tall and made of ivory, gold, and precious stones on a wood core. It was destroyed by fire in 475 A.D. The Temple of Artemis at

Ephesus was built in the 6th century B.C. by the architect Chessiphiron. It was burned in 356 B.C. and rebuilt to a size of 360 by 180 feet. It was again destroyed, by the Goths, in 262 A.D. The Hanging Gardens of Babylon apparently were ornamental gardens planted on a series of terraces along the Euphrates in the 6th century B.C. The 80 or so Pyramids of Egypt range from small to huge. The Cheops (Khufu) Pyramid alone is 481 feet high and 755 feet along each of the base sides, the corners of which are almost perfect right angles.

SFUMATO, in Greek sculpture, a stylistic technique of the Hellenistic period (330 to 100 B.C.). It is characterized by delicate modelling and a sensuous softness.

SHAFT GRAVES OF MYCENAE, deep, rectangular burial pits used by the warrior aristocracy of the Peloponnesus from the 16th century B.C. When Heinrich Schliemann, the pioneer German archaeologist, excavated here in the autumn of 1876, he discovered richly furnished graves that introduced Mycenaen civilization to the world—and at a point where it truly began, for the shaft graves mark the beginnings of that 600-year-old civilization. The treasure trove is mainly gold—exquisite brooches, pins and rings, silver and gold rhytons and

Shang Dynasty: Ku bronze. 13th century B.C. (Metropolitan Museum of Art, New York)

cups, ornate tiaras, decorated armor and weapons, and several golden "death masks," unlike any found before or since. The most sophisticated metalwork is on inlaid dagger blades: hunting scenes done in bronze, gold, and silver, with black niello for details. The "Silver Siege Rhyton," though in poor condition, must have been equally impressive with its crowded and dramatic battle imagery artfully worked in repoussé relief. This cup, like the daggers, blends Minoan form and motifs with a non-Minoan style. The limestone stelae (three to six feet high) that topped the graves carry crude, lightly incised hunting and war scenes and represent the only monumental art of the period. The rich and deep royal tombs of the 3rd millennium, discovered at Alaca Huyuk in Anatolia, may have been a prototype for the Shaft Graves of Mycenae.

SHAILENDRA DYNASTY, rulers in Indonesia, particularly in central Java, from 778 to 864 A.D. They are best known for their vast series of Buddhist and Hindu monuments on Java. The Shailendra kings claimed the title of Mountain Kings and built their pyramidlike temples on the basic pattern of repeated diminishing stories. The related concepts of Mountain King and temple architecture were borrowed by the Khmer rulers of Cambodia. Greatest among Shailendra monuments are the ornately carved Chandi Mendut and the last colossal building complex of the central Javanese school, the Lara Jonggrang, which incorporates 232 temples into one vast design, 120 feet high at its center. Shailendra sculpture was characteristically massive, lacking in visual movement, and bore a facial impassivity that embodied the Javanese concept of perfection.

SHAMANISM, a type of primitive religion characteristic of hunting cultures and practiced in various forms by nomadic and seminomadic peoples of prehistoric Europe, central Asia, Siberia, the Lapps of Finland, Eskimos, North American Indians, some peoples of Africa, and Melanesian islanders. Shamanism's world is populated with good and evil spirits who dwell in particular objects or locations. The shaman—or witch doctor—both priest and healer, communicates with spirits and is often possessed by them while seeking the well-being of his people. Shamanist art and artifacts include grotesque masks and costumes.

SHAMASH, the Babylonian and Assyrian sun god, one of a triad of gods, with Sin, of the moon, and Ishtar, of the earth. Shamash was the god of justice and healing. His wife was A or Aa. There were temples to him at Larsa, Babylon, and Nippur.

SHANG DYNASTY, the first historical Chinese dynasty (1500 to 1122 or 1027 B.C.); it marks the beginning of Chinese history and civilization. An advanced bronze-age society, showing both east and west Asian influences, the Shang had capitals at Anyang and Cheng Chou in Honan Province. Houses were pit types, while larger pillared palaces, roughly 26 by 92 feet, were of timber with rammed-earth walls. A white pottery with stamped patterns but no glaze was produced, and 2,000 characters existed for writing, as evidenced on oracle bones found at Shang sites. By the middle Shang, horses were introduced and a feudal society with hereditary kings developed. Magnificent Shang bronze ritual vessels, covered with intricate, incised, and high-relief designs, represent a superb development in bronze casting and are considered superior to European Renaissance works. The fusion of Shang cultural elements with those of the subsequent Chou Dynasty formed the basis for the ultimate flowering of Chinese civilization.

SHANGO. In Nigeria, West Africa, he was the deified fourth king of the Yoruba kingdom of Oyo. Worshipped at specially assembled shrines, he is known as the wrathful god of thunder and lightning. His symbol, the double-headed axe, adorns images dedicated to him.

SHEBA. See **SABAEANS.**

SHILOH, the central sanctuary of the ancient Hebrews, in the mountains west of the Jordan, a bit north of Bethel. When, around 1200 B.C., the Israelites had conquered the Canaanites, the Hebrew tribes, led by Joshua, set up the Ark and the Tabernacle in Shiloh, and it became the religious capital of the Hebrew tribal confederation. About two hundred years later the town was destroyed in the war with the Philistines.

SHINTO ART AND ANTIQUITIES. The ancient nature worship of Japan, Shinto—or the Way of the Gods— attributes divinity to the awesome and beautiful manifestations of nature. The introduction of Buddhism and Chinese ideas of ancestor worship into Japan spurred development in the mid-6th century A.D. of Ryobu Shinto, in which Shinto deities were identified with Buddhist deities. Many Shinto shrines were administered jointly with Buddhist shrines until the 19th century. Architecture of Shinto shrines before the introduction of Buddhism was based on the thatched-hut style, with a torii, or carved wooden gateway, at the shrine's entrance; the Great Shrine at Ise is a fine example. The Buddhist-influenced Shinto shrines were painted and had up-curving bracketed roofs and pagodas; the torii was finally displaced by two-story portals. Examples are the Kamo Shrine at Kyoto and the Kasuga Shrine at Nara. Thousands of smaller shrines, usually about six feet tall, were built throughout Japan. Shinto painting and sculpture did not appear until the end of the 9th century, simply because there was no established iconography before then. Subsequent Shinto art is of minor importance. Typical objects are the polychromed statues at the Hachima Shrine, Nara. Shinto painting, or *suijaku-ga*, is in two styles: scenic depictions of deities' dwelling places and representations of the symbol of a particular deity.

Shinto Iconography began to develop after the arrival of Buddhism. The basic Shinto deities are the *kami*, who dwell in various natural locations, such as in a tree or a mountain. Early Japanese literature refers to eight million

Shinto art: "Vermilion torii." Approach to the Fushimi Inari shrine, Kyoto.

kami; consequently their powers and dwelling places were never consistent. They rarely were represented as human, since the dwelling place was of primary importance. *Kami* were usually symbolized by swords, mirrors, and *magatawa* (curved jewels), or implied by a painting of their dwelling place. As the Shinto *kami* became identified with Buddhist deities they could be shown in human form. In some cases a deity was represented as a Buddhist priest; in others an emperor would be depicted as a particular Shinto divinity. The highest Shinto deity is the sun goddess, Ameratsu, who is represented by a sacred mirror in the Great Shrine at Ise. Other important deities are the moon god, the war god, and Inari, the god of rice, whose image is a fox.

SHOFAR. See RAM'S HORN.

SHUNGA DYNASTY, an Indian dynasty established about 185 B.C. by Pusyamitra Shunga and ended about 72 B.C., when the Andhras from the Deccan took control. Centered in Magadha, the dynasty was feudal. Shunga art is a merging of early, archaic forms with the high development of the classic Gupta period. Early Shunga art is crude but lively, and later it became more plastic and complicated. Buddhism was popularized under the Shungas with the development of the *jatakas* (stories about Buddha's earlier incarnations) and the nature spirits (*yashkas* and *nagas*). These iconographic elements are evident in the major monuments of the Shunga Dynasty—the carved gateways and railings at the stupas of Sanchi, Bharhut, and Amaravati.

SIBYL, in Classical antiquity, a female prophet and oracle. There were several sibyls, among them the Delphic, Libyan, and Erythraean sibyls. However, the most famous was the Sibyl of Cumae, who lived in a cave near Naples. Consulted in times of crisis, the Cumaean Sibyl uttered prophetic guidance to the troubled leaders of Rome. Her sometimes paradoxical statements were recorded in the Sibylline Books, which were said to have been destroyed in 83 B.C.

SIDON, a Phoenician city-state on the coast of Lebanon. The site, modern Saida, is still occupied and is about 25 miles south of Beirut. Ancient Sidon vied with Tyre, which it had founded, as the leading commercial settlement and seaport of the Phoenicians. It was renowned for its precious metalwork and its purple-dyed textiles, as well as its glassware, linens, and perfumes. Sidon, which dates to the 3rd millennium B.C., was dominated in turn by Assyria, Babylonia, and Persia and was captured by Alexander the Great in 333 B.C.

SIEMREAP, modern name for the area in Cambodia with the largest concentration of ancient Khmer sites, near the Siemreap River. The earliest buildings date from the 7th century A.D., but the great period of building began in the 9th century with the complex of Phnom Bakheng, a sacred "mountain-building" surrounded by walls almost two miles long. Best known of the Siemreap sites is Angkor Wat, built in the 12th century. The site is dominated by monumental Khmer hydraulic works, which include the east and west barays (reservoirs), the west baray measuring more than five square miles. There are thousands of smaller tanks and channels—all linked to the Siemreap River for irrigation purposes.

SIGIRIYA, the great rock, or Lion Mountain, which rises in the center of Ceylon 600 feet above the surrounding plains. During the reign of Kasyapa I (511–529), a great palace and fortress complex was built on the rock; only the foundations and a façade in the shape of a seated lion remain. The sides of the rock were covered with paintings of divinities, and although most of them have been destroyed by exposure, some paintings in a protected part of the rock have survived. The best preserved of Singhalese murals, they depict 21 apsaras in cloud banks. Although the faces have Singhalese features, the figures are painted in an Andhran-Indian style.

SILBURY HILL, in Wiltshire, England, is the largest prehistoric artificial mound in northern Europe, some 130 feet high and covering more than five acres. It is not far from several other prehistoric sites, including Avebury and West Kennet Long-Barrow. The exact purpose of Silbury Hill is still unknown, but it may be an immense grave-barrow. If it belongs to the period of the Megalithic Builders, it should be dated at some point after 2000 B.C. It is evident that the builders must have been able to call on a large and organized labor force from over a wide area.

SILLA, one of the three kingdoms of Korea, traditionally founded in 57 B.C. and overtaken by the Koryo kingdom in 935. Up until the 5th century, Silla culture was characterized by the barbaric grandeur of large burial mounds, containing the distinctively Korean gold antler-crowns with hanging decorations and curved jewels, like the Japanese *magatawa*. Chinese influences appear in the 5th century, and in 668 the Silla unified Korea, marking the beginning of the Great Silla period. The graceful, flowing art style of this period is represented by large bronze bells, often 11 feet tall; the cave temple of Sukkulam, containing a massive Buddha and reliefs; and the large stone pagoda of the Pulguk-sa monastery.

SIN, the moon god of Babylonia and Assyria. In art, he is represented in human form with a flowing beard and an inverted crescent above his head. Sin was the controller of the seasons, lord of wisdom, dispeller of darkness and evil, and giver of dreams and oracles. His father was Enlil, and his daughter was Ishtar. In later times Sin's identity was merged with that of Marduk. The festival of Sin, the Sabattu, was celebrated at the time of the new moon, when all human activities ceased. Hence, it is thought to be the source of the Hebrew Sabbath. Many temples were erected to the god Sin.

SINAI, the arid peninsula which links Asia and Africa, in Egypt, Israel, and Saudi Arabia; it is also the name of the sacred mountain where the Ten Commandments traditionally were revealed to Moses (Exodus 19 and 20). The exact location of Mount Sinai cannot be ascertained. In 1904–05 an expedition led by archaeologist Flinders Petrie found carved inscriptions at Sarabit al Khadim, which is the region generally thought to be at or near Mount Sinai. Although the Petrie inscriptions ultimately proved to

Siva: Head. Terra cotta. Khmer, 967 A.D. From Cambodia.

have no Biblical connection, they did turn out to be among the earliest known forms of alphabet script, dating from about the 16th century B.C. The mountains of the Sinai peninsula served ancient Egypt as a source of copper, turquoise, and malachite.

SINGHALESE. The majority people of Ceylon, they originally were Aryan-speaking people of northern India who settled the island in the 5th century B.C. About 200 B.C. Buddhism was introduced and the capital established at Anuradhapura—the site of almost 1,000 years of Singhalese history and monuments, including particularly large dagobas, or stupas, 370 feet in diameter and 400 feet high. Singhalese culture flowered from 150 B.C. to the 4th century A.D., strongly influenced by Indian styles. Southern Indian Tamils repeatedly invaded the Singhalese, and in the 11th century the Indian Cholas conquered the island. Although Singhalese building and artistic activity revived during the 12th century, another Indian invasion in 1213 forced the Singhalese south and ended this renaissance.

SITULA, in Etruscan archaeology, a deep circular, bucket-shaped vessel with a swinging handle. Apparently for some ritual use (as an urn for ashes), Etruscan situlae often have delicate relief decoration in bands around the outside. Este in northern Italy was a center of situla-making. There is a fine, late 6th-century B.C. situla in Providence, Rhode Island.

SIVA, one of the principal Hindu gods, is the Destroyer who recreates from his own destruction. A combination of the Vedic mountain god Rudra and a fertility deity, Siva is represented in many forms, including Natarja, Lord of Dance; an ascetic; and the great yogi. His symbol is the lingam, and he is often shown with a third eye and four arms.

SIX DYNASTIES PERIOD, a dark interregnum (221–589 A.D.) in Chinese history, following the collapse of the Han Dynasty. There was the Wei Dynasty in the north, the Chinese royal family in the south, and several smaller kingdoms elsewhere. Indian Buddhism was introduced into China during this period. Some of the best examples of Six Dynasties sculpture and painting are at the cave temples of Lungmen, Tunhuang, and Yunkang, showing central Asian and Indian influences. Also, fine pottery tomb sculpture was produced. In the south, the foundations of Southern-style landscape painting were laid by the artist Ku K'ai-chih (344–405).

SIYALK, one of the most ancient settlements in Iran; its earliest remains, which include fine gray-black pottery, date from the 6th millennium B.C. In the later half of the 2nd millennium B.C. the site, near modern Kashan, was abandoned and then reoccupied by people who are believed to have been the first of the Persian tribes to penetrate the Iranian plateau. These Persians produced unique funerary vessels which are a familiar feature in

exhibitions of ancient Near Eastern art. They are striking, painted jugs with a long spout, which imitates in shape and decoration the neck and beak of a bird. The body of the vessel was usually painted with distinctive, although somewhat awkward, animal designs. The Siyalk people also made small female figurines of copper. Siyalk art anticipates the feeling for decorative effect and concern for animal forms characteristic of later Persian art.

SKARA BRAE, a remarkably well-preserved neolithic village on the main island of the Orkneys, off the north coast of Scotland. The inhabitants are thought to have fled when the village was suddenly buried by a sandstorm. Another sandstorm in 1850 uncovered this village of well-furnished stone huts, with central hearths, stone bed spaces, shelves, and containers for food. Pottery similar to that found in the south of England establishes a date as early as 2000 B.C. for the site, whose inhabitants had hunter ancestors but themselves had turned to cattle farming.

Slavic peoples: Animal-style plaque. (Hermitage, Leningrad)

SKYPHOS, a Greek drinking cup shaped like a modern one but with two horizontal handles attached to its rim. On early (8th century B.C.) examples the handles were often affixed to the swelling base.

SLAVIC PEOPLES, a group of Indo-European tribes who, like their distant relatives the Celts and the Germans, had an ancestry related to the Battle-Axe culture of the 3rd millennium B.C. in south Russia. By the 2nd millennium B.C. the Slavs, identifiable as such, had occupied vast tracts of eastern and central Europe neighboring on Celtic and Germanic territories. Forest dwellers, farmers, and warriors, the early Slavs—whose descendants include the present Russians, Poles, Czechs, Slovaks, Slovenes, Croats, Serbs, Bulgarians, Ukrainians, and others—had established a more or less homogeneous lifestyle. Their pantheon included Svantevit, the god of harvest and war; Perun, the thunder god; and Svarog, the sun god. Not surprisingly Slavic deities were similar to those of other Indo-Europeans, as were their belief in a life after death, their practice of sun worship, and their holding of oak groves as sacred. Although authorities disagree as to the ultimate source of Slavic culture, most point to Lusatian remains as intrinsically Slavic in origin. Formed by about 1200 B.C., Lusatian culture, with its chief site at Biskupin in Poland, covered eastern Germany, northern Czechoslovakia, and Poland. Farther to the east, in Russia and the Ukraine, vigorous Slavic tribes, after centuries of farming and pastoralism, were building villages and towns, which frequently fell prey to the fierce horsemen of the Eurasian steppes, the Scythians, Sarmatians, Cimmerians, and finally the Huns. The Slavic peoples of Russia not only survived these waves of nomadic onslaught but, in the end, prevailed. In the early 1st millennium A.D. a major Slavic state, founded by the Rus, developed in and around Kiev. Other Slavic kingdoms were established in Bohemia, Bulgaria, Moravia, Croatia, and Poland. The Byzantine Church in Constantinople, sensing new fields of spiritual conquest, ordered the conversion of Slavic Europe, an event that lasted from the 9th to the 11th centuries A.D. and met with great success. After untold centuries of paganism the Slavs had become Christians.

Slavic Art and Antiquities. Unfortunately, due to the missionary zeal of the Byzantines, who destroyed much of pre-Christian Slavic art as the work of the devil, little remains of original Slavic art. From the artworks that do remain and from ancient written annals, it is clear that the Slavs had a rich art tradition. They built timbered temples, dedicated to their gods and decorated with painted walls, cloth hangings, and finely carved sculpture. The object of veneration was a huge cult statue, generally anthropomorphic but multiheaded in design. Sculpture was most often in wood, although stone was sometimes used. Totemlike poles, sacred shields and spears, as well as drinking horns, were also carved by the Slavs. Some sites in Rumania and Yugoslavia have yielded elaborate terra-cotta female figurines that are thought to be Slavic, while in Russia hoards of fine metalwork, clearly showing Eurasian art styles, have been unearthed. Several museums in eastern Europe have collections of ancient Slavic art, among which is the Slavic Antiquities Museum in Split, Yugoslavia.

SMITHFIELD CULTURE, a late stone-age culture discovered in southern Africa. It is known archaeologically through surviving stone tools and rock paintings. The Smithfield people, who were probably ancestors of the modern Bushmen, lived primarily by hunting. Named for the town in South Africa where remnants of the culture were first found, Smithfield in its later phases merged into another culture that has been called Wilton.

SMYRNA, ancient city on Asia Minor's western coast, at the site of modern Izmir, Turkey. It was controlled by Ionian Greeks from about the 9th century B.C., destroyed by Lydians in the 6th century B.C., and reconstructed some 200 years later to flourish during Hellenistic and Roman times. Most important remains are inaccessible to archaeologists because of standing modern structures. However, ruins of a 7th-century B.C. Greek temple have been partly explored, and remains of a Roman basilica, decorated with marble reliefs, are reasonably intact.

SOGDIANA, historic region north of Afghanistan between the Syr Darya and Amu Darya rivers in modern Russia, including the ancient city of Samarkand. Sogdiana had clearly defined borders before the 1st millennium B.C., although the history of the area—a succession of dominance by Persians, Bactrian Greeks, Huns, and Kushans—is known only from the 6th century B.C. Recent excavations in the area have revealed art forms influenced by Greek, Indian Buddhist, and Arab styles. Temple wall paintings generally depict people frontally in hunting, banqueting, or worshipping scenes. Sculpture of stucco and wood is in the round and highly developed. Plant and animal motifs, particularly fantastic beasts, predominated in architectural sculpture.

SOLOMON'S TEMPLE, the revered temple of the Israelites, built in Jerusalem by King Solomon in the 10th century B.C. Although no ruins remain, the temple is described in the Bible as being a splendid stone edifice, with Phoenician influence playing some part in its design. It was about 100 feet long and its central gate was flanked by bronze pillars. Behind the central hall was the Holy of Holies, a dark chamber holding the Ark of the Covenant. Destroyed by the Babylonians under Nebuchadnezzar II in the 6th century B.C., a second temple was built on approximately the same site around 520 B.C., following the return of the Israelites from their Babylonian Exile. Although less impressive than its predecessor, the second temple contained—according to the Bible—many fine menorahs and vessels, some of which had been gifts from the King of Persia. The temple was plundered and desecrated in the 2nd century B.C., and around 20 B.C. King Herod had it razed and replaced by a complex building of splendor, with several spacious halls—for a synagogue, for sacrificing animals, and for bazaars—and magnificent walled courtyards. The Herod Temple, never fully completed, was largely demolished during the Roman destruction of Jerusalem in 70 A.D. The famous "Wailing Wall" is from this temple. It is thought that the Islamic Dome of the Rock rests on the original foundations of Solomon's Temple.

SOLUTREAN, a culture named after Solutre in the Loire Valley of France and beginning about 18,000 B.C. Its distinguishing mark was great skill in the working of flint tools. One delicately chipped oval flint, with a cutting edge all round, is 14 inches long and only about a quarter of an inch thick at the center. Solutrean culture seems to have appeared and disappeared suddenly between the Aurignacian and the Magdalenian periods and to have been scattered over Spain, France, and southern England.

SOMME-BIONNE, an important Celtic burial ground, located in northern France and dating from the La Tene period of Celtic migration, or from the second half of the 1st millennium B.C. The site consists of five royal graves and perhaps 80 graves of ordinary tribesmen, cut into a chalk deposit. Of the royal graves, only one was intact at the time of excavation. It held remains of a chieftain, buried with his two-wheel chariot in a rectangular pit approximately two yards long and slightly more than three yards wide. Items buried with him included a sword and bronze scabbard, as well as amber and glass beads and bronze and brass jewelry, all of probable Celtic origin. Non-Celtic art objects included Etruscan gold jewelry and bronze wine vessels and an inscribed bronze cup of Greek origin, dating from the early 5th century B.C. These objects are now in the British Museum.

SONGE, an African people living in central Zaire. Several centuries ago the Songe migrated westward to their present home, where they settled among the Lubas. Similarities between the arts of these two peoples attest to their close cultural relationship. Nevertheless, Songe carved figures have a forceful, robust quality missing in Luba works. Notable among Songe art are striking wood fetishes, which often have a horn emerging from the top of the head, with strips of metal overlaying the face, and sometimes raffia or metal objects hanging from the body.

SONGHAI, a great West African empire which reached its zenith during the 16th century A.D. Filling the political vacuum left by the disintegrating Mali Empire, Songhai expanded to include the entire region from Senegal to Chad. This was accomplished largely through the expert military leadership of two rulers—Sunni Ali and Askia Mohammed. Under their aegis Gao became the capital city, and fabled Timbuktu flourished as a center of learning. Repeated invasions from the north during the 17th century brought the collapse of the empire, but the tomb of Askia Mohammed at Gao still remains as. a major architectural monument in Africa south of the Sahara.

SOUTHERN DEATH CULT, an unusual religious movement, which by 1400 A.D. covered much of the southeastern United States. Derived from Caddoan culture of earlier times, the Southern Death Cult showed profound influences from Mexico. Major centers of the cult were at Moundville, Alabama; Etowah, Georgia; and Spiro, Oklahoma, although Arkansas, the cradle of the Caddoans, may have been its heartland. Cult objects unearthed in this region include modelled clay skulls, elaborate flint blades, stone palettes, copper plates richly engraved with curvilinear designs, and incised conch shells. Constantly recurring death motifs were skulls, arm bones, fleshless hands, crosses, winged men, and eyes, especially the closed eyes of the dead. The most outstanding cult pieces, however, are in stone sculpture. Some of these depict kneeling men, approximately 18 inches high, with faces of almost portraitlike quality. Related to the stone figures are carved ceremonial pipes, some weighing as much as 10 pounds, which portray men engaged in a variety of activities, including human sacrifice.

SPARTA, a city of ancient Greece, located in a narrow, fertile valley of Laconia, in the southern Peloponnesus. Probably founded by the warlike Dorians, Sparta was to become the strongest city-state in Greece and the archrival to Athens. From the 8th through the 7th centuries B.C. Sparta, before it became completely devoted to the martial arts, enjoyed a period of wealth and culture. The poets Alcmaeon and Tyrtaeus lived and worked here, and fine Laconian ware was created. A black-figure pottery, the ware was decorated with brightly painted birds, fish, and animals set against an elegant creamy background. Architectural remains of the period, although not spectacular, include a very early stone temple to Artemis; in her sanctuary many ivory statuettes and reliefs dating from the 8th and 7th centuries B.C. have been unearthed. With the arrival of military dictatorship in about 600 B.C. the Spartan artistic impulse was stifled.

SPEAR-THROWER. See ATLATL.

SPECTROGRAPHIC ANALYSIS, a method for quantitative analysis of metals, pottery, glass, and minerals to provide information on the sources of the component materials. The method is quite accurate and can be used on samples as small as ten milligrams. Spectrographic analysis is based on the principle that characteristic spec-

Sphinxes: The Great Sphinx, the Great Pyramid (right), and Chephron's Pyramid (left). Giza.

trum patterns are produced by the light emitted from a vaporizing element. In practice, a sample is vaporized by an electrical discharge, and the light is refracted onto a photographic plate or viewing screen. The component elements of the sample are then identified by comparing the spectral patterns with control patterns. It is a method often used to identify an antiquity.

SPHINXES, monstrous creatures, usually with a man's head on the body of a lion, probably originating in ancient Egypt and found in Greece and throughout the Near East. Sphinxes can also have the head of a ram or that of a woman. Egyptian sphinxes, with the heads of deceased pharaohs, were used to guard tombs and temples and often lined avenues to temples, as at Thebes. Most famous of Egyptian sphinxes is the Great Sphinx at Giza, built during the 4th Dynasty (2680–2565 B.C.) and having the head of Chephren; it is 240 feet long and 66 feet high. Greek sphinxes, often bearing wings, are symbols of death and are found on ancient gravestones. Other examples were on the statue of Athena at the Parthenon and on the throne of Zeus at Olympia. Sphinxes also decorated jewelry and were carved in ivory and bone.

SRADDHA. See ANCESTOR WORSHIP.

SRIVIJAYA, an Indianized kingdom, centered around Palembang on Sumatra, which arose in the 7th century A.D. At its height, the kingdom dominated areas northwest to the Straits of Malacca, southeast to Java, and as far as Ligor on the Malay Peninsula. By the 9th century Srivijaya was assimilated by the Shailendra Dynasty of central Java. Most characteristic of Srivijayan art are the small bronze Buddhas produced in the style of the Indian Pala Dynasty. Finely cast, these figures contrast the precise details of the Buddha's hair and jewelry with the apparent softness of his flesh. They were exported throughout the Indonesian and Indian areas.

STABIAE, modern Castellammare di Stabia, in Campania, Italy, a small Roman spa long noted for its mineral waters. Just south of Pompeii, Stabiae was buried in the same eruption of Vesuvius in 79 A.D. Excavations here began in the 18th century, were discontinued, and then recommenced in 1949. Although smaller and less rich in art than Pompeii, Stabiae has nonetheless provided many fine examples of Roman wall paintings of the 1st century A.D. From Stabiae, and now in the Naples Museum, are the noteworthy "Harbor View" painting, perhaps depicting the Bay of Naples as it appeared then; the well-known "Primavera," so reminiscent of Botticelli's work on the same theme; and the impressionistic "Flora" and "Portrait of a Poet."

STANWICK BRONZES. A hoard of Celtic bronze work, mainly chariot gear of the 1st century A.D., was found near the earthworks of Stanwick, the largest earthwork fortification in Britain. The earliest part of Stanwick is a hill fort of moderate size, 17 acres, dating from the early 1st century. But in about 50 A.D. and again in 72 A.D. very large areas were also enclosed with a 16-foot ditch and a drystone-faced rampart. Stanwick, north of Richmond in Yorkshire, England, was a stronghold of the Brigantes, a British tribe who revolted against Rome in 70 A.D.

STARCEVO, a site in western Rumania where painted pottery of a distinctive type was discovered. Starcevo was occupied in about 4500 B.C. by neolithic farmers, but the pottery they made was quite highly developed. It is marked by a special form, that of bowls supported on pedestals, and by painted decoration in black, red, brown, and white, sometimes in angles and hatchings resembling basketry, sometimes in curving spirals. Starcevo, situated near the site of Vinca in Yugoslavia, was a major force in the development of early Balkan culture.

STEATITE, a soft red, gray, or green stone commonly called soapstone and used for seals, vessels, molds, and statuettes. Steatite artifacts are found widely in the ancient world.

STEATOPYGOUS, a style of female figurine with well-pronounced, large buttocks. It can be seen in prehistoric Venus figures as well as in African carvings.

STELE, or stela, any upright monolith bearing carved inscriptions or sculptural decorations and occurring in several different shapes. Common stelae are stone pillars or plaquelike stone slabs. They are found in many parts of the ancient world, especially in the eastern Mediterranean region, Mesopotamia, and in Pre-Columbian America.

STELE C. See TRES ZAPOTES.

STELE OF NARAMSIN, a Mesopotamian stone stele, measuring almost seven feet in height, now in the Louvre. Dating from the last half of the 3rd millennium B.C., it commemorates the victory of Naramsin, king of Akkad, over his enemies. Naramsin is depicted as wearing the horned crown of divinity; thus this monument may be the earliest known example of the apotheosis of a conqueror. The stele was unearthed at Susa.

STEPPE CULTURES OF EURASIA, a way of life shared by diverse peoples who, from remote antiquity, occupied the vast grassland plain extending from eastern Europe to central Siberia. As early as 4000 B.C. the steppes gave rise to cultures economically dependent on animal herding and, in many cases, agriculture. The most important among these, including the Tripolye and Usatovo cultures, had developed villages. After 2000 B.C. the Andronovo and Karasuk cultures brought Eurasia into the bronze age. The 2nd millennium B.C. saw the rise of tribes of nomadic steppe horsemen. The most powerful of these peoples—the Cimmerians, Scythians, Sarmatians, and, by the dawn of the Christian era, the Huns—tended to dominate the village cultures and contrived to harass the great bordering civilizations from the Mediterranean to China. During the course of their migrations the Asian nomads carried cultural influences across the length and breadth of Eurasia, bridging the gap between the great civilizations of East and West. Most of the steppe cultures shared the custom of kurgan—or barrow grave—burial; and these grave sites provide most of the important art

288

and artifacts relating to and identifying the various steppe cultures. The art of the Eurasian steppes is best reflected in animal-style metalwork.

STIRRUP-SPOUT, a characteristic vessel shape of ancient Peruvian ceramics. Vessels of this type have a spherical body, topped by a hollow horseshoe-shaped handle, with a spout projecting from the handle's center. Its body was often painted or elaborated into a sculptural form. A wealth of ethnographic information about life in ancient Peru has been gathered from the depictions on stirrup-spout vessels.

STOA. See **AGORA.**

STONE AGE, in archaeology, a term used to denote the earliest technological stage in human cultural development. Since the dawn of the stone age varies from region to region, absolute dating is not to be implied; for example, Pre-Columbian America was in the stone age until the Spanish Conquest, while the peoples of New Guinea are today in the stone age. Metal tools or weapons were unknown in the stone age, although wood and other

perishables were certainly used. Modern archaeologists classify the divisions of the period according to the growing sophistication of tools and weapons manufactured. Thus, there is the paleolithic, or old stone age; the mesolithic, or middle stone age; and the neolithic, or new stone age. The stone age appears to modern man as of incredibly long duration, in the range of half a million years. The dates given here are to some degree conjectural and may have to be altered considerably in view of excavations in Kenya and Tanzania and in the light of revisions now being applied to radiocarbon dating from new methods based on dendrochronology. The paleolithic age seems to have begun in Europe, at any rate, around 500,000 B.C. The tools used then and for countless centuries thereafter altered little. They were hand-axes, rocks suitable for hefting in the hand, with a round back to fit the palm and a sharper edge for chopping. By the mid-paleolithic, about 100,000 B.C., tools were being made from splinters of stone. Neanderthal man, first appearing in this period, began using objects of bone. By 35,000 B.C., or the upper paleolithic, the appearance of *Homo sapiens* in Europe (Cro-Magnon man) led to a quickening of culture, to flint and bone blades and the development of sophisticated cave art. The mesolithic, or middle stone age, began about 8000 B.C. and is marked by the making of microlithic, finely formed, flint tools. It also saw the beginnings of transport and the domestication of the dog. Hunting and fishing were still almost the only food-producing activities. With the coming of the neolithic, or new stone age, marked by polished stone tools, the momentous agricultural revolution began, in which man grew crops, reared livestock, made pottery, wove fabric, and was soon building cities and founding empires. The neolithic took place in the Near East about 7000 B.C. and in Europe about 5000 B.C. The stone age was succeeded by the bronze age and then by the iron age, a sequence of technology first suggested by the Danish pioneer archaeologist Christian J. Thomsen in 1836.

STONEHENGE, in Wiltshire, England, the most impressive bronze-age ceremonial center in Europe and probably the world's first solar observatory. Circles of immense, upright stones, some with giant lintels upon them, forming trilithons, stand in the middle of Salisbury Plain. The largest uprights are 22 feet high and bear a lintel 16 feet long and four feet thick. Two groups of stones are set in horseshoe form, and in the center of these is an altar stone. Standing at the altar stone and looking towards the entrance, one can see the sun rise over the so-called Hele Stone at dawn on midsummer day. The great open-air sanctuary is thus thought to reflect a widespread bronze-age sun worship, probably associated with the Megalithic Builders. The building of Stonehenge passed through several stages between 2000 and about 1400 B.C., when it probably reached its present form. At first there was only a circular ditch and bank

Stonehenge: Aerial view. Salisbury Plain, England.

with a ring of small pits for cremation burials. Later a remarkable people known as the Beaker folk brought bluestones of great size from the Prescelly Hills in Wales, 150 miles away, and erected them. Large blocks of sandstone, or sarsens, from Wiltshire, 25 miles away, were added in the final form of the sanctuary. The latest research on Stonehenge may require the dates above to be moved back several centuries.

STUPA, a hemispherical Buddhist monument, containing sacred relics and found widely in the Buddhist world. In Ceylon it is called a dagoba. Probably derived from pre-Buddhist burial mounds, the stupa form is a dome, crowned by an umbrellalike superstructure; it is surrounded by a gateway and fence, often carved ornately, and a ceremonial path. Stupas, for Buddhists, symbolize the attainment of nirvana. The Indian Emperor Asoka was the first to encourage the building of stupas, and those at Sanchi are probably the earliest.

SUI DYNASTY, 589 to 618 A.D., the rulers who reunited China after the Six Dynasties period, thus inaugurating the Second Empire, which flowered during the succeeding Tang era. The Sui are more noteworthy for their political and military prowess than their artistic output. However, some interesting work was produced. Buddhist wall paintings in the Tunhuang caves in Kansu belong to both the Sui and the Tang eras. Sui sculpture at this site shows a sense of volume and roundness of contour—qualities that were later carried to maturity and perfection by Tang Dynasty artists.

SULLA PERIOD, in Roman history, named for the general and military dictator Lucius Cornelius Sulla (138–78 B.C.). It was a period of Roman colonial expansion and extensive building, much of it initiated by Sulla, both in Rome and in newly Romanized cities. Coinciding with Roman conquest and territorial acquisition, large amounts of Greek sculpture and painting were imported to Rome, as were fine Greek silver and household furnishings, all of which were highly prized by Romans. Thus the Romans developed a taste for Greek art, an influence which later—during the reign of Augustus—became the dominant force in the flowering of Rome's golden age.

SUMERIAN CIVILIZATION, which arose in the fertile Euphrates River valley of lower Mesopotamia (now southern Iraq), was almost certainly the first civilization in world history, a civilization recognizable as such by about 3500 B.C. The influence of Sumeria on the early cultures of Egypt, to the west, and on those of Iran and the Indus Valley, to the east, is yet to be fully determined. Probably emerging from Ubaid culture of the 6th millennium B.C., Sumerian civilization was originally begun by a non-Semitic people from the Persian highlands. By the mid-4th millennium B.C. Sumeria consisted of a series of independent city-states, notably Ur, Uruk, Kish, Eridu, Lagash, and Adab, loosely confederated as a theocracy and bound together by a common language, culture, and religion. Each city was dedicated to a god of the Sumerian pantheon. This multitude of deities (including Utu, sun god; Sin, moon god; Ninhursay, earth mother; Iuanna, love goddess; etc.) was later inherited, with variations, by succeeding Mesopotamian civilizations—the Babylonians and Assyrians. Sumer's priesthood formed around these deities, providing the organization that became the cities' central political power; the bureaucratic needs of the ruling priesthood no doubt prompted the epochal invention of the first written language—cuneiform—before the end of the 4th millennium B.C. By about 3000 B.C. monarchic rule was firmly established in the major Sumerian cities, each of which vied with the other for dominance of Mesopotamia. First to approach suzerainty was Kish (about 55 miles south of modern Baghdad), under a king named Etana, in the early 3rd millennium. Subsequently, at Uruk, King Meskiaggasher established a powerful dynasty, his most famous successor being the near legendary Gilgamesh, who later became hero and namesake of the most important epic to emerge from Mesopotamian literature. Several centuries of violent three-way struggle for Sumerian supremacy, by Kish, Ur, and Uruk, ended around 2500 B.C., when King Lugalannemundu of the city of Adab temporarily united all of Sumer. Undoubtedly Sumer's greatest ruler was Sargon (about 2350 B.C.), the Semitic king of northern Sumer (called Akkad), who united the entire north through military might, then built a new capital which he called Agade, the remains of which have not yet been identified. His rule marks the beginning of Semitic absorption of Sumer. Sargon's empire disintegrated after his death, and around 2200 B.C. Sumerian cities were attacked by the barbaric Gutians, a tribe from the northeast. This was the first in a succession of military defeats that ultimately wrecked Sumerian civilization. Around 2000 B.C. Ur was destroyed by another band of outsiders, the Elamites of Iran, and soon after 1900 B.C. Amorites from the Syrian desert conquered Sumeria and built on its ruins the culture that ultimately became Babylonian civilization.

Sumerian Art and Antiquities herald the starting point in an almost continuous sequence of creativity that encompasses most of Mesopotamian art. Great advances in architecture and sculpture, in life-size statues and small figurines, were made by the Sumerians. Religious and political themes dominate Sumerian art, with stone statues, stele, and bas-reliefs mainly portraying deities, priests, kings, and nobles. Most famous of these is a 22-inch-high alabaster portrait statue of the son of Gudea, ruler of Lagash, which dates from about 2100 B.C. The statue's head is in New York's Metropolitan Museum of Art, while its torso is in the Louvre. Seal designs differ somewhat, with animals and monsters constituting the most frequent subjects. Graves of important personages, amid the ruins of Sumerian cities, have yielded fine examples of art from the dynastic era—wooden plaques illustrated in pigments and decorated with shell and lapis lazuli, apparently intended for use as inlays on furniture and soundboards of stringed instruments. Among the finest of these is the so-called Ur Royal Standard (around 2800 B.C.), which has double panels depicting a marching

Susa: "Susa vase." Painted terra cotta. 4th millennium B.C. (British Museum, London)

army and a lavish regal court scene. It is now in the British Museum. Perhaps Sumer's most famous bronze is a head measuring 13¾ inches and depicting an Akkadian ruler—possibly Sargon—now housed in Iraq's Baghdad Museum. Carved stone vases and fine vessels of copper, lead, and silver have also been unearthed in ancient Sumeria.

SUMI-E, a Japanese term for a style of Chinese painting in ink, introduced to Japan from the northern Sung in the late 12th century A.D. Characterized by free, spontaneous brush strokes of varying widths, the style was strongly influenced by Zen Buddhism in its simplicity. Often *sumi-e* paintings were landscapes accompanied by poems. The first important *sumi-e* Japanese painters were Shubun and Sesshu. Their work eclipsed the prevailing, more decorative, *yamato-e*, a purely Japanese style. *Sumi-e* reached its height during the Ashikaga period with the work of Kei Shoki. The *sumi-e* style was successfully combined with elements of *yamato-e* by the famous Kano painters.

SUNG DYNASTY, 960 to 1279 A.D., the beginning of China's modern history and a time of brilliant cultural achievement. Because the Chinese were cut off to the north and west by barbarian tribes and invaders, Sung culture, developed in isolation, is uniquely Chinese. Art was produced not only for religious purposes but also for its own sake. Sung porcelain—considered by many the finest of all—included pale-green celadons and white-figured pieces. Painting supported by the Court Academy was characterized by delicate nature studies. Painting outside the Academy became impressionistic, with landscapes rendered monochromatically in bold brush strokes; it was strongly influenced by Zen and Taoist throught and ultimately became the style of Japanese painters. Sung sculpture was elaborate and fleshy. The multistoried pagoda appeared during the Sung Dynasty.

SURYA, Hindu sun god who drove his flaming chariot across the sky to dispel the darkness. He is a combination of several Vedic gods, and his iconography is similar to that of Vishnu, with the addition of a sun disk. Surya was especially popular in the Gupta and medieval Indian periods and many temples were dedicated to him, including the 13th-century A.D. "Black Pagoda" of Konarak. Surya is also known as Savitr the Nourisher.

SUSA, a major archaeological site of the Near East, located in southwest Iran, and once the splendid capital of Elam. Susa reached its zenith in the 12th century B.C., and its remains are among the most artistic of the ancient Near East. Pottery from its earliest occupation level, dat-

Sumerian art: Ur Royal Standard, detail. Painted and inlaid wood. Ca. 2800 B.C. From the "royal cemetery" of Ur (British Museum, London)

ing to 5000 B.C., is notable for its balanced composition of stylized animal and geometric designs. In the 2nd millennium B.C. Susa became the capital of the Kingdom of Elam. Finds from Elamite times include cylinder seals, engraved gems, bas-reliefs, and great architecture, especially the world's best-preserved ziggurat. The Elamites of Susa also created an abundance of sculpture in the round, ranging from small votive figures of silver and electrum to the great bronze statue of Queen Napirasu; the largest metal statue found in the Near East, it weighs 3,860 pounds and now stands in the Louvre. In the 6th century B.C. the city came under the control of the Achaemenid Persians, and Darius I built his palace here. The palace is remarkable for its wall friezes of enameled bricks showing animals and royal bodyguards in a style that was probably inspired by the Ishtar Gate of Babylon. Also unearthed at Susa, and undoubtedly brought there as spoils of war, were the Babylonian Code of Hammurabi, the Akkadian Stele of Naramsin, and the Obelisk of Manishtusu. In later times the city came under Greek, Parthian, and Sassanian control. Many art treasures of Susa are now in the Louvre.

SUTTON HOO, on England's Suffolk coast, site of an Anglo-Saxon ship burial of about 650 A.D. While the royal ship had long since disintegrated, its treasure—one of the greatest ever found in Britain and certainly the richest collection of Anglo-Saxon antiquities unearthed anywhere—remained almost intact. The oar-driven ship, about 80 feet long, was apparently the grave of a wealthy Saxon chief. Its hoard, now in the British Museum, includes a gold purse inlaid with garnets, enamel, and blue and white glass and holding 40 Merovingian coins and two small ingots, all of gold; silver bowls and plates; mounted silver drinking horns; bronze cauldrons; silver and gold ship fittings; a battle shield with bronze and gilt decorations; and a sword with hilt of gold and jewels.

However, the two most impressive antiquities are a helmet of iron with bronze and silver fittings, nose piece, mustache, and eyebrows edged in garnets, and a great silver dish of Byzantine origin, stamped with the name of Emperor Anastasius (491–518 A.D.). The treasure of Sutton Hoo exemplifies the eclectic nature and taste of Anglo-Saxon art.

SWASTIKA, a hooked cross symbol, having obscure religious significance; perhaps intended to represent the wheel of the sun. It occurs as decoration on very early Greek weapons and as a secondary design, or within border devices, on later Greek vases, etc. It may share a common origin with an identical motif of the ancient Celts—called a *fylfot*—appearing on funereal urns and metalwork and surviving to European medieval times on church textile embroidery. A Hindu decorative motif—called an *arani*—is also of identical design and equally ancient and obscure in origin, although scholars believe it was first introduced during the Aryan invasions of the 2nd millennium B.C.

SYBARIS, ancient Greek colonial city in southern Italy. The earliest city of Greek Italy, it was founded around 720 B.C. as a port for commerce between Italy and Greece. In 510 B.C. it was totally destroyed by enemies from the rival city of Croton. The site of Sybaris has been identified but is buried beneath several feet of soil and still awaits full excavation.

SYRACUSE, town on Sicily's southeast coast, founded by Greek colonists from Cornith around 734 B.C. and probably the most important Greek city west of the Adriatic until the late 3rd century B.C., when it entered the Roman sphere. Settlement, having originated on the small offshore island of Ortygia, was predominantly on the Sicilian mainland by the 5th century B.C. A temple to Apollo (7th or 6th century B.C.) is probably the oldest major Doric-style ruin in Sicily. Other important ruins include a Doric temple to Athena on Ortygia (5th century B.C.) and a theater on the mainland, also 5th century B.C. but later rebuilt by the Romans.

SYRIA, an ancient region of the Near East, bounded on the west by the Mediterranean, on the east and south by desert, and on the north by the Taurus Mountains of southern Anatolia. Its position between Egypt and Mesopotamia made it an important crossroads for trade, and its oases often evolved into major commercial cities—notably, Palmyra, Damascus, and Antioch. The earliest known settlers in Syria were the Semitic Amorites in the mid-3rd millennium B.C. Parts of ancient Syria were successively occupied by Phoenicians and Aramaeans; conquerors of various Syrian territories were notably the Egyptians, Hittites, Assyrians, and Persians. Syria had no political identity until after its conquest by Alexander the Great in 333 B.C.; Antioch became the capital city of his Seleucid heirs. From 64 B.C. Syria was a Roman province. Syrian sites yielding antiquities from various civilizations include Antioch, Palmyra, Mari, and Ugarit. Probably the most outstanding of numerous Roman ruins of the region are those at Baalbek, in modern Lebanon.

Sutton Hoo: Shoulder brooch. Gold with cloisonne enamel. Anglo-Saxon, 7th century A.D. (British Museum, London)

T

TA. See **PAGODA**.

TABU, a Polynesian word meaning forbidden or restricted. As an anthropological term *tabu,* or *taboo,* is applied throughout the primitive and prehistoric world to certain acts or objects which could offend the supernatural powers. The killing of a sacred animal, for instance, would be a tabu. The term *tabu* is profoundly related to the idea of totemism and the concept of *mana*.

TAJ MAHAL, a magnificent Islamic edifice in Agra, India, built by the Moghul emperor Shah Jehan as a mausoleum for his favorite wife Mumtaz Mahal and for himself. Considered one of the most beautiful buildings in the world, it took 18 years (1630–48) to complete. The Taj Mahal is constructed of white marble and adorned with inlaid Arabic inscriptions and delicate naturalistic decoration. The main building (187 feet high) is octagonal in shape, with a large bulblike dome; it is surrounded by four 140-feet-high marble minarets. There is a walled garden, a reflecting pool, marble fountains, and dark cypresses. Though there are two sarcophagi in the mausoleum, the royal couple are actually buried in a vault beneath the floor.

TAMILS, a Dravidian people now living in the southeast of India and in Ceylon. Ancient Tamils were fierce fighters, and their three kingdoms—Cola, Kerala, and Pandya—were in almost constant war with each other. By the 2nd century B.C. the Tamils were a seagoing power and continually invaded Ceylon; they also reached the coast of southeastern Asia. By the 1st century A.D. they were trading with the Roman Empire via Egypt. The Tamils were known particularly for their remarkable religious literature and for their metalworking, which was of high quality and originality.

TAMMUZ, Sumerian and Babylonian fertility god prominent in fertility rituals as the husband of Ishtar. He is thought to represent the vegetation spirit who married the earth (Ishtar), producing both seed and harvest. On his death he became god of the underworld. He is represented either by manlike or goatlike images. Parallel to Ishtar and Tammuz are the Egyptian Isis and Osiris and the Greek Aphrodite and Adonis.

TANAGRA FIGURES, charming terra-cotta statuettes produced in the 4th and 3rd centuries B.C. at Tanagra, a small town near Thebes to the north of Athens. The hundreds of these graceful figurines that have survived vividly depict the everyday world of upper-class Greece. Most show women wearing elegant robes, quietly sitting or standing, holding children, dancing, or tossing a ball. Their delicacy and deceptive simplicity convey a serenity difficult to imitate. Though made from molds, different combinations of arms, heads, and attributes brought forth a variety of poses, and their soft but gay painted colors made each figure a fresh creation. The majority of these figures have been found in graves, but they were probably intended primarily as art objects for the home. Similar figurines have been found throughout the Greek world.

Taj Mahal, Agra.

Tang Dynasty: "Reliquary." Lacquered cloth on wood. Chinese, 7th century A.D. (National Museum, Tokyo)

TANG DYNASTY, a magnificent Chinese period that succeeded the Sui Dynasty and lasted from 618 to 907 A.D. At its height the Tang controlled Korea, Manchuria, Mongolia, Tibet, and Turkestan. Confucianism was re-established as the Chinese state religion. A cosmopolitan cultural force, in emulation of the great Han Dynasty, the Tang promoted art and enjoyed foreign influences. Sculpture, showing Indian Buddhist styles, was in the round; human figures were quite plastic, covered with thin draperies and jewels, and had an indolent air. Court portrait painters produced boldly outlined images, with some shading; and during the late Tang the art of true landscape on silk was developed. Tang pottery had a characteristic three-color, cascading glaze that left lower parts of the wares uncovered. At the turn of the 10th century pure porcelain was developed; Tang porcelain shapes and their naturalistic bird and flower motifs showed strong Persian influence. All aspects of Tang life and art were emphasized and reflected in remarkable Tang tomb pottery-figurines. Sculpted Tang horses are world-famous.

TANIS, an ancient Egyptian city, the Old Testament Zoan, situated at the mouth of the east branch of the Nile Delta. One of the chief trade cities from the time of the 19th Dynasty (1300 B.C.), it is the site of the great temple of Ramses II and of the tombs of 21st and 22nd Dynasty pharaohs (1090–745 B.C.). Fine gold, silver, and bronze metalwork have been unearthed here.

TANIT, supreme goddess of ancient Carthage, who appears in art after the 5th century B.C. She is a mother-goddess associated with the heavens, especially the moon, and the consort of the chief Carthaginian god, Baal Hammon. Archaeological evidence suggests that children were sacrificed in her worship. In art she is por-

trayed in figurines and on stele with her consort. Often she is represented only by her symbol, the sign of Tanit, a crescent topped by a disk from which it is divided by a horizontal arm.

TANJORE, city in southeast India and former capital of the Chola Dynasty (900–1150 A.D.). It is the site of the huge Rajajesvara temple dedicated to Siva and built in 1000 A.D. by Rajaraja the Great. The temple, which is 180 feet long, is dominated by a 190-foot-high, 13-story tower covered with decorations; the temple sculpture is massive and dynamic. Also at the site is the Bridesvara temple, with notable ancient south Indian wall paintings.

TANKA, a painted Tibetan religious banner showing Lamaist scenes, saints, heroes, and terrifying deities. Tankas decorated temples and homes and were carried on journeys to ensure divine protection. They were produced according to a strict iconography and under the supervision of monks. The tanka's surface almost bursts with recondite scenes, symbols, and colors; red is the chief pigment used. Because tanka painters remained anonymous under rigid monkish rule, tankas show little apparent originality and are difficult to date.

TANTRISM, a secret cult, centering around erotic and magical rites, that developed in northeast India about the 6th century A.D. Its sacred scriptures, or *tantras,* emphasized the worship of the female principle, or *sakti,* and the goddess Parvati was the chief devotional figure. Ritual ceremonies were held around a mandala and were followed by sexual union. The tantric forms of deities are usually represented with many heads and arms and in erotic positions. The popularity of the sect influenced the growth of Hinduism, Buddhism, and Lamaism.

TAOIST ART AND ANTIQUITIES cover the entire span of civilized China's history and were inspired by Taoism, a unique blend of mysticism, magic, and philosophy that crystallized into a body of thought during the era of its greatest teacher, Lao-tzu, who lived sometime between the 7th and 6th centuries B.C. Besides prescribing a way of life (*tao* means way, or road), Taoism has a rich body of legend, filled with mythical and semihistorical characters who constitute important subject matter for Taoist art. Dragons and other fantastic creatures were among the earliest images of Taoist art, but in the late Han era (roughly 2nd century A.D.) such Taoist figures as the Mother Queen of the West and the Father King of the East become more typical. Taoist sculpture dates from about the 3rd century A.D., but its most important examples are considerably later (e.g., eight of the Lungshan cave temples, completed 1234–39). Taoist printmaking dates from about the Sung Dynasty (1000 A.D.). Recurring Taoist motifs include *hsien,* mountains representing the ideal of man's unity with nature; and *po-ya,* two lute players, one teaching as the other listens.

TAO TIEH, a monster mask often used as a design motif on Chinese Shang and Chou bronzes. It consists of two stylized profiles of dragons in mirror image, which combine to form a single facelike design. The *tao tieh* added magical significance to the bronze and in some cases was repeated several times over the vessel's surface.

TAPA CLOTH, a cloth made from soaking and pounding the inner bark of trees, usually mulberry. Although often associated with Polynesia, this almost paperlike cloth is manufactured widely throughout the Pacific islands, southern Asia, and Africa. It was sometimes painted with decorative designs and used as clothing or as wrappers for sacred objects. Tapa is often called bark cloth.

TARA, in Ireland, about 20 miles northwest of Dublin, the site of a bronze-age fort whose exact date after 2000 B.C. cannot be determined. It was used not only as a citadel but as a royal residence and a burial place. The largest of six enclosures is known as Rath na Riogh, the Fort of Kings. Tara was the coronation site of the High Kings of Ireland until the 6th century A.D.

TARASCANS. The most powerful nation in western Mexico at the time of the Spanish Conquest, the Tarascans were one of the few peoples to resist subjugation by the Aztec Empire. Although their name is applied to much of western Mexican art, they probably arrived in this area only a few centuries prior to the Conquest. They are noted for a distinctive type of architecture called a *yacata*, examples of which can still be seen near their capital city of Tzintzuntzan. Yacatas were made of closely fitted stones and in ground plan resembled a "T" with a round platform at its stem. The Tarascans were also skilled metal workers who produced a vast amount of gold and copper ornaments in a wide variety of techniques.

TARENTUM, a Spartan colony founded around 700 B.C. on the southern coast of Italy. Tarentum (modern Taranto) reached its zenith in the 4th century B.C. and fostered a long and rich artistic tradition. Large numbers of terracotta reliefs ranging from the 6th to the 3rd centuries B.C. have been unearthed. The sculptured friezes and small plaques of soft stone used to decorate tombs show the influence of the great Greek masters of the 4th century B.C. Exquisite gold rings and fine coins also represent the purest and most perfect expression of the Greek spirit on Italian soil.

TARQUINIA, chief of the 12 Etruscan cities and reputed home of two kings of early Rome. Founded, perhaps, in the 9th century B.C., it lies about 60 miles to the northwest of Rome. In the 4th century B.C. Tarquinia was defeated by Rome, and by the 3rd century B.C. it had lost its independence. Tarquinia is most famous for its necropolis. Here a major series of painted chamber tombs, whose frescoes are jewels of Etruscan painting, were found. Colors are few, but the tones are bright and pleasant. Those of the 6th century B.C. (among them, the so-called Tombs of the Augur, the Baron, and the Hunters and Fishers) show the simplicity and naivete of archaic art. Themes are varied—scenes from daily life are

Tarquinia: "Revellers," detail. Fresco. Etruscan, ca. 470 B.C. The Tomb of the Leopards.

Tarquinia: "The Dancers," detail. Fresco. Etruscan. The Tomb of the Lionesses.

mixed with religious and mythological episodes. Later frescoes, such as those discovered in the Tomb of the Leopards and in the Tomb of the Triclinium, with their beautiful banquet scenes, are more sophisticated and subtle. In both earlier and later paintings, the Greek influence is obvious, but Etruscan love of the schematic—for movement and life—as well as Etruscan indifference to exact anatomy, mark these lyrical compositions as distinct from what we know about Greek painting. Tarquinia also had stone carving in the 6th century B.C., mostly seen as unusual stone slabs in relief—perhaps used to roof early chamber tombs. A carved stone slab, now in the Archaeological Museum in Florence, carries one of the few indecent scenes found in Etruscan art.

TARTARIA, a neolithic site in Transylvania, from which were excavated three clay tablets with incised symbols dated at some point after 3000 B.C. Some see in these symbols a form of writing said to have been derived from the pictographic Sumerian script of Mesopotamia, but many difficulties attend this theory. The latest scholarship is inclined to accept the signs as meaningful, since they have now been paralleled by signs at Karanovo.

TARTARS, or Tatars, a name that generally applies to Turkic nomads of Russian steppe origin. However, historians have sometimes used the word *Tartars* to denote widely diverse Asian nomads, including Mongols. From very early times Turkic Tartar artisans were highly skilled as leather craftsmen, pottery makers, iron forgers, and cloth weavers. Between roughly the 9th and 15th cen-

Tassili frescoes: Sefar cave painting. Tassili n'Ajjer, Sahara.

turies A.D. the Tartars became sedentary, taking up farming and livestock breeding on the steppes. In the 16th century they were absorbed into the Russian Empire, their leaders taking Russian titles. However, the people retained a large measure of their ethnic identity.

TARXIEN, the site in eastern Malta of a group of three stone temples built some time after 3000 B.C., to which a fourth was added in about 1500 B.C. At that time the ground over the earlier temples began to be used as a cemetery. The temples here, as elsewhere in Malta, were formed of gigantic stone slabs covered with capstones. The courts were open to the sky, the corridors roofed with large stones, and the sacred apses had carefully made corbelled roofs. The walls were decorated with geometric designs, spirals, and friezes of animals. The bottom half of a large stone statue of a mother-goddess figure was found here.

TASMANIA, a large island off the southern coast of Australia. Once called Van Diemen's Land, the area was the home of aboriginal inhabitants who had migrated from Australia. They lived in relative security until the 19th century, when they were virtually driven off their land by European settlers. Though the Tasmanians had a very simple material culture, they made decorated boomerangs and carved glyphs on rock shelters.

TASSILI FRESCOES, a profuse collection of prehistoric rock paintings and drawings found in the Saharan wastes of southeastern Algeria. They may span a period of some 8,000 years. The frescoes are located near the town of Tassili n'Ajjer, whose name means "Mountains of the Rivers," which hints at the time when lush vegetation supported a thriving animal and human population in the Sahara. The culture which left the major part of the rock art, showing scenes of everyday hunting life, probably reached its peak between 3000 and 2500 B.C. Colors for the frescoes were made from earthen oxides mixed with animal fat and blood. The earliest Tassili depictions of humans and animals, often with massive legs and rounded bodies, bear some similarities to prehistoric cave art found in northern Spain and in southern France.

TAXILA, a once prosperous city and center of learning in ancient northwest India, now sited in modern Pakistan near Rawalpindi. It was invaded by the Achaemenid Persians in the 6th century B.C., and in 326 B.C. it was conquered by Alexander the Great. Archaeological digs reveal two cities here. The earlier, called Bhir Mound, dates from the Persian and Greek invasions and consists of a town of narrow, irregular streets. The later, called Sirkap, dates from about 100 B.C. to 100 A.D. and gives evidence of careful town planning around a straight main avenue some 20 feet wide. Taxila was destroyed by the White Huns in the 5th century A.D. Ruins of several buildings here show a curious clash of Indian and Greek ornamentation. Great numbers of small art objects have been found.

TEKE, an African people who live chiefly on a secluded plateau, north of Brazzaville, in modern Zaire. Much of their history is still obscure, but it is known that they established their kingdom here during the 15th century A.D. and, due to their isolation, were able to carry on a brisk commerce while avoiding many of the European entanglements that affected their neighbors. Their most outstanding artistic carvings are their fetishes, which take the form of stiff, frontal male statues, often adorned with beards, accurately portrayed hair styles, and tribal markings. Fetishes are admired by these people as much for their aesthetic quality as for their magical powers. Teke metalwork is also noteworthy and consists of statuettes of men and women, magnificent jewelry, ceremonial axes, and fly whisks with anthropomorphic handles.

TELL, an archaeological term, used in the Near East, for a mound created by the accumulation of debris at a centuries-old but no longer existent settlement. Tells often rise to great heights. Since tells are built up in consecutive time layers, archaeologists can obtain fairly precise dates and associations for the wealth of objects found in them. The word *tell* is from the Arabic; *huyuk* and *tepe*, from the same area, are, respectively, Turkish and Persian equivalents.

TELL ES-SULTAN. See JERICHO.

TEMPERA, type of paint having a gelatinous base, notably egg yolk, but sometimes certain saps or gums. Tempera hardens quickly, leaving clear and air-resistant colors. From early times it has been a favored medium for mural painting.

TEMPLE OF CONCORDIA, a 5th-century B.C. Doric temple at Acragas (modern Agrigento) on the southern

Teohuatihucan: Effigy vessel. Terra cotta. 400–600 A.D. (National Museum of Anthropology, Mexico City)

coast of Sicily. Because it was turned into a church in the 6th century A.D., the temple is well preserved. The cella walls still stand to their full height, and the pediments are intact. The present name of the temple is traditional, but the original dedication is unknown.

TEMPLE OF HERA, at Paestum (ancient Poseidonia) in southern Italy, one of the best preserved Doric temples found anywhere. Formerly called the Temple of Poseidon, it dates from 460 B.C. and is the only Greek temple in which part of the second tier of the interior cella columns still stands. Another larger and earlier temple of Hera, called the "Basilica," stands alongside it.

TEMPLE OF THE TOOTH, Buddhist shrine in Kandy, Ceylon, and repository of a sacred tooth believed to have come from the mouth of Buddha. The temple is a large wooden structure of 17th-century A.D. origin, fronted by a stone archway. It is the focus of Ceylon's most important yearly religious festival, called *Esala Perahera*, and the terminal point for a procession that marks the feast. The temple is a major tourist attraction.

TENOCHTITLAN, the capital city of the Aztec Empire; its ruins are buried beneath modern Mexico City. Tenochtitlan was founded around 1350 A.D. on a swampy island in the middle of Lake Texcoco. The Aztecs attributed their choice of the site to divine instructions from their god, Huitzilopochtli, but in reality this was the only land their more powerful neighbors would allow them. As the Aztec Empire grew, so did its capital. With a population of 300,000 and an area of 20 square miles, Tenochtitlan was as large as many European capitals at the time of the Spanish Conquest. The Spaniards were overwhelmed by its regular plan, enormous markets, broad causeways, numerous canals, and brilliant white buildings which contrasted with the brightly painted ceremonial precinct at its center. This sacred precinct was enclosed by a wall, and just beyond it stood the palaces of the nobility. It is thought that each of the 20 clans of the Aztec nation lived in a different section of the city. After a long siege, Tenochtitlan was completely razed by the Spaniards and its canals filled in. Recent subway construction in Mexico City has unearthed many unusual works of Aztec sculpture.

TEOHUATIHUCAN, also spelled Teotihuacan, one of the most splendid and powerful cities of ancient Mexico, located approximately 25 miles north of modern Mexico City. Teohuatihucan's major ceremonial structures, the Pyramid of the Moon, 140 feet high, and the world-famous Pyramid of the Sun, 210 feet high, were built in the 2nd century A.D. At the height of its power, from 400 to 600 A.D., Teohuatihucan covered nine square miles, housed 85,000 people, controlled most of central Mexico, and made its influence felt as far away as Oaxaca, the Gulf Coast, and the Mayan areas of Guatemala. The origins of the Teohuatihucan people are shrouded in mystery. The foundation of the city has been variously attributed to the Totonacs, Toltecs, or a people as yet unidentified. The ruins of Teohuatihucan so impressed the Aztecs that they believed it was built by a race of giants or gods. The art of Teohuatihucan is highly symbolic, yet serene and austere. The few free-standing stone sculptures that survive have an architectonic quality. Among them is the monumental "Water Goddess," a blocklike statue eight feet high and weighing 22 tons, which now stands in the site museum. The outstanding sculptural expressions of Teohuatihucan are the beautifully simple greenstone face masks, which were probably used to cover the faces of the dead. Statuettes unearthed here have faces very much resembling the masks. Fresco murals, usually depicting the gods, including Quetzalcoatl, richly embellished the interiors of palaces. On a much smaller scale, mural paintings decorated a fine, thin orange pottery vessel, which frequently appears in areas subject to Teohuatihucan influence. The site was abandoned and burned, for still unknown reasons, around 800 A.D.

TEPE, the Persian term for a tell, or mound, created by the accumulation of centuries-old remains, at the site of an ancient settlement. Although dimensions may vary, Persian tepes are distinguished by their massive size. The tepe at Susa, for example, rises to a height of 115 feet and includes the remnants of a large acropolis.

TERP, a mound or hillock, site of a prehistoric village, especially in Scandinavia, the Low Countries, and Germany. In many ancient settlements it was customary to continue building on the same site for centuries, even when this involved building on rubbish thrown out by previous generations. The mound thus formed was often used by farmers to fertilize their fields. Interesting archaeological objects are often excavated from terps.

TERRA COTTA, baked clay objects, including pottery, inscribed tablets, and figurines, the latter often having religious significance. Terra cottas are found among the remains of most cultures and can be an important source of archaeological data, as well as much sought-after art objects.

TERRAMARA, an important culture of around 1500 to 1000 B.C. in northern Italy. A highly developed bronze industry brought about the ultimate fusion of this culture with that of the Apennine culture to the south, with far-reaching effects for the subsequent iron age in Italy.

At its height, in about 1400 B.C., Terramara culture was under the influence of the Urn People.

TESSERAE, small cubes of marble, colored stone, terra cotta, or glass, set in wet cement and used in the making of mosaics. The name is derived from the Greek word for four.

TEUTONS, the first of the Germanic peoples to come into conflict with the Romans. They are mentioned in 345 B.C. as living on the west coast of Jutland. Encroachments by sea may have caused them to migrate, and they requested and were refused Roman-controlled land for settlement. Provocation of the Teutons by several Roman generals, combined with incompetence, led to Roman defeats, the most serious being at Arausio in southern France in 105 B.C., which cost many thousands of Roman lives. The archaeology of the Teutons is but little known.

TEZCATLIPOCA, a major Aztec god, known as the "smoking mirror." Although he has many iconographic forms and representations, he is often recognized by a mirror he wears in place of a leg; his leg, it seems, was bitten off by the earth monster. Taken from the Toltec pantheon, Tezcatlipoca symbolized, in Aztec times, the night.

THAIS, a people who held a kingdom in southern China before the 8th century A.D., when they were driven into northern Siam, then part of the Khmer Empire. They assimilated into Khmer society and by about 1400 replaced the Khmers as the dominant power, founding their own Thai—or Siamese—dynasty. A change in art style from Khmer to Thai is apparent, although subject matter in both is Buddhist. Khmer stone sculpture was replaced by bronze casting. Several Thai art schools evolved, notably that of the Chengmai. Chengmai Buddhas have somewhat conventionalized faces—sharp noses, delicate, curving lips, and almond-shaped eyes.

THEBES, ancient city in central Greece, inhabited from perhaps the 3rd millennium B.C. Important among its early remains is a royal palace of the Mycenaean era. Approximately 80 vases of Mycenaean workmanship have been found in these ruins. Ancient chroniclers credited Thebes with having seven famous gates, but only one—the Elektra Gate—has been found. It stood between two circular towers of undetermined height. A temple to Apollo dates probably from the Geometric period but was rebuilt in Doric style during the 4th century B.C. Remnants of that structure still stand.

THERA, a volcanic island, now called Santorini, in the Aegean, about 75 miles north of Crete. In the mid-2nd millennium B.C. the island was the home of an exceedingly sophisticated people who used special techniques to make their buildings earthquake-resistant and produced pottery similar to that found in Knossos on Crete. Recent excavations have unearthed a palace, with frescoes painted on its walls, most depicting scenes from nature in a delicate but active style. They are believed to surpass in beauty all frescoes found to date in the Mediterranean region. Thera erupted around 1450 B.C., destroying its native culture and wreaking havoc on neighboring Crete. Many scholars believe the eruption may have played a major role in the fall of the brilliant Minoan civilization. It is also thought that Egyptian accounts of the destruction of Thera were the basis for Plato's story of Atlantis. Excavations on Thera, first begun in 1967 by the noted Greek archaeologist Spyridon Marinatos, have also revealed a fine city and theater of Hellenistic and Roman times.

THESEUM, the alternate name for a well-preserved marble temple in Athens, dating from about 440 B.C. and more properly called the Hephaisteion, since it was dedicated to the deity Hephaestus. The name *Theseum* derives from the temple's 18 frieze panels depicting the adventures of the Greek heroes Theseus and Herakles. The temple was thus once thought to have been dedicated by the Greeks to Theseus. Additional temple sculpture includes images of Hephaestus and Athena and a relief showing the legendary birth of their son, Erichthonius. Influence of the master sculptor Phidias is apparent throughout the Theseum.

THOTH, ancient Egyptian god of writing and of wisdom, equated with the ibis, a long-billed African bird. Egyptian artists depicted Thoth either as ibis-headed or completely in the form of that bird.

THOLOS, from the Greek for "dome," an archaeological term describing ancient communal burial tombs found in the Mediterranean region, principally in Mycenaean Greece, Asia Minor, Malta, and the Balearic Isles. Shaped like a beehive, tholos tombs, or tholoi, are built of regular courses of masonry, have a domed or corbelled central chamber, a passageway, and a tumulus or mound covering them in whole or in part. Similar tombs of the Megalithic Builders, elsewhere in Europe, have an almost identical plan but are built of great slabs of stone on end or on edge.

THOR, one of the chief gods of the Nordic pantheon, son of Odin. He was the god of thunder, a great fighter, physically powerful, and with his magical hammer, Mjollnir, protector of gods and men. He is represented as red-haired, fond of eating and drinking, and sometimes rather naive. Thursday is his name day.

THRACIANS, an ancient semibarbaric people of southeastern Europe who occupied territory north of Macedonia and east of the Black Sea during the 1st millennium B.C. They were seminomadic and probably related to the Scythians, who were their neighbors to the northeast. They were conquered by Philip of Macedon and again by the Romans, but in culture and language they remained distinct from the Greco-Roman world. Nevertheless, they had commercial contact with the Greeks as early as the 7th century B.C. Art objects and artifacts in Thracian tombs are mainly of Greek or Greek-Scythian origin.

THULE CULTURE, an Eskimo culture that appeared around 900 A.D. and soon spread over the Arctic from Siberia to Greenland. The Thule people lived in a highly specialized society that revolved around whale-hunting. Thule art is considered much less impressive than that of the preceding Ipiutak culture. Forms are simple, and the motifs are few and very general. One of the characteristics of Thule art is a great variety of human and animal figurines, carved from wood and ivory, which are decorated with small drilled holes. Although only a few inches high, they display the monumentality common to most Eskimo art. Around 1700 A.D., with changes in climate and the consequent disappearance of the whale, Thule art and culture disappeared.

TIAHUANACO, one of the least known of the great Pre-Hispanic cities, located on the shores of Lake Titicaca, high in the Bolivian Andes. The site was first occupied around 200 B.C., and most of its monumental structures

Tiahuanaco: Tapestry. (British Museum, London)

Tibetan Civilization: Neck ornament. Gold inlaid with coral. (British Museum, London)

were built before 600 A.D. At that time the city's influence began to spread, and eventually the region from northern Chile to the Peruvian city of Cuzco became part of the Tiahuanaco Empire. The most famous monument of the city, known as the "Gateway of the Sun," is a massive stone carving, 10 feet high and 12 feet wide. Over its lintel is a frieze sculptured in the manner of a tapestry, with a deity known as the Gateway God—flanked by winged attendants—in its center. Although his function is uncertain, this deity is the most important element of Tiahuanaco iconography. The vast majority of ceramics, sculpture, and fabulous tapestries · produced at Tiahuanaco depict the Gateway God, although with local variations and different degrees of abstraction. Tiahuanaco ceramics are especially famous for their luxuriant colors and for a form known as a *kero*, a beaker with a flared mouth. Although the empire did not last more than two centuries, its influence, especially in the form of iconography, can be seen on South American art objects until the 11th century A.D.

TIBETAN CIVILIZATION is recognizable as such from about the late 6th century A.D., in the form of a feudal monarchy dominating the high plateau region of Asia's Himalayas. Despite that natural mountain barrier, Tibet had contact with neighboring countries and possessed a considerable military force that periodically attacked adjacent Indian, Nepalese, and Chinese states. Tibet reached its peak of power during the reign of Kri sron lde btsan (755–97), at which time Mahayana Buddhism was introduced from India and embraced by the monarchy. The native religions predating Buddhism were varieties of shamanism (worship of nature spirits thought to reside in mountains, forests, etc.), including Bonpo, and a yet more primitive shamanism of the ordinary people, called *mi cos*. By the 9th century Tibet's monarchy had deteriorated and the country began breaking into small states. However, the successful merger of Buddhism with local faiths had already produced a distinctive new social order, which endured. It was based on what was ultimately called the Yellow Sect—remnants of the old feudal system, mainly preserved in the small western kingdom of Guge, combined with a flourishing Buddhist monastic society whose religious belief, ritual, and art were strongly colored by shamanism. This distinctive form of Buddhism is called Lamaism. From about the 13th century Mongol incursions affected Tibetan culture, and in 1578 a Mongolian prince conferred the mantle of deity upon Tibet's head lama and ruler, giving him the hereditary title Dalai Lama, which endures to the present day.

Tibetan Art and Antiquities, with only few exceptions, fall into the classification of Lamaist art and antiquities and are mainly discussed in an article under that heading. This is because Tibetan civilization was monolithic, and its only important art and antiquities were expressions of its official religion. However, there are some interesting albeit relatively minor items that fall beyond that realm. Ancient Tibetan metal craftsmen made a variety of small bronze and copper objects that are occasionally unearthed by local farmers who regard them as magic objects fallen from heaven. Mainly shamanist-inspired, they bear representations of animals (monkeys, horses, or a mythical bird called *Kyun*) or abstract magical symbols. Finely crafted products of Tibetan civilization of nonreligious nature were mainly objects for aristocratic households or personal items. These include distinctive brass and copper food vessels and teapots, often gilded or embellished with silver and decorated with intricate dragon motifs. Also of note is the *gau*, a small, delicate charm case, usually of silver and copper, and worn around its possessor's neck.

TIKAL, the largest and most important Maya city of the Peten area of Guatemala. The earliest dated monument at the site corresponds to July 6, A.D. 292. Ten years of excavation here makes Tikal one of the best known of Maya sites. The remains of over 2,500 buildings have been uncovered in a six-and-a-half-mile area. Tikal is best known for its architecture. Its pyramids, the highest in the Maya world, are topped with temples, which in turn are crowned with elaborately carved roof combs. The roof combs were functionally unnecessary but served as visual devices to increase the height of the pyramid. At Tikal, these combs sometimes rise to almost twice the height of the temple. Carved wooden lintels from temple doorways provide some of the few examples of Mayan sculpture in this medium. Several royal burials, found in the pyramids, have yielded fine pottery and a treasury of art objects carved from jadite, shell, flint, and bone. A series of stelae and altars was erected at regular intervals at Tikal. These are thin stones with low, flat relief, in contrast to the almost three-dimensional carving found at sites like Copan. Tikal was mysteriously abandoned in the 9th century A.D. Its preeminence was probably based on the existence of a plentiful water supply and on the presence of an abundance of flint and obsidian, which were in high demand.

TIKI, the name given to a Polynesian mythic hero and to any wood or stone image of this hero. Although tikis were made throughout Polynesia, those best known were the ones used by the Maori of New Zealand. Carved from precious jade, with eyes of inlaid shells, these small figurines were worn as pendants.

TIMGAD, a Roman colony in what is now Algeria, 100 miles from the sea. It was founded by the Emperor Trajan in 100 A.D. to house veterans of the 3rd Augustan legion in a regimental environment. The nearly square layout shows Roman town-planning in its simplest form, neat chessboardlike streets carefully divided. Timgad's monumental gates (the west one is a triumphal arch), its colonnaded roadways, attractive temples and fountains, markets, shops, baths, and houses, all invite the often-made comparison with the more famous site of Pompeii.

TING, a type of Chinese porcelain manufactured from the 10th through the 14th centuries A.D. and used in imperial households. It is usually off-white, with floral designs molded onto its surface. Ting ware is occasionally found in black, red, or purple. The term is also used to describe bronze or lacquer vessels mounted on legs, produced from the Shang through the Han eras.

TIRTHANKARAS. See JAIN ART AND ANTIQUITIES.

TIRYNS, a Mycenaean fortress-town dating from the early 2nd millennium B.C., located on the Gulf of Argos, Greece, and probably a satellite of the city of Mycenae to the near north. It was destroyed in the 12th century B.C., probably by Dorian invaders. Its well-preserved main fortress has an outer wall up to 19 feet thick. The palace, arranged around courtyards, contains numerous Minoan-inspired frescoes. The best of them shows a procession of women dressed in bright ceremonial costumes.

TISZA WARE, also known as Theiss ware, takes its name from a Hungarian river in the Moravian region and represents a late phase of Danubian culture. The beginning of the production of Tisza ware is dated about 3000 B.C. A crusted pottery, generally anthropomorphic in shape, it bears an incised style of lines, dots, and, later, elaborate designs of ribbons or bands.

TITUS' ARCH, one of the most important creations of Roman monumental art, erected by the Emperor Domitian in 81 A.D. It became a model for numerous commemorative arches in ancient and modern times. Titus' arch spans the Sacred Way between the Colosseum and the Roman Forum. A single-opening archway, it is faced with reliefs of the Emperor Titus entering Rome after his conquest of Judaea in A.D. 71; his soldiers, in procession, offer the spoils of victory. The deliberate emphasis on the figure of Titus, incongruously facing full front in his

chariot while the procession moves to the side, reveals how far the emperor-cult had come in the 90 years since the reliefs of the Ara Pacis, where Augustus is nearly anonymous. Never again did Roman relief strive so boldly for the effect to which painting regularly aspired —to hold the spectator to a brief moment of complete illusion.

TJURUNJA, or churinga, an object held sacred by Australian aborigines as representing their ancestral spirit. An oval or elongated slab of stone or wood, the tjurunja is decorated with incised linear designs. Some have a hole drilled in one end and can be whirled around, producing a humming sound. This kind of tjurunja is known in Australia and in many other parts of the primitive world as a bullroarer.

TLALOC, a beneficent Aztec god of rains and lightning. Known as "he who makes things grow," Tlaloc was among the most ancient of all gods worshipped in Mexico and Central America. He was generally depicted with a mask that gave the appearance of his wearing goggles and a mustache. This mask and most of his garments were painted blue.

TLATILCO, an ancient village site, just north of present-day Mexico City, which dates from about 1000 B.C. The numerous Pre-Columbian graves excavated here have yielded lavish offerings of ceramics and figurines. The figurines, which display a great variety of dress, ornament, and pose, are mainly female, a characteristic typical of prehistoric sites throughout the world and thought to be related to fertility cults. Tlatilco art style shows definite Olmec influence. Moreover, a number of typically Andean traits appear at Tlatilco, such as the presence of stirrup-spout vessels. This has led to speculation about contact between the Valley of Mexico and Peru.

TLESON PAINTER. See LITTLE-MASTER CUPS.

TLINGIT. A North American Indian tribe, the Tlingit lived in southeastern Alaska and its offshore islands and shared in the culture of the Northwest Coast. Along with their neighbors, the Tsimshian and Haida, the Tlingit were noted for wood sculpture that combined technical excellence with powerful design and refined color. However, their most original creation was the "Chilkat blanket," a type of shawl made from goat hair and cedar bark and named after one of the Tlingit clans. The back of the blanket is divided into three panels and decorated with highly abstract and symbolic designs usually in blue, white, yellow, and black.

TOKUGAWA SHOGUNATE. See EDO PERIOD.

TOLTEC CIVILIZATION, a civilization of ancient Mexico, founded prior to the 10th century A.D. At their height, from the 10th through the 12th centuries, the Toltecs ruled most of central Mexico from their flourishing capital at Tula, about 40 miles northwest of modern Mexico City. Renowned in legend as a nation of great artists, builders, poets, and scientists, the Toltecs were in

Toltec art: Vase. Plumbate ware. 900–1200 A.D. From Tula. (National Museum of Anthropology, Mexico City)

fact a people of mixed barbarian origin who acquired their cultural accomplishments from the more civilized peoples they conquered. To the further contradiction of legend, Toltec civilization was marked by extensive human sacrifice, war, and militarism, cultural traits which profoundly altered the mainstream of ancient Mexican life. So great was the military prestige of the Toltecs that a few centuries later the Aztecs amended their history to prove direct descent from the Toltecs. Quetzalcoatl, the old god of the Toltecs, a god of peaceful pursuits, was said to have been driven from Tula in the late 10th century and replaced with a pantheon of new, more bloodthirsty, gods. At about the same time the Toltecs invaded the Yucatan and occupied several Mayan cities. At Chichen Itza, for example, evidence of Toltec control is seen in several buildings that are almost exact replicas of structures at Tula. In the late 12th century Toltec power declined, and finally the nation fell. Tula was destroyed in 1224.

Toltec Art and Antiquities. The best expressions of Toltec sculpture, reliefs, and architecture are at Tula, their capital. Distinctive forms of Toltec sculpture can be seen there: enormous atlantean figures used as columns to hold roofs or, on a smaller scale, to support altars; and Chacmools, reclining anthropomorphic figures with elevated knees and heads and with a bowl on their stomachs. Another characteristic form of Toltec sculpture is a relief panel, on which eagle, jaguar, or human skull motifs are constantly repeated. Although the Toltecs claimed to have introduced metalworking to Mexico, the technique was known before their era. Toltec artistic influence was important in the Yucatan peninsula, most notably at Chichen Itza, where Toltec styles were skillfully mixed with existing Mayan art forms, thus creating a new, if temporary, vigor in architecture, sculpture, and metalwork. Toltec pottery was typically Mazapan ware.

TOMB OF SETI. See **SETHI TOMB.**

TOMB 7. See **MIXTEC CIVILIZATION.**

TORII. See **SHINTO ART AND ANTIQUITIES.**

TORI TRIAD. See **ASUKA PERIOD.**

TORQUE, a type of necklace fashioned of twisted metal, especially popular as personal adornment in bronze-age European cultures. The most commonly used materials include bronze and gold.

TOTEMISM, in primitive religion, the belief that a human or tribe of humans can have a mystical and ancestral relationship to a creature of nature, such as a bird, an animal, an insect, or, even, a plant. Usually there is a prohibition (or tabu) against harming this creature, or totem. Prehistoric and primitive art were oftentimes influenced by totemism. There is sufficient evidence to

make probable the belief that totemism preceded the rise of high civilizations in Sumeria and in Egypt.

TOTEM POLES. The most spectacular art form of the American Northwest Coast Indians, totem poles are elaborately carved posts that rise to lofty heights. The many figures represented on the poles may be animals, humans, or fantastic hybrid creatures. They do not actually represent totems but rather specific family crests and myths. At times the poles were erected as burial memorials or commemorative objects. The production of totem poles reached its height in the 1860s when new tools and artistic influences arrived from the white man's world. Several poles were generally erected around each family house, thus transforming simple coastal villages into surreal forests.

TOTONACS, a people living in the Mexican state of Veracruz at the time of the Spanish Conquest. They were organized into a society with a complicated system of social classes, and the population of their major city, Cempoala, numbered about 30,000. Although they probably arrived in Veracruz during the 11th century A.D., their name, Totonac, has been applied to a vast body of antiquities of much earlier date and wider provenance. Among these are the "laughing head" figurines, yokes, hachas, and palmas, unearthed in Veracruz. They are said to have founded the city of El Tajin, whose construction dates back to the 2nd century A.D. This confusion might have been started by the Totonacs themselves, who boasted to the Spaniards of having built the magnificent ancient city of Teohuatihucan.

TOWER OF BABEL, a monumental structure mentioned in the Old Testament (Genesis II), believed to be the ziggurat of Marduk—called Etemenanki, House of the Foundation of Heaven and Earth—at Babylon. Today little remains of this particular tower, which was described on cuneiform tablets, then again by Herodotus around 460 B.C. The tower apparently was built in seven stages, with a temple of enameled blue brick at the top. A clay tablet dating from 229 B.C. states that the tower was 294 feet square at its base and 294 feet high. A triple staircase leading from the ground to the tower has been excavated, although Herodotus described the structure as having a spiral ramp. Construction of the ziggurat was begun during the reign of Nebuchadnezzar. The structure was destroyed by Xerxes of Persia and cleared on order of Alexander the Great, with local builders hauling the bricks away. There is alternate evidence suggesting that the Tower of Babel might have been a different ziggurat, constructed at Borsippa, seven miles southwest of Babylon.

TRAJAN'S COLUMN. Erected in 113 A.D. in the forum of the Emperor Trajan in Rome, it bears the most elaborate relief composition remaining from the Roman world. About 130 feet high, the stone column has a continuous spiral frieze (over 600 feet long) vividly depicting the victorious campaigns of Trajan in Dacia, a Danubian region. Scenes of battles, sieges, suffering, and surrender unfold dramatically from base to top against a background enriched with landscape and geographic allusions. The whole composition was once painted and is, indeed, a translation of the tradition of triumphal column-painting into stone carving—a natural, if audacious, step forward. Plaster casts of the "unwound" frieze can be studied at eye level in the Museum of European Civilization in Rome. The monument became the emperor's tomb in 117 A.D. when his ashes were interred in its base. The statue of Trajan atop the column was replaced by one of St. Peter in 1588.

TRAKIEU, located in central Vietnam, site of an ancient Cham capital from about the 7th through the 11th centuries A.D. Some of the best examples of Cham sculpture were found here, including depictions of human figures in high relief, which served as ornamentation for sandstone capitals. The best figures, dating from about the 10th century, have near-classic proportions. Most objects have been removed from the original site and are housed in a museum at nearby Danang.

TREASURE OF PRIAM. See TROY.

TREASURY OF ATREUS, the most spectacular structure of the Greek Mycenaean period. It is a royal burial chamber, which was cut in a hillside outside the citadel of Mycenae sometime after 1300 B.C., and represents the best preserved example of a tholos ("beehive") tomb known. The main chamber is a circle 49 feet in diameter, roofed by a 45-foot-high dome of dressed ashlar blocks. Concentric circles of stones (without mortar) rise in ever-narrowing diameters (corbelling) until they form a dome sealed by a single capstone. There is a 20-foot-square side chamber cut into the rock. This monumental tomb is approached by a long (120 feet) entranceway (dromos), lined with rectangular, saw-cut blocks, and entered through an ornate and colorfully decorated doorway 18 feet high. The doorway is topped by two giant lintels, the inner one 24 feet long and estimated at over 100 tons. Weight on the lintel was relieved by leaving an open triangular space above, concealed by the facade plaque. Looting through the ages has left only the grandeur of the construction to hint at the riches this royal tomb once held.

TREE OF LIFE, also the Sacred Tree, a recurring motif in ancient Mesopotamian and Palestinian art, consisting of a highly conventionalized tree and based on a Mesopotamian belief that divinity is manifest in plant life. It occurs frequently on Assyrian reliefs, often accompanied by griffins; on Babylonian seals; on capital pilasters at various ancient Palestinian sites; and even on the antiquities of Russian steppe peoples.

Trajan's Column: Detail. From the forum of the Emperor Trajan, Rome.

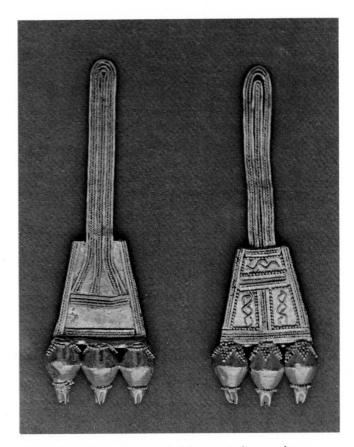

Troy: Trojan earrings. Gold. (Acropolis Museum, Athens)

TREE-RING DATING. See **DENDROCHRONOLOGY.**

TRES ZAPOTES, a major Olmec site, in the Mexican state of Veracruz, 100 miles northwest of the ruins of La Venta. Tres Zapotes stretches for more than a mile and in ancient times was occupied twice: the first, contemporaneous with La Venta; the second, after La Venta's fall. Tres Zapotes has a large number of earthen mounds, as well as various kinds of monumental sculpture. One "colossal head" was found which is from the first occupation. Tres Zapotes, however, is most famous for the so-called Stele C, the earliest dated monument in the New World; a "bar and dot" on one side of the stele is set at 31 B.C. Although no similar Olmec monument has been found, Stele C suggests that writing and a counting system based on the so-called bar and dot were principal Olmec contributions to Pre-Columbian culture. Many small Olmec art objects have been discovered at Tres Zapotes.

TRIALETI, the site of bronze-age kurgans, or barrow graves, in Soviet Georgia. These royal tombs appear to range in date from the late 3rd through the mid-2nd millennium B.C. The site's 42 graves have yielded unusually fine objects, now housed in Soviet museums. Most valuable among the objects are drinking goblets of silver and gold. Embossed animal and possibly human figures on the goblets are of uncertain cultural origin but may be related to styles found in Anatolia.

TRIGLYPH, the rectangular, slightly projecting slab between the metopes of the frieze of a Doric temple. Two vertical grooves divide it into three parts. Purely decorative, it is of no structural importance in the Classical Greek temple of stone. Triglyphs stood over each column and over the middle space between columns.

TRIPOLYE CULTURE, an early agricultural culture of the Soviet Ukraine between the Dniester and Dnieper rivers. From approximately 3500 to 1900 B.C., the Tripolye people built permanent settlements, mainly along riverbanks; their largest known settlement was found at Vladimirovka on the Bug River. Houses were made of packed clay and timber. Objects found in the barrow-type graves here include terra-cotta statuettes in human and animal forms and an expertly fired and painted pottery having elaborate ornamental motifs. Northern Tripolye regions have yielded pottery with mainly geometric designs. In the south and around the Dnieper, the designs tend to be spiral or meander.

TRIPTOLEMUS. See **DEMETER.**

TROIS FRERES is the name of a large cave complex in the Department of Ariege, France, in which are many prehistoric engravings cut into the rock face. They are dated in the mid-Magdalenian period about 12,000 B.C. A large variety of animals of the chase, mammoth, rhinoceros, bear, wild horse, reindeer, and musk ox, are depicted with freedom and delicacy. A lion and two snowy owls are drawn in full-face position. The most celebrated engraving is that of a wizard, in stag-antler mask and horse tail, enacting a hunting-magic dance.

TROY, called Ilion by the Greeks, fabled city of Homer's *Iliad*, the site of which was discovered in 1871 by the inspired and determined German archaeologist Heinrich Schliemann. Located on the Dardanelles, near modern Hissarlik, Turkey, this powerful city once controlled trade to and from the Black Sea. Between 1871 and 1890 Schliemann excavated nine separate occupation levels —designated Troy I through Troy IX—at this major coastal site in Asia Minor; they provide an almost complete picture of bronze-age development in western Asia Minor. Troy I was settled soon after 3000 B.C. and Troy II a few centuries later. It was during this 3rd-millennium period that Trojan metal workers produced their finest works, in particular the famous hoard—the so-called Treasure of Priam—unearthed by Schliemann at Troy II's level. A wooden chest was found to contain silver and bronze vases packed with gold objects (one vase contained innumerable gold rings, earrings, etc.), two diadems, an electrum vase, and weapons of bronze. Trojan goldsmiths were probably the most advanced in their world, and expert Trojan bronzework became one of the main sources for the introduction of bronze weapons to central Europe. Depictions on many of the metal objects—as well as on wheel-made Trojan pottery—were of ships and dolphins. The earliest full-scale city ap-

peared with Troy VI (about 1900 B.C.) and had walls of cut stone, enclosing a 300,000-square-foot area, on which terraced houses and a palace stood. Homeric Troy seems to have been Troy VII. Traces of burning and pillage, probably from the Greek siege, date from around 1250 B.C. The last Troy languished and quietly disappeared at about the dawn of the Christian era. Schliemann removed the Treasure of Priam from Turkey, and, not surprisingly, it became part of the collection of a Berlin museum. When the Second World War broke out, the treasure, one of the most historic in the world, was secretly hidden in a deep bunker beneath the Berlin Zoo. Immediately before, or soon after, the Soviet occupation of Berlin in 1945, the fabulous "gold of Troy" vanished.

TRUJILLO, an archaeological region of northwestern Venezuela, which may have once been a cultural crossroads for influences from Colombia to some Caribbean islands. Finds in Trujillo cover a 2,500-year period, from 1000 B.C. to the Spanish Conquest. The most characteristic art expression of Trujillo is in ceramics, especially in its clay female-and-male figurines. These were decorated with a distinctive gray-and-white painting. Female figures tend to have a strange-shaped wide head, while males are depicted with normal-size heads and seated on stools. The ancient people of Trujillo also produced miniature clay figures, which were probably used as charms, and carved stone fetishes.

TRUNDHOLM. In a field here in Zealand, Denmark, a small, 10th-century B.C. model of a solar chariot from the bronze age was found. A gilded bronze disc, representing the sun, was mounted on six wheels and drawn by a bronze horse. Apparently a full-scale version of this chariot, representing the daily journey of the sun across the heavens, was customarily pulled across the field at the solstice feast as a magic aid to the fertility of the crops.

TSIMSHIAN. A North American Indian tribe of British Columbia, the Tsimshian shared in the culture of the Northwest Coast. Their art style, closely related to that of their neighbors, the Haida and Tlingit, is characterized by technical skill, powerful design, a limitation to the basic form of the material, and a sense of restraint. The importance of clans in Tsimshian society is reflected in the production of a great number of totem poles. In addition, they adopted many decorative ideas from the Athabascan tribes of the Canadian interior, including beadwork, leatherwork, and porcupine quilling.

TSUN, type of Chinese Shang bronze vessel having an animal form for its base. The term also applies to a very large goblet-shaped bronze from the same era.

TULA, an archaeological site some 40 miles northwest of modern Mexico City and once the capital of the Toltec Empire. Founded in 980 A.D. by the legendary priest-king Ce Acatl Topiltzin Quetzalcoatl, whose name and deeds

Tula: Atlantean columns from the Temple of Tlahuixcalpantecuhtli. Toltec, 10th–12th centuries A.D.

Tula: Wild boar. Terra cotta with mother-of-pearl. Toltec, 10th–12th centuries A.D. (National Museum of Anthropology, Mexico City)

were later attributed to the god Quetzalcoatl, Tula was in the 11th century a splendid city of considerable size. It was built atop a high hill and enjoyed a large central plaza, surrounded by pyramidal structures, fine palaces, and sacred ball courts. However, with neither streets nor residential neighborhoods, the city lacked the monumentality of its greatest predecessor, Teohautihucan. Tula is best known for its building colonnades and for its massive sculpture, including atlantean columns, often depicting warriors, which rise to a height of 18 feet. There are great stone Chacmools and numerous relief slabs with carvings of the feathered serpent, the symbol of Quetzalcoatl, and of fierce jaguars, coyotes, and eagles devouring the hearts of sacrificial victims. The art of Tula was

strongly felt in the Mayan city of Chichen Itza after the Toltec conquest of the 10th century A.D. Tula and the Toltecs flourished until the early 13th century, when the city was destroyed by invaders.

TUMBAGA, an alloy of gold and copper in which the surface copper is removed to leave only the gold. Tumbaga was used extensively in the Pre-Columbian world to make exquisite art objects in the form of pectorals, pendants, figurines, masks, and, occasionally, ceremonial vessels.

TUMULUS CULTURE. About 1500 B.C., during the bronze age in central Europe, there developed a regular practice of honoring the dead by burying them under great mounds, or *tumuli*. From its center in southern Germany the culture spread east, west, and north, until it became almost universal in Europe. The Tumulus culture period immediately precedes the rise of the Urn People. The contents of Tumulus tombs in bronze weapons, drinking vessels, jewelry, amber plateware, and embossed bronze plaques—the accompaniments of war and peace—provide important evidence for archaeology.

TUNHUANG, an ancient Buddhist site in north-central China, of importance from roughly the 4th through the 10th centuries A.D. Built during the Wei Dynasty, it has numerous Buddhist temple caves with wall paintings, as well as paintings on silk, paper, and wood. Rediscovered in 1900, the caves had been walled up since the 11th century. Tunhuang was on a major trade route between China and the West and became a center of cultural interchange. Its cave-temple art shows cosmopolitan influences. The wall paintings at Tunhuang are said to be the earliest in Chinese art history.

TUREHOLM. One of the largest of Sweden's hoards of ancient gold objects was found in 1774 in Tureholm in Sodermanland, some distince west of Stockholm. The weight of the hoard totalled 12 kilograms. This indicates the considerable wealth of some Swedish chieftains in the period from the decline of the Roman Empire in 400 A.D. to the rise of Charlemagne near 800 A.D.

TURIN ROYAL CANON, modern name for what is perhaps the most important of the many Egyptian papyrus documents ever discovered. It offers an authoritative listing of the Egyptian pharaohs from Egypt's earliest times until the New Kingdom. The compilation itself dates from the New Kingdom era, probably about 1250 B.C. The manuscript, in Italy's Turin Museum, is in poor physical condition.

TURKIC PEOPLES, a generic term for certain central Asian nomadic tribes (Kirghis, Uigurs, Uzbeks, etc.) recognizable by the 6th century A.D. in Siberia, Mongolia, and on the Russian steppes. They were horsemen, cattle breeders, and had an advanced iron-working technology. Before 800 A.D. they split into eastern and western groups, the eastern tribes periodically struggling against Chinese civilization, while the western Turkic tribes were, by the 9th century, largely incorporated into Islamic civilization. Turkic art includes jewelry, metalware,

and unusual stone sculpture. Distinctive among Turkic jewelry are belt plaques of gold or silver, usually bearing a flower motif and worn suspended from a belt on leather strips. Fine silver vessels, bowls, bottles, etc., have been found in Turkic tombs throughout central Asia. Turkic stone statues of human figures are found in the open—notably in the Tuva region, east of the Altai—and probably represent important tribal leaders.

TUTANKHAMON'S TOMB, the only nearly intact tomb of ancient Egyptian royalty ever found by archaeologists. Located in the Valley of the Kings at Thebes, it was discovered in 1922 by the Englishman Howard Carter of Lord Carnarvon's archaeological team. The tomb has four chambers, and although thieves of the remote past had done some pilfering, the priceless treasure hoard that remained was huge, capturing worldwide attention. The antechamber included portraits of Tutankhamon and his queen, Ankhesenamun, and chariots, jewels, gold statuettes, and gold-inlaid furniture. An inner chamber holding Tutankhamon's mummy was also filled to capacity with gold and other precious articles. The treasury chamber was dominated by four life-size goddess figures guarding the alabaster canopic chest. Mummies of two infants, apparently Tutankhamon's stillborn offspring, were also found. The fourth chamber served as a storage room for food, wine, oils, etc. Tutankhamon was an 18th Dynasty pharaoh who reigned around 1350 B.C. His treasures are now in the National Museum, Cairo.

TYCHE. See **FORTUNA.**

TYRE, a major Phoenician city, once located on a coastal island, off Lebanon, about 45 miles south of modern Beirut. A sea power and colonizing center, Tyre reached its peak of prosperity around 1000 B.C., and around 814 B.C. it sent colonists to the North African coast to found the city of Carthage. Tyre successfully resisted attempts at conquest by the Assyrian and Babylonian empires, but in 332 B.C. it fell to Alexander the Great after a bitter siege and was destroyed. The city was revived during the Roman Empire and again became an important trade center, exporting murex, the Phoenician purple dye, as well as silk and glass products. Excavations at Tyre, now covered by sand and sea, have yielded few remains predating the Roman era.

Tutankhamon's tomb: Tutankhamon's golden coffin, detail. Gold inlaid with semiprecious stones. Egyptian, 18th Dynasty. (National Museum, Cairo)

U

UBAID CULTURE, a southern Mesopotamian culture dating from the mid-5th millennium B.C. and the immediate predecessor of Sumerian civilization. Remains of the major Ubaid settlement—at Al 'Ubaid, near the site of Ur—show evidence of reed huts and have yielded pottery with painted monochrome designs and implements for hunting and fishing. The Ubaid culture lasted for at least 400 years and marked the dawn of the copper age in Mesopotamia. Friezes and statues showing animals have been found at Ubaid and are of copper. Monumental temples of mud brick were set on mounds or platforms, which were the precursors of the ziggurats of Sumer.

UGARIT, an ancient Canaanite city on the coast of northern Syria, six miles north of modern Latakia and presently occupied by the large tell Ras Shamra, which was excavated by C. F. A. Schaeffer between 1929 and 1939. The earliest settlement at Ugarit—a pre-pottery, flint-working culture—dates from the 7th or 6th millennium B.C. Bronze-age settlements at the site produced the characteristic Halafian pottery, having burnished polychrome decoration of animal images and geometric patterns. Ugarit had close diplomatic and economic relations with Egypt during the early 2nd millennium B.C., and many Egyptian statues have been discovered here. By 1450 B.C. Ugarit was a rich commercial center, and remains from this era include several palaces, temples to Baal and Dagon, and burial vaults. It was destroyed around 1200 B.C. by Sea Peoples from the Mediterranean.

UGARIT TEXTS, inscribed clay tablets dating from around 1450 B.C., found at Ras Shamra, site of the ancient Semitic city of Ugarit, on the Mediterranean coast of Syria. Tablets from the temple and palace are in a decipherable alphabetic cuneiform script of 29 characters and shed light on the city's political, economic, and social life. At least equally important is the information the tablets yield on the polytheistic Canaanite religion and Semitic mythology. Prominent are stories and poems in which the god Baal occupies a major role.

UIGURS, a Turkic people who were military allies of China's Tang Dynasty in the 8th century A.D. By the 9th century they had their own nation in wimhat is now China's Sinkiang Province, but by the 13th century they were joined to the Mongol Empire. The Uigurs were predominantly Buddhists and had several important cultural and intellectual centers, including Tarfan, Bezeklik, and Koco. Many finely executed paintings survive from these and other sites.

UJJAIN, a sacred city in north-central India, considered during Buddha's time as one of the holiest of Indian cities. Archaeologists have found three distinct phases of ancient occupation beneath the modern city. Ujjain's peak of cultural importance coincides with the second phase, in the late 1st millennium B.C., and shows predominantly brick structures, varied pottery, and ivory seals with script dating from roughly 200 B.C. The third phase contains ruins of Buddhist structures from the early centuries A.D.

ULTRAVIOLET-RAY EXAMINATION, a technique used in conjunction with other methods of examination to reveal information about the age and authenticity of an antique art object. As a general rule, a surface exposed to filtered ultraviolet light will effloresce in differing colors that are fairly predictable, depending on age. For example, a recently cut marble surface will usually give off a purple glow under ultraviolet light, while an apparently similar marble surface that has been exposed to the atmosphere for several centuries or more will take on a green-to-yellow glow. Pottery and porcelain will also effloresce in varying colors, depending on age.

UNETICE CULTURE, also known as the Aunjetitz culture, is named from a great ancient cemetery excavated south of Prague in Czechoslovakia. This bronze-age culture (1800–1400 B.C.), arising in the fertile Danube region of Bohemia, subsisted on pastoral and agricultural activity but also had important trade and industry, which had wide effects across Europe. In the Unetice cemetery bodies of long-headed persons of moderate size are laid in a crouched position on their right sides facing south. The pottery found with them includes jars, bowls, amphorae, and broad-rimmed dishes. A gold ring for the hair was found, which is clearly a copy of better goldsmith work from Troy. There are many bone and stone tools, but bronze had become common, in the form of strong flanged axes, daggers of triangular form, and pins and jewelry of widely varied shapes. These bronze types were exported and copied broadly over Europe.

UPPSALA, in Sweden, near Stockholm, a former royal center and site of an ancient temple and of burial mounds of impressive proportions marking the graves of kings. The largest mound is nearly 40 feet high. The royal dynastic name was Ynglingr, or Englander. The graves belong to the Swedish pre-Christian period from the fall of Rome in the 5th century A.D. to the rise of Charlemagne.

UR, a major center of Sumerian civilization whose site, the tell el-Muqaiyar, is located about 220 miles south of modern Baghdad, in Iraq. The Biblical Ur of the Chaldees, said to have been the homeland of Abraham, the first Hebrew patriarch, Ur was a brilliant city-state of the ancient Mesopotamian world. At its height, in the 3rd millennium B.C., Ur was a large oval-shaped town—protected on three sides by the Euphrates River—which housed a population of about 250,000. There were splendid temples, palaces, public buildings, and canals. Excavations begun here in the 1920s by C. L. Woolley, the famous British archaeologist, and continued by the University of Pennsylvania have revealed occupation levels dating from the 5th millennium B.C., when the people of

Ur lived in mud-coated reed huts, produced clay figurines, and made a richly decorated pottery, since identified as Ubaid ware. Covering the earliest level of occupation was a deep layer of river silt, the residue of a once great flood; it is thought that this catastrophe was the ultimate source of the Biblical Flood. Among the many discoveries at Ur, the so-called royal cemetery, dating from about 2800 B.C., proved to be the most spectacular. An extensive burial ground, with brick tombs supported by arches and topped by domes, the cemetery yielded a treasury of precious antiquities: gold and silver statues, vessels, and weapons; inlaid jewelry; richly embellished musical instruments; and lapis-lazuli mosaics. Also unearthed were the remains of royal attendants, who apparently were sacrificed so as to serve their king or queen in the next world. This wealthy, if somewhat cruel, culture came to an end in about 2300 B.C., when the Akkadians, a Semitic people, invaded non-Semitic Sumeria and conquered Ur. Some 300 years later, Ur, then a blend of Semitic and non-Semitic peoples, enjoyed another period of greatness under the 3rd Dynasty. Founded by Ur-Nammu, who came to power in about 2000 B.C., the dynasty established the Sumerian capital at Ur. The great ziggurat to Nannar, the moon god, which still dominates the site of Ur, was built, while literary works, such as the Gilgamesh epic, were composed or written for the first time. Some 2,000 cuneiform tablets, dating from the 3rd Dynasty, have been found and include works of literature and accounts of taxes,

economics, and an inscription of the code of Ur-Nammu, the oldest known legal code. Of the few remaining artworks of the period, the most famous is the large white limestone stele depicting Ur-Nammu building the great ziggurat. Ur was destroyed in about 1700 B.C., probably by Elamites, rebuilt by Kassites in about 1400 B.C., and became a major religious center under the Babylonians of the 7th century B.C. However, the splendor of ancient Ur had long since vanished, and in the 4th century B.C., when the Euphrates changed its course, the city was abandoned. Antiquities from Ur can be seen at many museums but especially in the collections of the British Museum, the University Museum, University of Pennsylvania, and in the Baghdad Museum.

URARTU, the Biblical Ararat, an ancient kingdom of eastern Anatolia, Turkey, centered around Lake Van. Still largely unknown, the Urartians may have entered this area early in the 13th century B.C., but by the 9th century B.C. they had developed a flourishing kingdom. It lasted until the 7th century B.C., when, it is thought, Armenians from Phrygia supplanted the native Urartians. Continuing excavations near Erivan in Soviet Armenia may shed light on the origin and nature of the Urartians. Ancient Urartu was renowned for its metal craftsmanship, especially in bronze. Characteristically, metalwork was carefully engraved with a richness of detail, set with inlays of precious stones, and was often used to embellish furniture. Metal helmets, arms, cups, tripod cauldrons, and candelabra have also been found at

Ur: Helmet. Gold. (Baghdad Museum, Iraq)

Uxmal: "Queen of Uxmal," detail. Carved stone. Mayan. (National Museum of Anthropology, Mexico City)

Urartian sites. The Urartians had a strong influence on later Persian culture, especially in the use of terraces and cyclopean architecture at Persepolis. A beautiful statuette of a Urartian deity, standing on the back of a bull, is in the Metropolitan Museum of Art, New York; however, the art of Urartu can be best seen at the British Museum.

URN PEOPLE. The study of graves and methods of disposing of the dead has given important clues to the life and civilization of various peoples. In the bronze age in central Europe and in Italy a new funerary practice was introduced. Instead of simple burial the body was cremated and the ashes placed in an urn. Large numbers of these urns were buried, often very close together, in a field. Sites of those who followed this new practice, the so-called Urn People or Urnfield People, have been found in Hungary and in the middle and upper Danube region dating from 1400 B.C. The new rite spread to Italy, where it is found in Terramara settlements of the Po Valley. At the best known of the Terramara sites, Castellazo di Fontanellato, the settlement is surrounded by a moat and rampart, and the urn cemetery outside it is likewise protected by a moat. There are urnfield sites in Spain and France and other parts of western and central Europe.

UR ROYAL STANDARD, a double inlaid panel of Sumerian origin, discovered in the Ur royal cemetery and dating from about 2800 B.C. The panels are of white shell, lapis lazuli, and pink limestone, set in bitumen and wood. One panel shows the Sumerian king in battle; the other shows him at a feast in celebration of the victory. The panels, now in the British Museum, are considered to be the best illustrations of Sumerian life to survive from the 3rd millennium B.C.

URUK, one of the oldest and greatest of Sumerian city-states, located 35 miles northwest of Ur in what is now southeastern Iraq. It was the Biblical Erech and is now encompassed by the town of Warka. Excavations at the site since 1912 have revealed 18 layers of occupation spanning more than 4,000 years of history. The earliest level, dating from the mid-4th millennium B.C., marks the beginning of Sumer civilization. Wheel-made pottery, cylinder seals, and early forms of cuneiform writing—possibly the earliest in the world—were all introduced at Uruk. Also unearthed at Uruk were city walls, six miles in circumference, and several large temples, including one in an extraordinary state of preservation now known as the White Temple. This mud-brick structure occupied an area of 60 by 70 feet and was built on a platform some 45 feet high. Uruk's buildings were decorated with cone mosaics, characteristic of Sumerian art. These are clay cones about four inches high, colored black, red, or buff, and set in mud plaster to form geometric patterns. Sculpture in the round, bas-reliefs, deco-

rated stone vases, and vessels of copper, lead, and silver have been discovered at Uruk.

USHABTI FIGURES, ancient Egyptian funerary statuettes, generally sculpted from stone or wood or molded from terra cotta or faience. They range in size from about four inches to nearly a foot high and have been found in numerous Egyptian tombs. Many bear inscriptions from the Book of the Dead. Ushabti were intended as substitutes for the deceased, when, in the afterlife, he was called on to perform menial tasks for the gods. The finest figures, dating from the New Kingdom, were shaped to bear a close resemblance to the mummified corpse.

UXMAL, one of the most accessible and frequently visited Mayan sites, near the city of Merida in the Yucatan. Uxmal is noted for its architecture, most of which dates from the 10th century A.D., and provides outstanding examples of the Puuc style. The building complex known as the Nunnery, as well as the so-called Palace of the Governor building, display the typical Puuc traits of long, low façades broken by doorways, with plain walls topped by incredibly elaborate mosaic friezes. The friezes are composed of geometric designs alternating with masklike faces of gods. Two other buildings, the pyramids of the Magician and of the Dwarf, dominate the site with their great height. One of the few portable sculptures from the site, known as the "Queen of Uxmal," was found beneath the central doorway of the Pyramid of the Magician.

Uxmal: Detail of the central entranceway, eastern edifice, of the Nunnery Quadrangle.

V

VALLEY OF THE CAVES. See **MOUNT CARMEL.**

VALLEY OF THE KINGS, a desert necropolis of ancient Egypt's pharaohs of the New Kingdom, situated on the Nile's west bank, opposite Thebes. Probably the first important tomb there was for Amenhotep I, dating from the 16th century B.C. Most famous from the modern viewpoint is that of Tutankhamon, discovered nearly intact in 1922. Most tombs were cut into the valley's rocky wall and consisted of several descending chambers joined by corridors, the final chamber holding the sarcophagus and lavish treasure. Interior walls were decorated with carved and painted scenes and funerary texts. Numerous memorial temples were constructed adjacent to the riverbank. The Valley of the Kings was extensively plundered in ancient times.

VALLTORTA, a gorge in the province of Castellan in eastern Spain whose rock shelters contain a large number of paintings dating from the end of the paleolithic and into the mesolithic period. In contrast to the cave art of northern Spain and southern France, these paintings show numerous human figures hunting game, running and leaping, many armed with bows and arrows and some wearing feather headdresses.

VANDALS, a Germanic tribe from Jutland who were settled in the valley of the Oder River by the 5th century B.C. At the time of the dissolution of the Roman Empire, with its ensuing barbarian invasions, the Vandals moved farther in their migrations than any other northern tribe. Crossing the Rhine into Gaul in the 5th century A.D., they swept through Gaul and Spain. In 429 Boniface, a rebel

Roman governor in North Africa, invited them there to help his cause. They stayed to conquer, fanned out to Sardinia and Italy and sacked Rome in 455. They were defeated in North Africa by Justinian, the Byzantine emperor, in the 6th century. They have been saddled with the reputation of being mere destroyers (vandals, vandalism) but were probably no worse than other tribes in this respect. The Vandals left little in the way of permanent institutions or monuments.

VAPHEIO CUPS, the famous Minoan-Mycenaean goblets, named after the site in Sparta where two such cups—dating from the late 2nd millennium B.C.—were discovered. Both of the original cups are made of gold and are richly decorated with scenes of bulls. The cups are straight-sided and widen slightly towards the rim. They have a single handle. Recent scholarship tends to the opinion that one of the cups is Minoan in origin, while the other is most probably a Mycenaean copy. The Vapheio cups are in the National Museum, Athens.

VARANGIANS, the Greek word for the Scandinavians who traded and ultimately settled in Russia. They developed several settlements along two trade routes, one following the Volga, the other the Dnieper. The identification of the Varangians with the people known as the Rus and the part they played in the foundation of the early Russian states are matters of controversy, but the tradition that Scandinavians in fact founded the ruling houses of the cities of Novgorod and Kiev is correct.

VAT PHRA KEO, the royal temple in the eastern portion of the Thai Royal Palace area in Bangkok, dating from the 18th century A.D. The temple is built within a rectangular gallery, the walls of which are covered with frescoes depicting scenes from each episode of the *Ramakarti,* which is a Siamese adaptation of the Indian epic the *Ramayana.*

VEDIC PERIOD, in Indian history, roughly from 1500 to 800 B.C.; the period that followed the destruction of the Indus Valley civilization by Aryan invaders and preceded that of the pre-Mauryan dynasties. It takes its name from the *Vedas,* sacred Hindu scriptures which were composed

Vapheio cups: Gold with repousse decoration. (National Museum, Athens)

Venus of Willendorf: Carved limestone. Aurignacian culture, 25,000–20,000 B.C. (National History Museum, Vienna)

during this time. Vedic India was probably ruled by Aryans, and most structures were built of perishable materials, such as wood. Known exceptions include a few rock-cut tombs (e.g., at Mennapuram)—simple domed chambers having a monolithic stone column at their center. It is difficult to date art objects and antiquities as specifically Vedic, although such classification applies to some figures in terra cotta or, more rarely, in precious metals. These icons closely resemble the deities and fertility spirits of Indus Valley origin and have been found in many parts of India.

VEII, Rome's most powerful and wealthy Etruscan rival, located across the Tiber, ten miles to the north of Rome. In the 6th century B.C. Rome called the famous Etruscan artist Vulca from Veii to decorate the Temple of Jupiter on the Capitoline Hill. Veii fell to the Romans about 400 B.C. after a ten-year siege; ruins and Etruscan tombs remain. Excavations here since 1916 have turned up a series of exquisite, almost life-size, terra cottas which once stood on the roof crest of the great Veian Temple of Apollo. Four are the masterpieces of one artist (generally thought to be Vulca) and include a powerful, striding Apollo; a Heracles, trampling the sacred hind; a Hermes; and a headless woman holding a child in her arms. The artist employed the accepted traditions of archaic Greek art, but his individual native genius can be felt in the statues' colorful and vivid exuberance. These, the finest and most famous of Etruscan terra cottas, are now in the Villa Giulia Museum in Rome and date from 500 B.C.

VENDEL, in Uppland, Sweden, the site of several magnificent Viking ship burials of the 5th and 6th centuries A.D. The dead, buried in superb armor and surrounded by their household goods, their weapons, horses, and dogs, testify to the wealth of Viking chiefs. One fine iron helmet from Vendel closely resembles a helmet from the Sutton Hoo hoard in England.

VENUS. See APHRODITE.

VENUS FIGURES. These small female statuettes in bone, ivory, and stone have been found all the way from southern France to Lake Baikal in Siberia and in western Asia. The head, arms, and feet are unimportant, but the female sexual characteristics, breasts, genitalia, buttocks, and abdomen in a state of pregnancy, are exaggerated. The figurines mostly date from the Aurignacian period, usually from the early Gravettian phase (about 25,000 B.C.) and are thought to be associated with hunting magic. Venus figures are not to be confused with mother-goddess cult statues, which first appeared in the 7th millennium B.C., in Anatolia and the Near East, and are profoundly related to the neolithic agricultural revolution, when farming displaced hunting as the chief means of life support.

VENUS OF LAUSSEL. In the Laussel rock shelter near Cap-Blanc in the Dordogne region of France a number of

stone carvings were found, of which the most famous is the 18-inch-tall Venus of Laussel. This opulent female figure holds a bison horn upraised in one hand, while her other arm lies across her body. Her head is held to one side in a natural and somewhat appealing pose. The generous hips and breasts of this Venus figure indicate a fertility cult of the Gravettian period about 22,000 B.C., to which this masterly carving is attributed. It can be seen in Bordeaux.

VENUS OF MELOS, a 2nd-century B.C. statue of Venus (Aphrodite), now in the Louvre. While not the finest, it is surely the best known of the statues that have come down to us from the Greek world. Found on the Aegean island of Melos in 1820, the "Venus de Milo" caught the imagination of the world as the personification of the Greek ideal of feminine beauty. The goddess stands taller than mortal woman (six feet eight inches) and is carved from two main pieces of Parian marble joined at the hips. The now missing left arm reached upward and was separately joined by a dowel. The pose, though statuesque, still conveys a feeling of movement through the twist of the torso to the left and the slightly raised left leg. The somewhat heavy and awkward drapery contrasts with the softly modelled flesh of the Venus.

VENUS OF WILLENDORF. This figure, the best executed and most famous of all Venus figurines, was found in the village of Willendorf on the north bank of the Danube River. It is carved in limestone, about five inches high, and still bears traces of red paint. The figure exhibits great vitality and realism. The head is faceless but the hair elaborately braided. The buttocks and abdomen are prominent and the breasts large and pendulous. This,

along with other Venus figurines, seems to have been a cult object of fertility rites practiced by Aurignacian hunters around 25,000–20,000 B.C. The Venus, one of the masterpieces of prehistoric art, is in the Natural History Museum of Vienna.

VERAGUAS, an indigenous art style of Panama that flourished in the centuries prior to the Spanish Conquest. Veraguas graves have yielded splendid goldwork, in-

Vikings: Ceremonial axehead. 10th century A.D. From Mammen, Denmark.

cluding fantastic pendants of eagles, men, and animals. These pieces were frequently rendered in gilded copper rather than solid gold. The Veraguas gold style bears a strong resemblance to that of Cocle and Chiriqui.

VIA APPIA. See **APPIAN WAY.**

VICTORIA. See **NIKE.**

VIJAYANAGAR PERIOD, named for the 16th-century A.D. city and principality in southern India, the last major Hindu outpost against the Islamic invasion that opened India's Moghul period. Vijayanagar is a period of heroic sculpture and florid architecture. The city's famed Vitthala temple was a typical structure, having an immense pillared hall, each pillar actually being a fantastic sculpture of such subjects as battling warriors and rearing horses. Vijayanagar was methodically reduced to rubble by its Islamic conquerors in 1565.

VIKINGS, the warriors of Scandinavia whose sea raids inspired terror among the dwellers on the coasts of Europe and Britain during the Viking age from the 8th to the 11th centuries A.D. The most accomplished shipbuilders and sailors of their time, the Vikings penetrated as far west as Greenland and North America (Vinland) and as far east as Russia. Their oceangoing "long ship" had a high prow and stern, carved and painted, a single mast and colored sail carried on a single long yard, and a large steering oar on the starboard. The Viking ship, often ornately carved, bore painted round shields along each gunwale and had capacity for a crew of 90, of whom 30 were oarsmen. Their raids were prompted by population pressure and motives of trade but perhaps principally by the desire for loot, adventure, and glory. The Vikings were also known as Varangians, Norsemen, Normans, and Danes. Viking art, of which there is little, includes carved woodwork and decorated metalwork, especially in weapons; a frequent motif was that of intertwined animals. Their greatest contribution was the creation of the Norse sagas.

VILLANOVAN CULTURE shows the transition from the bronze to the iron age, about 1000 to 750 B.C., in north-central Italy. The use of iron spread from the Near East along a northern route through the Balkans and a southern lane by sea; the two influences met and merged in the cultures of Italy, particularly in that of the Villanovan. This culture is named for a village near Bologna and covered the present regions of Emilia, Tuscany, and Latium. The Villanovans were known for their fine metalwork, characterized by bronze pins and ornaments of repousse, and by the gradual introduction of iron to the point where even chariot wheels were made of the new metal. They cremated their dead, though the earlier practice of burial survived in places. Decorated burial urns have been found in Villanovan cemeteries. The Villanovans may have become the Etruscans of later history.

VINCA, a site near Belgrade in Yugoslavia, the first neolithic settlement to be excavated in the Danube region. Vinca was a village raised on a mound formed by the old buildings and discarded rubbish of earlier generations. Painted and burnished pottery from the earliest levels, of about 4500 B.C., and male and female figurines show affinities with Asia Minor. The neolithic farmers of Vinca, among the earliest in Europe, used stone tools and bred stock animals. They also hunted and fished for sturgeon in the Danube. About 20 other settlements of the Vinca type have been identified in the Danube region.

VINLAND. See ANSE AU MEADOW.

VIRU CULTURE, also known as Gallinazo, was centered in the Viru Valley on the Peruvian north coast, where it flourished in the centuries around the beginning of the Christian era. This was a time of great Peruvian population expansion, and the Viru people were able to build fortified pyramid sanctuaries and large irrigation systems. Their pottery, along with the Salinar, is transitional between the Chavin and Mochica styles. It portrayed a great variety of subjects, including plants, animals, houses, and men, in a charming and anecdotal, if non-realistic, manner. The chief contribution of the Viru to ancient Peruvian ceramics is the decorative technique of negative painting.

VISHNU, beneficent Hindu god of preservation; with Brahma and Siva, one of the three major deities of the Hindu pantheon. He usually takes a human form in Hindu iconography, although sometimes he is pictured as a regal lion or a boar. In full reign, Vishnu is depicted as crowned and seated on his throne, bearing in four hands his symbols: the conch, the solar disk, the mace, and the lotus.

VIX TREASURE, found in a rich Celtic burial barrow in the Rhone Valley of northern France. In the 6th century B.C. a young princess, with a gold diadem on her head, was buried on a cart and surrounded by silver and bronze cups, Athenian black-figured ware, flagons for wine, and the largest bronze krater, or wine-mixing bowl, known from antiquity. This famous krater, standing over five feet high and now in the museum at Chatillon-sur-Seine, probably came from Massilia (Marseilles). It was made about 520 B.C. in a Greek colony of southern Italy. The vessel has lavishly decorated handles and a vigorous frieze of Greek soldiers on foot and in horse-drawn chariots.

VLADIMIROVKA. See TRIPOLYE CULTURE.

Vix Treasure: Greco-Scythian, ornament, 6th century B.C. (Musée de Châtillon-sur-Seine)

VOLUTE, a scroll-like, ornamental motif, sometimes compared in shape to the horns of a ram. It is a distinctive feature of the Greek Ionic capital.

VOODOO. See FETISH.

VOTIVE, an offering to a god or gods in return for a favor. This ancient religious custom has been practiced in many different places and at many different times. In art, a votive figure is usually, but not always, a statue or statuette of the god himself, a priest, or a worshipper. Votive deposits, a collection or hoard of votive objects, were sometimes buried in a sacred precinct for the use of a god.

VULCA. See ETRUSCAN CIVILIZATION.

VULCI, an ancient Etruscan town in northern Italy, with burial sites dating from around 900 B.C. By the 7th century B.C. it was a prosperous trade center, as evidenced from finds of many Greek vases. Bronze figurines made by Vulci craftsmen—dancing figures, animals, monsters, warriors, etc.—were exported as far as Greece and central Europe. Among Vulci's important tombs is the so-called Francois Tomb (5th century B.C.), with wall paintings showing the sacrifice of Trojan prisoners—a Greek theme but executed in Etruscan style. Other noteworthy tomb art includes a 3rd-century B.C. stone sarcophagus lid showing an embracing husband and wife, now housed in the Museum of Fine Arts, Boston.

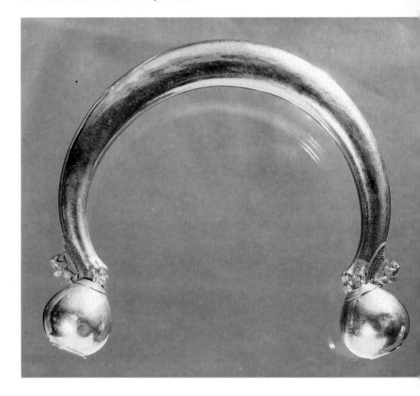

W

WALDALGESHEIM, on the Rhine in Germany, the site of an elaborate Celtic burial between 325 and 250 B.C. In the double grave of a man and woman of princely rank were found much pottery, a chariot with its fittings, gold ornaments, bronze plaques with human figures, and other fine metalwork. The Waldalgesheim tomb is one of the latest in a series of rich burials of this date found in the Rhine Valley.

WAREGA. See LEGA.

WARI, or Huari, one of the most extensive urban centers of Pre-Incan Peru, located near the modern city of Ayacucho. After the 7th century A.D. Wari was the center of a great military expansion, contemporary with that of Tiahuanaco, and the ruling city of most of highland and coastal Peru. Wari people produced truly spectacular polychrome pottery mostly in the form of large ceremonial urns. These were decorated with Tiahuanaco motifs, including the Gateway God and his attendants. Wari collapsed in the 8th century, but its influence on the pottery of the region continued until the 11th century.

WARKA. See URUK.

WARRING STATES PERIOD, in China, extends from the disintegration of the Chou Dynasty, around 480 B.C., to consolidation of China under Ch'in rule around 221 B.C. Despite violent political disruption this period marks the birth of Confucian thought. The era is not notable for its art, although some interesting bronzes resembling those of the preceding Chou date from the Warring States period. Typical bronzes are decorated in the so-called Huan style, which uses interlocking snakes as a motif.

WEI DYNASTY, a dynasty that arose in northern China from about 386 to 535 A.D., during the Six Dynasties period; it partly filled the vacuum left by the collapse of the Han Dynasty. Post-Han China was a period of cultural eclipse, somewhat similar to Europe's Dark Ages. The most important constructive influence was Buddhism. Wei rulers were predominantly ardent Buddhists, and their major contributions to Chinese culture are the Buddhist cave temples at Yunkang, Tatung, and Tunhuang, containing massive stone Buddhas and countless small sculptures. The earliest known Chinese wall paintings, at Tunhuang, date from the Wei Dynasty.

WESSEX, the historic name given to the southern section of England, with occupation sites dating from the 2nd millennium B.C. The name has not survived in the designation of any present-day county, in contrast to its counterpart, Essex. Wessex culture was important in the Eng-

lish bronze age of about 1600 B.C., for it was the people of this region who undertook the impressive final stage of the construction of Stonehenge, adding lintels to the outer ring of stone uprights and setting up five enormous trilithons in a horseshoe shape. In the 9th and 10th centuries A.D. Wessex was the kingdom of King Alfred the Great and his successors. King Alfred rallied resistance against the Danes. He had to concede to them his eastern region, called the Danelaw, but the powerful kingdom of Wessex extended along the whole of the south coast and included the west coast up to the modern Chester. Wessex has rich barrow graves, and discoveries here—especially objects of amber and faience—indicate a wide international trade, as well as the wealth of ancient Wessex chieftains.

WHITE HORSE OF UFFINGTON, colossal rock engraving in Berkshire, England, between Swindon and Oxford. It was cut in a chalk hillside between the 3rd and 1st centuries B.C. The free, flowing form of the horse, possibly a tribal badge or a fertility symbol, is typically Celtic and is found also on pre-Roman coins. Folk festivals down the centuries are probably responsible for keeping the large effigy clean and free from obscuring vegetation.

WILTON. See SMITHFIELD CULTURE.

WINDMILL HILL, in Wiltshire, England, the site of a neolithic corral or causewayed camp. Numerous gaps in the three concentric circles of ramparts and ditches here show that the site cannot have been a fortification. It was apparently used by early farmers about 2500 B.C. for rounding up their flocks and herds at certain seasons, for slaughter, feasting, and preparing the skins. Within the second circle are two round graves of the later Beaker folk.

WINGED VICTORY. See NIKE OF SAMOTHRACE.

WOAD. See PICTS.

WODEN. See ODIN.

WOODLAND INDIAN CULTURE, a way of life that appeared in eastern North America about 1000 B.C. and included Hopewell culture with its distinctive burial and effigy mounds. The entire culture of the region reflected its forest and riverine environment; food was obtained by corn farming and by seasonal hunting and gathering. Wood and bark were the chief materials used by the Woodland peoples. Their art was developed, and examples of wood carving, decorative household objects, porcupine quilling, and beadwork exist. In more historic times the Iroquois became the most important of Woodland people. Their most striking creations were the wooden "false-face" masks worn during religious ceremonies. Carved from live trees, the masks, with distorted, grotesque features, are powerfully expressive. They were actually believed to house spirits and when not in use were carefully stored and even regularly fed.

Wei Dynasty: Buddha's head. Stone. From a temple at Yunkang. (National Museum, Tokyo)

XYZ

XANTHUS. See LYCIA.

XIPE, terrifying Aztec god, known also as "the flayed lord." Proper sacrifice to Xipe entailed flaying a live human victim, after which a priest would wear the bloody skin. Images of Xipe often show him wearing a flayed skin with his mouth stretched wide in anguish.

XOCHICALCO, a fortified hilltop site in the Mexican state of Morelos, near the modern town of Cuernavaca. Although occupied several centuries earlier, Xochicalco reached its peak from the 7th to the 11th centuries A.D., when it was a major center for the flow of ideas between the Maya to the south and the peoples of central Mexico, especially the Toltecs. As such, its architecture and art style reflect the influence of both groups. The most important monument at the site is a square stone platform in its center, decorated with reliefs of the Toltec god Quetzalcoatl.

X-RAY EXAMINATION, a modern method of examining antiquities to determine age and authenticity. A common use of X-ray is the visual probing of an object's interior structure without having to dismantle and perhaps damage it. If, for example, a bronze statue claimed to be from an ancient civilization proves, under X-ray examination, to be joined in its interior with bolts of modern vintage, the object is probably fraudulent—or, at the very least, has been subject to modern tampering. A highly specialized technology called X-ray spectroscopy is also used to examine the physical structure of a fragment of substance—e.g., bronze, porcelain, etc.—and can shed some light on the substance's probable age or occasionally on its source of origin.

YAHWEH, modern transliteration of the ancient and ineffable Hebrew name for the one and only God, who is said to have revealed himself in about the 13th century B.C. By the time of the prophets of Israel, the Yahweh name had taken on a philosophical connotation, meaning "I am that I am" (Exodus 3:14). By then the word was considered too holy to be spoken—and Adonai (my Lord) and Elohim (the common Semitic noun for God) were used instead. The artistic impulse of the Israelites was restricted in the same way as the verbal, with the making of images of the deity being forbidden by law. Thus the God of Israel, along with Allah of later Islamic religion, were probably unique among the gods of ancient cultures in that they were not given artistic representation. Another form of Yahweh is Jehovah.

YAKA, an African people of southern Zaire and Angola. The Yaka are said to be descendants of a people who invaded and settled in the kingdom of the Congo during the 16th century A.D. They were primarily a hunting people. Their works of art comprise small standing figurines, carved wooden containers, and masks of raffia and wood. Both in style and function these objects are clearly related to those of such neighboring peoples as the Pende and Suku. Polychromed masks, used in initiation ceremonies for young men, have an alluring serenity. Masks and figurines often feature a sloping, upturned nose and ears that stand out horizontally from the head. These are unmistakable signs of the Yaka style.

YAKSHI, a Dravidian Indian female fertility spirit, originating in the Indus Valley culture, where she was portrayed as a tree-dwelling female figure. Yakshis are also depicted in Buddhist art as tree spirits. These sensuous nymphs are a common subject in Hindu Indian sculpture.

YANGSHAO CULTURE, also called the Painted-Pottery culture, one of the two major ancient Chinese cultures (with Lungshan) that prefigured the rise of civilization in the Yellow River Valley. The Yangshao people occupied modern Honan Province in northern China from roughly 2000 to 700 B.C.; their last phase overlapped the Shang and Chou eras of early Chinese civilization. The culture is known mainly through its pottery, an excellent red earthenware with animal or geometric designs, painted in black, white, or red. Its later shapes, including tripod types, may have been conscious copies of Shang and Chou bronzes. Jade carvings were also made by the Yangshao, who may have been settlers from central Asia.

YAYOI CULTURE, a culture developed by prehistoric Mongoloid people who settled the Japanese islands around the 3rd century B.C., displacing the more primitive inhabitants on all islands except Hokkaido. The Yayoi introduced rice growing, bronze and iron making, and pottery into Japan. The pottery is of red clay with slight decoration or none at all. Bronze objects dating from the Yayoi era, including great bells and spearheads, appear to have had ceremonial uses. The culture's name derives from Yayoi, a section of Tokyo, where in 1884 the pottery was first found.

YAZILIKAYA. See BOGHAZKOY.

YEAVERING. See ANGLO-SAXON PEOPLES.

YEHA, a northeastern Ethiopian site with several ancient structures, the earliest dating from perhaps the 5th century B.C. The culture of the early Ethiopians who built these structures remains largely unexplored, and thus the full significance of the site is unknown. Classified as South Arabian in style, the buildings are massive and rectangular, largely constructed of limestone blocks.

YELLOW SECT. See TIBETAN CIVILIZATION.

YI DYNASTY, a period of rule in Korea from A.D. 1392 to 1910. Politically and culturally it was influenced by China's Ming and Ching dynasties. Early Yi painting

Yayoi culture: *Dotaku* (bell). Bronze. Japanese. Found at Sumiyoshi-cho, Higashinada, Kobe. (National Museum, Tokyo)

is—despite some Japanese influence—very similar to Chinese Ming work. However, by the 18th century a distinctive Yi genre painting had emerged, using charming, intimate subjects absent from Chinese work. Early Yi porcelain resembles Ming, although decoration is more sparse. Late Yi pottery, while showing a technical decline, takes on a characteristic Korean flavor, both in shape and decoration.

YOKE, a horseshoe-shaped stone object used in Pre-Columbian Mexico. Yokes are often intricately carved to represent a snake, frog, or human form. When viewed from below, some yokes seem to represent a jaw with fangs. It was formerly throught that they were placed under the head of a corpse to represent the mouth of a monster receiving the dead. However, since the discovery of clay figurines with U-shaped objects around their waists, yokes are now thought to be stone replicas of belts worn in the ceremonial ballgame. Although found over a wide span of time and place in Mexico, yokes are usually associated with the Totonac people of Veracruz.

YONI, Hindu symbol of the female sexual organ, often shown as a ring. It is an object of cult worship, as is the male lingam, which together symbolize the creative power of the deities.

YORUBA, an African tribe living principally in southwestern Nigeria and southeastern Dahomey. Although unified by common language and traditions, the populous Yoruba were organized into many distinct kingdoms such as Oyo, Ijebu, Ife, and Ketu. Their complex religion, which required the cult worship of various gods, or *orisha*, stimulated a rich and varied artistic tradition. Among the better known of their splendid wood carvings are the *ibeji* or twin figures; dance wands used in the worship of Shango; and anti-witchcraft masks of the Gelede Society. Beads were used for royal crowns.

YU, a type of Chinese ceremonial bronze vessel dating from the Shang and Chou eras. It is a low-bellied, bucket-shaped container, meant for use as a wine container. It has a tightly fitting lid and a swingable handle.

YUAN DYNASTY, a period of Mongol rule in China, beginning in the 13th century A.D. and prevailing until the restoration of native Chinese rule under Ming leadership around 1368. Artistically, the Yuan era was bleak. The only activity of major importance was in porcelain, which underwent marked transformation from the previous Sung style. Yuan porcelains are generally more heavily decorated than Sung. Many pieces have raised, unglazed designs set against a glazed background. A Yuan-era porcelain center at Kiangsi produced *Shufu*, a hard, white porcelain having an unusually heavy glaze.

YUEH CULTURE, a little-known culture that developed along the coastal regions of China, Korea, Southeast

Asia, and in parts of Indonesia from the 2nd millennium B.C. By around 500 B.C. Yueh was a formidable maritime state to the south of the Chou and, later, Han Dynasty territories. Yueh potters produced a quality ceramic ware superior to Han pottery, which it influenced. Yueh ware

is considered the direct predecessor of porcelain. By the 8th century A.D. the Yueh were absorbed by the Chinese.

YUNKANG, a Buddhist cave-temple site near Tatung, in China's northern Shansi Province. Construction was undertaken by the Wei Dynasty around 460 A.D., but the temples were gradually abandoned and virtually forgotten after 493. In 1961 restoration was begun by the Chinese People's Republic. Yunkang consists of 20 major shrines and innumerable small ones. There are five huge stone Buddhas—the largest some 45 feet high—and about 51,000 smaller images, which adorn the cave walls.

ZAKROS, a Minoan palace site on the extreme edge of eastern Crete. First built in about 1600 B.C., the palace was destroyed by a seismic catastrophe in 1450 B.C. Excavations begun here in 1962 have revealed hundreds of cult vessels in marble, a rarity in Minoan art, and in rock crystal, obsidian, and ceramic. A treasury building at Zakros contained ivory tusks and copper ingots for international trade. Major finds from the site are on exhibit in the Herakleion Museum, Crete.

ZAPOTEC CIVILIZATION. Still to be found in the Mexican state of Oaxaca today, the Zapotec people probably originated as far back as 1500 B.C. Evidence suggests that even as early as that time they had a society divided into different classes, considerable wealth, and some knowledge of irrigation control. Their rise to greatness begins with the construction of their hilltop ceremonial center, Monte Alban, in about 700 B.C. The oldest buildings there are faced with relief panels depicting dancing men. These panels, known as *los danzantes*, were probably influenced by Olmec art styles. Although ancient Oaxaca's geographic position led to cultural and commercial contacts with the great city of Teohuatihucan to the north and the Maya to the south, the Zapotecs remained a distinct cultural entity. The emphasis of Zapotec society was on the worship of the gods, and authority was divided between two rulers. A secular monarch controlled the military, but the great power belonged to a high priest whose office was hereditary. The Zapotecs are credited with a high level of scientific achievement. They had a 260-day ritual calendar and were familiar with the solar calendar, as well as with hieroglyphic writing. They are also thought to be among the first of the Mexican peoples to work metal. Their achievement in architecture can be seen at Monte Alban and at Mitla, another major Zapotec site. Zapotec culture began to decline around 900 A.D., when Monte Alban was abandoned, probably due to problems of water supply and erosion of nearby farmland. Shortly thereafter the Zapotecs were overrun by Mixtec peoples from the highlands.

Zapotec Art and Antiquities. Although the Zapotecs produced outstanding architecture and stone carvings,

Zapotec art: Funerary urn depicting Xipe. Painted terra cotta. 600–900 A.D. From Monte Alban. (National Museum of Anthropology, Mexico City)

probably their most famous and distinctive art objects were large funerary urns of baked clay. Characteristically these are cylindrical with an extremely elaborate false front, representing human beings or, most often, the gods. Usually the principal figure is seated cross-legged in a rigidly frontal position. Zapotec pottery included vessels in the form of a shoe and many forms of effigy pottery. The elaborate tombs at Monte Alban show many examples of large-scale wall painting, as well as stele and slabs carved in a stiff but bold style. After the Mixtec invasion Zapotec art becomes indistinguishable from their conquerors' style.

ZEALOTS. See **MASADA.**

ZEMI, a Pre-Columbian sculpture of the Caribbean. Created by the Arawak people of the Greater Antilles, Zemis took the form of wooden idols or images carved on three-pointed stones. Arawak religion was based on a belief in the spirits of natural phenomena or the ghosts of the dead which could be communicated with through the use of a Zemi. Although every household had several Zemis, those of the Arawak chiefs were considered the most potent and were worshipped in special temples.

ZEN ART AND ANTIQUITIES derive from the Buddhist sect called Chan in China and Zen in Japan, where it took hold from the 13th century A.D. Zen discipline stresses meditation, while its philosophy attempts to reconcile contradictions. Thus, Zen artworks are objects of meditation and dynamic exercises in the resolution of the specific and the general, the large and the small. The most common medium is ink on paper or silk; frequent subjects are portraits, although landscapes with minutely small human figures are also typical. Zen painting techniques were established in Sung Dynasty China (after 1000 A.D.), as was the peculiarly flowing Zen calligraphy, later adapted for Japanese use. Zen temple sculpture dates from Japan's Muromachi era (14th–16th centuries).

ZEUS, the supreme lord of the heavens, the greatest god of the Greek pantheon, and, like Jupiter for the Romans, the essence of all divine power. The most famous rendition of Zeus was the colossal gold-and-ivory statue by Phidias in the Temple of Zeus at Olympia. The noble, benevolent, and bearded face of the god, as seen in the Vatican bust found at Orticoli in northern Italy, is thought to be an imitation of Phidias' masterpiece. A seven-foot-high bronze, now in the Athens Museum, is the most impressive of surviving Zeus figures; it dates from about 450 B.C. The statue is sometimes identified as a Poseidon figure.

ZEUXIS, a celebrated 5th-century B.C. Greek painter. A well-known anecdote, attributed to Pliny, describes Zeuxis' work as so realistic that birds, deceived by his masterly illusion, attempted to eat his painted grapes. Zeuxis' art style came to dominate Hellenistic painting. His portrayal of Helen for the Temple of Hera near Croton was especially famous. The Roman writer Quintilian credits him with discovering the principles of light and shade. None of his work survives.

ZIGGURAT, a stepped brick temple-tower, which was the characteristic architectural and religious feature of Sumerian, Babylonian, and Assyrian civilizations. Its towerlike shape is thought to have represented the gateway or stairway to heaven. Ziggurats evolved from 4th-millennium B.C. temples that were built on raised terraces. Around 2150 B.C. a many-staged edifice was built at Ur by the Sumerian king Ur-Nammu; this may have been the earliest true ziggurat. Typical ziggurats usually had seven stages with a small shrine at the top; the stages were connected either by ramps or stairs. Remains of about 25 ziggurats survive to the present. The largest (342 feet square at the base and 135 feet high) is at Choga Zanbil, in Elam, Iran. Probably the most famous ziggurat was that of Marduk at Babylon (modern Iraq), thought to have been the Biblical Tower of Babel.

ZIMBABWE, fabled ruins of an ancient African culture located in southern Rhodesia. These impressive ruins, first described to Europeans by the German geologist Carl Mauch in the 1870s, cover about 60 acres and contain several buildings. Perhaps the most famous is the so-called Temple, a massive stone enclosure with walls 24 feet high and 17 feet thick at the base; one long section of wall was decorated with chevron designs. Although some legends have linked the founding of Zimbabwe with the Biblical King Solomon, its origins are still enigmatic. The area may have been settled in two major waves of occupation, the first about 320 A.D. and the second about 1075 A.D. Many small art objects from Zimbabwe survive. The most important are stylized soapstone birds with straight backs, folded wings, and articulated beaks and legs. These carvings were perched atop stone pillars and may have had religious significance. Gold ornaments, female fertility figures, stone bowls, as well as Chinese, Persian, and Indian artifacts, have been found at Zimbabwe.

ZIWIYE HOARD, a treasure of gold, silver, ivory, and terra-cotta objects dating to the 7th century B.C. that was discovered in 1947 near modern Saqqez, in northwest Iran. The pieces show a varied blending of Middle Eastern stylistic influences and reflect the many artistic currents in Persia of that time. Typically Mesopotamian are gold bracelets that end in snarling lion's heads and ivory plaques carved with reliefs of goats and sacred trees. A large silver dish, 15 inches in diameter, is embossed with Scythian motifs, and gold pectorals and weapons show the influence of Urartu. The objects are now scattered among the private collections and public museums of three continents, most notably the Archaeological Museum in Teheran and the Metropolitan Museum of Art, New York.

ZOROASTRIAN ART AND ANTIQUITIES. Zoroastrianism, the ancient religion of Persia, was founded by the prophet Zoroaster, or Zarathustra, in the 6th century B.C. It reached peaks of popularity under the Achaemenids and, later, under the Sassanians. The holy book of Zoroastrianism was the *Avesta*, or book of wisdom, which foretold of the eternal conflict between the forces of good and evil, between Ahuramazda, the god of light, and Ahriman, the god of darkness; Ahuramazda, according to the *Avesta*, would ultimately reign supreme. The holy scriptures held fire as sacred—a religious concept probably derived from Iranian sun worship—and the earth as pure. Human burial was forbidden for fear of contaminating the earth; thus, Zoroastrians raised their dead on high to rot in the open air. This ritual is still practiced by the Parsis of India, the last of the Zoroastrians, who expose their dead on so-called Towers of Silence. Also prohibited by the *Avesta* were the making of idols and the building of temples, a stricture that profoundly affected the course of ancient Persian art. The central symbol of Zoroastrian art was fire, usually depicted on coins and reliefs as rising from an altar, while the god Ahuramazda is often shown as a winged solar disk. The fire altar and the winged solar disk are therefore the major icons of Zoroastrian art. A significant religion, Zoroastrianism influenced the development of Judaism and Christianity. The god Mithra, whose cult was so popular among the legions of Rome, was acquired from the Zoroastrian pantheon.

ZUNI, a Pueblo Indian tribe of the American Southwest, living along the Rio Grande River of New Mexico. Modern Zuni culture had its beginnings in the centuries prior to the Spanish Conquest, but its roots can be traced back to the prehistoric Anasazi culture of this area. The Zunis are an agricultural, pueblo-dwelling people who have a complex religious life centered around rainmaking and crop fertility. For their religious ceremonies they produce an abundance of kachina masks and dolls. However, their major art form is pottery, generally slipped in black or brown and decorated with floral and geometric designs. Handcrafted silver and turquoise jewelry are sold commercially by the Zuni.

Zuni: Water jug. Polychrome slip ware. (Private collection, Paris)